Patricia Madoo Lengermann

Ruth A. Wallace

George Washington University

GENDER IN AMERICA
Social Control
and
Social Change

PRENTICE-HALL, INC., Englewood Cliffs, New Jersey 07632

Library of Congress Cataloging in Publication Data

LENGERMANN, PATRICIA M.
  Gender in America

  Bibliography: p. 259
  Includes index.
  1. Sex role—United States.   2. Sex differences.
3. Sex discrimination against women—United States.
4. United States—Social conditions.   5. Social
control.   6. Equality.   I. Wallace, Ruth A.   II. Title.
HQ1075.5.U6L46   1985   305.3'0973   84-13383
ISBN 0-13-347493-3

To Jill, Paul, and Jim

Editorial supervision and
  interior design: Serena Hoffman
Cover design: Joe Kurcio
Manufacturing buyer: John Hall

PRINTED IN THE UNITED STATES OF AMERICA

10 9 8 7 6 5 4 3 2 1

ISBN 0-13-347493-3   01

PRENTICE-HALL INTERNATIONAL, INC., *London*
PRENTICE-HALL OF AUSTRALIA PTY. LIMITED, *Sydney*
EDITORA PRENTICE-HALL DO BRASIL, LTDA., *Rio de Janeiro*
PRENTICE-HALL CANADA INC., *Toronto*
PRENTICE-HALL OF INDIA PRIVATE LIMITED, *New Delhi*
PRENTICE-HALL OF JAPAN, INC., *Tokyo*
PRENTICE-HALL OF SOUTHEAST ASIA PTE. LTD., *Singapore*
WHITEHALL BOOKS LIMITED, *Wellington, New Zealand*

CONTENTS

PREFACE

This book is a description and explanation of the institution of gender in America society. It provides the reader with a theoretical framework that explains, first, the persistence of gender inequality, and, second, the growth of gender equality as the result of recent changes in beliefs and structures. We are aware, however, that this book is being published at a time when the limited gains in gender equality are threatened by the mobilization of conservative interest groups, and we take this backlash seriously in our discussion of resistance to change.

We describe and explain the American gender institution from three perspectives or levels of analysis: the level of individual subjectivity, of individual interactions, and of macro organizations and institutions. Woven throughout this tripartite analysis of gender are data from the 1980 census and recent empirical studies. We do not pretend to offer an exhaustive summary of all post-1975 research in the area of gender. What we offer here is a strong theoretical framework to help the reader uncover the social control factors maintaining gender inequality and the social change factors fostering equality.

In Part I we focus on social control and gender inequality. In Chapter 1 we define gender inequality and briefly review the sociological theories that inform our three-level analysis. Our social control theory is presented in Chapter 2; Chapters 3 through 5 are applications of that theory. In Chapter 3 we explore the individual beliefs that maintain gender inequality; in Chapter 4 we look at the acting-out of these conventional beliefs in everyday interactions; and in Chapter 5 we look at the large-scale social institutions that ensure women and men will remain in their proper places in society.

In Part II we explore the changes underway in America's institution of gender. Our social change theory is presented in Chapter 6; Chapters 7 through 11 are applications of that theory. In Chapter 7 we explore new beliefs about gender, in particular contemporary feminist beliefs; in Chapter 8 we examine micro and macro structures that facilitate change for women, in particular the contemporary women's movement; in Chapter 9 we look at women's new arrangements in the paid labor force, in education, and in the family; in Chapter 10 we turn to an examination of the new feminist male, in particular his source for new meanings and his pressures for power sharing; and in Chapter 11 we discuss the resistance to gender equality. Finally, in Chapter 12 we take a look at some of the feminist utopias and make some projections regarding gender equality in the year 2000.

The two sections of the book do not depict a chronology in which a conventionalized system of gender inequality is replaced by a new system of greater equality. Rather, the two sections constitute an analytic breakout of social processes all in place at present in American society. Putting it more concretely, there are many millions of Americans today who experience gender in the form described in Part I of this book; there are millions more who experience the changing system described in Part II; and equally significant numbers live in situations that combine elements from the two patterns of gender. Parts I and II depict what sociologists call *ideal types,* formal models of human activity and relationship that are abstracted out of the complexity of daily experience. Because of your particular social location, one or other of these "types" may seem unreal to you. But they do both exist, now, in the United States. We shall present data that demonstrates this. And in the process we hope that you will learn something else about sociology—that it not only enables people to suddenly see the familiar, but that it also enables us to go beyond our particular experiences to a wider grasp of the complex society in which we live.

Patricia Lengermann took primary responsibility for Chapters 1, 3, 6, 7, and 11. Ruth Wallace took primary responsibility for Chapters 5, 9, 10, and 12. Lengermann and Wallace share responsibility for Chapters 2 and 4. Wallace provided the initial data base for Chapters 8, 9 and 12. Lengermann and Jill Brantley, of Northern Virginia Community College, wrote the analysis for Chapters 8 and 12. Brantley wrote the analysis for Chapter 9.

Special recognition for contributions to this book goes to Janet Hunt of the University of Maryland, College Park, for her very thoughtful criticisms and suggestions on earlier drafts of the manuscript. We also want to thank anonymous reviewers chosen by Prentice-Hall: Maxine Atkinson, North Carolina State University; Sharon Guten, Case Western Reserve University; Linda Haas, Indiana University; Janet Hunt, University of Maryland; Ross A. Klein, Iowa State University; Judy Long, Syracuse University; Pamela Oliver, University of Wisconsin; Rita Sakitt, Suffolk County Community College; Neil Smelser, University of California-Berkeley; Barrie Thorne, Michigan State University; and Beth Vanfossen, SUNY Brockport. Thanks are also due to our students whose reactions to the early material improved our revisions, and to the Graduate School of Arts and Sciences at George Washington University for a summer grant in the early stages of the project.

Finally, we thank Cynthia Gaizband, Barbara Marshall, Donna Henderson, Claudia Southcott, Roberta Bixhorn, Alice Wilding-White, Audrey Goldman, Mary Alison Albright, Mary Beth Hooban, Donna Aldridge, Pat Donat, and Doris Summers for their typing help, and our

Prentice-Hall editors, Serena Hoffman and Jeannine Ciliotta. We owe a special debt to family and friends, whose encouragement and moral support helped us to complete this project—in particular, those to whom we dedicate this book.

Patricia Madoo Lengermann
Ruth A. Wallace

1
A SOCIOLOGICAL PERSPECTIVE ON GENDER INEQUALITY

Of the various issues that have held the attention of the American public in the last twenty years, some—like Watergate and the oil crises—have been debated intensely for a time and then quickly allowed to become "past history." Others—like environmental protection, the growth of government, and the rights of racial minorities—have persisted and seem to promise to be centers of concern for the foreseeable future. Our interest in this book is in one of these areas of continuing public debate, the so-called "woman question"—or, more precisely, the question of the place of women, and also of men, in contemporary America.

Women have protested their situation and formulated a feminist perspective almost continuously over the past three hundred years (Spender, 1982). It is the public that periodically rediscovers the gender issue, each time in the belief that the issue is new. The past twenty years constitute the contemporary phase of debate on gender.

The contemporary debate has grown in complexity during its recent history. During the turbulent sixties, vocal groups and dramatic gestures drew public attention to the gender issue. The mass media, often exploitatively, zeroed in on the "women's libbers"[1] and have kept the "woman question" before the public ever since. Public debate on the issue took place within a framework of seemingly irreconcilable values that time has only served to intensify. Political mobilization began within the major parties and through special interest groups either "for" or "against" significant changes in women's situation. Governmental policies were set at local, state, and national levels. All this activity has been accompanied by a flood of information and speculation: government investigations, academic research, the growth of women's studies programs on college campuses (at last count there were almost 500), theoretical debate. There has been a steady flow of all this data and debate through journals, magazines, books, television, and movies to specialized and general publics.

This book is an attempt to help the reader develop a sociological perspective with which to evaluate the continuing debate about our gender arrangements. In this introductory chapter, we undertake three important tasks: a detailed specification of our approach to the study of gender; a brief, critical review of biological explanations of gender, the chief rival to the sociological approach; and an overview of the sociological theories that provide the basis for the descriptions and explanations we offer in the following chapters.

DEFINING THE TOPIC

In order to make sense of all the research, debate, and speculation about women's place in our social life, we have limited and focused the scope of this book. Our first step has been to identify precisely what it is we are investigating. Our concern will be with *the phenomenon of gender inequality*. For we, like everyone else, have arrived at our interest in gender because of a social movement by and on behalf of women, a movement that claims that women's situation is not only different from but inferior to that of men in terms of material resources, power, valuation, and autonomy. Much contemporary debate and research has centered on this claim. Moreover, we believe this claim is a valid one, and in the main body of the text we will present the data that support it.

This text is anchored not only in the assumption that gender inequality exists, but in the value position that it is harmful to both women and men, but particularly to women. There are those who argue that holding a value position on an issue makes it impossible to describe or analyze that issue objectively. We do not agree. In other areas of social inequality, such as class, race, and age, sound scholarly work is produced by people with strong value positions. Indeed, it is hard to believe that there are people who have no values that bear on the issues they study (though they may have unconfronted ones), or that pure objectivity is, in fact, possible. One must simply try to be as objective as possible, staying close to the data and to scholarly writings on the topic. Being objective is facilitated by confronting one's value position and making one's audience aware of it. Our intention is to present as objective an analysis as possible of gender inequality.

To study gender inequality, we need to explore *the social institution of gender*. Exploring the gender institution means looking at the identity of females in relation to males, and vice versa, at the relations between females and males, and at the relations of females to each other and of males to each other in the context of a two-gender social reality. We focus on one striking feature of that institution, gender inequality. Because of the focus on inequality, we emphasize the situation of women, the subordinated gender, and deal much more selectively with men. They are a foil, contrast, explanation, and indispensable reality for understanding women.

Our analysis is also limited to a particular time and place. There is enormous scope for comparative work in the study of gender. Women's unequal and inferior status is a nearly universal social fact; despite myths about matriarchal societies, no documented case exists of a society in which women are dominant over men. There are variations from culture to culture and time to time only in the degree of subordination. But our study is not comparative; we emphasize the typical patterns of gender relationship in American society in the 1980s. Yet even with this emphasis, we include some comparative work. We try to show how American gender arrangments vary by region, class, race, and ethnicity. We explore the history of our gender institution, particularly since 1900, to make the present understandable. And we look at the future of gender in America by comparing it to the present. But by any measure, comparative work is secondary: our focus is on the here and now of the American gender situation.

The fourth step in limiting the topic was to select a disciplinary base from which to begin our exploration of gender. *We base our analysis in sociology.* Many readers will already know what sociology is; others may need a brief definition of the discipline.

Sociology is the social science that attempts to describe and explain the relationships of human beings to one another, and human actions as they are affected by these relationships. The study of social actions and relationships involves both observable interpersonal behaviors (the social)[2] and the ideas people share and out of which they act (the cultural). Sociology, then, is the science of the sociocultural experiences and products of human beings. It differs from psychology because its primary interest is the individual's social environment, rather than her or his psychic structure; from economics and political science because it focuses on *all* social relationships; from history because it focuses on the present and the general rather than the past and the particular; and from anthropology because of its primary interest in modern complex societies.[3]

As many of you know, however, the discipline of sociology is not constructed around a unified core of theory and method. It is marked by competing subgroups, each of which advances a distinctive type of theory and method. Our decision to anchor our analysis in sociology forces us to another and final step in limiting the topic. We have to identify the sociological concepts and hypotheses that guide us, and how we have selected them out of the competing schools of sociological theory. Before turning to that task, however, we will first take a critical look at the explanation of gender inequality most frequently opposed to the sociological—the biological explanation.[4]

BIOLOGICAL EXPLANATIONS OF GENDER INEQUALITY

The biological explanation has two broad strands. The first identifies biologically determined differences between the sexes that affect our social arrangements. (In this text, *sex* is the term used for the biological differences between females and males, and *gender* is the term used for the sociocultural differences.) The second strand attempts to explain the ways in which biology determines social institutions by tracing these biological determinants back to the early evolutionary experience of the species. This approach is an aspect of *sociobiology*, the discipline that uses biological principles to explain the behavior of all social animals, including human beings (Robertson, 1981). In these two areas, certain factors have been identified as significant for the institution of gender.

The Biological Factors

Reproduction. The crucial biological difference between females and males is their different functions in the reproduction of the species. Like every other mammal, the human male impregnates the female, who produces ova, incubates the fetus within her body, and can produce milk to nourish the newborn infant until it is capable of using nutritional resources in its environment. These reproductive functions have biological effects for the two sexes not only on basic and secondary reproductive organs, but also on anatomy (the wider pelvis of the female which allows for the birth canal), body rhythms (the female menstrual cycle), and hormonal structures. These sex-related traits are all transmitted by the DNA genetic codes at the moment of conception.

Research shows that the different codes associated with maleness and femaleness begin to move the fetus along its distinctive developmental pattern from as early as the third week after conception (Baker et al., 1980:58). Of these sex-related differences, the most significant is the hormonal profile. The dominant female hormones are estrogen and progesterone. The dominant male hormones are androgen and testosterone. *All individuals, however, have all four hormones, and each individual has a particular profile of them, determined by that individual's genetic heritage.*

Appearance. The average male is bigger than the average female from birth, the American male baby averaging 19.8 inches and 8.4 pounds at birth and growing by adulthood to 70.9 inches. The average female baby at birth is 19.3 inches tall and 7.5 pounds in weight, growing in adulthood to about 65.3 inches (Bayer and Bayley, 1959, cited in Baker et al., 1980). Additionally there are different genitalia, different secondary sexual characteristics like breasts and facial hair, the wider shoulders of the male, the wider hips of the female, different voice tones, the greater visibility of muscular development in males, the more rounded contours (resulting from a greater mix of fat with muscle) in the female. Biologists trace most of these differences to the effects of the sex-related hormones.

Physical Strength.   Biologically it does appear that the greater muscular upper body development of the male gives him greater short-term strength in lifting and throwing. Females however, because of reserves of energy stored in fat, have greater physical endurance, another dimension of strength (Selden, 1981, in Richardson and Taylor, 1983). Female endurance is also manifested in longevity. In the United States, the average life expectancy of the white female is 78.3 years and of the black female 74.5 years; the average life expectancy of the white male is 70.6 years, that of the black male 65.5 years (Bureau of the Census, 1980, in Robertson, 1981:521). Biologists point to the effect of the sex hormones as one explanation of these differences between genders.

Mental Abilities.   Research shows the following differences between females and males. Females outpace males in verbal development between infancy and adulthood (Baker, 1980:83). Males in high school and college outscore females in mathematical ability (Maccoby and Jacklin, 1974), and over the whole period between infancy and adulthood show superior skills at tasks requiring spatial perception, judgment, and manipulation (Buffery and Gray, 1972). Females lose visual acuity more rapidly than males (Alpern, 1967); males lose hearing ability more rapidly than females (Corso, 1963, in Baker et al., 1980); females have more sharply developed senses of taste (Meiselman and Dzendolet, 1967, in Baker et al., 1980), and of temperature variation (Kenshalo, 1970, in Baker et al., 1980). Biological explanations for these differences include different male-female patterns of left and right brain development and hormonal effects.

Hormones and Emotions.   High levels of the female hormone estrogen are said to produce a general sense of energy and well-being. Low levels produce feelings of anxiety, fear, and depression. Women typically have high estrogen levels in the first half of each menstrual cycle, and during pregnancy. Low estrogen levels are typical late in the menstrual cycle, after childbirth, and at menopause. This has been translated into theories about women being more susceptible to mood swings than men. On the other hand, the male hormone testosterone has been related to aggressive feelings and actions (Goldberg, 1974). Testosterone is present at particularly high levels in adolescent and young adult males—a fact biological theorists have used to explain everything from crime rates to career achievement.

Sexuality.   Scientific study of the physiology of human sexual response, an issue long shrouded in taboo and myth, has been fairly recent. We now know that almost all men experience full sexual release (orgasm) during heterosexual coitus, while about a third of women rarely or never do, and another third do so only occasionally (Kinsey, 1948, 1953; Hite, 1976). This disparity exists despite the fact that females and males are physiologically equal in their capacity to achieve orgasm, females in fact possessing a capacity for multiple orgasms over a short period, unlike males (Masters and Johnson, 1966). The disparity uncovered by Kinsey and Hite is explained by the Masters and Johnson finding that the primary organ for female sexual arousal is the clitoris, an organ only secondarily involved in coitus.

Other interesting male-female differences are that females experience secondary sexual stimulation over a much greater body area (including skin, breasts, and vagina) than men (Masters and Johnson, 1966); that with stimulation of these secondary areas they may have several nonorgasmic levels of arousal and pleasure, but will achieve orgasm, if they do at all, less rapidly than men do (Masters and Johnson, 1966; Rossi, 1977); and that females achieve more rapid and intense orgasm with direct clitoral stimulation through masturbation or manipulation than they do through the indirect stimulus of coitus (Masters and Johnson, 1966; Hite, 1976). Biologically speaking, then, there is not a perfect complementarity between female and male sexuality.

Associational Patterns. Sociobiologists argue that females and males, because of biological "programming," show different patterns of bonding to others of their species. The root of these differences is traced to the survival needs of the emerging human species. Hormonal and sensory factors are said to predispose women to a primary, near-instinctual bonding with their newborn offspring (Rossi, 1977). Males, who in evolutionary prehistory are thought to have survived in defensive and hunting groups, are said to have a "biogrammer" predisposing them to large-scale purposive grouping (bonding) with other males of their age (Tiger and Fox, 1971). This predisposition is used to explain boys' play groups, male juvenile gangs, male adult team sports, clubs, and political and economic associations.

Biology, then, seems to demonstrate that males and females differ in reproductive function, appearance, kinds of physical, sensory, and intellectual strength, patterns of mood and emotion, sexual need, and associational tendencies. A biologically inclined theorist would argue that these fundamental differences would result in sociocultural arrangements which differentiate between males and females. It seems a strong argument, and we take it fairly seriously. But the biological argument is not as overwhelming as it first appears. Let us see why.

A Sociological Appraisal

Biologists identify a large number of traits on which females and males differ. But even if we accept these data, it seems hard to explain why these differences give one gender, males, a consistently superior social position. Review the points above with an eye to explaining, first, why females might be biologically superior, and then why males might be biologically superior, and you will see what we mean. Why, on the basis of these differences, do men get paid more for their work (see Chapter 5)? Why do women not only bear children, but rear them and do housework without being paid? Why do parents prefer to have boys than girls (see

Chapter 3)? Why has no woman ever been president? Why are menstruating women, in many cultures, viewed as unclean and polluting, while ejaculating men are considered virile and powerful?

The elaborate cross-cultural phenomenon of powerful, positively valued males and subordinate, less valued females cannot be explained directly from the "facts" of biological difference. We must turn to social arrangements, as they interact perhaps with biological differences, to explain gender inequality.

The biological "facts" just presented often rest on questionable research and logic. The finding on differential vision, for example, rests on a study which noted the number of men and women wearing glasses in each age group. The sociobiological arguments about biological differences in associational behavior are particularly suspect. The thesis about male bonding seems to rest on little more than a linkage of the observation that men do form all-male groupings of various types to some mythic vision of prehumanoid hunting bands. The thesis about mother-child bonding links maternal commitment to high estrogen levels, a sense of well-being and sensual arousal in pregnancy, high estrogen in the hours immediately following birth, and the sensual pleasure of breast feeding (Rossi, 1977). We will mention only a few of the many objections that could be made to this thesis. Why, for example, should high estrogen produce commitment toward the unborn fetus rather than toward persons surrounding the pregnant woman? What are the effects of low estrogen, depression, and anxiety on maternal commitment in the postpartum period? What about women who are sick during pregnancy, who do not experience sensual pleasure when suckling a baby, or who adopt a child? Is their maternal commitment less?[5]

Many of the male-female differences isolated by biologists may not be biologically caused. As an example, look at the issue of lesser physical strength in the female. This is a belief so strong in America that women are assumed to be incapable of opening a jar or lifting a stack of books— and the truth is that American women often lack the strength to do these things. But are women biologically weaker? Americans traveling abroad are often startled at the sight of Asian women carrying enormous loads, African women doing the most grueling agricultural work for long hours, Russian women using heavy machinery. Would these women faint at the sight of a jar or a pile of books? In America itself, modern sports medicine has thrown the whole issue of woman's frailty into question by showing that women have certain physical advantages in flexibility, endurance, and fluid conservation, and that good nutrition, information, and exercise can greatly increase their strength and athletic capabilities. As one writer puts it: "Women are the most exciting side of athletics today. Men are fairly close to their limits; women have scarcely begun to imagine theirs" (Selden, 1980, in Richardson and Taylor, 1983).

We have to understand the physical weakness of American women as a complex interplay between cultural belief and social acts that make the belief come true: prohibitions against tomboys and against aggressiveness in females, lack of athletic training, protection against physical exertion. Male strength and aggressiveness are deliberately fostered by social arrangements, of which the sanction against the "sissy" is the most obvious. Observable differences in strength may be socially produced. Plausible arguments might also be developed to explain differential longevity, mental and sensory abilities, aggressiveness, emotional "swings," mother-child bonding, male-male bonding, and perhaps even sexuality. In other words, measurable differences *may* be socially produced.

The differences between males and females identified by biological theorists are generalizations made about two huge categories of human beings. Individuals within each of these categories will vary tremendously on how much or how little of a particular trait they have. There are, for example, individual males who are smooth-skinned and rounded in contour, and individual females who are deep-voiced and angular. For the various traits associated with behavior—size, strength, sensory acuity, and verbal, mathematical, or spatial judgment; tendencies to anxiety or aggression; parental commitment or same-sex sociability—individuals in each category show a normal curve distribution. And there is considerable overlap in the normal curve distributions of the two populations (see Figure 1–1).

Why then is a man valued as bigger, stronger, more intelligent, less moody, and so on, when in a large population like that of the United States there will always be some women bigger, stronger, smarter, and less moody, and when overall most people possess average amounts of whatever the valued or nonvalued trait is? The answer is that it is not the *trait* that is the primary object of valuation, but the *category* male or female. And this is a socially rather than a biologically determined fact. Biologists themselves fall into the trap of social determinants when they emphasize within-category sameness but cross-category differences in the study of gender, rather than the opposite. As one leading biologist talking about modern science shows, this is bad biology.

> Darwin revolutionized our study of nature by taking the actual variation of things as central to reality. That revolution is not yet complete. Biology remains in many ways obdurately Platonic. . . . Geneticists, who are supposed to know better, will sometimes talk about a gene's determining a particular shape, size or behavior instead of reminding themselves that if genes determine anything it is the pattern of variation of a developing organism in response to variations in the environment. (Lewontin, 1983)

Finally we want to question an implication of the phrase "biologically caused," the implication captured in the cliché "biology is destiny." The popular assumption is that "biologically caused" means unchangeable. But this is nonsense! Society and culture have been reworking biology since the emergence of the human species. Social norms and rituals can curb, channel, or heighten aggression, anxiety, sociability, or parental commitment. In intelligence testing, it is nearly impossible to separate what is innate (ability) from what is training (achievement). Strength is in large measure socially cultivated or prevented. And modern science has altered longevity patterns and reproductive constraints and is gaining the capac-

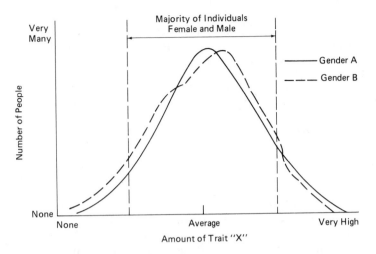

FIGURE 1–1: Typical Distribution of a Sex-Linked Trait in the Overall Population of Human Beings

ity for constructive intervention in hormone disorders. Society, then, may be as much a determinant of biology as vice versa.

Is our position, then, that biological explanations of gender are to be discounted? No. We are not so radical. Males and females have different experiences of themselves as biological organisms because of their different reproductive functions, appearance, body rhythms, sexual physiology, and hormonally affected emotional states. This input from bodily experience may have a significant effect on the consciousness and sense of self of the two genders. But neither the biological differences nor the possibly different personalities that might be shaped by biological factors give us a biological explanation of *gender inequality*, of the enormous superiority in power and valuation almost universally attached to maleness. That superiority, since it is not biological, must be socially constructed and maintained.

Yet we still have to deal with the facts that gender inequality and male superiority are almost universal to human societies. Can biology help us to understand why this is so? Tentatively we would suggest, first, that the typically different appearances of the two sexes provide a visual starting point for social classification and stratification. Second, until recently women have been hostage to their fecundity; frequent childbearing might seriously limit women's capacity for unhampered action. Third, men have not had this biological constraint, and do have greater short-term strength and perhaps more aggressiveness. Fourth, males might have not only physical advantages for domination of an easily identifiable "other" category, but also interests in domination that are in part biologically derived. These interests are to control sexuality for their own gratification, and to control reproduction.

These biological parameters may have set in motion, in society after society, the processes of male domination over females. What societies have then done nearly universally until very recently is to construct an *institution of gender* in which male-female differences are heightened rather than muted, in which a vast array of other differences have been imputed, in which male domination is sustained and strengthened, and in which males are judged superior and females inferior.

SOCIOLOGICAL THEORIES AND THE STUDY OF GENDER[6]

As we said earlier, any attempt to make sense of the world by means of systematic description and explanation begins with some theory. Certain theoretical ideas have guided our attempt to provide a sociological answer to the central questions of this book. Sociology, as we have indicated, contains within itself a large number of theories, often in apparent competition with each other. In our view, the many theories in sociology can be classified under one or the other of three broad theoretical orientations that jointly constitute the theoretical landscape of contemporary sociology: the natural science approach, the critical conflict perspective, and the viewpoint of the interpretive theorists.[7] We have drawn upon ideas from each, as the following discussion shows.

Selections from Natural Science Sociology

Natural science sociologists assume that sociocultural phenomena are like all other aspects of nature, and that they can therefore be studied using the methods of the natural sciences. These methods include a commitment to precise measurement, a quest for generalizations that are universally applicable, a standard of strict objectivity toward the issues under exploration, and an assumption that the elements in society (or nature) are part of the same system. Most natural science sociologists study large-scale social phenomena, but some work, such as exchange theory, is done at the micro level. The classic founders of this branch of sociology are Comte, Spencer, and Durkheim. The most visible and impressive theoretical work in modern times has been that of Talcott Parsons,[8] and it is his ideas from natural science sociology that we use here.

Parsons's theories are particularly useful for understanding the organization and persistence of our gender institution. Three aspects of his work are especially relevant: his concepts of the social system and of social control, and his latent ideology of sexism, which reveals in microcosm the ideological underpinnings of our gender system.

The Social System.   Parsons's social system model provides us with a number of useful guidelines. Parsons conceptualizes society as a system of interlocking status roles. *Statuses* are positions that individuals fill in relation to one another and to collective tasks, such as parent/child; clerk/customer; doctor/patient. *Roles* are the behaviors expected of persons in particular statuses. Statuses and roles are derived from the shared expectations of a group. Parsons depicts each of the commonsense spheres of social life (family, economy, religion, education, and so on) as an arrangement of status roles, an institution, and society as a system of institutions. Individuals, over the course of their days and lives, shift from one status role to another, each individual being sociologically defined in terms of her or his distinctive cluster of status roles. Parsons argues further that there is a natural social tendency toward equilibrium, toward a harmonious and stable complementarity of roles within each institution, and of institutions in society.

This model of the social system suggests several strategies for analyzing gender. Gender itself may be depicted as an institution centering on the complementary status role sets of male and female. Each of these social identities is then to be understood as associated with its own distinctive constellation of expected behaviors. The institution of gender itself may be viewed as one that affects and is affected by most other social institutions. The theory also suggests that we study the stability of the gender institution in terms of complementarities between male and female behaviors, and in terms of the buttressing effect of other institutions. Most generally, and most usefully, Parsons's analysis of social organization alerts us to the need for analyzing social arrangements at at least two levels: the grand level of institutional interrelationships, and the more small-scale, detailed level of role-mediated interpersonal dynamics. One of the hypotheses central to Parsons' social system model, that of a natural complementarity between status roles in an institution, and between institutions in a society, also gives us one explanation for the enduring quality of an institution like gender.

Social Control.   Parsons's social control theory provides us with a second and major explanation for the stability of the gender institution. Basically this theory says that social arrangements are anchored in consensual social support so broad and basic that those who query the arrangement in action, or even in thought, are subjected to society's control pressures. Some of these are external pressures. The person who questions finds herself or himself labeled as deviant and is negatively sanctioned, both materially (such as by loss of income or the inflicting of pain) and psychologically (such as the extraordinarily potent sanction of social disapproval). Other controls are internal. The questioner may be someone who has been socialized into certain beliefs and norms. Challenging these generates inner tension—guilt, anxiety, self-doubt. Parsons places great emphasis on the functions of internal social control and of socialization as stabilizers of society. We pay close attention to external and internal social control as key processes that perpetuate our gender institution, and throughout this book we take a deep interest in socialization and its relationship to gender continuity and change.

Sexism.   Sexism, a belief that the separate and inferior status of women is natural and right, is evident in much of Parsons's theory. The theory mirrors the society it seeks to understand and unintentionally provides us with a clear statement of the conventional ideology surrounding gender.

At the core of Parsons's theory is a deeply held belief in the fundamental importance of the family for overall social well-being. The family is the primary socializer of children, the wellspring for internalized social control. The family is also the major sphere for the emotional sustenance and renewal of adults. As such, it possesses formidable resources for external social control of a psychological nature, as well as being vital for the siphoning off of individual tensions that might otherwise disrupt society. The family is therefore the primary source of social order.

Parsons argues further that for the family to perform its vital social functions, it is essential that adult males and females play very different roles within it. Men serve as the primary link between the family unit and the wider social and natural environment. It is important that they bring to this task, and to their other function of creating and maintaining the key public institutions, an "instrumental" orientation. That is, they must have the qualities of ambition, forcefulness, and self-reliance. Women, however, maintain the internal functioning of the family. They are socializers and sustainers. It is essential that they be supportive of the male actors and "expressive"—that is, affectionate, gentle, and sympathetic—in their orientation. Too much similarity in male and female family roles, Parsons argues, will produce unhealthy competition and will erode the capacity of the family to perform its vital functions (1954:79).

Here, in particularly clear form, we find the pattern of belief that helps to explain the resistance to gender equality by both women and men: the belief that reworking male and female roles in the direction of greater equality affects not only those roles, but threatens family stability and societal well-being.

Parsons's natural science theory gives us useful tools for the analysis of gender and several hypotheses for explaining the persistence of our gender institution. But his work leaves us with some crucial questions:

1. Does normative consensus anchored in socialization and social control provide us with a complete explanation of the persistence of an institution like gender, even with its dynamics of male-female inequality?
2. What exactly does normative consensus mean, apart from agreement on the rules of social behavior? How does it work as a social process, and how do social institutions relate to this process?
3. How does change occur in an institution? Can the processes of normative consensus themselves somehow generate institutional change?

Answers to questions 2 and 3 are provided by interpretive theory. Answers to all three questions are provided by critical conflict theory. But since the latter perspective draws on the insights of the former for its explanations, we will begin to answer these questions by looking at the answers provided by interpretive sociology.

Selections from Interpretive Sociology

Interpretive sociologists view human societies as unique, as distinct from all other natural phenomena. The uniqueness of human groups stems from the species' distinctive capacity for complex communication, thought, and idea creation. Human groups are depicted by interpretive sociologists as bound together by these processes of communication and idea creation. Human actions are guided by ideas, or by *meanings*. In order to explain human actions, sociologists need to understand the meanings that motivate the particular subjects under study. They must seek an empathetic understanding of the subjects' world by immersion in their group life and in the situations particular to that life.

Empathy, participation in the life of those being studied, an interest in the microdynamics and situational specifics of group life, a lack of interest in the quest for "univeral social forms" are all hallmarks of interpretive sociology. Its classic formulators are Weber and Mead. In modern sociology, interpretive theory has several famous proponents and comes in many varieties; it includes the work of such thinkers as Blumer, Goffman, and Garfinkel. For our purposes, however, the most significant contemporary formulator of interpretive theory is Peter Berger (1967). We use two themes in his theory, his thesis of everyday reality as socially constructed knowledge, and his view of the individual as active.

Everyday Reality as Socially Created Knowledge. Berger's central proposition is the assertion that the individual in her or his daily life acts on the basis of taken-for-granted knowledge about reality, knowledge arising primarily from social processes that create and sustain meaning. What the individual experiences as reality is largely a social construction of knowledge and meaning so deeply held by the individual that it appears real.

What processes construct this system of taken-for-granted knowledge? Here we come to the key proposition in Berger's theory—the circular dynamic between individual and collective life. We can begin at any point in this circle; for convenience, we start with the individual. Individuals create knowledge as they confront the problems of living. At any moment in time, the individual brings to bear on experience a system of meanings that pattern and make sense of it. These meanings, the individual's understanding of experience, have been created by the individual or learned from other individuals. What individuals believe subjectively they make visible to others through words, actions, and products (like this book!). These externalized ideas now are objects (words, activities, books, laws, doctrine) forming part of the social environment of other individuals. As these others relate to these objects, their own perceptions and ideas about reality are affected. They take into their consciousness, or internalize, the objectified ideas of the first individual, who is also being affected and has always been affected by the externalized ideas of others.

For Berger, as for Parsons, internalization of social meanings, or *socialization,* is a basic social process. He too sees primary socialization—the learning that the child does—as very significant. It is infused with the child's need for some basic patterning of the chaos of primary experience, with the child's emotional dependence on adult family members, and with the intertwining of the child's emerging sense of identity with this primary learning of the world. But Berger sees learning as a process that goes on through life and as occurring in all situations an individual may encounter. What each individual learns may then be somewhat distinct from what others learn, and what has been learned may be restructured by later experience. There is room for both institutional variation and institutional change in this formulation. Internalization, moreover, is only one basic social process. Equally important is externalization of what is subjectively believed, and the making of these into the "objects" which are society. For, as Berger puts it: "Society is a human product. Society is an objective reality. [The individual] is a social product" (1967:61, phrasing altered to nonsexist language).

This view of society has several implications for our study of gender. It suggests most obviously that our gender arrangements, our assumptions about the "realities" of male and female roles, natures, needs, and social placement, are constructs, as are all social institutions. It shows us that these constructs are both resilient and fragile. Our gender institution is resilient because it is knowledge intertwined with all we know about reality and self. A threat to that system throws up the terror of knowing nothing. So simple legal or technical changes will not automatically transform our gender system. Deeper change requires reworking our knowledge of self and the world. Our gender institution is fragile because we see it as dependent on ongoing relational and definitional processes, as always confronting new definitions discovered by individuals whose life experiences are different from those in the mainstream. Anyone can introject new meanings into the social process, and this introjection can occur at any point in the social fabric.

Finally and most generally, interpretive theory suggests that in addition to analyzing social life in terms of its big structural arrangements and the microdynamics of interpersonal relations, we also study what people believe, their subjective reality.

The Active Individual.   Although interpretive theory has much in common with Parsons's focus on norms, institutions, and cultural consensus, social change figures much more prominently in its view of society. Theorists like Berger in fact have a double vision of society as potentially both self-perpetuating and transformative. The key to this view is the assumption that the individual is an active (and not merely reactive) being.

Individuals act. They pursue goals. They relate to each other: they operate, negotiate, get into conflict. Above all, they reflect on their experiences in a continuous interlocking sequence with overt activity. They define their situations and act on the basis of those definitions. Society itself is this constant process of individuals in activity, and it is reaffirmed or reconstructed by that activity. There is also a strong emphasis on "situation" in this approach. Activity, definition, and reaffirmation or reconstruction of knowledge arise in concrete situations. There is a dialectical tension between overarching systems of societal knowledge and situationally grounded knowledge in process. Stability and change are in tandem, rather than in sequence.

Selections from Critical Conflict Theory

Critical conflict theorists, like natural science sociologists, are primarily interested in large-scale social phenomena, in which they discern patterns of interrelatedness.[9] Critical conflict theorists, however, differ from natural science sociologists in three crucial ways. First, they argue that societies should be analyzed in specific historical terms, as well as in terms of universal social processes. This balancing of the historically specific with the universally visible is somewhat like interpretive theory's focus on specific situations against a backdrop of what is universally known about social processes. Second, they start with the assumption that the central social process is not equilibrium but conflict between groups. Through exploitation of others, some groups have a great deal of power and material resources and seek to preserve them; other groups seek to escape exploitation and improve their life experiences. The analyst of society, then, confronts basic issues of value: between privilege and equality, between domination and freedom, between the interests of overdog and underdog. In addition to studying society, critical conflict theorists argue that the social scientist needs to confront its inequalities and seek to dissolve them. This is their third basic difference with natural science sociologists who emphasize objective, value-free analysis. The classic source and still the vital center of critical conflict theory is to be found in Karl Marx's writings. For our purposes, the most important contemporary proponent of this viewpont is Jurgen Habermas. The description that follows is drawn from both writers. It focuses on two themes: the linked concepts of class, power, and conflict; and the thesis about ideology.

Class, Power, Conflict.   In contrast with the other two orientations in sociology, Marx and his intellectual heirs focus not on socially shared ideas, but on the material conditions of human existence. Marx argues that the basic social process is the capacity of a group to produce what it needs for continued existence. Material production involves the application of technology and labor to environmental resources. These techno-economic factors, labeled by Marx the "means of production," lie at the center of social organization. Around them cluster the processes that form personality and the key social relationships, which affect the shape of all other aspects of society. Each historical epoch is marked by a distinctive pattern of techno-economic processes.

Control over the means of production—technology, raw materials, energy, labor—is the primary source of power in society. Every society is characterized by a *stratification* or *class* system in which some groups control the means of production, forming a ruling class; others exist as labor, just eking out a livelihood and constituting a powerless or subordinate class. A basic source of social conflict and antagonism is the gap between powerful and powerless classes. The dominant class will use its resources to buy other forms of power: political, legal, coercive, ideological. All these means of control are used to protect its own position and to keep the powerless class docile and productive. But however docile and manipulated, the powerless class has at some level an interest in its own emancipation. Its docility is not to be counted on. Periodically, when a complex of historical factors is "right," the subordinate class erupts into revolution against the conditions producing its exploitation.

Marx and Habermas are not primarily interested in gender inequality; their focus is the class stratification of men. But all kinds of implications for the study of gender flow from their theory. First, it gives us a model of society that focuses on inequality—a theme largely missing from the other perspectives. Next, it argues that each historically concrete society will be in many ways unique in its dynamics of inequality, a position that helps us justify our focus on one society in one time frame. Critical conflict theory, moreover, engages our values on behalf of those who are the subordinates, a neat coincidence with our own values on the gender issue. It explains that a system of inequality is really a system of differential power, and that the primary source of power, economic resources, can buy many other kinds of power, including the ability to define a situation. Through this lens we can hypothesize that women have an inferior social position because they are powerless, because as poorly paid wage-sector workers or as unpaid domestic homemakers they can be dominated, manipulated, and rendered docile through the application of law, coercion, politics, and ideology.

Yet, if the critical conflict theorists are to be believed, powerlessness produces a counterforce, the wish for emancipation. Using this viewpoint, we can argue that change is and always has been a possibility for our institution of gender. We need only ask what constellation of social, technological, and economic factors has produced the present thrust toward egalitarian change. The concept of differential power grafted onto the theories of socially constructed knowledge and consensually anchored institutions suggested by the other frameworks is the model used throughout this book.

Of the many other implications of this model, one deserves particular attention: the connection between the Marxist model of economic classes and the phenomenon of gender. This connection makes us see how gender is an essential support of a class system, for the most powerless men can experience power over women. And we can see how class divides women, who, despite the fact that they have historically been denied direct economic power, identify with the class position of their husbands and fathers. So we have women who are wives and daughters of the propertied class, women who are wives and daughters of wage earners (both white collar and blue collar), and women who have their own independent locations as wage earners. In America this situation is further complicated by the conflict-laden diversity of ethnic and racial groupings. We will try to keep this diversity of women's experience and interest before the reader by showing the contrasts between, say, highly educated professional women, wealthy wives, and welfare mothers. But we never lose sight of the commonality among these groups of women: their powerlessness in relation to men.

Ideology. With the concept of ideology, critical conflict theorists link their exploration of the material and power dimensions of social organization to those ideational aspects on which Parsons and Berger place so much importance. Marx's interest in ideas is secondary. Habermas, however, has been influenced by the philosophers whose ideas have fed interpretive sociology, and he gives socially constructed meanings equal weight with material and power factors. For Habermas, society is both the material production of life and the social construction of reality. Both processes help to produce inequality. Regardless of emphasis, however, both Marx and Habermas draw similar maps of the structure of ideas in society.

Ideas arise from people's experience of life and from their communication with others. At one level, then, a society is a collage of idea systems, anchored in the different life experiences of groups. At another level, a society is characterized most of the time by a dominant system of ideology or knowledge, anchored in the interests and experiences of the dominant power groups. Access to the educational and religious systems, the mass media, the political leadership, and so on give these groups channels through which they can disseminate their views of what is true, good, "real."

Powerless groups live caught between two visions of the world, that of the dominant ideology and that arising out of their own experiences and kept alive, often in half-articulated form, in the communities in which they live. The penetration of their consciousness by the ideology of those with power over them is one of the main ways in which they are controlled. An explicit, systematic articulation of their own beliefs and values is necessary for their emancipation. What saves their own beliefs even at the worst of times from being extinguished, and what makes these beliefs periodically bloom in the cause of liberation, is the basic drive toward emancipation that Habermas sees as part of human nature. Fed by this drive, consciousness, or knowledge, or ideology is always potentially critical of the social world in which it is located.

In the chapters that follow, we present an empirically informed analysis, first, of our conventional system of gender inequality (Part I, Chapters 2–5), and then of the various changes presently visible in that system (Part II, Chapters 6–12). The theories we have briefly reviewed here will both frame and be expanded upon in this analysis.

NOTES

1. "Women libbers" and "women's lib" are media-popularized terms of disparagement for feminists who seek women's liberation.

2. Our definition of *social* as "visible interpersonal behaviors" is admittedly narrow. Most sociologists use the term as an umbrella for the sociocultural world. We use the term in this broader sense elsewhere in the book.

3. Even when anthropologists study sectors of modern complex society, they view the groups they study as total or near-total societies or communities. This contrasts with the sociological assumption that any group studied, except for the world community, is part of a bigger social complex and only partly explainable in terms of its intragroup processes.

4. Two other influential explanations of gender inequality are the religious and the psychological. We describe the former in Chapters 3 and 11. A partial presentation of psychological and psychoanalytical theories appears in Chapter 4.

5. For a full evaluation of the Rossi thesis, see *Signs* 4, 4 (Summer 1979): 695–718.

6. This section draws extensively on Lengermann, Marconi, and Wallace (1981).

7. This view of the three basic orientations in sociological theory is now fairly widely used. See, for example, Habermas (1975), Poloma (1979), and Ritzer (1975).

8. Parsons, though he believed in formal, universally applicable theory on a grand scale, was nevertheless sensitive to the limits of a rigid natural science approach, as he demonstrates in his first major work, *The Structure of Social Action* (1937).

9. We focus here on critical rather than analytical conflict theory (for the distinction, see Wallace and Wolf, 1980). But analytical conflict theory, particularly as represented in the writings of Randall Collins, also contributes significantly to an analysis of gender, and its relevant ideas are used later in the book.

Part I:
Social Control

2
THEORETICAL
OVERVIEW:
SOCIAL CONTROL

Picture yourself in the following situation: You have been given a summer job by the public relations department of a large corporation to act as a tour guide for visitors to the organization. One day you escort a delegation from the planet Androgenia, which is interested in comparing American business organization practices to those of their own planet. Over coffee in the cafeteria, after a day of visits to several departments in your building, the delegation's leader comments:

> By and large, your office organization is similar to ours. You have large numbers of people doing the routine tasks of typing, filing, or word processing and so on. They take orders from a smaller number of persons in authority. In contrast to the average paper processor, these bosses have private work space and considerable freedom to determine their use of time. They are the experts to whom we were constantly referred. They are treated with deference by their subordinates. But there is one striking difference between your practices and ours: The subordinates are all female. The bosses are all male. We think this indicates a most fascinating difference between your world and ours. On your planet are females and males two distinct populations? Are males by nature better at leadership? Are females by nature better at typing, filing, and paper processing? What happens to males who are good at paper processing, or to females who are good at

decision making? Doesn't this dilemma ever occur? You see, on our planet the females and the males are so similar in their job capacities that they each can and do perform both kinds of jobs. Please explain your situation to us.

What would you say?

What you are being asked to do is to explain the phenomena of gender differences and gender inequality. You are not being asked about our system of occupational inequality—that is, about the fact that some categories of workers are so much better off than others. That is an issue for another book, though in our exploration of gender inequality we will note the connections between gender inequality and other patterns of stratification.

In this chapter we attempt to answer the questions the Androgenians raised by defining more clearly terms like *gender differences* and *gender inequality*. Next, we state a key assumption: that the consequences of our present gender arrangements are impoverishment for males, for females, and for society. Finally, we look at why our gender institution, with its pervasive inequalities, persists. We call this explanation a theory of social control.

Before we proceed, however, we need to make a very important point. This section of the book describes and explains gender inequality in America; later sections of the text describe and explain contemporary trends toward gender equality. Earlier and later sections, however, do not depict a chronology, in which a conventionalized system of gender inequality is replaced by a new system of greater equality. Rather, the two sections constitute an analytic breakout of social processes all in place now in American society, or what sociologists call *ideal types*—formal models of human activity and relationship that are abstracted out of the complexity of daily experience. Putting it more concretely, millions of Americans today experience gender in the form described in Part I of this book; millions more daily experience the changing system described in Part II; and equally significant numbers live in situations that combine elements from the two patterns of gender. For the moment, though, let us focus on inequality.

GENDER INEQUALITY

The pattern of the relationships between males and females and the characteristics of these two genders are so pervasive and universal that most of us have difficulty seeing them clearly or dealing with them analytically. The Androgenians seem to be blind to occupational inequality, seeing only the dissimilarities between their gender arrangements and ours. More to the point, how did you in your imagination "see" the Androgenians? Were they all male? Did you assume the leader was male? Do you begin to see how ways of thinking and acting may be so taken for granted that you are unaware of them?

If you assumed the leader to be male (as we suspect most of our readers did), you were operating with two taken-for-granted beliefs about males and females: first, that they typically perform *different* functions in society, and second, the dominant positions such as those of leader are usually held by men. It is this pattern of female subordination that makes us speak of gender *inequality*. Embedded within this concept are six themes: categorization, functional differentiation, segregation, unequal access to material goods, differential value, and unequal power. Let us look at what we mean by each of these terms.

Categorization

All societies have two mutually exclusive categories—"male" and "female"—into one or other of which all members are placed from birth to death. The placement of each individual is done by means of a series of cues, most of which are social constructs. Any member of a society can, from an early age, distinguish between males and females.[1] The cues for this recognition are not primarily physiological. Normal dress hides genitalia. We can quickly identify children as female or male, although they have not yet developed beards or breasts or distinctive voice pitch. We "place" individuals without seeing or hearing them. The cues to gender categorization are, by and large, socially constructed signifiers: names, titles, styles of dress and ornamentation, learned modes of gesturing, of interacting with others, of moving.

Most of you probably remember the scene in *Huckleberry Finn* in which, having dressed like a girl and after attempting to pass as "Sarah Williams," Huck was told:

> You do a girl tolerable poor, but you might fool men, maybe. Bless you, child, when you set out to thread a needle, don't hold the thread still and fetch the needle up to it: hold the needle still and poke the thread at it— that's the way a woman most always does; but a man always does t'other way. And when you throw at a rat or anything, hitch yourself up a-tiptoe, and fetch your hand up over your head as awkward as you can, and miss your rat about six or seven foot. Throw stiff armed from the shoulder, like there was a pivot there for it to turn on—like a girl; not from the wrist and elbow, with your arm out to one side, like a boy. And mind you, when a girl tries to catch anything in her lap, she throws her knees apart; she don't clap them together, the way you did when you catched the lump of lead. Why, I spotted you for a boy when you was threading the needle; and I contrived the other things just to make certain. (Twain, 1943: 236–237)

Placement of each individual begins at the moment of birth and is done on the basis of genitalia. By and large this method works, but even when it does not, as in the case of infants with birth defects, the categorization is still made (Money and Tucker, 1975: 55–57). Societies appear not to be able to tolerate ambiguity on the issue of sex-gender identity.

After initial placement, the infant will have attached to it, for the rest of its life, an elaborate sytem of social cues, starting with names, pink and blue clothing, and the repeated assertions of certain characteristics, such as prettiness or toughness, to confirm and make easily recognizable her or his gender identity. A variety of social processes maintain this system: irritation with parents who insist on unisex outfits for their children, hostility toward young people whose dress and hairstyle are not easily placeable, open sanctioning of transvestites as deviant. Most insidiously, our socialization makes every one of us feel embarrassed when occasionally we slip and miscategorize an individual.

In every society, then, we find a situation like that between blacks and whites in America. We find two mutually exclusive social categories. Each individual, from birth to death, is continuously placed into the appropriate category. Placement is facilitated by a series of visible "signifiers," some of which are phsyical, but many more of which are tagging processes created and maintained by the members of the society.

Functional Differentiation

All societies make clear distinctions between the activities and personality traits typically expected of individuals placed in the category "female" and those placed in the category "male." As we saw in Chapter 1, there is a biological base for the association of a few of these activities (or functions) with one or the other sex. For example, only women bear children, and men generally have greater short-term physical strength. But in most societies an enormous number of functions is reserved exclusively or almost exclusively for one gender or the other. Women not only bear children, they raise them. Women do most domestic tasks. Women do secretarial and clerical work. They are also nurses and elementary school teachers. Women are supposed to be warm and emotionally supportive. Males are reared to leave the home daily to procure the means of family subsistence; they are the "breadwinners." They are supposedly better at mechanical and technical activities. They are expected to be physically brave and emotionally tough. Consequently, a range of jobs, from production-line manufacturing to engineering, architecture, and medicine, is identified as men's work. Men are supposedly better equipped for significant decision making and leadership, both in the home and in the public sphere. Indeed, placement in the category "female" almost destroys an individual's chances of being president, senator, corporation or university president, bishop, priest, rabbi, general, admiral, and so on.

Nothing more clearly underscores this taken-for-granted system of gender differentiation than the reactions of people to individuals whose behaviors do not fit into the conventional scheme: to women who dislike mothering or domesticity, to men who enjoy "mothering" or sewing, or women heads of state and male secretaries. Such people are not quite "right." We feel uneasy about them; there is a lurking suspicion even about their sexuality. So an individual's placement in the category of "male" or "female" has deep, fundamental consequences for the activities society will allow her or him to perform and the personality society will encourage her or him to develop.

Segregation

All human societies reserve certain spaces for "males only" or "females only." Persons of the excluded gender who enter these spaces are subjected to severe social sanctions. Functional differentiation produces a de facto gender segregation. During the working day, residential suburbs are populated largely by women, construction sites or financial centers largely by men. Our discussion of gender segregation is not primarily concerned with this pattern of de facto segregation, but rather with what might be termed de jure segregation: segregation formally established and maintained by law, by regulation, and by custom.

In many tribal societies, male or female initiation areas were sealed off from individuals of the opposite sex by a combination of religious ritual and doctrine, physical force, and social ridicule. In present-day traditional Islamic societies, law and custom rigorously separate the sexes in practically every aspect of life. In our own society, the contemporary feminist movement has, for over a decade, attacked the structure of gender segregation. As a result, our system is in flux. Some arrangements until now supported formally by law are maintained more by informal social custom—for example, all-boys schools and all-girls schools, sororities and fraternities, male and female changing rooms in athletic facilities and in department stores, "ladies" rooms and "men's" rooms, men's clubs, bars, the structure of men's events and women's events in the Olympic Games, fire departments, and seating arrangments in Mormon or Orthodox Jewish congregations.

We can summarize this theme of gender segregation as follows: all societies bring men and women together for sexual relations. Heterosexuality is universally approved; homosexuality is very often strongly disapproved. Universally, the two genders mingle within the confines of the home and family, although even here "men only" and "women only" areas may be formally maintained. Outside the family, societies vary markedly in the degree of spatial segregation of the two genders formally imposed by the general population. American society has always allowed considerable gender interaction. But even in America, spatial segregation persists, primarily in relation to "intimate" personal functions, recreation, and religion.

Unequal Access to Material Goods

Within any social class, gender arrangements in our society give women less access to money than men. In advanced industrial societies like our own, money is the universal medium of exchange. To speak of the distribution of material goods is essentially to speak of access to money. Direct access to money is provided by two routes: for a minority of the society, through the ownership of income-generating property (stock in business conglomerates, commercial or manufacturing enterprises, rentable land or buildings); for the vast majority, through working for a wage, salary, or fee. Men have much greater access to both routes, and therefore much greater access to money.

Let us first consider property ownership. How does an individual in this society become an owner of property? She or he may do so by working to acquire it, through savings, investment, and trading and dealing, through generally demonstrating "business acumen." But women have less access to incomes that facilitate savings. Moreover, functional differentiation defines them as "unfit" for business dealing on a big scale. This belief, a belief in which they often share, has in effect excluded women from corporate board rooms, from financial centers like Wall Street, and from educational programs that would give them the necessary skills. Until very recently, for example, women constituted a tiny minority of those enrolled in economics, accounting, or business administration programs.

A second means of acquiring property has been through inheritance of what has been accumulated through the savings and business acumen of an earlier generation. Here again women have not been treated equally. Propertied fathers (or mothers propertied through inheritance), realizing the advantages their male children have had for expanding property, tend to leave the major part, or the vital and active part of a business enterprise, to their sons. The daughters inherit small portions or peripheral sectors of a property system.

Moreover, until 1895 married women could not be independent property owners. (Babcock et al., 1975: 187). Upon marriage, their right to property was transferred to the control of their husbands. The cumulative effect of this on the distribution of property by gender is still with us, and reaffirms the idea that we need to understand our past if we are to know our present. It is not that there are not today women who own and manage property; it is rather that among the population of those actively acquiring and expanding property, women are a small minority. Men dominate. Women's prime avenue to income from property is through marriage to a man of property. This is, however, an indirect route, influenced more by the quality of the personal relationship than by women's control of property itself. When a marriage ends through death or divorce, women are left vulnerable and frightened, as the multitude of arguments over inheritance and alimony indicate.

But people who live off property-generated income are a minority of the population. Most people work—for a wage, a salary, a steady flow of fees. Here the difference between men and women is dramatic. Functional differentiation means that women are seen as better suited for domesticity, men for being breadwinners. Even today many women (45 percent of married women) stay home to rear children and keep house (Smith, 1979: 14), a job that does not bring a wage or salary or fee. In the past, the proportion was much higher—55 percent in 1968 and 80 percent in 1947 (Hayghe in Aldous, 1982: 28–29). These women are financially dependent on a man's (usually a husband's) wages and therefore, like the wives of propertied men, are dependent on their relationship to the wage earner during his lifetime, and are vulnerable to considerable deprivation after his death. Pension benefits to widows in the Chicago study of Lopata (1979: 338) were minimal. Only 9 percent of her respondents reported receiving veterans' widows' pensions, and only 10 percent reported receiving employee pensions. Lopata found 44 percent of the widows she studied living in poverty.

An increasing number of women, though, are going out to work for a wage, salary, or fee. Projections are that two-thirds of all married women under 55 years of age will be in the labor force by 1990 (Smith, 1979: 18). But overall, women do not go to the same jobs men go to. Few women are in manufacturing (except garment manufacturing); in transportation; in skilled mechanical services like plumbing, electrical work, carpentry; in construction; in supervisory administrative positions; in business; in the independent professions. Women take jobs as clerks, typists, service workers, and waitresses, in the lower echelons of health delivery systems, and as teachers (see Chapter 5). All are low-paying jobs—sometimes because they require little skill, sometimes because they are in low-return economic sectors, sometimes because they are underunionized, and sometimes because they are simply undervalued—"women's work," done by women with husbands who are the primary wage earners.

Some women do enter the better-paying occupations traditionally monopolized by men. But they do not receive equal treatment. The accumulation of unequal opportunity in training, recruitment, promotion, and salary allocation (see Chapter 5) means that women have less overall access to these jobs and to the best incomes these jobs can generate. It is on this part of women's inequality that the whole range of affirmative action policies is focused. The overall result is the "startling statistic" that women in the wage sector earn 59 cents for every dollar earned by men.

Differential Valuing

Almost all societies believe males are more important and more valuable than females. Material goods are not the only rewards people seek; people also seek social approval. They get that approval when what they do or what they are is perceived by a group as fitting into its classification of valued things. For example, an individual will get approval for behaviors that make others laugh in those situations where a sense of humor is held to be a valued trait. The same individual may also be approved for seriousness in situations where group members feel that the tasks at hand demand all the participants' resources. To be or to do something others value means that those others will direct a variety of signs of approval, both implicit and explicit, to the person. A flow of these "warm strokes" is essential to the growth and well-being of the human personality.

> "What woman," mused a young Northern Melpa man, "is ever strong enough to get up and say, 'Let us make *moka*, let us find wives and pigs, let us give our daughters to men, let us wage war, let us kill our enemies!' No, indeed not! . . . they are little rubbish things who stay at home simply, don't you see?" (Strathern, 1972: 161, in Jagger and Struhl, 1978: 160)

This statement dramatically captures a stance toward valuing that is almost universal. It is an attitude that lurks, we believe, unexpressed and unacknowledged in the hearts of a majority of our own population. It is the attitude that to be female is not as valuable as to be male, and often that to be female is to be of no value at all.

Fortunately for the female psyche, it is rare to find a group or society that finds nothing about women that deserves some approval.

Minimally, women are usually valued as sources of sexual pleasure for men and as bearers of children.[2] Without them, as every group has perceived, the group would not survive. Moreover, males do not always find that maleness brings approval. Remember this nursery rhyme?

> What are little girls made of?
> Sugar and spice and all things nice,
> That's what little girls are made of.

> What are little boys made of?
> Snips and snails and puppy dog tails,
> That's what little boys are made of.

The point, then, is that the categories *male* and *female* are not value-neutral. Around each category in our own society swirl a curious mix of positive and negative evaluations, an overall attitude of ambivalence. Another general point is that the category *female* is surrounded by more ambivalence and has attached to it many more negative judgments than the category *male*. These evaluations are communicated to males and females by a variety of signals. Some are obvious; some are so subtle that one does not even know one is getting a message—though one gets the message. And these signals are sent to individuals over the whole course of their lifetime. Indeed, they begin from the moment of conception (see Chapter 4).

Unequal Power

A variety of resources makes it easier for men to work their will in the world. The commonsense definition of *power* is that it is the ability to realize one's will, to do what one wants. The sociological definition is that power is the ability to impose one's will on others, to get them to do what one wants, despite their resistance. In our society, as in almost all others, men have more power than women, both in the ordinary sense and in the sociological sense. And that power is often exercised as power over women.

Functional differentiation, for example, equips women to be competent in the domestic sphere, while equipping men to be competent in the outside world. Trained skills are a power resource. Women exercise power over men within the home (a situation caricatured for us in domestic comedies). Men exercise power over women in such institutions as the economy. This, however, is not a simple power equivalence. In big industrial societies like our own, the world of economy, politics, and big organizations is the powerful sector in the society. The domestic worlds of family, home, and neighborhood possess certain reserves of resistance, but overall they are vulnerable to economic conditions, legislation, and organizational pressures. In other words, the spheres in which men have power are the spheres which, if we take a more general look at social organization, have power over the areas in which women have power resources. At the interpersonal level, this is visible in the power men wield in the family as primary wage earners.

Other factors, too, explain the unequal power of males and females.

Take, for example, what we might call *personality differentiation*. Our society prepares women to be supportive, caring, nonassertive; it expects men to be independent, tough, effective, capable of making decisions. It negatively sanctions women for showing male personality traits, and vice versa. In other words, males have, through socialization, traits that will make them effectively powerful in any situation, even in the overall running of family life. Women have been trained to step back, to defer, to behave in ways that open the way for leadership by a man. Have you ever served on a committee of men and women and noticed, if you were male, that women seemed to be passively leaving the work of decision making up to you? Or felt, if you were female, all choked up as you wanted to say what you thought, but somehow felt uncomfortable speaking up?

Now let us consider the implications of differential valuing. The advantage that maleness confers is an enormous power resource. Why else do women fill out application forms using only their first initial, not their first name, if not in the hope of "passing" as a male? Also, a man's voice will get attention in almost any situation—and not just because a deeper voice carries better.

Two other power resources need to be looked at. The first is the resource given by superior physical strength. In interpersonal relations, this is the ultimate power resource. It is the source of coercive power. As we will see in detail in later chapters, all the statistics on rape and wife battering show that men use this power resource over women. It is a power resource men have within the family, that sphere in which it has been argued that women exercise power. And men have this power partly because of biology (because on the average they are physically bigger and stronger), but also partly because of social gender arrangements (because males get more training in physical skills).

A final power resource is control over the formal organizations of power in society—the legislative process, the courts, the police. These are male-dominated institutions. The consequences of this arrangement will be discussed more fully in Chapter 5; at this point it is enough to say that in a social confrontation between male and female interests, these institutions are usually used for male interests. Think about the process of a rape case, where the abuse is usually simply talked away, dismissed, or treated as trivial by the male authorities involved.

GENDER IMPOVERISHMENT

The major assumption of this book is that American gender inequality impoverishes both women and men. Under our present gender arrangements, both women and men remain partly stunted, some of their potential for full personal growth stifled. A society of stunted personalities is an impoverished society.

What is "full personal growth"? What possibilities for human development are thwarted by our gender arrangements? Philosophers, psychologists, and humanists argue endlessly about this (see Maslow, 1955 and 1969; Degler, 1980; Smith-Rosenberg, 1975; Mahowald, 1978). Our definition is somewhat arbitrary and simple, but it does not contradict the main drift of this debate, which is that gender arrangements are a hindrance to full personal growth.

The first part of our definition is based on the assumption that people are all much alike in their potential for happiness. In other words, men and women are potentially capable of happiness produced by the same sources. One primary source is the experience of loving: of giving and receiving love, warmth, affection, and friendship in an open, uninhibited way. Another primary source of happiness is meaningful work: work that allows the personal experience of autonomy, independence, and self-sufficiency; work that allows the externalization of one's energies and creativity; work that, however modest, is publicly approved as worthwhile (Glennon, 1980). Both men and women are potentially capable of experiencing deep personal satisfaction of both types. And both men and women in our society are presently denied access to some part of this range of experience simply because they *are* men or women.

Men in today's society are forcefully restrained from open emotional expression. Take, for example, the following accounts. One male, as an adolescent, was told to "be a man" when his mother died. Recalling this period, he said, "I felt resentment at not being able to cry for my own mother's death" (*Newsweek*, June 15, 1981:107). Another man, who was "equal parenting," tells a poignant story about sharing his son's experience at the X-ray department of a hospital, where his son was to have an arthurogram to check a growth on his knee. He describes it thus:

> Aaron grabs my arm and hangs around my neck. I feel what he feels. I do not want to leave him any more than he wants to leave me. He looks straight into my eyes and speaks with his eyes before his words repeat, "Dad, I'm scared."
>
> Uncharacteristically my words dissolve in my gut. I hug him firmly as he cries softly. As I search for words, I realize the embrace is enough. Vainly looking for nonexistent casualness, I say, "It will be over in a half-hour." He hugs me hard. He leaves with the white-robed stranger behind a "No Admittance" door.
>
> The intensity of my love for my son nearly overpowers me. I wait alone. I let in the feeling of how important he is to me. The doctor returns to tell me the growth is not malignant and that Aaron has been a brave and calm patient.
>
> When I am an old man the memory of our X-ray day will help me feel warm and full, just as it does now as I write this. I am grateful that I did not "have to work" that day. (Ray Lovett, *Washington Post*, January 23, 1980:E-5)

On the other side of the coin, women are restricted in their access to meaningful work. It is true that domesticity can give some outlet for creativity, but housework is heavily shot through with an unending round of drudgery. Despite the romantic image of absolute satisfaction projected in *Family Circle* advertising, doing laundry for a family, or washing dishes, or washing and waxing kitchen floors is very, very dull work. Nor does housework bring much public approval. And since it is unpaid, there is no potential for making the worker feel autonomous and independent.

In the area of wage work, as we have seen, women's access to the range of jobs is restricted. True, many men are also restricted by class, race, age, and ethnicity. But this does not mean we can discount the restrictions imposed on half the population because of gender.

The second part of our definition of full personal growth derives from the assumption that each individual is different in physical, intellectual, and emotional traits. For full development, each individual should be able to explore the entire range of social opportunities and to choose those activities and ways of being that best fit her or his personal traits. Lack of material affluence and educational opportunity limits the access of individuals in our society to this kind of development, as do undervalued racial, ethnic, or age characteristics. But our interest here is in the restrictions posed by gender. Gender identity throws up massive barriers to free individual choice for both males and females. Being tagged male or female limits one's choice in style of dress, mannerisms, degree of physical activity, choice of sexual partner, and kinds of education, recreation, and work. In many ways, the negative sanctioning for males who cross the lines of gender restriction is far more severe than it is for women. This is because aspiration to downward mobility—that is, deliberately moving to the undervalued category "female"—is more shocking than its opposite.

The third and final theme of our definition of full development is that of an absence of chronic pain—pain growing out of the organization of our psyches and of our emotions. Our present gender arrangements create a situation of chronic psychic pain for both women and men. We will take up this issue more fully in Chapter 4. Here we need only point to the pain and anger that females all experience at some level because of the ongoing experience of being undervalued and relatively powerless, to the consequences of this pain and anger for relationships to males (sons, fathers, brothers, husbands), and to the responsive anger, guilt, and ambivalence men feel. Our gender arrangements create a psychological pain like that caused by our arrangements of black-white relations.

In addition, our present arrangements create bodily pain for both women and men. The very same prejudices that select men as better suited for leadership, for decision making, for "breadwinning," for heavy labor, for mechanical jobs, produce the negative consequences for men of combat duty in war and of stress-filled and often dangerous and always exhausting work in the civilian economy. Women, though seemingly protected from these life-threatening occupations, experience the bodily pain of rape and spouse abuse.

Our conventional gender arrangements, then, impoverish both females and males by denying them the full range of happiness, by restricting the choices they can make for individual growth, and by generating chronic emotional pain. Cumulatively, this process of individual impoverishment adds up to a tremendous social cost. Lost to society are vast amounts of talent—the men who could have nurtured their children lovingly, the women who could have been scientists or poets. As Virginia Woolf said long ago, Shakespeare may have had a sister as talented as he. But we will never know, for circumstances kept her silent. (1929:117, 118)

Embedded in society is an explosive amount of unhappiness and anger: alienated housewives, emotionally inhibited men, frustrated mothers living vicariously through their children, men defensively locked into rigid sexist prejudices, women whose repressed anger leads them into deep depression, men whose explosions of anger lead to wife abuse and homicide or rape. Is it possible to find a better situation than our present one? In Part II of this book we will look at the arguments presently raging on this question. But first we need to understand why the present situation persists.

SOCIAL CONTROL: THE THEORETICAL MODEL

We will use a rather schematic and formal model to answer the question of why the system persists. We call this a model of *social control,* meaning the array of social and social-psychological processes by which a society sustains or reproduces a complex set of social arrangements.

To arrive at a sociological explanation of any situation, one must look at it from a variety of angles—or from *three levels,* as sociologists say (see Figure 2–1).

Three Angles on the Problem

First, there is what we will call the *X-ray approach.* To explain the recurrence of a complex social situation, one must investigate how individuals in the situation think and feel. This kind of investigation we call the

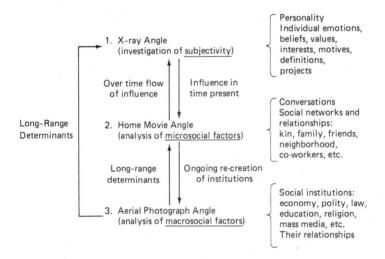

FIGURE 2–1 Three Levels of Sociological Analysis

investigation of *subjectivity*. We attempt to answer the question, "What is going on inside people's heads?" We look at each individual's processes of self-interaction—that is, at what each person is saying to herself or himself as he or she interprets a particular situation and acts within it. At this level of inquiry we ask questions about a person's personality and emotional nature, about beliefs, values, interests, and motives, about how individuals define their situations and how they plan courses of action.

Second, there is what we call the *home movie approach*. Here we attempt to answer the question, "What is going on around each of the individuals that would help us to understand the situation?" It is as though we could follow individuals around with a movie camera to record their movements, their conversations, their demeanors toward each other, and the positive and negative sanctions they give each other. Sociologists call this the *microanalytic approach*. It involves the study of the individuals' immediate milieu—relationships in family and kinship groups, and with neighbors, peers, friends, co-workers, networks, and cliques. There is a great deal of interaction between these phenomena and individual subjectivity. An individual's personality, emotional nature, and beliefs get molded in these environments, and at any moment in time the particular shape of one or other of these relationships results from the interplay among the various individuals' personalities, emotions, and beliefs.

Third, there is what we will call the *aerial photograph approach*, in which we try to answer the question, "What's going on in the society that would help us to understand the persistence of this situation?" Think, for example, of the office situation described at the beginning of this chapter. To take an "aerial photo" approach to that situation would require us to try to see things going on elsewhere: in other departments in the same organization, in the relationship between the organization and other business enterprises, and in the fit between those office routines and what goes on in the "big" social arrangements of the society, like the educational system and legal system. This is what sociologists call the *macroanalytic approach*, or the study of social institutions and their relationships.

There is some disagreement in sociology about how these institutions relate, and also about how this level relates to the other two. We can answer this question in several ways. First, at any moment in time these large social arrangements massively influence all the situations and environments in which individuals live their lives. The particular forms of our relationships to family, co-workers, and friends are influenced by our economic arrangements, our educational system, and so on. The same is true about the link between these macro arrangements and subjectivity. Institutional arrangements enormously affect what we believe and how we act in our own personal environment.

We reject the notion, however, that institutional arrangements totally determine either milieu or subjectivity. Each of these levels has its own dynamics, a degree of autonomy, and a great deal of unpredictability. For example, how will groups react to a condition of economic scarcity? By breaking down and fighting? By joining together more tightly for mutual self-defense? By rationally dividing up what is available? All these outcomes are possible and will happen in different groups. From our perspective, institutions are in part a collage of milieus in which relationships and actions take on predictable and patterned form. It is in these milieus that institutions are reproduced or changed. In other words, microanalytic factors and subjectivity, although deeply affected by macrostructures, also have significant effects on what we call institutions.

The Major Social Processes

The next stage in the development of our model of social control is to relate the three levels of analysis just described to some concepts about social processes. The processes are external social control, sanctions, coercion, internal social control, socialization, authority, and dualism.

External social control is the term for the relationship between a society or group whose members want an individual to act in a prescribed way and an individual who actually or potentially resists acting in that way. The group seeks to stop this resistance by the use of positive and negative *sanctions*—rewards for conformity and punishments for resistance and deviance. Positive sanctions include material goods like food or money, social approval, social prestige, and the possibility of social influence and power. Negative sanctions include withholding of all these rewards, as well as the use of physical force that threatens the deviant's life, physical well-being, or freedom of movement.

External social control can operate between people of roughly equal status, as in a group of friends; and it can operate between people of different social status and different social power, as between a supervisor and a subordinate or a teacher and a student. Situations of unequal power are those in which the superordinate's will prevails over that of the resisting subordinate. When that power relationship rests on the superordinate's use of social sanctions, particularly on the use of the more painful negative sanctions of physical force and material deprivation, we have *coercion.*

Internal social control refers to the situation in which the individual does not resist the group, even when the prescribed behaviors seem not to further the individual's needs and interests. Indeed, the prescribed behaviors may be costly to the individual. The individual conforms because those prescribed behaviors strike her or him as good, sensible, meaningful, or because the individual, though aware to a degree of the cost of conformity, feels that it is right to conform, that nonconformity will make her or him uncomfortable and guilty. This attitude is usually not just a happy coincidence between individual and group. It results from a long relationship between the individual and group, as a result of which the individual absorbed the views of the group and in effect exercises control over herself or himself.

The process by which the individual internalizes group attitudes is *socialization,* or social learning. It begins at birth, is particularly effective in childhood, and continues throughout life. It occurs informally in microsocial settings and formally in schools, churches, and other large organizations. Internal social control will operate in groups of equals and

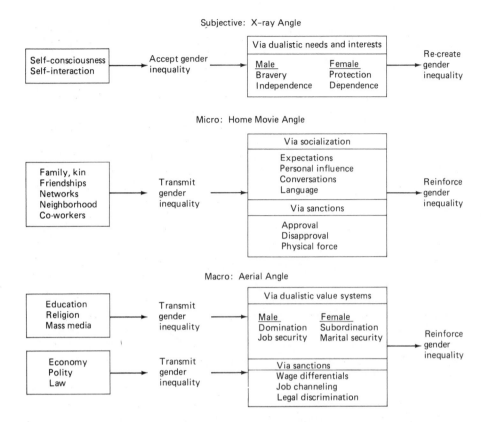

FIGURE 2–2   Gender Inequality and Levels of Sociological Analysis

in situations where individuals are unequal in wealth, status, and power. In situations of unequal power, when both superordinate and subordinate accept their relationship as right, we have a situation of *authority*. Super- and subordinates may not have identical outlooks; their motives, values, and beliefs may differ. But the differences are complementary; they fit their bearers to their different situations in a relationship both see as correct. It is this difference in outlook, with its peculiar complementarities, that we call *dualism*.

We have now presented all the tools or concepts of our analytic model of social control. Figure 2–2 relates these concepts and groups them around the issue of gender inequality. This formal chart is supplemented by Figures 2–3 and 2–4, which show how these processes work together in two concrete situations.

Applying the Model

Internalized social control is depicted in Figure 2–3, where we use our *X-ray view* to look into the mind of a secretary and see that she is happily doing her typing chores and reacting to her situation with thoughts that

FIGURE 2–3 Internalized Social Control and Gender Inequality: The Happy Secretary

can be summarized by the remark, "This is wonderful!" There is perfect harmony between her thoughts and actions because she has fully accepted the values, laws, and formal sanctions of the larger social structures, as well as the informal sanctions in her immediate surroundings. Her unquestioning compliance derives from her view that her male superior has authority; he represents a legitimate power source.

Now let us think back to the opening scene of this chapter, when the Androgenians asked why there was this peculiar set of gender arrangements in the office, where the paper processors were female and the leaders male. Internalized social control is half the answer to that question. The macro and micro structures have done their job so well that the happy secretary re-creates those very structures impinging on her by reinforcing, through her words and actions, the beliefs of others. She is thus helping this situation to persist. We do not intend to imply that the happy secretary is happy every moment of the day. There are bound to be moments of frustration, of questioning, of being tired of getting kicked around. But her general posture is a satisfied one; she generally sees her place as meaningful. She has been successfully socialized in the way her society wants her to be.

Figure 2–4 shows a situation of external social control. Our unhappy secretary depicts the other side of our social control model. The chief source of her unhappiness is on the subjective level, where her consciousness of her subordinate position is acute; hers is *not* a conforming consciousness. Unlike her counterpart in Figure 2–3, she is questioning the legitimacy of her boss's power; in fact, she sees his position as coercive. Though she continues to type, her self-interaction (what she is saying to herself, the X-ray view) regarding her actions is negative, and the macro and micro structures are experienced by her as pressures rather than reinforcers. For instance, she is no longer thrilled about the size of her

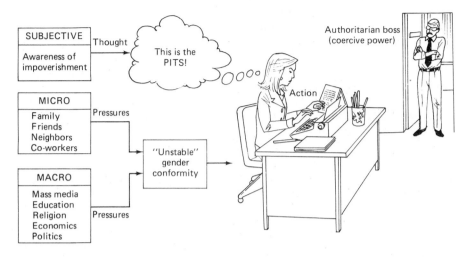

FIGURE 2–4 Externalized Social Control and Gender Inequality: The Unhappy Secretary

paycheck; she reflects on and questions the job counseling she received in high school; she is critical of the way TV ads depict women in jobs like hers. In addition to feeling these pressures from what sociologists call macro structures (economy, education, and mass media), she also feels pressures from friends, family, and co-workers, who urge her to "be a good girl" and to "keep smiling." All this results in unstable gender conformity. Since her thoughts and actions do not match, she must constantly repress the side of her that says "This is the pits" in order to stay on the job. The social control mechanisms are external, not internalized. She is a potential rebel.

To see how the social-control model can be applied to a male position, let's focus on the boss in Figures 2–3 and 2–4. Assuming that the same macro and micro elements are working to keep the boss at his job, the internalized social control picture would be that of a "happy boss"—a satisfied man whose consciousness about his job matches his actions. Everything about his situation reinforces his conformity. For example, his paycheck is sufficiently rewarding; his educational and religious background have prepared him to take on the task of breadwinner, and the mass media communicate approval of his dominant position (all bosses and breadwinners are male). In addition, micro-level structures (family, kin, and friends) are constantly "patting him on the back"; his co-workers are giving him "warm strokes" as long as he continues to make good decisions, exhibits the leadership qualities and expertise they expect of him, and puts in his 40-hour (or more, as the case may be) week. Thus the boss is saying, "Wonderful!" to himself most of the time.

Suppose, however, that this apparently happy boss becomes aware of the fact that he is turning into such a workaholic that he is missing out on precious time with his family. He realizes that he really wants to be a loving father and husband, to be with his wife and children more, to take an equal share in the upbringing of the children. Now the newly unhappy boss no longer has a conforming consciousness. His decision regarding equal parenting puts him in a deviant position with regard to the macro and micro structures, and they will attempt to inhibit him. For instance, his decision to pass up a promotion and/or to change to a 60 percent work-week schedule so that he will have more time at home will be met with disapproval by his company. There is little or no reinforcement for him in the mass media, either. In fact his wife, if she is a full-time house-wife, may react negatively because she sees him trespassing on her turf at home. She may put pressure on him to go back to full-time work because she wants to protect her home turf and also because she disagrees with and disapproves of his decision to reduce the family's financial resources and objects to making the sacrifices involved. While he may be saying "This is the pits!" to his full-time job, she may be rejecting the hardships caused by his change of mind.

Other micro structures also pressure him to return to or to stay on the job. Friends and neighbors may label him as an "adult sissy" because he wants to do more nurturing of his children; his parents and siblings may want him to be a financial success; members of professional organizations may want him to remain an active participant; some female PTA members may isolate him when he arrives at an afternoon luncheon and finds himself the only male present. All these people convey the undeniable message that he is perceived as a deviant, that his thinking is muddled, that he should conform by staying on or returning to his full-time job. As we saw with our unhappy secretary, the key to understanding his situation is the X-ray view; that is, being able to see whether an individual is aware of the impoverishment caused by gender inequality.

SUMMARY

This chapter began with a claim that gender inequality exists in American society today, where women are generally subordinate to men. We then elaborated on our meaning of subordination by introducing the themes of categorization, functional differentiation, segregation, unequal access to material resources, differential valuing, and unequal power. This was followed by a discussion of the consequences of gender inequality: impoverishment for both females and males and for society. We then presented a model of the social control processes that keep this inequality in place.

At the beginning of this chapter an extraterrestrial visitor asked you why our office routines were arranged as they were by gender. We think that you could now offer a general answer to that question. You could say that these arrangements reflect and are partly caused by a much more general, society-wide set of gender arrangements in which males and females are perceived to be different and unequal. You could go on to show that many people accept and are content with the pattern of gender arrangements because of the cumulative effects of a complex of institutional and interpersonal influences. Finally, you could point out that even when some individuals reject these arrangements, institutional and interpersonal influences work to keep them in line. In the next three chapters we will use available information about gender in America to show in detail how these processes work.

NOTES

1. By age 3, children know their own gender, and by age 4 or 5, they learn to label the gender of others correctly (see Kohlberg, 1966:104).

2. Not always, though. The Greeks were an exception. For example, see Pomeroy (1975).

3
CONVENTIONAL BELIEFS ABOUT GENDER

In this chapter we use what we described in Chapter 2 as the X-ray approach to take a look at what goes on inside the heads of conventional women and men as they act out their gender roles in our society. Our argument is that an enduring institution of relationships and inequalities like gender derives much of its stable character from the fact that people have *internalized* (that is, incorporated into their personalities) beliefs that lead them to act in the patterned, predictable ways that constitute the institution. Now we describe in some detail what conventional women and men think—that is, the patterns of subjectivity that lead people to act in ways that reproduce our system of gender inequality, to perceive their actions as "right" or legitimate and to imbue the system itself with authority.

We use the terms *subjectivity* and *meaning system* as labels for the ideas, beliefs, and assumptions people use to make sense of their observations and experiences in the world. We are particularly interested in what people take for granted, and beliefs about gender offer us a rich lode of taken-for-granted assumptions.

Sociologists who focus on individuals' meaning systems follow some basic rules when investigating a group's meaning system: (1) strive to perceive and describe the world *as the subjects themselves experience it*—that is, try to put oneself in the place of the people whose beliefs one is seeking to know; (2) describe the whole cloth these beliefs form, rather than imposing preconceived analytic distinctions; (3) attempt to create a sympathetic portrait of the subjects' viewpoint, in the belief that people hold their deepest, taken-for-granted beliefs in good faith.[1]

Our description is guided by the assumption of *dualism;* that is, men and women do not necessarily have identical outlooks on gender, but rather have views which are, in many instances, different but complementary. We will also discuss the causal connections between the beliefs we have described and the micro and macro social systems in which American women and men live. We will look, in other words, at the links among our X-ray, home-movie, and aerial photo factors.

GENDER AS A BELIEF SYSTEM

We begin by letting our subjects speak for themselves. Remember the happy secretary and her equally satisfied boss (Figure 2–3)? Let us assume that she is also a happy wife and mother, and he a happy husband and father. Let us imagine that we can catch them each in a reflective moment. We ask her to sum up what it means to her to be a woman, and we ask him to sum up what it means to him to be a man. What do they say? We hear first from our conventionally situated woman, the happy wife, mother, and secretary.

THE HAPPY SECRETARY SPEAKS:

A woman is basically different from a man. A man's born to rule the world, as they say, but a woman rules the hearth. In other words, a woman's place is in the home, looking after her husband and her children. In many ways, that's what holds the world together.

How come I'm working, you ask, if I feel like this? Well I may be working, but don't think of me as a career woman! I'm working because of inflation. I'm working to help pay the mortgage. But the minute Tom, my husband, wants me to quit, or the minute my children need me at home full time, I'll quit. We'll manage the mortgage some other way.

And I never forget that Tom is the breadwinner, that because of him we are financially secure. Even though I've gone out to work, I've seen to it that things haven't changed around here, at least in the essentials. Tom and the children come home to the clean, comfortable, loving home they have a right to expect. I may grumble a bit when I'm tired, but mostly to the children. Tom gets all the respect that he's due. He is basically the boss in his own house. A man needs to feel that he's looked up to. And Tom knows I love him, that I keep myself looking attractive for him.

I see my boss at work much the same way. He's a breadwinner too. He's got to succeed. As a man it's easy for him to take charge and make decisions—and somebody has to. I try to follow orders, to make him feel respected, to do little things to make his life more comfortable. After all, isn't that what a woman's for? To stand behind her man—be it boss or husband—and help him in his struggle with life? Knowing this is maturity.

I guess I've been mature ever since I was a kid. I always expected to marry and be a homemaker first. Work's always been a secondary consideration for me. Career women really bother me. It flies in the face of nature, and takes good money away from a man. Anyway that's how I see it, and it's how I'm raising my daughter. Maybe the world will make it through if we women keep raising our daughters to be real women, like us.

It would take the happy secretary about five minutes to tell us all this. She probably would not use as many clichés as we have included, but we chose the clichés deliberately. We wanted to bring home to you the fact that these ideas are as commonplace as the phrases that express them. But though commonplace, the ideas are not shallow or superficial. Like the iceberg's tip, they are the visible expression of a huge and complex system of beliefs about gender.

Now we hear from a conventionally situated man. The happy boss, husband, and father gives his views on what it means to be a man.

THE HAPPY BOSS SPEAKS:

Men and women are basically different. A man's lot in life is a tough one. He has a hard row to hoe. As the Bible says, "By the sweat of thy brow shall thou eat bread all the days of one's life." That's man's lot.

A man's got to work hard all his life. He's got to be the breadwinner for his family while a woman's born to be the homemaker. A man's got a terrible responsibility.

It's a tough, dog-eat-dog world out there—a world where there are only winners and losers. I've tried all my life to stay on the winning side. I worked hard at school, majored in college in a field that would help me get ahead, and now I try to stay on top of the information in my field. I act decisive, as though I'm in control. It doesn't do to act soft in business. You've got to look strong and act tough. And it's paid off. My employees respect me, I've gained quite a reputation in my field, I make good money for myself and my family.

. . . My family—I'm a lucky man. Three healthy children, a lovely wife. Mary's done her bit for my career. She's a great cook. Loves entertaining. Looks after the house and kids and leaves me to get on with the job. Even when I'm putting in twelve-hour days. It's good to know when you're out there that your home is a little oasis where you can get peace, respect, and love. It's good to have a wife who looks up to you, a wife you can trust.

Mind you, I'm good to Mary too. She's never had to work a day in her life. I see to it that the little woman has everything—all the labor-saving conveniences, pretty things, little considerations like the unexpected bunch of flowers, the weekend holiday for two, and protection from the rough and ready of life. Above all I let her know she's special to me, that whatever happens she's my wife. Women are such delicate, lovely creatures. They put all the color and warmth in life. They deserve to have someone to look after them. My Mary knows I never forget that.

Obviously, this too is a caricature. But we make our happy boss think in clichés for the same reasons we made our happy secretary do so—to emphasize the commonplace nature of their ideas. Those of you who doubt that people think this way should check Rubin (1976), Shapiro and Shapiro (1979), and Terkel (1974), as well as the quotations in Chapter 11 of this book.

We need to explore the wider meanings that frame these two statements. For a general overview, look carefully at Table 3–1. In the first column are phrases used by our happy secretary. In the second are phrases used by our happy boss, phrases that complement the conventional woman's views and communicate essentially the same general belief

TABLE 3–1 Conventional Beliefs About Gender

	Woman's View (Quoted from the "happy secretary's" speech)	Man's View (Quoted from the "happy boss's" speech)	Underlying Belief
I	"A woman is basically different from a man.... In many ways that's what holds the world together...."	"Men and women are basically different.... As the Bible says...."	The belief in *natural differences*
II	"A man is born to rule the world ... Tom gets all the respect that's his due...."	"It's good to have a wife who looks up to you...."	The belief in *male authority* (patriarchy)
III	"A woman's place is in the home...."	"A man's got to be the breadwinner."	The belief in *public vs. private space*
IV	"I'm not a career woman.... (My family) comes home to the clean, comfortable, loving home...."	"A man's got to work hard all his life.... [My wife's] never had to work a day in her life...."	*Man's work vs. "woman's work"*
V	"Tom knows I love him...."	"Home ... an oasis of love. It's good to have a wife you can trust...."	The belief in *love*
VI	"Ever since I was a kid ... I always expected to marry and be a homemaker first...."	"I worked hard in school, majored in college in a field that would help me get ahead...."	*Schooling: male and female views*

about gender. In column 3 we identify each of these underlying beliefs with a sociological label, such as "natural differences," or "public vs. private spheres."

THE BELIEF IN NATURAL DIFFERENCES

At the foundation of conventional perceptions of gender is the belief that there are *real, significant, and immutable differences between men and women.*[2] "You can't expect men and women to do the same things" both our happy secretary and our happy boss would say; "It's not natural. Men are better at some things, women at others. *Vive la différence.*"

How are men different from women, you might ask? Well, they would answer, men are bigger and stronger, more physical, more decisive; better at fighting, and at leading and making decisions; less emotional and intuitive, less aware of the feelings of others around them; better at achievement and worse at nurturance; better at technical things and at mathematics; and so on. Women are smaller and softer and prettier, good at caring and loving, at supporting and quietly enduring, and ill equipped for the intellectual and physical rough and tumble of the world. And reality supports this description of the distinctiveness of men from women. Men (as a group) do appear to have more of some qualities and less of others in relation to women (as a group), exactly as the conventions say they do.

Of course, there are those who depart from the rule—big, strong, physical, decisive, achieving women, and small, soft, caring, loving, nondecisive, nontechnical men. But conventionally situated people either do not see these unexpected types or else see them as deviant, as "not normal." Sociologists will say that men and women have the traits they are culturally supposed to have because of the working through of the process known as the *self-fulfilling prophecy*—that is, the adjustment of society and of people to prescriptions in the culture. These people, however, never for a moment believe that the differences between women and men are products, artifices, or group creations. They affirm that the differences are "natural," that the beliefs merely map reality.

What is meant by the term *natural*? In the first place, natural means anchored in biology. Conventional people believe that the different tasks, activities, and social functions of women and men have a physiological, biological cause as concretely real as the differences in genitals. In the newborn infant, different genitals are taken as the signs of those basic, inborn differences. In the second place, natural means something which, at least in embryo, is there from the start and which unfolds and elaborates inevitably with maturation. Male and female babies, in other words, are somewhat similar (though the experienced eye can spot the crucial differences). Adult males and females are dramatically different. The period between infancy and adulthood is one in which these differences come visibly "to the surface." Third, natural means, for most people, willed by God or divinely ordained. An aura of sanctity and awesome power surrounds the term. Questioning what is natural is profane, sacrilegious, dangerous. Finally, natural means part of a bigger design, part of the intricate, massive pattern of life-sustaining, God-given nature. One believes that the details of the design may not be fully known or understandable, but that the fact of interconnectedness has to be accepted and taken seriously. To tamper with an important feature of this design risks destroying the whole system, and that way lies chaos and terror.

Two quotations from Whitehouse (1977:88, 251) summarize this complex belief about "natural":

We set a disaster course if, as the liberationists do, we aim to eradicate the physical, psychological and emotional differences between men and women. Men and women *are* different and our world has no future if this basic fact is twisted and ignored. The woman is essentially the mate, the home maker and the mother. What happens to her, how she sees her role, will determine the happiness, stability and creativity of society. Without a woman who is prepared to be a woman, to fulfill her role as child-bearer, a man can see no human fulfillment of his sexuality . . . he might as well be impotent. . . . For a woman to deny maternity . . . is to dissociate herself from the most crucial of acts—the perpetuation of the species . . . then society itself cannot long survive. . . .

Respect for women and for the family lies at the heart of the Christian faith so that when we destroy one, we destroy the other.

THE BELIEF IN PATRIARCHY OR MALE AUTHORITY[3]

One of the natural differences between men and women, our subjects believe, is that males are, by right, the powerful ones. In part, that power is understood by both genders to be "raw power": power based on greater strength, greater aggressiveness, greater ability to fight—greater coercive capacities, in other words. A variety of researchers have shown that lurking deep in the myths and fantasies of both women and men is a terror or fascination with that possibility of male coercion, symbolized in the act of rape. Males who rape have been found, in most cases, to be acting out that fantasy, affirming that fundamental, raw male power rather than responding to sexual deprivation.[4] And women's "typical" passivity, the very ways in which they move and hold their bodies, protectively closing inward, has also been shown to be based partly in fear or caution toward that threat of power.

But the belief in male power is more than a partly repressed belief in male coercion. It is much more explicitly and openly a belief in man's natural right to lead, to take command, to be superordinate—it is the belief in male authority. We call this belief in male authority *patriarchy*, which means "the rule of the father." It is a particular vision of the nature of the male-female power relationship. "A man," our secretary and our boss agree, "has to be boss in his own home." Behind that statement lies a system of beliefs conjured up by phrases like "God, the Father," ". . . and God gave man dominion over all the earth," "Father knows best," and "Just wait till your father comes home." Male authority, it is believed, is physiologically anchored, divinely ordained, part of the life-sustaining design of nature: "Acceptance of the divinely ordered hierarchy means acceptance of authority—first of all, God's authority and then those lesser authorities which He has ordained. A husband and wife are both under God, but their positions are not the same. A wife is to submit herself to her husband. The husband's 'rank' is given to him by God" (Elliot, 1976:141).

The belief in male authority carries rights and obligations for both men and women. Men have the right to command; women must submit to those commands. Women, in turn, have the right to expect protection, and men are obligated to provide it. Indeed, on this dimension woman-man relations are defined as similar to child-parent relations. The child is little, helpless, loved, charming, protected, free from responsibility; the parent is big, resourceful, benevolent, protective, burdened with responsibility, but always in charge.

The belief in male authority is almost universal in societies. Various theories seek to explain the origins of patriarchy. Sociologists speak of male strength and female reproductive functions, social evolutionists of the division of labor in the tribe, Marxists of the emergence of property relations in early agrarian societies, and Freudians write about the male child's quest for autonomy from the mother. But whatever the cause, this belief pervades our social fabric. Think, for example, of the seating arrangement at the family table, of the changeover in drivers when a wife picks her husband up at the office or subway stop, of the tendency of the woman to refer important family decisions (and minor ones too) to the "male head of the household," and of the assumption both share that he will go downstairs at night to check on a strange noise (although he is as vulnerable to the intruder's bullet as she is). Look at advertisements in magazines. Almost invariably the man is taller than the woman. His appearance is more serious. His hand may be protectively on her shoulder, while she looks up shyly at him. She sits on the floor; he sits, slightly apart, on a chair. Her toes turn in and she grimaces in a childlike way, while he smiles with amused adult tolerance.

The belief in male authority also has more dramatic implications. Partly because of it, bosses in offices are usually male, their clerk-typist subordinates female, and this arrangement is taken for granted as normal and natural. Because of it, conventional people find it almost impossible to envisage a woman as president or general, corporation head, bishop, or rabbi. Those are positions of power. It "flies in the face of nature" to put a natural subordinate in such positions. Both conventionally situated women and men hate "domineering women" who "emasculate their men," and they hate "henpecked men," those "Dagwoods in aprons." Because of this belief, a woman who in the ordinary run of things finds herself in control will seek to hide this competence both from herself and from the man (husband, boss) by actions that consciously make the man feel his authority and male identity are protected, unchallenged, intact. And because of these actions by conventional women, conventional men perhaps never realize that women can be competently in control.

PUBLIC VERSUS PRIVATE[5]

"Woman's place is in the home." "A man has to be the breadwinner for his family." Those two strongly held conventional beliefs are our entry to a third major theme in the meaning system that anchors our institution of gender: the theme that maps the area, or space, or universe of our life experiences into two spheres, private and public, and that unquestioningly assumes that men and women have different locations on the map.

Private versus public is a map we have collectively made of the psychological, social, and physical space of our lives.[6] The baseline for this mapping process is our sense of the private; the anchoring concept for our notion of the private is the image of the "home." We perceive our private space as centered on the area we regard as home, the place where we are safe, where we can let down our guard, where, as one poet has said, "we don't have to deserve to be." The other members of our private world are those who have access to our home either by "natural right" or by concession: husband or wife, children and parents, kinfolk, friends and neighbors. We perceive our relationships to those others as one of closeness, of social and psychological intimacy. And we assume that these others perceive their relationships to us the same way.

In our culture, the private sphere is loaded with emotional significance. It is the world that we believe will endure for us, in the face of all evidence to the contrary. It is therefore a world in which we experience a sense of security. It is also seen as a social-psychological womb in which we take shape as personalities, a sanctuary in which we can reveal those personalities, an enclave of emotional expressiveness, and a source of daily physical and emotional renewal. Our "home" (that is, our private world of family, friends, and kin) is our "castle," our bastion against all foes, and we believe we have the right to kill in order to protect it. Private space is sacred.

Public space, in contrast, is not. Public means away from or distant from home. In our minds, we see the public sphere as a world of strangers, some of whom we may relate to over an adult lifetime (as, for example, co-workers), but toward whom we feel we must always be, to a degree, on guard. Public is the sphere in which we must constantly prove ourselves. In the public sphere, we locate our economic, political, educational, and other bureaucratized services. We think of public as a zone of transients, of relationships that will not endure.

If our collective position on the private sphere is one of deep approval, our position on the public is best understood as one of ambivalence. At one level, we engage with the public world only out of necessity, to get whatever is necessary (money, goods, education, legislation) for survival. The vision here is of forced separation from our private home base, and of weary, grateful return to it. At another level, we all experience the deep satisfactions of the public world: self-testing, practical achievement, clear expectations, freedom from the obligations and restraints of "home," and tangible, heady rewards like money, power, rank, and applause. We crave and pursue such satisfactions, but often without a clear acknowledgment that they are legitimate. Our conventional beliefs about gender are very much influenced by this cultural map of public versus private spheres.

Conventionally situated people firmly believe that woman's "natural" characteristics—her reproductive functions, her emotionality and capacity for nurturance, her sensitivity to relationships and to emotions, her predispositions toward domesticity, her lack of toughness and of technical talent—mean that her primary functions and location are in the private sphere and that her ventures into public space are secondary, short-lived, unimportant.[7] Men, in contrast, are "born to rule the world." Their birthright is public space. Men are pushed into the public sphere by necessity, and pulled by its positive satisfactions. For a man to acknowledge the pull of those public rewards is legitimate and applauded, just as long as he does not at the same time deny the sanctity of private space. Men expect, and are expected, to leave the private sphere regularly for the public world, to conduct the business of that world in a sustained and serious way, returning periodically to the private sphere for physical and emotional renewal. Men's "natural characteristics" suit them to this role. All in all, then, there is a pleasing symmetry in this design between the different requirements of public and private worlds and the different yet complementary qualities of men and women. The whole pattern seems natural and right.

One major consequence of this complex of ideas has to do with the judgment that conventional people make about the lot of women and men. Since the private sphere is idealized, women are perceived as fortunate. To a degree, they seem to possess that sacred aura with which we imbue the private world. Since the public sphere is viewed with ambivalence, men are, to a degree, less fortunate. It is true that their nature suits them to public life, that they find satisfaction there, but to do this they must leave the sacred area of home. Constrained not only by their nature, but by the needs of their dependent women and children to spend most of their lives in the wilderness of public toil, they have a right to expect compensation, to expect something significant in return. And that compensation is authoritative power, the right to command and the right to respect, both in the public *and* in the private domains. Women may do most of the practical management of the home, but only in the role of steward.

The second major consequence of these beliefs is dualism—very different orientations to the zones of human activity in our society. Conventional men are oriented primarily to wage work; they know its dynamics in detail and view other institutions—politics, law, education, and family—primarily in terms of their interaction with work. Conventional women are oriented primarily to family; they are absorbed in the details of that world and view through that lens such institutions as education, economy, religion, health, and community. Conventional men and women exist side by side—as husband and wife, brother and sister, parent and child, relations or friends—their daily life experiences enmeshed in different motivations and different structures of interest and relevance.[8] Each has only a sketchy knowledge of the other's primary and absorbing concern. Each accepts this lack of shared interest and experience as natural and right, as a complementary division of labor that jointly reproduces the world they value.

MEN'S WORK VERSUS WOMEN'S WORK[9]

When conventionally situated men and women hear the word *work*, they initially think of the same things. They think of what we will throughout this section call "Work" with a capital "W." After this first wave of shared images, however, conventionally situated women may begin tentatively to describe something else that they feel may be labeled work. They *may* do this. But they will be quick to concede that this other thing may not be "real work," that it is merely "women's work." In this section, we first talk about people's idea of Work, and then we try to see what women are thinking about when they think about their own activities as "women's work."

The key to the conventional perspective on work turns on a belief that the things produced by human labor fall into two distinct and mutually exclusive categories. One may produce things that satisfy one's own needs or needs existing in one's circle of intimates. These products are for *private consumption.* Or one may produce something that one believes meets a public need, a need made evident by the fact that the public or market will pay money for such an activity or product.

For centuries now, in our society money has been the universal medium of exchange. Money can buy almost anything. And in our complex urbanized world, we are acutely aware of the fact that we would die without money. Labor that generates money for the worker—a wage, salary, fee, payment, or cash return—is vital. From the conventional viewpoint, only labor that produces money for the laborer is really Work. So Work is labor that takes place within the market economy—production for money.

Work, thus perceived, has several other distinctive features. It occurs in a space that is not private but public. One may have an office in the home, but even in these circumstances, one closes the door on one's private life and space when one "goes to Work." And for most people, the sense of a physical separation between the location of Work and that of private life is underscored by travel over considerable distances. Work is formally scheduled around some variant of the 9-to-5 day and the 40-hour week. Work outside this schedule is overtime or moonlighting or workaholic behavior—an aberration.

Work also has the characteristic of *componentiality;* that is, it is perceived as consisting of discrete units (of time, materials, organized effort), brought together in structured sequences in the building of the product. Work has a general flavor of discreteness: of separate, identifiable work places; of separate, identifiable work times; of separate, identifiable work components, work tasks, work stages, work groups; of separate units of reward.

Conventional people believe that men and women stand in dramatically different relationships to Work. For men, Work is the unavoidable, essential condition of life. The rationale is that a woman's nature links her unavoidably to producing children, caring for them until they reach adulthood, and maintaining the home. Since modern circumstances make a steady inflow of money essential for survival, the task of leaving the home to work for money for the household falls to men. There is also a vague but fairly strong belief that men are, by nature, better suited to the activities which constitute most types of Work.

Men's Work: Public, Paid, Serious

For men, Work is not only unavoidable, it is central to a sense of identity. Most know themselves and are socially identified in terms of occupational role—lawyer, plumber, sales manager, construction worker. This Work-anchored identity is always perceived against a backdrop of who other people "are" in terms of their Work—what jobs they hold, and how those jobs measure up in terms of income, prestige, and power. Man's job-anchored identity is knowledge of his place in the social stratification system. "Who will I be when I grow up?" the little boy asks, and what he means is what Work he will do.

Since Work and identity are so closely linked in the male perspective, a man perceives his personal investment in Work as the central investment he makes in life. That investment will give him and his family its sense of its social worth. He must therefore give more of his time, energy, and commitment to his job than to any other area of his life. Often a man's investment in Work far outweighs the sum of all his other investments. In the conventional male vision, Work is, by choice or necessity, the central life experience. Success in Work is a goal to be pursued as hard as possible and as long as possible; it is a goal relinquished only with pain, with a sense of failure, with a crisis in identity.

In contrast to all this, conventional people perceive women's Work as voluntary. Male children grow up with a dawning realization that wage work is an unavoidable necessity of adult life; female children typically grow up believing they will marry and be financially "looked after" by a man who will Work. Wage work, for conventional women, is something with which to fill up the days in that short period between the end of schooling and the beginning of marriage, something she may perhaps choose to do during marriage as a means to secondary income (so long as her spouse approves, his job demands come first, and she continues to provide quality care for the children). In one recent (1978) survey, 78 percent of Americans surveyed believed fully or partially that "A wife should put her husband and children ahead of her career" (Tarshis, 1979:113).

This belief in the voluntary relation of woman to Work exists despite the fact that throughout history, women have worked out of necessity rather than from choice. To sustain this belief, the evidence of women working out of necessity has been defined not as a general feature of women's experience, but as the accumulation of individual "exceptions to the rule": women who have had the misfortune not to marry; to be widowed, deserted, or divorced; or to marry a man who, for some reason, cannot earn sufficient income. Even women working out of necessity have so interpreted their situation.

Several consequences flow from the belief in man's involuntary and women's voluntary relation to wage Work. Men are perceived to be less free than women, and deserving of a reward, in terms of respect, authority, and domestic convenience, for this "unfreedom." Since men at Work maintain the public sphere and financially support the private world, they are perceived as "serious." Women are seen as "unserious," almost childishly free from responsibility, useless though decorative things, not only by men, but sometimes by women themselves, as this statement shows: "I know it's old fashioned, but I do feel that women just are inferior to men—in almost every way. So women should concentrate on being just that—women—and leave the rest to men. I'm sure everybody would be a lot happier" (Janet Pearce, "Pet of the Month," *Penthouse,* December 1969, quoted in Jaggar and Struhl, 1978: 79). This aura of unseriousness extends to women's wage Work. As we shall show in Chapter 5, the jobs typically filled by women are almost always poorly paid and poorly esteemed. The belief in women's voluntary relationship to Work means that they are located in the community stratification system through the Work status of the man (husband, father, son, deceased husband or father) who heads or headed the household. This placement holds even when the woman engages in wage Work. So we have the urge among young women to "marry well," to marry someone whose Work status is as good as or better than that of their fathers—a motivation that has inspired countless legends and fantasies on the Cinderella and Prince Charming theme.

Women's Work: Private, Unpaid, Nonessential

Work, then, is wage work. But what about the conventional woman, married, with children, at home full time? How does she pass her time? What does she think about her activities in the home?

One of the interesting by-products of our traditional and collective absorption with Work is that we know next to nothing about housework, or "women's work." The wage sector has been systematically described by academics and government agencies, but to describe woman's work in the home we have to fall back on an unsystematic listing based on first- or second-hand experience. We have used as a baseline the young, middle-class, married housewife, with a couple of school-age children and a young child at home. Here is how she would describe her "job":

> Round-the-clock care of the young child: feeding it, cleaning, dressing it, toilet care, care in illnesses, playing with it, teaching it, taking it out on a regular basis, being permanently "on call."
>
> Most of the same duties toward the school-age children outside of school time, *minus* the toilet care and perhaps the play, *plus* chauffeuring to ball games and ballet classes, conferences with teachers, volunteering for the school bake sales, for Girl Scout leader, for preparation of the school's spring luncheon, for Sunday School teacher.
>
> Housework, including sweeping, dusting, scrubbing, polishing, waxing, cleaning baths and toilets, changing beds, washing dishes after each meal.
>
> Meal preparation, three times daily, if possible offering variety and nutrition.
>
> Care of the garden, including mowing, raking, weeding, planting.
>
> Cleaning, mending, sorting, purchasing, and making clothes for the family.
>
> Shopping for food, clothing, toys, appliances, and furniture, and for services such as medical and dental care, plumbers and electricians, auto mechanics, roof and gutter repair, appliance repair, and so on.
>
> Periodic entertaining (in which a dinner for six will take three days' preparation) and organizing the festivities of the year (birthdays, Christmas, Hannukah, Thanksgiving, and so on).
>
> Sorting out the social or emotional problems of all family members.

Maintaining through letters, cards, phone calls, invitations, and visits the links to kinfolk and friends.

And this is only a partial listing. Each woman would want to add to this list. Here, for example, is how one mother recalls the situation of being permanently "on call" (Rich, 1976: 3–4):

> I remember a cycle. It began when I had picked up a book or began trying to write a letter, or even found myself on the telephone with someone. The child might be absorbed in busyness, in his own dream world; but as soon as he felt me gliding into a world which did not include him, he would come to pull at my hand, ask for help, punch at the typewriter keys. . . . And I would feel the futility of any attempt to salvage myself . . . my needs always losing. I could love so much better, I told myself, after even a quarter-hour of peace, of detachment from my children. . . . I waited with impatience for the moment when his father would return from work, when for an hour or two the intensity between us (would) slacken. . . . And yet there *was* authentic need underlying my child's invented claims . . . a need vaster than any single human being could satisfy, except by loving continuously, from dawn till dark, and often in the middle of the night. . . .

There are also systematic variations. Those with less income will find themselves working harder at creating the basics; those with more income will be caught up in the expectations for realizing a "higher standard of living." Those with husbands in certain occupations, such as clergy or the diplomatic corps, find themselves functioning as essential adjuncts to their husbands' jobs.

All this is surely work, and women at one level recognize it as such. They know that they labor at home, just as men and women labor in the wage sector. They know that their labor produces things that are vital to their families' needs, just as wage labor produces vitally needed money and market products. They know that their sense of identity and self-worth is as closely bound up to their effectiveness in this work as that of their husbands is linked to job effectiveness. And they know that their link to these activities is as absolute and determined by their gender as is their husbands' to the wage sector.

Yet they know too that this kind of work has several features that make it distinct from wage work. This is work in private space, not public; work done largely in isolation from all others except children; work that has no time limits or vacations; work that is always woman's lot, even when she enters the sphere of wage work. This is work for which there is no program of study, but rather a long apprenticeship throughout childhood, and then dramatic and total immersion, a sink-or-swim experience, in early marriage and parenthood. It is work for which there is no wage, but where the tasks are mandatory for female gender, and the rewards are (or are said to be) intrinsic. Whereas wage work has the characteristic of discreteness from self and private space, woman's work is inseparably intertwined with those structures—so much so that when woman's work is at its most demanding, it consumes both self and private space.

Women's work then is work, but different from wage work. Conventional women know this, for they live in a world where women's work is the daily pattern of their lives. Yet they know this in a half-recognized, unsystematic way. The male-dominated organized structures of social communication, religion, education, scholarship, publishing, and mass communication do not pay sustained attention to this area of human labor; instead, these structures of communication identify significant human labor with wage Work. Any labor that is not wage Work is something less—a choice, a volunteer activity, a hobby. Women's work is depicted as something less than Work—merely a cluster of choices, hobbies, and voluntary activity—nonessential, unserious. It is "women's work," diminished in the very phrasing. Women learn this master mapping of the world of human labor, and their actual daily experiences take on an unreality in the face of it. Conventional women, while periodically "grumbling when they are tired," accept the old saws about themselves as "just housewives" who do not, like men, have "to work for a living," and who busy themselves with a daily round of "women's work."

LOVE: MALE AND FEMALE VIEWPOINTS

Conventional beliefs about gender emphasize the differences between men and women: their different natures, their separate spheres of activity. These beliefs produce real differences in daily experience and different perceptions based on those experiences. What then links men and women together? The themes we have just explored suggest several possibilities: complementary functions, reciprocal need, authoritative power. But ask our happy secretary what binds her to her husband, or our happy boss what links him to his wife, and both will answer "love." And with this response we come to another significant belief complex in the system of conventional gender subjectivity, the belief that love is the ultimate natural tie between man and woman.

The list that follows gives some of the key elements of this belief complex, and some of the differences between conventionally situated women and conventionally situated men in their understanding of what love, in the context of gender, means.

1. Gender-specific love is an adult experience and an adult relationship, distinct from love relationships between parent and child, friends, God, and humankind. One of the special features of gender-specific love is that it contains an important element of erotic feeling. Gender love is, to a significant degree, erotic love—love centering on sensual and sexual pleasure.

2. Sensual and sexual pleasure is, in and of itself, deeply suspect. In the religious outlook on which our conventional gender system is anchored, sexual pleasure is perceived as the most obvious path to sin and personal corruption. Sexual pleasure is only "right" when it has been subordinated to God's (or Nature's) design for human continuity, and to the sacred institutions of marriage, family, and home. Gender love finds its only good expression in adult heterosexual marriage.[10]

3. One outcome of the combination of (1) and (2) is that conventionally situated people resist anything that appears to bring the possibility of erotically charged gender love to those they see as children. They resist sex education in schools, the availability of birth control resources to teenagers, the presentation of sexual love in films, on TV, and in literature accessible to young people. All these things appear to threaten and pollute the "natural innocence" of children.

4. Another outcome is that conventionally situated people have a deep abhorrence of homosexual love. To them this is wholly sinful and unnatural love, since it is separated from God's (or Nature's) reproductive design. The idea of marriage, family, and home between homosexuals is, in the deepest sense, a profanity, a violation of sacred themes and sacred institutions.

5. The ambivalence that people have toward erotic experience has, moreover, created a deep suspicion among persons of each gender that those of the opposite gender are by nature the more sensual and lustful beings, the source of temptation, corruption, and personal loss of innocence. Through our culture flow such repeated themes as that of Eve in the Garden of Eden, Circe, the Sirens, and the Lorelei—temptresses who have lured men to sin and death—and of centaurs, satyrs, and minotaurs, half-man, half lustful beast, who have devoured or seduced innocent, virginal girls. From the male side, this idea of female temptation has ranged from the numerous tales of male enchantment and male loss of self-direction when under a "woman's spell," to the mumbled excuse, "She made me do it," which rapists have used with such startling effectiveness before male jurors, male judges, and male police.[11] From the female side, this suspicion of men as lustful devourers of women has sustained an age-old rule among mothers that one should "lock up one's daughters," a long-standing, ever-popular melodramatic literature about seduction by "dirty old men" or "ruthless, experienced men of the world," and a deep protectiveness toward one's daughters, who are perceived as the embodiment of purity and innocence.

6. The belief that it is only in marriage that gender love is pure and good has created general rules that a person should be chaste before marriage and faithful to his or her partner after marriage. But male power in our society has softened the application of these norms to men. Men who "play around" before or after marriage are doing something wrong, it is true, but the wrong is at the level of a misdemeanor, deserving only mild reproof. For, conventional people agree, "a man is a man," "men deserve a little bit of fun," "the world is full of temptations," and ultimately, "it was the woman's fault." This, in case you haven't spotted it, is what is meant by the *double standard*.

7. Within marriage, conventional beliefs about behavior are in a state of flux. Until recently, it was believed that: (a) direct discussion of sexual matters was inappropriate between marriage partners; (b) husbands were the active initiators; (c) wives, as part of their acceptance of their husband's authority, should submit, in a natural but fairly passive way, to their husband's rights in this area of marriage. But the so-called sexual revolution of the past two decades has begun to transform these beliefs. Conventional women are now being told to be actively sensual—not only as a means to their own pleasure, but as a way of keeping their husbands happy—as their wifely duty. Here are the steps one recent best seller, clearly located in the broader conventional approach to gender, spelled out: (a) begin in the morning by being good to look at, to be with, to talk to; (b) call your husband at work during

the day with some sexually tantalizing message; (c) meet him on his return with flowers, candlelit dinner, and frilly new night clothes; (d) be prepared to seduce him seven nights a week; (e) seek professional help, medical or psychological, it you have a deeper problem (Morgan, 1973: 163–164).

So far we have described the belief in gender-relevant love as a belief in an erotically charged bond between an adult man and an adult woman, a belief shot through with ambivalence toward sensuality, and consequently a belief that contains a long list of proscriptions and a single prescription—that gender-specific love should be manifested only in heterosexual marriage. Our happy secretary and our happy boss would, we think, recognize their views about love in what we have said. But at the same time they would both also protest that "Love is a lot more than a sexual bond sanctified by marriage." If we could draw them out on this, we would hear them mention many things common to all love relationships, not just gender love: companionship, supportiveness, loyalty, kindness, and so on. But in the flow of their talk we would also identify a theme about love that does seem to be peculiar to gender love—that is, the belief in "romance."

How would conventionally situated people describe romance? How would you describe it? You are surrounded with images of it: on television, in movies, in stores, in advertising. Romance, it seems, is how gender love between a man and a woman is supposed to begin; it is about "falling in love." It is apparently a mysterious attraction that will spring up between a man and a woman, elusive, enchanting, pulling them irresistibly to marriage. (Romance without the possibility of marriage is perceived as a great tragedy.) Romance is indeed much more than open sexual attraction; it is magic, tenderness, eternal commitment. "A diamond is forever"; the advertisement, with its misted photographs, captures the essence of the ideal of romance.

The theme of romantic love figures much more significantly in literature aimed particularly at women. Research (Modleski, 1980; Radway, 1983) has shown that the ideal of romantic love looms much larger in women's views about gender love than it does in men's, for whom the sexual theme is more central. Tarshis (1979:251) reports that a 1973 poll found that 50 percent of women surveyed said that they were "in love" with the first man they slept with, while 10 percent of the men surveyed were "in love" with the first woman they slept with. A 1979 study of 4,000 married men and women showed that 56 percent of the women and 39 percent of the men believed they had married because of "love."

It is true, people believe, that anyone can have a romantic experience—that the magic connection may occur between the most unlikely possibilities. But it is also true, in the conventional viewpoint, that romance is more likely to be the experience of physically attractive people, in particular of beautiful women. Conventional women believe that their chances of finding and keeping romance are more likely if they conform to prescribed standards of attractiveness and beauty. A whole industry of fashion, beauty products, published advice, advertising, weight-loss programs, and even cosmetic surgery and dentistry draw the parameters of that ideal for women. Women, young and old, stare anxiously into their mirrors, worrying about weight, blemishes, glasses, hair color, wrinkles, age spots, unfashionable clothes, and so on, certain that their chances of finding or holding love hang in the balance. The belief that physical attractiveness is a prerequisite for gender love also operates among men, particularly young men, but far less forcibly. Indeed, men learn that being a man is its own attraction—being strong, assertive, and, with age, increasingly successful at Work. A man can devote his energies to being what he's been taught a man should be, and he believes this will also bring him gender love. A woman, however, will strive to appear youthful and beautiful, whatever else she must be and do, or else she feels herself insecure in love. And—for this is the wonder of collective definitions of the situation—they are both right!

SCHOOLING: MALE AND FEMALE PERSPECTIVES

By schooling we mean attending school—elementary, secondary, college—and obtaining knowledge and certification. Why do conventional females and males seek schooling in our society? What are their perceptions of its significance?[12]

Initially, of course, young children go to school because their parents insist they should. We therefore need to inquire into the perceptions of conventionally situated parents about schooling. A great deal of habit shapes their thinking—that is, they take it for granted that children go to school. They also know that it is legally required, and the mother finds it desperately convenient. But over and above all this, schooling is perceived as having intrinsic value for children. Probably for all parents, elementary education is seen as the way in which children acquire necessary basic skills and knowledge for dealing with the world in which they must live— numerical and literacy skills, and knowledge of one's world as a natural, cultural, historical, and technical phenomenon. This perception will continue to operate for steadily decreasing proportions of parents through high school and even college. Moreover, in the early stages of schooling, in the early grades, parents will not distinguish in any important way between why boys or girls should go to school.

On all these dimensions, young children's perceptions of school will mirror the perceptions of their parents. In addition, young children increasingly perceive school as a place where they find their own community, the social world of their peers, a world that begins to give them a sense of independence. Much of this basic core of significance (general preparation for life, social ties to age peers) continues for both girls and boys through high school and college. But the belief that the relevance of schooling is different for males and females begins to appear as early as the fourth grade, both among conventional parents and among their children. The belief sharpens steadily from then on.

For boys, schooling is defined as an important preparation for manhood. This includes the realization of the male's "natural" capacities for physical prowess and aggression, expressed in the emphasis on athletics at school, and of his "natural" talents in formal abstraction and in technical matters, expressed in curriculum selections. School is also an arena for developing and testing one's intergender skills with an eventual eye to finding a wife. Above all, schooling is perceived, with increasing emphasis and centrality, as essential preparation for the male's destiny: Work. Because of this perception, conventional parents will be prepared to sacrifice in order to "invest" financially in their sons' education and future. Because of this perception, their sons will, with increasing purposefulness, "invest themselves" in schooling as a means toward a career in the wage sector. Also because of this perception, boys and young men will orient themselves throughout schooling toward achievement and success in competition with others.[13] And it is here, in school, that many males will taste the bitter fruit that is the inevitable consequence of our conventional beliefs about males: failure in competition, failure to succeed, and the sense of emasculation that failure brings.

For boys then, schooling appears to be directly and vitally related to what is to be their primary activity in adulthood—Work. For girls, and those who raise or counsel girls, schooling does not appear to have a similarly direct relationship to their adult destiny—marriage, family, care of the home. Training for this destiny is given within the home itself and in a more diffuse way by community, kin, friends, and the mass media. For girls, schooling has what they and those around them consider to be a set of useful but secondary relevances. It is perceived as giving them basic skills, which are necessary if one is to run a home in today's complex, urbanized world. These same skills, together with a reasonably broad "general education," also enhance one's capacity to be wife and companion to a man who is making his way in a complex, urbanized world, so schooling is useful in this way too. Conventional girls anticipate that they may have to work before marriage, or to generate secondary income in marriage. Schooling is perceived as a way to get training for Work, essentially for the jobs women traditionally fill (hence the slant of their curriculum choices in high school and college). Finally, schooling gives them access to a social world in which they learn from girlfriends the nuances of "being a woman," and where they will, most likely, find romance and marriage with someone suitable.

But although girls will seek schooling, they will do so in ways very different from their brothers. If marriage comes along, they will feel safe and right about dropping out. If resources have to be funneled to a brother's education, it will seem right to them that they defer their own educational demands on family resources. They will avoid traditionally male subjects and disciplines. They will focus on acquiring skills in areas that can lead them into typically female work. They will avoid at all costs the appearance of being overly competitive, overly successful in academic work, for doing so makes them appear "unfeminine." And here many of them will feel for the first time, though perhaps only dimly and fleetingly, the pain that our conventional gender beliefs create for women: the realization of some talent or capacity in themselves simultaneously with the knowledge that that capacity must be restrained, hidden away, lest they appear unwomanly.

SUMMARY

What we have done so far is take an X-ray perspective on our conventional gender arrangements. That is, we have described what people are thinking as they relate to life and each other along conventional lines, and we have dug down to explore sociologically the deeper structures of belief out of which those thoughts arise. At this point, three questions arise. First, why do these beliefs exist in our culture? Second, how do these conventional beliefs affect our gender arrangements? Third, how do people come to hold these beliefs?

A variety of explanations have been offered for the existence of the complex of beliefs just described. Historians point to the consequences of Christian beliefs about sex, sin, and death, to the medieval tradition of courtly love, and to industrialism's effects on the patterns of our life. Marxists have traced the effect of the emergence of private property on human relationships. Freudians explore the deep emotional undercurrents in parent-to-parent and parent-to-child relations. Feminists see patriarchy as a universal social form creating its own legitimations. At later points in the text, we shall explore some of these theories more fully.

Here we provide a modest addition to these explanations. What we have been describing is an age-old complex of beliefs about gender. Such a belief system will continue in place so long as people are motivated to reaffirm it rather than deny it. One of the most influential of sociologists, Max Weber (1968), proposed a long time ago that four motivational clusters may prompt people to act in ways that reaffirm a cultural system. First, people may do so out of practical self-interest, resulting from their location or position in society. For example, for practical reasons, men may support a belief system that confers a privileged position on them. Second, people may affirm a belief system because of a deep commitment to underlying basic values. Women, for example, may adhere to beliefs that devalue them because of deep religious commitment. Third, people will hold to a set of beliefs out of habit and an unreflective attachment to tradition. And finally, people may be motivated to act in ways that reproduce a belief system because of deep emotional impulses.

In Chapters 4 and 5 we look at some of the group processes and institutional arrangements that generate these motivational patterns. Chapters 4 and 5 also deal with the other two questions posed above. Empirically speaking, the three answers are practically the same. That is, the same observed sequences of social activity will tell you how people's beliefs about gender produce the visible institutions of gender, how those institutions mold people's motives, and how people come by their beliefs. For one of the basic truths that sociology has discovered is this: *people create society; society creates people; both processes of creation are going on simultaneously and constantly* (Berger and Luckmann, 1967).

People like our happy secretary-wife and our happy boss-husband externalize their perceptions and beliefs in their actions. That is, their perceptions and beliefs become visible in the world in their actions. When very large numbers of people act and relate to one another in terms of their beliefs and perceptions, the outcome is what people call society. *People create society*. At the same time, those aggregated actions and relationships help to put motives and beliefs into people. The actions of our happy secretary-wife and of our happy boss-husband, what they say and what they do, transmit their beliefs to their children and confirm each other's beliefs in the office. *Aggregated human actions (society) creates people*. In the next two chapters we explore this two-way process.

NOTES

1. Our approach to interpretive sociology is guided by the writings of Max Weber, *Economy and Society*, vol. 1 (1968), and *The Methodology of the Social Sciences* (1949). Throughout this chapter and particularly in our introduction and conclusion, we are heavily in debt to Berger and Luckmann (1967), and Berger and Kellner (1981).

2. This belief has been so deeply engrained in our culture for so long that an attempt to cite proponents of the argument would read like a "Roots of Western Civilization" reading list. For a good sampling of these statements, see Agonito (1977). This book presents selections from the book of Genesis in the Bible, Aristotle, St. Paul, St. Augustine, Thomas Aquinas, Rousseau, Kant, Hegel, Darwin, and Freud—all arguing the case for natural differences. In contemporary discussion, that argument is advanced by sociologists like Steven Goldberg, *The Inevitability of Patriarchy* (1974), by spokespersons from the conservative religious community like Mary Whitehouse, *Whatever Happened to Sex?* (1977), and by spokespersons for the antifeminist movement like Anita Bryant, *Bless This House* (1976) and *Mine Eyes Have Seen the Glory* (1970); Marabel Morgan, *The Total Woman* (1975); Phyllis Schlafly, *The Power of the Positive Woman* (1977). A thoughtful if critical assessment of the natural differences theme is given in that feminist classic, Simone de Beauvoir, *The Second Sex* (1952), especially in the chapter called "The Data of Biology." A useful bibliography of medical and biological writings on the issue is given in Chapter 3 of Judith Long Laws and Pepper Schwartz, *Sexual Scripts* (1977).

3. On patriarchy generally, see Kate Millet, *Sexual Politics* (1970); Mary Daly, *Beyond God the Father: Towards A Philosophy of Women's Liberation* (1973); Adrienne Rich, *Of Woman Born* (1976). On coercive power, rape, and rape-related fantasies, see Susan Brownmiller, *Against Our Will: Men, Women and Rape* (1975). For women's bodily stance in relation to the fear of male violence, see Janet Wedel, "Ladies, We've Been Framed! Observations on Goffman" (1977), and Iris M. Young, "Throwing Like a Girl" (1980); for the parent-child analogy of patriarchal authority and for the depicting of this in advertising, see Erving Goffman, *Gender Advertisements* (1979).

4. See William Fuller, "Why I Raped," in Shapiro and Shapiro (1979:139–140).

5. For a review of the generality of this dichotomy in both Western and sociological thought, see Glennon (1979); for the long-standing nature of this dichotomy and of the ideology that reveres "the home," see Agonito (1977). Jessie Bernard, *The Female World* (1981), Chap. 4, thoroughly maps the contemporary ideology of "home." Feminist writers like Rich (1976) and Dinnerstein (1976) have explored the cognitive and evaluative patterns in this belief.

6. The term "we" is used deliberately. For whatever you, the reader, and we, the authors, may think about natural differences and male authority, we'd wager that we all operate with the belief in public versus private. On this belief we are all "subjects."

7. "The primary role of women is in the home and family . . . men still need a good mother to come to with their little troubles. Women should provide a place of refuge where the husband and children can return from a busy, confused and complex world" (Belle

Spafford, president, Women's Auxiliary, Church of the Latter-Day Saints, quoted in Jaggar and Struhl, 1978: 218). A 1978 survey shows that 53 percent of Americans still believe "Marriages are stronger when the wife stays home," and 69 percent believe that "Children suffer when the mother goes to work" (reported in Tarshis, 1979: 114).

8. The theme of relevance structures is an important one in interpretive theory; see Berger and Luckmann (1967), Berger and Kellner (1981). The theme of separate spheres of attention and the exploration of woman's institutional map is worked out in detail by Bernard (1981). The male absorption with work is presented in a series of papers in Shapiro and Shapiro (1979). The contrast between male and female perceptions of life is sharply drawn in Rubin (1976).

9. The distinction between private-consumption labor and market labor was originally made by Karl Marx in *Capital*, vol. 1 (1967). It has been applied to the conceptualization of female-male work in Zillah R. Eisenstein (1979) and in Kuhn and Wolfe (1978). The perception of wage work as made up of discrete components is described in Berger, Berger, and Kellner (1976). The pain and the significance of wage work for men is graphically presented in Parts I and II of Shapiro and Shapiro (1979). The ideology of women's peripheral relationship to wage work is brilliantly explored in Betty Friedan's classic statement, *The Feminine Mystique* (1963). The theme of women as unserious is developed in Goffman (1979). The low value given to women's wage work is well demonstrated in the study of trends in our wage structure done by Emma Rothschild, "Reagan and the Real America" (1981). Housework as women's experience is explored in Lopata (1971), Oakley (1974), and Glaser (1976). Mothering as work is brilliantly explored in Rich (1976) and Glubka (1983). For women's role in the organization of holidays, see Caplow, "Christmas Gifts and Kin Networks" (1982).

10. On the ambivalence toward sexual love and the belief that marriage is the only legitimate setting for its expression, see Elliot (1976), Whitehouse (1977), Dinnerstein (1976), Friedan (1969), de Beauvoir (1952), Rich (1976), and Marina Warner (1976). On romantic love, see Friedan (1969), Laws and Schwartz (1977), Rubin (1976), and Modleski (1980). Bernard also discusses the association between beauty and romantic love. On this issue see also Banner (1983), Chernin (1981), Lurie (1982), and Millman (1980).

11. Said one male juror, who had served on a famous rape case: ". . . the guy's not trying to kill her. He's trying to give her a good time . . . giving a girl a screw isn't doing her bodily harm" (Shapiro and Shapiro, 1979: 137).

12. Extensive bibliographies of the impact of gender on educational behavior and attitudes are to be found in several sociology of education texts; see especially those in Parelius and Parelius (1978), Scimecca (1980), and Hurn (1978).

13. We admit the middle-class bias in this statement. Everything we say about gender is complicated by social class. Working-class males may not associate school with Work as much as middle-class males do.

4
SOCIAL INTERACTION AND GENDER INEQUALITY

This chapter takes what we called in Chapter 2 a "home movie" approach to gender inequality. In other words, it focuses on the routine activities by which people maintain our gender institution in their face-to-face relationships. Sociologists call these sequences of activity and relationship *interaction*. Our subject in this chapter is conventional gender interaction.

One basic advantage of an interaction approach is that, in its account of what people actually say and do, it brings a social institution vividly and graphically to life. In doing this for gender inequality, we will describe actual conversations and activities in which people engage as they act out conventional gender roles. As we have said in earlier chapters, these descriptions are an ideal type. They focus exclusively on the conventional features of our present gender institution, omitting the elements of change that are now mingled in with those conventional arrangements. But the descriptions focus on certain features of the current situation that are real and significant.

Because we want not only to describe but also to explain the persistence of our gender institution and of gender inequality, the descriptions of gender interactions focus on their *socialization* and *sanctioning* functions (see Chapter 2). Our method of describing and explaining gender inequality at the level of interactional dynamics is based on a sociological concept, that of *social scripts*. Sociologists have taken this idea from the theater. They often depict patterned social interactions as an everyday drama in which people act out their roles, guided by a script they have memorized and made their own. It is easy to see how this metaphor can be extended to interactions among conventional men and women, who may be viewed as acting out a script about gender. At the same time, however, it is important to know that new players learn the script not only by direct instruction, but also by observation and participation.

This chapter describes how people act out scripts about gender and how people are taught gender scripts in an ongoing process over the entire course of their lives. But first we set the stage and introduce you to the technique of describing a social situation in script terms by looking at the pattern of gender expectations into which most members of our society are born:

Prologue

A hospital delivery room at the very moment Baby is born. Both parents are present, and the doctor announces, above Baby's wails, "It's a boy!" or "It's a beautiful little girl!" This is the very first pronouncement made about Baby, even before its parents are reassured about the health of their new offspring. It seems to be what they want to know first.

After they have held and inspected their new baby, the three principal actors separate. Mother is wheeled off for a few hours' rest. Father goes home to send telegrams, make phone calls, have his hand shaken by friends, neighbors, and workmates. In each separate communication, he begins by restating the doctor's pronouncement, "It's a girl!" or "It's a boy!" And what of Baby? Baby has been placed in a bassinet in the hospital nursery, to which, as a matter of routine, the staff have attached a blue bow or a pink bow, so that strangers, peeping through the glass at his or her wrinkled face and swaddled form, will be certain to know that he or she is a boy or girl.

In summary, Baby has been born into an atmosphere of intense curiosity and anxiety about her or his sex. Depending on circumstances, Baby's parents are relieved and happy or secretly disappointed by Baby's sex. To better understand the drama we have just witnessed, it is important to know what research tells us about the typical American family.

Average family size in America is 1.9 children—that is, two children is the average number for an American family (U.S. Census Bureau, 1980). Forty-five percent of women surveyed in a nationwide poll by Princeton University's Office of Population Research wanted their first-born to be a boy, while only 20 percent wanted a girl as firstborn (Cohen, *Washington Post*, July 20, 1982). The majority of couples wanted a mix of boys and girls. Boys, however, are the preferred sex when prospective parents are forced to limit gender choice to one child (Tarshis, 1979: 143–144).

Baby's conventional parents have an ideal design for the family they are in the process of creating: Father as the primary breadwinner; Mother at home as primary childrearer; two, maybe three children, at least one boy and one girl, hopefully with the firstborn a boy. When Mother became pregnant, both parents repeatedly declared that they "didn't care what it was so long as it was healthy."

But despite their protests, the parents do have a preference for a baby of one or the other gender. What the preference is will be determined by whether Baby has an older sibling or siblings and by the gender of the sibling or siblings. But anyone knowing these facts knows what their preference will be, for the gender script is very clear on this point. Baby's parents and all their friends and relations have been secretly keeping their fingers crossed that the ideal family design, or its closest approximation, will be realized in their case. In all this they are absolutely typical. The doctor, who knows next to nothing about their particular family details, will unerringly and routinely speak to their chief and overriding anxiety when making the first pronouncement about Baby.

INFANCY: ACQUIRING AN EMOTIONAL SCRIPT

In this section, our home movie camera follows Baby home from the hospital and records the gender-relevant events that occur in the first two years of life. During this time Baby is essentially preverbal; that is, even at the end of the period, she or he lacks a vocabulary of any significant size. Empirically this poses a major problem, for one cannot interview Baby, and one's interpretation of his or her actions is always open to question. Sociologists, in other words, lack the tools for discovering what Baby learns about gender in this period.

For help with this task we turn to another discipline, psychology, and in particular to psychoanalysis. Ever since Freud, psychoanalysis has focused on discovering areas of human experience not easily accessible to human verbalization, either because they occurred early in life or because they have been so deeply repressed. Psychoanalysis maps these areas of marginal consciousness by linking the data from long-term, intensive clinical studies of individuals, most of whom have emotional problems, with an elaborate theory of the development, structure, and dynamics of the human psyche. On this basis, psychoanalysis has constructed a detailed account of people's emotional development, one in which the experience of the preverbal early years plays a significant role.

Psychoanalytic work has been heavily tinged with sexist and patriarchical assumptions, and has given little attention to the issue of female psychic development. Recently, however, several scholars have begun to rework earlier findings with an eye to reconstructing the different psychic and emotional experiences of females and males in our society (Miller, 1973; Mitchell, 1974; Gayle Rubin, 1975; Dinnerstein, 1976; Chodorow, 1978). Though we take full responsibility for any flaws in the following account of Baby's early years, it has been heavily influenced by Dinnerstein and Chodorow.

First Scene: Nine Months

This is really a selection of scenes during Baby's first nine months of life. The sequence attempts to capture the rhythm of life in Baby's home, as it impinges on Baby. Father, it appears, is a relative stranger. They interact infrequently and intermittently. The film shows Father leaving home early in the morning while Baby is having a first feeding, returning home late in the evening to peek in at the sleeping baby, going off on weekends to the office, to weekend courses, to business golf games. Father is working hard at being a breadwinner. We catch a glimpse or two of him walking Baby around when she or he is fretful, and another shot of him playing with Baby in a free weekend hour.

By contrast, Mother and Baby are locked together in a close and continuous interaction. Mother is essentially Baby's social environment, and while Mother still has contacts with husband, kin, and friends, Baby is clearly her primary round-the-clock job and her primary source of social interaction. The film shows Mother feeding, changing, bathing, soothing, talking to, smiling at, playing and strolling with and teaching Baby, who sleeps and walks, eats and defecates, whimpers and yells, gurgles and smiles, grows, and moves with increasing effectiveness over the course of the film. When Baby is asleep or placid, Mother gets on with other chores, or chats to other adults. There is one scene of an infuriated Mother slamming the door on a crying Baby, and several shots of Baby and Mother obviously enjoying each other, their actions and gestures meshed in almost perfect unison.

Now let us pretend we have two reels of film running side by side, projected on two separate screens. In the first film we see Mother relating to Baby Girl, in the second film to Baby Boy. The interactions are almost identical, but in the first film Mother seems more frequently to hold Baby gently, close to her body, to call her "Momma's little girl" when she is comforting or approving of her—even, in the Christmas portrait session, dressing Baby and herself in look-alike outfits. In the second film, Mother seems more frequently to bounce Baby Boy vigorously up and down, refers in a jocular tone to his strength and physical development, uses the phrase "Momma's boy" when she is irritated or disapproving him, and provides him at Christmas with a football sweatshirt almost identical to the one she gives Father.

Sociologically speaking, two things underway here need our attention. The first has to do with what Mother is feeling and doing. Mother's feelings toward Baby are pretty clear from the film: occasional anger, frequent exhaustion, and occasional desperation for time for herself, love, pride, commitment, responsibility, and a sense of deep empathetic fusion with Baby (Glubka, 1983; Rich, 1976; Bernard, 1972). Mother also acts differently toward Baby, depending on whether Baby is a boy or girl. Mothers perceive boy babies as "other," destined for a role and experiences very different from their own. They identify with girl babies as "self," as a being whose basic life experiences will replicate their own. In small, subtle ways this affects a mother's actions toward her baby, even in these early months: what she says to Baby, how she touches and holds Baby, how she plays with Baby, even the tone of her voice. In other words, the mother will feel a more intense sense of empathetic fusion with Baby Girl. A sense of time limits, of an inevitable parting of the ways, colors her feeling of fusion with Baby Boy. And in a multiplicity of almost indiscernible ways, this percolates into her actions toward Baby. Let us call this Process A.

Our second interesting topic is Baby's feelings and development.

Baby, in these early months, lacks all conceptual categories for making sense of experience. Baby is even unable to distinguish between self and environment. For example, Baby is unaware that the hands moving in front of his or her face are his or her hands, and that the hands holding him or her belong to a separate being, Mother. Experience is unpatterned, a blurred, undifferentiated, "booming, buzzing confusion."

But Baby does experience. There are bodily sensations, some unpleasant, like pain, hunger, cold, the impact of harsh light or sound; some intensely pleasurable, like feeding, suckling, being warm and full. There are also emotions: fear and rage at bad sensations, pleasure and love of good ones. Baby acts on these sensations and emotions, and Mother responds. So one of the first things Baby learns is that the undifferentiated "thing" which is experience can suddenly change from badness, fear, and rage, to goodness, satisfaction, and love, or vice versa, and that the transformation is associated with the presence or absence of a reassuring sound (Mother's voice), a reassuring face (Mother's), and the feel of reassuring hands, arms, body, breast (Mother's). Baby learns to crave that reassurance, to feel fearful and lonely in its absence.

By 9 months of age, Baby is beginning to distinguish between self and environment, between self and other. Baby may also be saying a word or two. In other words, Baby is taking the first steps toward autonomous identity and cognitive experience. But from those early months of life, Baby takes away a complex of primeval, unlabeled "feeling memories": of pain, rage, and loneliness experienced without contrast, "in themselves," as ultimate pain, rage, loneliness; of pleasure, love, security, again experienced "in themselves," as ultimate pleasure, love, security. These sensual-emotional "feeling memories" will be almost irretrievable cognitively, for the words and categories on which cognition is based come after they happen. They will, however, persist as sensual-emotional parameters in Baby's later life, affecting action, perception, need, and desire. And because the constant caretaker was Mother, that substructure of sensual-emotional "feeling memory" will be permanently intertwined with one's sensual-emotional "feeling recall" of a woman. The consequences of this will vary, depending on whether Baby is male or female. But male or female, Baby at the sensual-emotional level has become inextricably intertwined with woman. A sequence of interaction between mother and baby has produced a structure in Baby's psyche. From now on, the latter (subjectivity) will affect the former (interaction). Let us label this sensual-emotional involvement with Mother Process B.

Second Scene: Two years

A year later, Baby is having a temper tantrum. Face flushed and contorted, Baby is yelling "No! No!" Mother is trying everything except concession. Eventually, patience exhausted, Mother picks screaming Baby up, carries the child upstairs, dumps her or him in the cot or crib, and slams the bedroom door shut. Mother sits downstairs, tight-lipped, as Baby howls away. Father comes in from work and there is some conversation about "the terrible twos." There is now only an occasional hiccuping sob from upstairs. Mother goes back up. Baby peers at her bleary-eyed from the cot, Mother picks Baby up, they cuddle, and Mother carries Baby downstairs. Baby is delighted to find Father. Baby and Father play while Mother fixes dinner. Everyone seems to have forgotten the tantrum.

In making sociological sense of all this, we focus on Baby. Baby's experience and situation is best depicted as a cluster of contradictions. On the one hand he or she now clearly has a sense of separate identity. The 2-year-old can distinguish between self and environment. On the other hand, Mother, whom Baby perceives as the major feature of that environment, is still so closely and symbiotically linked to Baby in emotions and in daily interactions that she or he cannot yet clearly draw the boundary between self and Mother. It is as though the psychic fence that separates different people from each other has a big gap in it in this case. Baby is separate from Mother, yet open to her. And if you factor in Process A, Mother's greater closeness and intimacy toward a daughter than toward a son, you will see that the gap in this fence will be wider for a girl baby than for a boy baby.

Another crucial cluster of contradictions is the emotions Baby has toward Mother. Baby's daily experiences and needs produce the same emotional mix we described earlier: rage, fear, and loneliness versus love, security, and satisfaction. Baby, however, now knows when she or he is directing these emotions to that ever-present being, Mother. And Baby now directs bad feelings toward Mother not only when reacting to discomfort, but when in the more active pursuit of identity, Baby's will clashes with Mother's (the tantrum). When that happens, and it seems to happen all the time, for Baby is a "terrible two," exploring and testing the power of personal will, Mother almost always wins. For Mother is stronger, more resourceful, more powerful. Baby rages against Mother's power, and yearns for greater power.

Yet Baby is totally dependent on Mother for the satisfaction of daily needs. Emotionally she or he craves the comfort and reassurance of Mother's presence. In this egocentric way, Baby loves Mother with a deep, desperate love. Also, as we have seen, Baby is not quite sure where he or she leaves off and Mother begins, emotionally speaking. Raging against Mother and encountering Mother's responsive rage makes Baby feel bad: scared, guilty, lonely. It almost feels as though in hating and raging against Mother, one is hating and raging against oneself. How does a 2-year-old handle this explosive swirl of emotion? By a complex series of maneuvers, the literature tells us.

First, Baby discovers and turns to a countervailing and greater power, Father. Look back at our scene. Baby finds Father at home and Mother, placid now instead of terrifyingly angry, busy fixing dinner. At 2, Baby's instinct for power is almost unerring, and he or she perceives, by observing the interactions between Father and Mother, that Father has power over so-powerful Mother. Baby is enamored of Father's power and wants to be just like him.

Second, Baby is becoming verbal and learns from language that there are two categories of people, male and female, and that Father is male, Mother female. Baby connects all her or his feelings about Father and Mother to gender categories. Males are Fathers, a focus for one's clean-cut unambivalent attraction to a power independent of and superior to mother-power. Females are Mother, a focus for very ambivalent feelings: deep rage and fear of a totalitarian and arbitary power that thwarts one's will and actions; deep desire for the comfort, nurture, and security which they (Mother) provide. As language guides Baby deeper into the culture, he or she discovers that "reality" defines males and females in much the same way. Baby's emotions and sociocultural "reality" mesh neatly together.

Third, because Baby still loves and needs Mother in a vital way, because Baby still feels fearful and "bad" at his or her bad feelings toward Mother, Baby represses those feelings. Anyway, life is providing Baby with more opportunities to feel autonomous as she or he gets older (Father, playmates, nursery school). The docile 3-year-old emerges from the turmoil of the terrible twos. Baby feels only obedient love for Mother—most of the time. The category "female" provides the necessary tension release; it is a peg on which one can hang all one's bad memories and bad feelings about Mother. So an emotional structure is set in place in Baby's subjectivity because of the intersection of microsocial processes (Baby's relationships with parents) and macrosocial arrangements (cultural beliefs about gender). From now on, the former will help shape the latter. Let us call this process of bad-good feelings toward females and attraction to male power Process C.

Different Emotional Development

It would seem that our story has a neat if unhappy conclusion. But, like a detective story, we now come to an addendum that unsettles our neat solution. For at the same time Baby is linking emotions to gender categories, she or he discovers that he or she too is a gendered being. Our solution works cleanly if Baby is male. But what if Baby is female? For Baby Girl, the experience of contradictory feelings continues: love and resentment of Mother, desire of and anger at that out-of-reach male power, and mixed feelings about being female and about the category female.

After the second year, Baby—female or male—is caught up in verbal, cognitive life and socialization. Emotional development continues, but beneath cognition, at a level the child cannot identify and know. The consequences of this continued but unrecognized emotional development will be an adult male personality or an adult female personality. The three processes identified here, however, fix the direction for this development and its personality outcomes. Let us see where the three processes we have described lead Baby, in terms of emotional development.

We start first with Process C, bad-good feelings toward females and attraction to male power. This process, as we have already shown, becomes for a male child the underground source of a lurking hostility to women, a fear of female domination, and an accelerated identification with Father, male identity, and male power. For a female child, this process creates a mixture of fascination and estranged resentment of male power, and a mixture of sympathetic identification with and yet distrust of femaleness. The outcome is uncertainty and division in her own selfhood, in contrast to a male child's confident assertion of his male identity.

These different courses of personality development are reinforced by Process A, Mother's different feelings and actions toward a son and daughter. Seeing it in her own mind as teaching her son to be tough and independent, Mother's signals to him that he is separate from her become increasingly clear as time passes. The psychological fence around the boy's separate identity, therefore, is built up quickly. By age 6 or 7, he is a fairly self-contained personality. Seeing it in her own mind as keeping her daughter protected, loving, and attuned to the feelings of others, Mother's signals that the girl is "almost-self" continue throughout her relationship to her daughter. The girl will experience herself as fused with Mother into adolescence, will then struggle crudely and fiercely for separateness, but will never fully separate, never fully close the emotional fence around her identity. The outcome for a boy is greater self-confidence and lower empathetic qualities toward others; for a girl, it is less self-confidence and more emotional openness toward others, including the babies for whom, as a conventional wife, she will be primary caretaker.

And what of Process B, Baby's preverbal sensual-emotional recall of and craving for Mother/woman? This becomes entangled with the child's development as a sexual being in a world where heterosexuality is the rule. For a boy, what is required is that he give up his sensual craving for Mother, while hoarding this recall of her to help fuel his later adult sensual-emotional preference for women. Freud called this the Oedipal process. In the typical course of things, a boy will move successfully through this process by age 6 or 7, assisted by processes A and C, which effect his dissociation from Mother and his identification with Father and maleness. For a girl, what society requires is that she renounce both Mother *and* female as sensual-emotional goals, and that she direct those feelings toward males. Given that the demands are more radical, and that they interact with the consequences of Processes A and C, it is not surprising that a girl's Oedipal process takes longer, apparently until well into adolescence.

Some experts argue that the girl's transfer of sensual-emotional loyalties is only partial. Prompted by her attraction to male power and by signals from Mother, Father, society, and perhaps biology, the girl in adolescence directs her sensual preferences toward men. But her emotional needs still stay partly directed toward women. As we will see in later chapters, these gender differences in emotional configuration significantly affect adult social patterns like male-female interaction, parent-child relations, and same-sex friendships.

In sum, then, experiences in the first two years of life have major consequences for the formation of male and female personality. Basic emotional processes, distinctively different for females and males, are set in motion in this early period, processes whose lifelong effects take males and females along very different paths of emotional and personality development. These emotional dynamics are internalized learning of the deepest sort. They are acquired by the infant in interaction with immediate caretakers—that is, through microsocial processes. Yet those microinteractions are embedded within macrosocial structures: the system of beliefs described in Chapter 3; the institutionalized patterns of family life; and the fact that almost without exception, in the person of Mother or a mother substitute, an infant's primary caretaker is a woman.

CHILDHOOD: LEARNING GENDER ROLES

In this section we focus on how children between the ages of about 2 and 11 learn conventional gender roles. The increasing control over language that develops in this period is the crucial factor which, for our purposes, differentiates childhood from infancy. Acquisition of language makes possible the conceptualization of experience in precise, organized forms that contrast with the "feeling experiences" of the infant. This new conceptual life is greatly influenced by the child's social environment. For the facility for language is the means by which the child now enters into intense interaction with others, absorbing in this interaction the meaning systems of those others. Growing mastery of these social meanings opens up to the child the additional possibility of self knowledge, of understanding who he or she is in the context of social and cultural arrangements. A central feature of this emerging cognitive map of self and society is knowledge of gender. Childhood is the primary and formative phase of cognitive socialization into the gender script and one's role in that script as female or male.

One by-product of the child's growing verbal capacity is that she or he can now be studied by the conventional methods of social science research: observation of his or her spontaneous activities; interpretation of her or his spoken and written communications, and even of his or her drawings and paintings; interviews; surveys using questionnaires. In contrast to infancy, then, childhood gender socialization is the subject of a vast research and speculative literature, as bibliographies in Baker (1980), Bem (1983), Laws and Schwartz (1977), Maccoby and Jacklin (1974), and Walum-Richardson (1981) indicate. Our brief attempt to report here on this research has therefore to be highly selective. In making our selections we have had to come to terms with the implications of three major controversies concerning: (1) the processes by which the child learns; (2) the stages through which that learning progresses; and (3) the crucial agents of gender socialization.

There are three different approaches to the issue of how the child learns social scripts, including the gender script. The first approach is that of *psychoanalytical theory*, which focuses on the child's emotionally ambivalent, triangular relationship to parents, its struggle for a sense of identity separate from parents, and throughout all of this, the experience of emotional conflicts that permanently shape adult personality. A second approach is that of *social learning theory*, which traces the effects of the child's observation of its environment, its imitative behavior, and its experiences of rewards and punishments for conformity and nonconformity on its acquisition of the gender script. From this vantage point, the child is a fairly passive being affected by the patterns and dynamics of its social environment. A third approach to the issue of gender learning is that of *cognitive development theory*, which sees the child as an active agent who learns gender roles in the course of attempting to pattern experience and to arrive at a sense of selfhood. This thesis leads to the question of why this active work by children produces over and over again a consistent pattern of female and of male selfhood. The answer brings us back to gender patterns in society itself, and to the fact that the child's active work at patterning experience interacts with a patterning of experience which is socially provided.

Our position is that all the learning experiences identified by these theories affect a child's acquisition of gender-role knowledge. The first part of this chapter focused on the dynamics identified by psychoanalytic theory. Here we will look at the effects of observation, imitation, and sanctioning (rewards and punishments), as well as the child's active search for knowledge of self and society on the learning of gender roles. We see the child as both impinged upon and molded by its social milieu, and more continuously, actively engaged in comprehending that milieu and its place in it. Essentially our position is anchored in the theories of George Herbert Mead.

Mead offered a guideline that helps to bridge the division between social learning and cognitive development theories. He pointed out that the child's mental powers develop significantly over the period we are looking at, partly because of pure physiological maturation, and partly because of the child's ongoing relationship to society. Younger children do learn extensively from a kind of blind imitation (the imitative stage). As they mature, however, they become increasingly active in knowing the world and themselves—first in terms of fairly concrete, specific details (the play stage), and then in more abstract and generalized terms (the game stage). Many other writers have said much the same thing, notably Piaget. A second major controversy in the gender socialization literature in fact centers on the specification of stages in cognitive learning. Here, however, we are guided by Mead. We argue that the young child learns primarily by imitation, and that the older child through an increasingly more effective search for knowledge of self and society. But even in these later stages, and indeed through life, imitation and reward-punishment experiences continue as a mode of social learning.

The third major area of controversy and diversity in the childhood gender socialization literature is in identifying the aspects of social life that are most influential. Whole scholarly communities focus on the role of language, of nonverbal signs and gestures, of parents, siblings, school, peer groups, play, and the mass media in teaching gender roles. In this description we chart the effect of language and gestures, family and playmates on the child's developing consciousness of gender and of self.

First Scene: From Two to Six

What we have here is really a selection of episodes during the first half of the childhood period—that is, when the child is between 2 and about 6. In fact, we have two reels of film. One captures the typical experiences of girls, another those of boys. But there is considerable similarity between whole portions of these films, and we will describe their contents jointly.

We see the child listening to what people say. He or she notes the overwhelming fact that people are identified first by gender, that she or he is above all a "good/bad girl" or "good/bad boy." The child hears adult males referred to as men, but adult females more frequently called ladies or girls. In speech people link females and males together as "he and she," "boys and girls," "men and women," "Mr. and Mrs." Females are described as small, cute, sweet, pretty; males as big, tough, strong, powerful. Humankind is referred to as man or mankind, or he. Women avoid bad language, use qualifers like "such" and "quite," phrase assertions in questions. Men speak more directly and interrupt more frequently (Spender, 1980; Miller and Swift, 1977; Thorne and Henley, 1975).

The child also notes people's gestures. Father sitting at the head of the table, taking over at the wheel when Mother picks him up from work, retreating at home to his private study or workshop or den. Men touching women more frequently than vice versa. Women lowering their eyes or averting their gaze from men. Men using aggression as a form of play, while women cower and shriek. Father putting his arm around Mother's shoulders or leading her protectively by the hand (Goffman, 1977; Walum-Richardson, 1981).

Our film shows us the child playing—alone, with parents and baby-sitters, with siblings and friends. Sometimes the child uses household objects in play, sometimes the gender-appropriate toys she or he has been given. Sometimes the child merely rushes or putters around, making noises and chattering in intensely absorbed, imaginative involvement. Finally we see the child getting instruction and correction:

"Don't cry over a little thing like a scratch. Boys are tough."

"Let's get cleaned up and into a dress. Grandma is coming over. We don't want her to think you're a tomboy."

"Not Mrs. and Mr. Jones, dear, Mr. and Mrs. Jones."

"Say the 'lady at the Post Office,' not the 'woman at the Post Office.' It's more polite."

The child is similarly taught to refer generally to nurses, clerks, and teachers as "she," and to doctors, police, and mechanics as "he." The boy is instructed to give up his seat or open doors or carry heavy things for "ladies." The girl is taught to accept such favors graciously, like a "lady." She is also taught prescribed ways for presenting herself to others; girls must look not only clean and neat, but dainty and pretty. To the extent that she conforms, she is approved as "a proper little lady."

The boy, on the other hand, is encouraged at most to be clean and neat. People seem to get some pleasure out of his occasional grubbiness and dishevelment, his frequent noisy boisterousness. He is "all boy." If he expresses any strong clothes preferences he is begged not to be "fussy." People applaud him for his size (or bemoan his smallness), his energy, his sportsmanship. A confident and energetic posture to the world is what the boy must strive to acquire, whatever his shyness or physical limits. The girl, in contrast, prays for "petiteness" and cultivates a shy, pleasant manner.

Obviously, our "film" shows only a tiny selection of a child's gender-linked experiences in the home. Even so, there are so many implications in what we have seen that our sociological discussion too must be selective.

At the most general level, what we have seen is a child learning about the world of gender (gender categories and gender relations) and simultaneously learning about her or his location in that world (gender role and gender identity). Five features of this complex learning process deserve comment: gender categorization and self-placement; appropriate gender behavior; gender as a basic organizational principle for understanding the world; the construction of a personal identity heavily influenced by gender; and recognition of the facts of gender inequality. Let us briefly explore each.

By age 4, children clearly differentiate males from females, and equally clearly place themselves in the appropriate gender category. They do not yet fully grasp that placement in these categories is irreversible, for they associate the classification of individuals into gender categories with changeable social cues like hair style and clothing, and not with an immutable biology (Baker et al., 1980). In one study, when children were asked how they distinguished between males and females, they responded that they studied the grownups' shoes! (Kohlberg, 1966, in Laws and Schwartz, 1977:31). By the end of the first scene, however the 6-year-old understands the permanence of gender placement (Baker et al., 1980).

With the knowledge that there are males and females and that she or he is one or the other, the child learns to act in gender-appropriate ways. Usually observing parents and same-sex persons in his or her milieu, the child strives to imitate them in speech, gestures, actions, behavior, and relationships with others. This is probably more difficult for the young boy, whose mother is always present and whose father is often absent. But when either child diverges too widely from gender-appropriate behavior, she or he is brought back to the script by gentle but firm adult sanctioning. As social learning theorists argue, the child's environment teaches gender-appropriate behavior. Eventually what is learned becomes so deeply engrained that it is acted upon unreflectively.

At the same time, however, as cognitive development theory argues, the child is actively working at developing a more general understanding of its world and its identity. Observation of others' gender-linked actions leads it even in this early period to a grasp of some general principles. Knowing these, the child can respond with gender-appropriate behavior to situations for which it has had no direct teaching. One principle the child deduces from everything it observes is that gender is not just one social classificatory system; it is a basic principle in the organization of social life. Taking its stand on this principle, the child proceeds to relate all sorts of subsequent experience to it, to pattern the world with it (Bem, 1983). From this so-important adult criterion too, the child will learn to pattern its own relationships to others.

Grasping the importance of the gender principle, the child, in its drive toward achieving a separate identity, struggles to incorporate its gender into that identity. Much of this involves mastering gender-appropriate behaviors and of being sure that when she or he engages in them, she or he is seen by others as appropriately female or male. For as Mead and Cooley have pointed out, we arrive at our knowledge of self from the signals other people send us. And so we see the child "playing gender." The girl first imitating Mother sweeping or cooking, and later playing complex games in which she is mother, nurse, teacher, or in Mother's clothes and makeup, "Little Miss Beautiful"; the boy first imitating father driving or hammering, and later playing father in the office, fireman, race car driver, or, wearing a cape, Superman, the world's strongest mortal. In all this the children are not only internalizing gender-specific behaviors, they are beginning to see who they are in a gender script that will continue through life.

Finally, we observe children learning that the two gender categories not only identify different types of people, they also map a basic power relationship. The routines of speech and gesture convince the child that men take precedence over women, go first, lead, are dominant; that maleness is a safe, acceptable identity in the world, the ideal type of human; that men must show toughness, efficiency, strength, confidence, power, and adulthood. They also show the child that although a man's physical strength is his source of power, that strength creates an obligation to protect the weak. Women follow, and should be associated with men through marriage. Femaleness is a quality about which people feel ambivalent, seeing it as aberrant, wishing it to be curbed and muted by "ladylike" traits. Women should be small and soft; cute, graceful, and pretty; youthful or childlike in mannerisms; they should move with caution and decorum in the world, avoiding assertiveness, accepting male power and male protection as an obligation and a right. This is the pattern of gender power relations social interaction suggests to children. Both girls and boys may find it hard to fit into the role assigned them in life. The girl will probably find it harder, for subordination is a tougher role. Each of them, though, will be carrying an emotional "baggage" that eventually provides motivations which fit them to their roles.

Second Scene: School

Over the course of a day, our "camera" records the activities, apart from formal learning, of boys and girls in the third through the fifth grades. In the classroom we see the girls bustling around, busy with "helping" and "housekeeping" chores (Best, 1983:89). Boys are typically the passive recipients of this help, and on occasion they defy the teacher (a woman), insisting on repeatedly going to the bathroom or claiming to have turned work in when they haven't (Best, 1983; 12–14).

Both in the classroom and outside, the girls openly express emotions. They cry and comfort each other. They hug each other and the teacher. They go around in intense little "best friends" groups, swearing eternal devotion. They even terrify the boys at playtime by ganging up and chasing them, threatening to kiss them. Boys, in contrast, keep a tight lid on emotions and express affection only in rough play (Best, 1983).

Outside the classroom, a system of voluntary gender segregation is in force in seating arrangements in the cafeteria and on the playground. Boys tend to monopolize the central play areas with group games; girls cluster around this area in small units playing hopscotch and jump rope (Best, 1983; Lever, 1978). Typically boys play in larger groups. Younger boys are engrossed in creating various "clubs," which have a definite hierarchy and clear principles of exclusion. Excluded are boys perceived as sissies, crybabies, mama's boys, and teacher's helpers (Best, 1983:35). Play within the clubs stresses toughness, daring, fighting, and bearing pain without flinching (Best, 1983). Older boys are busy with long, competitive team games emphasizing skill. For them, the game is the thing. Quarrels are quickly settled by an appeal to the rules, and the game is resumed (Lever, 1978). In contrast, girls of all ages play in small groups of two to four friends. Their play deemphasizes competition and is often intensely verbal and imaginative. For recreation, the girls often "just talk." Keeping the relationship going is the important thing for them. If a quarrel breaks out during a game, the game is abandoned (Lever, 1978).

Let us now make some sociological generalizations about what we have observed. First, we see the continuation in intensified form of everything we noted about the younger children in the first scene. Knowledge of gender differences is now rigidly objectified in patterns of voluntary gender segregation. Each gender is busy conforming in exaggerated ways to what they perceive to be appropriate gender-role behaviors. If anything, the girls seem further along in their internalization of appropriate gender behaviors, engaging in these in a spontaneous and relaxed way. The younger boys still seem to be trying to learn what is appropriate to maleness in a highly stereotyped way, and will inflict fierce peer group sanctions for deviation from the stereotype. The greater availability to girls of same-sex role models resulting from our conventional organization of work, family, and school makes this understandable.

The most fascinating development in what we have observed is in female-male differences in patterns of play. Here we see in embryo the adult male's facility for purposive, large-scale organization and networking, and the adult female's ability for friendship (see Chapter 8). Especially significant are the differences among older, fifth-grade children. Mead has argued that children at this age are intellectually mature enough to move beyond an understanding of their world and themselves phrased in terms of particular, concrete details of experience. They are, in fact, moving toward a general theoretical and moral understanding of and orientation toward self and society. Mead also says that this emergent orientation is visible in the way children play. If this is so, then what we have seen suggests that real differences exist between the generalized orientation to society and self of girls and of boys.

This possibility is more fully explored in a recent influential book, Carol Gilligan's *In a Different Voice* (1982). Gilligan does research on patterns of moral judgment among both children aged 8 to 11 and adults. She finds among both children and adults two sharply contrasting modes of seeing and resolving moral dilemmas. The first moral stance articulates a hierarchy of general principles, organized logically and in terms of degrees of abstractness and moral absoluteness. From this vantage point, things go wrong because people depart from these principles; things may be put right by reaffirming the principles. One is a good person if as an individual one's actions and judgments are guided by these principles. The second moral stance emphasizes that human relationships, communication, and cooperation are essential to collective well-being. Things go wrong in the world because this web of relationships is ruptured, often as individualism collides with the fact of interdependence. Things may be put right by reweaving the web of relationship and mutual interdependence. One is a good person if one's actions are guided by a concern for preserving the relational webs of life and a sensitivity to the variable needs and perspectives of all those within it. As Gilligan says, these are alternative views of the world to which both men and women may be drawn. Empirically, though, males in our society tend toward the first view, females toward the second. Their different patterns of socialization from infancy on explains why this is so.

Childhood is the period in which people internalize their basic knowledge of gender roles, and a vision of the world heavily tinged with gender issues. In this period, too, they develop a sense of self in the world—that is, how to be in the world in terms of appearance, actions, relationships, and moral principles. All this development helps to produce conventional women and men who differ markedly from each other. And much of this development results from the interactions children have with parents, teachers, relatives, siblings, and peers.

ADOLESCENCE: AUDITIONING FOR ADULT GENDER ROLES

During childhood, individuals acquire a clear sense of how to be a "good girl person" or a "good boy person." They do so, however, by focusing on what the gender script requires of *them*, and disregarding what is going on with peers of the other gender. This exclusionary focus is objectified in gender-segregated patterns of peer relationships. What still has to be fully worked out is (a) how to relate to individuals of the other gender, and (b) what it will take to be a good woman or a good man. These are the lessons of adolescence, a period in which significant dimensions are added to gender identity and selfhood. To an important degree, these lessons are taught through interactions with specific others. To see this, let us look at some adolescent experiences. Remember that our focus is still on one part of the contemporary gender picture: the survival of conventional mores.

Scene: High School

The "camera" records the activities of teenagers in grades 9 through 12. Here we see a world very different from that of the elementary school. For one thing, the girls and boys look physically adult. Their movements and conversation show that they have mixed feelings about their changing appearance. Sometimes they seem awkward and uneasy with their increasing physical size and their development of the visible sex-linked characteristics of breasts, beards, and deepening voices. Yet they also seem eager to affirm the sense of adulthood these body changes signify, with movements and dress style that accent their maturing bodies. The girls in particular are obviously experimenting with adult fashions, hair styles, and cosmetics.

Patterns of interaction in the classroom also differ from those in the elementary school. In place of the passive and occasionally rebellious small boys, we see some teenage boys basically indifferent to academic routines, while others are the most active participants in the class. The latter respond first to teachers' questions, raise points for discussion, and indicate in a variety of ways their sense of control over class materials. In place of the bustling, talkative little girls, we find teenage girls on the whole hesitant and restrained about class participation. A few girls are as actively involved as the boys, and a variety of glances, facial expressions, and body movements by their peers signal that their assertiveness is inappropriate. Most teachers seem to focus their attention and activity on the boys (Sadker and Sadker, 1982; Dweck et al., 1978, cited in Hall and Sandler, 1982:5).

Outside the classroom too, things have changed. The male child's spontaneous interest in competitive team games has now been channeled into organized school athletics and male sports like football and basketball. These games, as well as the boys who do well in them, are the center of the school population's attention. When not engaged in organized activities, the boys—the days of special clubs far behind them—now tend to cluster in small talking groups. The girls continue their childhood pattern of passing free time in small, intensely conversational groupings. This small group activity is visible everywhere: in halls, cafeterias, classes, and open areas outside the school buildings.

As we focus on this small group activity, we find the most striking contrast with the elementary school. The teenage girls and boys have become intensely aware of each other. Groups of one gender spend a lot of time studying those of the other, commenting among themselves on their observations, exchanging banter with each other. The girls' conversation alternates between discussion of modes of enhancing their own appearance with fashionable clothing, makeup, and dieting, and avid attention to issues of sex, changing patterns of boy-girl interest, and quarrels among girls over all these issues. The boys alternate between discussion of school activities and sports, on the one hand, and sex, evaluative rating of particular girls, and joking references to their own dating experiences on the other. We also see that several girl-boy couples have formed and are publicly acknowledged by the school community, which studies these relationships with keen interest.

The key to understanding what we have seen is the following fact: These teenagers have been given a clear, unequivocal message by adults, peers, and the general culture that their bodily changes signify they must shortly assume an adult status in society. Guided by their lifelong observations of adults, by the direct and indirect messages of those around them, and by the mass media, they have arrived at a sense of what adulthood means. All the behaviors we observe are attempts to prepare for adulthood, guided by that sense of what it will mean to be an adult.

Becoming a Breadwinner and Husband

The boys understand that adulthood will require them to be "breadwinners." This role is perceived as having two components. First, they must be effective wage earners. Second, they will have to acquire a wife and family. Pushed by the first requirement, the boys are gearing up for achievement in some area of the occupational structure. For some boys, and this typically follows class lines, the occupational goal requires no great investment in education. These boys are indifferent to academic routines. Other boys see that school achievement leads to college and career; these are the mobilized achievers in the classroom. Peers and adults actively encourage this mobilization, and their earlier socialization has equipped them for individual competition (Kaufman and Richardson, 1982). At this stage they do not envisage the possibility of failure. The pain of personal failure will be, for some, an experience of adulthood.

Recognizing the second requirement of male adulthood, acquiring a wife and child, leads the teenage boy to that cultural complex discussed in Chapter 3, the interrelationship of marriage, love, and sex. This is a puzzling complex for the boys, for which they receive only the vaguest instruction (Litewka, 1972). What we see them working out in high school are the following conclusions: a heterosexual coupling is essential to adulthood; to achieve that relationship, the male must act as initiator, essentially choosing a marriage partner; that partner should be physically attractive and, in terms of personality, complementary to maleness. The individual's actual choice, however, will be affected by a complex process that rates both the boy and the girl (Scanzoni and Scanzoni, 1981), a rating process they must struggle to understand. The long-range outcome of all this, as the boy sees it, will be marriage, which brings with it the rewards of love and sex. Dating in high school is a process of experimentation with all this.

The teenage boy labors under certain handicaps in his role of pursuing a mate. Being cast in the role of initiator can be frightening and on occasion embarrassing, and his earlier socialization has not prepared him for the nuances of exploring and maintaining close relationships. Emotionally, though, he is comfortable with the quest for a wife who will substitute for the original source of sensual and emotional gratification

(Dinnerstein, 1976; Chodorow, 1978). Practically, he can bring his skills of assertiveness and competition to bear on this new problem. And the double tasks of achievement and heterosexual prowess work in harmony. The former enhances one's rating in the sexual game. Above all, the role of initiator, however frightening to particular individuals, puts them in a position of power. They may act or even for a while choose not to act in the maneuver for a sexual partner, for they have considerable control of the game.

Becoming a Wife

The teenage girl also recognizes what her primary adult role will be—that of wife to a man in marriage. This recognition generates a whole complex of problems, all centering on the fact that her role in the mate selection game is culturally prescribed as a fairly passive one (Laws and Schwartz, 1977). From a position of visible inaction she must somehow contrive to be selected by a suitable mate, for that is her basic route to adulthood. This puzzle leads her too to the cultural complex of marriage, love, and sex. But given her situation, she sees the relationship among those factors in a rather different way from the teenage boy. To her, love and sex lead to marriage—or more precisely, marriage will come to the woman who can appear to the male to be attractive as a love and sex mate.

Everything in her culture and peer group tells her what qualities males require of a love partner. To be attractive in this way, a girl must be pleasant and easy to be with, not overly assertive, never in competition with her partner, interested in what he is and does, and able to make him feel emotionally secure (Laws and Schwartz, 1977; Kaufman and Richardson, 1982). Independent achievement at school is a liability in the conventional girl's quest for marriage; it makes her look unattractively competitive. Indeed, the educational and career-linked aspects of school are irrelevant to her goals. High school may provide a suitable mate, or it may lead to college, where the choices may be even better. This overall calculation explains the low profile most girls maintain in the classroom (Rivers, Barnett, and Baruch, 1979; Kaufman and Richardson, 1982).

Being perceived as sexually attractive brings the girl under the tyranny of existing standards for female beauty (Laws and Schwartz, 1977; Millman, 1980; Chernin, 1981; Lurie, 1982; Banner, 1983). Whole industries make their livelihood by assisting women in this search for a beautiful appearance. The teenage girl, a novice at this game, is particularly vulnerable to its pressures. Her concern with appearance, weight, clothes, hairstyle, makeup, and personal adornment is intense, anxious, continuous. For together with cultivation of the appropriate mannerisms, this will be her major resource for achieving her goal, marriage.

To work her way through the maze that constitutes her movement toward adulthood, the girl can draw on certain assets. These are the emotional openness to others we explored in the first part of this chapter, and her relational skills. Caring for the other, understanding that other, and binding him to her are all abilities she has been acquiring since infancy. But the girl also labors under very real handicaps in this effort.

Emotionally, she finds herself in a painful situation. Until this point, her emotional development has been closely associated with her links to other females—her mother and her friends. As an emergent adult, she must establish an identity separate from her mother, and must in the search for a mate compete with her friends. Yet as we have seen, relatedness is at the very center of her moral sense, and individualism and competition are foreign modes. Adolescence is for the girl a time of emotional turbulence.

More practically, the girl has to bring the idiosyncracies of her personal appearance into line with the norms of fashion and also to abandon activities that might lead to achievement in the public sphere. The latter course will make her economically dependent on male support. She also experiences the frustration of not being able directly to pursue her life goal, a marriage partner. She must achieve that end by tactics of maneuver and indirection, the strategies of the powerless. Adolescence, in fact, is the time when the selfhood of the conventional female comes practically in touch with the powerlessness that is to be her adult destiny.

Adolescence is an important phase in the development of gender personalities that will conform to conventional gender mores. In this period, males and females begin to grasp the nature of their adult roles and the qualities of their future interrelatedness. Here again, interaction with others has been a major route to learning the gender script.

ADULTHOOD: KEEPING TO THE SCRIPT

Adulthood in our society conventionally begins when a person leaves high school for college, work, or marriage. By this time personality is fairly completely developed, and conventional men and women have fully internalized the beliefs and prescriptions for action described in Chapter 3. By and large, they will now spontaneously conform to the conventional gender scripts. Should they on occasion stray, however, others will quickly prompt them back to the script.

In this brief final section we look at how this prompting is done at the interactional level. Instead of decribing a scene, we report to you what people have actually said. Our statements are taken from research done in the last decade, and they describe the experiences of men and women from a variety of backgrounds. Primarily, though, they let us look at women in the three institutional areas of higher education, work, and family.

Education

Female: One woman earned high grades in a traditionally male field. Her professor announced to a mostly male class that this represented an unusual achievement "for a woman" and was an indication, first, that the woman student was probably not really feminine, and second, that the males in the class were not truly masculine, since they allowed a woman to beat them. (Franklin et al., 1981, quoted in Hall and Sandler, 1982:30).

Female: I told my adviser I wanted to continue working toward a Ph.D. He said, "A pretty girl like you will certainly get married. Why don't you stop with an M.A.?" (Bogart, 1981, quoted in Hall and Sandler, 1982:10).

Female: A few years ago, my husband took on a very important job that kept him busier than ever. So I decided that was a good time to go back to school and get a master's degree in psychology. By the time the first term was over, things seemed to be going downhill at home. Carl seemed snappy and angry. He worked even longer hours than before, and was almost never home. Then, in the middle of my second term, I found out he was having an affair. I was just devastated. The message was very clear for me. If I didn't devote all my attention to him, there would be another woman in the picture. (Rubin, 1979:143)

Work

Female: I was really crushed that he didn't seem to care, in that all the interactions that I'd had with him over a couple of months meant nothing to him. And if I wasn't going to sleep with him, I wasn't going to get my promotion . . . it made me feel so dehumanized. It made me feel like I wasn't a person—that no one really cared what I was like or was interested in knowing me. (Speak-Out, Working Women United Institute [now Working Women's Institute], 1975:35, quoted in MacKinnon, 1979:88)

Female: I,————, do hereby testify that during the course of my employment with the [company], I have suffered repeated and persistent sexual harassment by Mr. X, [head] of the [company]. Mr. X has directly expressed prurient interest in me on several occasions when he called me into his office as an employee, in his capacity as my superior, during normal working hours. I have been made audience to sexually explicit language and imagery in Mr. X's office during normal working hours. I have been intimidated by his power over my job and future, his connections in [the local government], his reputation for vindictiveness, and the gun he carries, often visibly. In his office, Mr. X has initiated physical sexual contact with me which I did not want.

    I believe, and have been made to feel by Mr. X, that my well-being on the job and advancement as an employee of the [company], as well as my recommendations for future jobs, are directly contingent upon my compliance with Mr. X's sexual demands. It is my opinion that Mr. X's hiring procedures are directly influenced by his sexual interests and that most if not all women who work for the [company] undergo some form of sexual harassment. (MacKinnon, 1979:45)

Male: I don't mind what she does during the day. But a woman has to be sensitive to how her husband feels when she comes home talking about things he doesn't know anything about. No matter how excited she is about what she's doing, she's better off to tear that page out of the book and come home quietly without saying much about it. (Rubin, 1979:116)

Male: I have always thought that I would be the primary breadwinner and even though I don't have to be, I can't get over the idea that I should be . . . I am used to having everyone rely on me, and when they can't—even if they don't need to—it's very upsetting . . . I don't mind her success, but I need my own . . . I don't want to feel dependent, that there is a safety net out there. It's not really masculine. . . . When I see myself as less masculine, I see her as more self-sufficient and more masculine, which isn't so great. . . . It affects my sexual interest and the way I feel about the relationship. (Blumstein and Schwartz, 1983:73)

Family

Male: A wife's got to learn to be number two. That's just the way it is, and that's what she better learn. She's not going to work. She's going to stay home and take care of the family like a wife's supposed to do. (Rubin, 1976:183)

Male: I couldn't stand being home every day, taking care of the house, or sick kids, or stuff like that. But that's because I'm a man. Men aren't supposed to do things like that, but it's what women are supposed to be doing. It's natural for them, so they don't mind. (Rubin, 1976:105)

Female: I begin to worry what's going to happen to me after the kids are grown up. I don't want to be like my mother, just sort of hanging around being a professional mother and grandmother. So I thought I could go to school—you know, take a few courses or something, maybe even be a teacher eventually. But he says I can't and no matter how much I beg, he won't let me. (Rubin, 1976:96)

Female: I don't like women who want to be men. Those libbers, they want men and women to be just alike, and I don't want that to happen. I think men should be men and women should be women. They're crazy not to appreciate what men do for women. I like my husband to open the car door for me and to light my cigarettes. It makes me feel like a lady. (Rubin, 1976:131)

Implications

The sociological implications of all this are quite clear. When conventional adults stray from the gender script, those around them bring them back into line very rapidly by applying a variety of sanctions. When women seem too ambitious and able in higher education, when they venture into the public sphere by taking a job or pursuing a career, when they insist on too much independence in their role as wife and mother, they will be punished by teachers, other students, employers, spouses, family, and friends. Although we have no excerpts to illustrate this, the same would also hold for men who pursue "feminine" subjects at college, fail at or give up on job aspirations, or try too hard to share in household duties and child care. The sanctions applied can include physical violence, threats to one's job, public ridicule, belittlement of one's aspirations, withholding affection, and the termination of important personal relationships. These are very powerful pressures for keeping behavior in line. They are all the more effective because those applying them believe unquestioningly in the absolute rightness of their position.

There are two other noteworthy features of this process of social control. First, women are clearly perceived as sexual objects who, once they stray outside the home, are targeted by other men for sexual innuendo and harassment. If they appear excessively ambitious in their public sphere achievements, they call into question not only their own sexual identity, but that of the men around them. This last process is very visible in the professor's remarks to his class in the first excerpt, and in the pain experienced by the husband whose wife had her own career.

The other feature of these excerpts that deserves comment is particularly visible in the statements of the husband with the career wife, the woman whose husband lost interest in her after she ceased being a full-time wife, and the woman who hates those "libbers." They show the other social control process, self-monitoring on the basis of internalized beliefs and values, at work. All these people would not only be sanctioned by others if they deviate from convention they would or do sanction themselves by feeling that they are deviants, that they are personally not a whole person, that they deserve the punishment their nonconformity calls forth. In these two very effective ways—external sanctioning and internalized attitudes—adults are held to their roles and lines in the conventional gender script.

SUMMARY

In this chapter we set out to answer the question, "Why do people conform to conventional gender expectations?" In developing an answer, we have tried to show how from infancy on, people develop emotional predispositions, selfhood, a sense of appropriate behavior, and knowledge of gender roles through interactions with those around them. Over the whole period, those others not only instruct them directly in the details of the gender institution, they show them indirectly, by an elaborate process of demonstration and sanctioning, how they must behave as beings with gender. The result is people who accept gender inequality as natural. We have, in other words, taken a close look at the dynamics of social control. We have traced some of the relationships between social interaction on the one hand, and socialization and sanctioning on the other. In the next chapter, we turn our attention to gender inequality and control as it is visible in the macro structures of our society.

5
SOCIAL INSTITUTIONS AND GENDER INEQUALITY

What is going on in the larger society that would help us to understand the persistence of gender inequality in America? To answer this question, we abandon the home-movie vantage point of the previous chapter and switch to the technique of aerial photography to see the large-scale patterns of behavior typical of the entire society. More precisely, in this chapter we change our focus from a microsocial to a macrosocial level of sociological analysis; we concentrate on social structures and institutions.

In this chapter, the terms *social structure* and *social institution* are used interchangeably. Both refer to large-scale regularities or widely dispersed patterns of interaction and relationship, like the national economy, the educational system, religion in America, the mass media, and the American family. There are many ways to discover these patterns. One can, for example, study a society's laws, its recorded religious doctrines, the content of its mass media, or the policies adopted and implemented by its government. But the most common way to see the big pattern is to draw on the data of large-scale surveys like the national census. We will utilize data from the United States Census, the Bureau of Labor Statistics, and national surveys[1] so that we can map the extent to which conventional patterns of gender inequality persist in American society.

Why study social institutions? Why look at the larger society? First of all, we want to see how gender inequality appears at this level of analysis. Without the macro view, we have only a partial picture of any social phenomenon. Stepping into the shoes of conventional women and men to study their thoughts and observe their interactions in everyday situations reveals a lot about the maintenance of gender inequality. But this is only a part of the description of gender. Macro analysis can enable us to go beyond individual experiences and get a wider view. It can help to cure us of the "blindness" of our own everyday experiences by extending our vision beyond our own personal turf. For instance, you may feel you have never seen, experienced, or witnessed any form of racial, ethnic, or sex discrimination in your own life. But you cannot claim on this basis that there is no discrimination in our society.

Our second reason for using a macro approach is to see if the study of American social institutions can help to explain gender inequality at any of the three analytical levels: attitudinal, interactional, and structural. The argument throughout this book has been that these three levels of analysis—the subjective, the interactional, and the structural—reciprocally influence one another. What an individual person with conventional attitudes believes both affects and is affected by her or his relationships with the people in her or his immediate environment and by large social institutions. According to our theory of social control (Chapter 2), social institutions ensure the maintenance of the present system of gender by two processes: socialization into particular configurations of motive and belief, and the sanctions on nonconformity. Here, we will see in more detail how these processes work.

It has been our intent throughout this section of the book to describe the conventional, long-standing patterns of gender inequality still visible in contemporary American society. We do so again here, abstracting out of the complex flow of national life data about current patterns of gender inequality. It is, however, impossible to present a comprehensive picture of gender inequality as it appears in each of our social institutions in a single chapter. We focus therefore on institutions and patterns suggested by the analysis of earlier chapters. Specifically, we describe macrosocial patterns of gender inequality as they are visible in the central institution of "private space," the family, and in the central institution of "public space," the economy. Other institutions are dealt with more selectively as they help to explain inequality in the institutions of family and economy.

PRIVATE SPACE: INEQUALITY IN THE FAMILY

Before we look at the first aerial photograph of the family in America, let us return to social control theory, and in particular to Figure 2–2, where we depicted the relationship between social institutions and gender inequality. One of our arguments there is that those social institutions whose primary function is the transmission of cultural values operate to transmit dualistic value systems to women and men that reinforce gender inequality. Males who internalize these values learn to value domination and job security; females who are perfectly socialized learn to value subordination and marital security. At the root of these different values for women and men is the American belief in patriarchy, the belief that men are born to rule and women to serve, that women and men have different destinies.

Family Income and Work Patterns

How is this dualistic value system reflected in the family? Within the family unit, the expectation is that the male, not the female, should be the breadwinner. The idealized image of the conventional American family is of a husband working full time for pay to support his family, while the wife works at home caring for the children and doing housework. If the wife works for pay it should, from this viewpoint, be only part time or for a period when the family needs her help. It is not "appropriate" for her to be the chief financial support of the family. Now let us see if current social statistics show such a pattern of family life in America. Since there are important differences by race in American family types, we present an overview of white, black, and Spanish-origin households.

Figure 5–1 shows the four family types: (1) married couple families, wife in paid labor force; (2) married couple families, wife not in paid labor force; (3) male householder, no wife present; and (4) female householder, no husband present. Keep in mind that unrelated persons living alone (divorced, widowed, separated, single) are not included in these data because the U.S. Census Bureau labels the latter as nonfamily. Family, according to the Census Bureau (1980, Series 60-127:40), "refers to a group of two or more persons related by blood, marriage or adoption and residing together; all such persons are considered members of the same family."

The first pattern emerging from Figure 5–1 is that white and Spanish-origin households are composed predominantly of married couple families (85 and 73 percent, respectively); black families are more evenly divided between married couples (54 percent) and single-parent households (47 percent). The evidence of racial inequality with regard to family income is, of course, very strong in Figure 5–1, where nonwhites have lower income in every family type. The image of the conventional family where father is breadwinner and mother is full-time housewife fits 43 percent of white families, 39 percent of Spanish-origin families, and 22 percent of black families. We can also see that 42 percent of white families, 34 percent of Spanish-origin families, and 32 percent of black families are two-paycheck families.

With so many wives in the labor force, we might want to conclude that the belief in patriarchy has been eroded and/or that gender inequality no longer persists in the family. However, if we examine Figure 5–1 more closely, we can see that the male breadwinner is still dominant in three of the four family types. The Census Bureau assumes that the male is breadwinner in both married couple types; otherwise, the labels would read "married couple families, *both spouses* in paid labor force," and "married couple families, *one spouse* not in paid labor force." The underlying assumption in the phrase "wife in paid labor force" is that the male should be the breadwinner.

Married couple families are, in general, better off financially, especially when the wife is in the paid labor force. However, we can see that the paychecks of wives typically add less to total family income than do the husbands' paychecks. Among white married couples, the wife's pay-

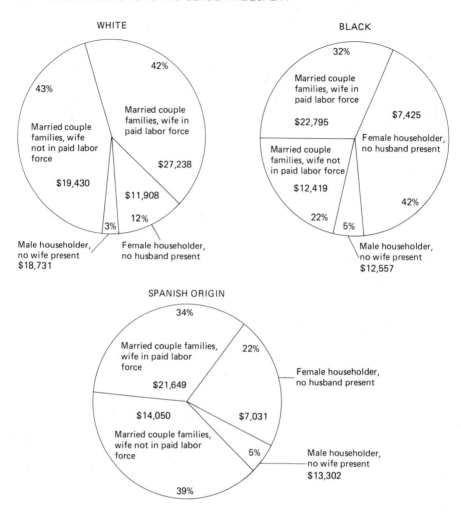

FIGURE 5–1 Type of Family and Median Family Income by Race, 1980
Source: U.S. Bureau of the Census, "Money Income of Families and Persons in the United States, 1980." *Current Population Reports,* Series 60-127:8–9.

check adds $7,808, or 29 percent of total family income; among blacks, $10,376, or 46 percent of family income. Among Spanish-origin couples, the wife's paycheck typically adds $7,599 and represents 35 percent of total family income. The male *is* the chief breadwinner in the two pay-check families. He is also the chief breadwinner in all but one family type (female householder, no husband present). If we collapse the three categories in which the male is breadwinner, we can say that the male is dominant in 88 percent of white families, 58 percent of black families, and 78 percent of Spanish-origin families.

What we want to focus on now are single-householder families. Families headed by female householders with no husband present accounted for 53 percent of families with incomes below the poverty level[2] in 1980 (U.S. Bureau of Census, 1980:3). It follows, then, that the greater the proportion of female-headed families, the lower the family income. In Figure 5–1 we see that black families not only have the largest percentage of single householder type families (47 percent, compared to 27 percent Spanish-origin and 15 percent white), but they have an alarmingly large percentage of families headed by single females and a larger portion of families living on low incomes. The "feminization of poverty" is not an abstract concept for those individuals (children and perhaps older relatives) in approximately half of black families headed by single women, where the median income is $7,425 (see Pearce and McAdoo, 1981). This "startling statistic" on female-headed black families is an illustration of the constraints of the double-minority situation. We do not intend to downplay the serious constraints of the other double-minority situation depicted in Figure 5–1, the Spanish-origin families headed by single females, where the income level is even slightly lower ($7,031). They do, however, represent a smaller proportion of families, because only about one-fifth of Spanish-origin families are headed by single females.

If we compare the differences in income among single householder families by gender, we see further evidence of gender inequality. For white families, the income difference between single male householders and single female householders is $6,823; for black families, it is $5,132; and for Spanish-origin families, $6,271. So among all three racial categories, families headed by single females have less access to money and all that it buys than those headed by single males.

The cultural ideal of a male "breadwinning" head of household and an economically subordinate wife still holds for a majority of American families. Of the four types of households shown in Figure 5–1, families in which the man works for a wage and the wife stays outside the paid labor force still constitute the most prevalent family form for whites and Hispanics. In the growing population of two-income families, the wife's income remains typically much lower than her husband's, for reasons to be discussed below. Families without a male household head constitute a minority of families among whites and Hispanics; among blacks, they constitute a majority and typically endure serious financial hardship.

Moreover, in all family types with a woman present, she assumes primary responsibility for childcare and housework (Ferber, 1982). This is true whether or not she works. Married and working women show a marked decrease in leisure as their income increases, a fact not true for men (Gronau, 1977), and working wives and mothers show visible signs of role overload (Reilly, 1982).

Yet another pattern of gender inequality within the family is revealed by recent studies of spouse abuse (Breines and Gordon, 1983; Zeitlin, 1983; Scanzoni and Scanzoni, 1981). Violence may occur in as many as one in six marriages in any one year (Gelles, 1979; Strauss, Gelles, and Steinmetz, 1980), and in 28 percent of all marriages over the life of the marriage (Gelles, 1979). The majority of these episodes, and certainly the overwhelming amount of physical damage resulting from them, are endured by wives who are abused by husbands with beatings, marital rape, and sadistic sexual practices (Scanzoni and Scanzoni, 1981: 486–499).

To an observer, then, the institution of the American family clearly shows patterns of female subordination. Males in families remain economically dominant, women dependent or deprived. Women shoulder the burden of unpaid household labor, often with the threat of physical abuse from their spouses. Why then does the institution endure? Why do we have women like our happy secretary-wife-mother of Chapter 2? The answer lies in the social control processes of socialization and sanctioning. We turn now to these processes for a macro-level explanation of the persistence of gender inequality in the family.

Education, Religion, and the Mass Media

There is strong evidence that our educational and religious institutions still reflect the belief in patriarchy. For instance, although over 80 percent of elementary school teachers are female, only 12 percent of elementary school principals are women. At the secondary school level, almost 50 percent of teachers are female, but only 6 percent of principals are women (National Educational Association, 1977, in Walum-Richardson, 1981:64; and Rytina, 1982). At the college level, women are 29 percent of the faculties, but only 7 percent of college or university presidents. Women presidents are more visible at women's colleges (67 percent) and less visible at four-year public institutions (3.8 percent) (Vetter, 1981:140; and Rytina, 1982). In addition, the latest census shows only 4 percent of clergy are women (Rytina, 1982). Since most churches require that the most important leadership position be filled by members of the clergy, there does not seem to be a serious threat to patriarchy in this institution. In theology schools, women in 1981 were 23.1 percent of the student population, and almost one in four receiving graduate degrees from professional and graduate theological schools (Taylor, 1982: 9–10). Males are still in the dominant positions in these schools, as female faculty were only 8.9 percent of total theology faculty in 1981 (Taylor, 1982: 33–34). Leadership positions in schools, colleges, universities, and churches across the country are predominantly male, an observation with a message that cannot be missed by the next generation.

Are high school students still learning that job security is a male value and marital security is a female value? Evidence regarding vocational education programs is illustrative. The Department of Health, Education and Welfare (1978) reported that within vocational education programs, girls represent 75 percent of students in consumer and home-making courses, occupational home economics, health, and office occupations, whereas 75 percent of the students in agriculture, technical, trade, and industrial programs are boys. High school students in these programs are internalizing the belief that the home-related courses are more appropriate for girls, and that the higher-paying, job-related courses are more appropriate for boys.

This message is conveyed much more directly by organized religion. By some standards, Americans are highly religious, for 90 percent of the population professes a belief in "God or some universal spirit," a level of faith outranked only by Hindu India. Forty percent of the population attends weekly religious services—in contrast to, for example, 15 percent in Britain (Robertson, 1981: 419). A few liberal religious groups may affirm gender equality, but traditional religion in all its forms transmits as one of its basic messages the theme that women's status is, by divine decree, a subordinated one. In Chapter 3 we noted the influence of religious beliefs in natural differences between the sexes and religious ambivalence toward erotic love. Within Christianity, much of the sinfulness associated with sexual love is also associated with Eve, the first woman, and with womankind generally, a theme captured in the following traditional verse:

> I am Eve, the wife of noble Adam, it was
> I who violated Jesus in the past; it was I who
> robbed my children of heaven; it is I by right
> who should have been crucified.
> I had heaven at my command; evil the bad
> choice that shamed me; evil the punishment for
> my crime that has aged me; alas my hand is
> not pure.
> It was I who plucked the apple; it went past
> the narrow of my gullet; as long as they live in
> daylight women will not cease from folly on
> account of it.
> There would be no ice in any place; there
> would be no bright windy winter; there would be
> no hell; there would be no grief; there would
> be no terror, but for me.
>
> A Golden Treasury of Irish Poetry,
> Greene and O'Connor eds.,
> (quoted in Warner, 1983:50)

This theme is discussed more fully in Chapter 11. We also look there at religion's message that woman's sacred duty is to be submissive to male authority.

Is this message also being conveyed by the mass media, our third socializing institution? A recent book by Erving Goffman, *Gender Advertisements* (1979), is illuminating with regard to the influence of the ads that are omnipresent in America. Goffman presents 500 black and white reproductions of magazine advertisements, photographs, and prints, and analyzes the often unspoken social assumptions about gender conveyed by these pictures. His aim is not to present the pictures as representative of gender behavior in real life. Assuming that the ads pictured represent (1979:25) "advertiser's views of how women can be profitably pictured," he challenges the reader to imagine the sexes switched in each picture, to imagine the appearance of what results from the switching, and thereby "to jar oneself into awareness of stereotypes."

Some of the themes pictured and discussed are:

1. *Relative size:* Men are shown with greater girth and height, with one exception; if the man is of lower class than the woman, for example, a servant, the woman is taller.
2. *Feminine touching:* A tracing, cradling, or caressing of an object as opposed to strongly grasping, manipulating, or holding it.
3. *Ritualization of subordination:* Picturing children and women on floors and beds more than men; bashful knee bends, whining or begging postures, and unserious clowning on the part of women.
4. *Function ranking:* The male performing the executive role both within and outside occupational specialization.

We will elaborate on this very important theme by quoting from Goffman directly. He asks (1979:36–37) how males are

> . . . pictured when in the domains of the traditional authority and competency of females—the kitchen, the nursery and the living room when it is being cleaned. One answer, borrowed from life and possibly underrepresented, is to picture the male engaged in no contributing role at all, in this way avoiding either subordination or contamination with a "female" task. Another answer, I think, is to present the man as ludicrous or child-like, unrealistically so, as if perhaps in making him candidly unreal the competency image of real males could be preserved. A subtler technique is to allow the male to pursue the alien activity under the direct scrutiny of she who can do the deed properly, as though the doing were itself by way of being a lark or a dare, a smile on the face of the doer or the watcher attesting to the essentially unserious essayed character of the undertaking.

By distancing himself from "female" work, then, the male in the ad is saying that women's work is beneath him; it is less important than his own work. Correspondingly, Goffman points out that when females are pictured engaged in a traditionally male task, a male may attempt to parenthesize the activity by looking on appraisingly, condescendingly, or with wonder. In either case, picturing the male with "tongue in cheek" is a subtle but very powerful way that advertisers have of reinforcing conventional roles, of keeping both women and men in their "proper places."

This traditional depiction of women is also presented in media other than advertising. Studies of women's magazine fiction shows little change since the 1950s in the depiction of women as essentially defined by their relation to men—their husbands, or lovers, or missing companions. Only 45 percent of the people appearing on television are women, and only 20 percent of those are in the wage work force. Women still appear there primarily in situation comedy, or as the victims of male aggressors in adventure-style presentations (Tuchman, 1979). In popular romances published for the mass market, women are depicted both as victims of male aggression and as determined by their relationship to their aggressors. These books reach a tremendous market. Harlequin Romances, just one of the publishing companies, markets 168 million books a year, almost entirely to women (Radway, 1983; Modleski, 1980).

All three socializing institutions, then, continue to convey the message that the male should be dominant and that it is appropriate that males value job security and females marital security. The success of this socialization, the fact that socializing institutions have done their job well, is one reason why gender inequality persists in the American family.

Sanctions: The Economy and the Law

What about those women and men who are not "perfectly socialized," who have not internalized the beliefs about gender, and who tend to deviate from social expectations? If socialization does not work, social control theory tells us to look to the sanctioning institutions that deter potential deviants from engaging in nonconforming behavior. Both the economy and the law are important providers of sanctions that tend to keep the present set of gender arrangements in place in the American family.

If we look back for a moment to Figure 5–1, we can see a very powerful economic sanction operating—namely, family income. The deviant family type is clearly the type headed by a female "with no husband present." Among white, black, and Spanish-origin families, the type with the lowest income is also the deviant type, the female householder. Negative sanctioning in the form of lower income operates to deter potential deviants (women) from engaging in nonconforming behavior (acting as heads of households). Families where the male is the head of household (as the belief in patriarchy dictates he *should* be) have higher incomes. The wage differential operates as a powerful sanction supporting marriage to a male breadwinner.

How does the law provide sanctions to ensure gender conformity in the family? Weitzman et al. (in Richardson and Taylor, 1983: 95–96) argue that when two people marry, they are legally committing themselves to a series of duties imposed by law, although the provisions of this "contract" are unwritten. The four essential provisions of a traditional marriage contract, as outlined by Weitzman et al., rest on the beliefs in patriarchy and in different destinies for men and women. They are: (1) The husband is head of the household. (2) The husband is responsible for family support. (3) The wife is responsible for domestic services. (4) The wife is responsible for child care. We would add a fifth provision—namely, that the wife is responsible for sexual services.

Legal discrimination is practiced against both men and women as a result of these provisions. For example, in 90 percent of divorce cases, custody of the child goes to the mother. Unless it can be proved that the mother is morally unfit, the father is not awarded custody on the grounds that it is in the "best interest of the child" to be taken care of by the mother (Orthner et al. in Walum-Richardson, 1981:120; Grossman, 1983). This deference to the mother serves as a deterrent for fathers who may disagree with the belief in different destinies, and who want to have a larger share in the nurturing of their children. On the other hand, mothers who are awarded custody often have a difficult time obtaining the postdivorce child-support payments from the fathers, who have low rates of compliance with support orders. In fact, a 1976 report (Griffiths, in Walum-Richardson, 1981:210) found that "less than half of the mothers who were awarded child support received it on a regular basis."

The laws regarding violence in the family are another case in point with regard to the persistence of inequality. Although all but five states have enacted some form of new legislation to deal with spouse abuse, and courts in thirty-four states can issue orders to restrain batterers, the loopholes in the law almost encourage potential abusers. For instance, in many cases police officers cannot make an arrest unless there is a witness to the abuse, or unless the injuries are extremely obvious and severe. Even when there is an arrest, approximately one in a hundred goes to court. If the wife has enough financial resources to get a restraining order (which typically cost $75 and are issued only during office hours), she still lacks protection. If the husband violates the order and beats his wife, he is usually only cited for contempt of court (Martin in Richmond-Abbott, 1983: 295). All in all, laws concerning spouse abuse tend to support patriarchy in that they tend to dissuade potentially deviant wives who question the extent of their husband's domination.

Medicine

Another institutional source of sanctioning is found in medicine. Women tend to cluster toward the bottom of the prestige ladder in the field of medicine, where 96 percent of registered nurses are women, and 88 percent of physicians are men (Rytina, 1982). Male control over medicine reinforces women's subordination within the family in numerous ways (Fee, 1983). We will give only a few examples here.

Within the family, the decision to limit family size is as much a male decision as a female one, based on a calculus of the cost of childrearing (Folbre, 1983). Yet the drift of medical practice and research places on the woman the health risks associated with birth control. Families who choose birth control typically use the contraceptive pill or the intrauterine coil, both of which pose long-term health hazards to the users (Kasper, 1983). The medical profession, moreover, has assumed control over childbirth, defining it as a medical "problem" requiring the extensive use of drugs and surgery harmful to both mother and child (Rich, 1976; Wertz and Wertz, 1977; Leifer, 1980; Paige and Paige, 1981; Roberts, 1981). Women who complain of anxiety or depression because of experiences generated by their social situation within the family are typically defined by doctors as emotionally ill and treated with drugs, psychotherapy, or moral lectures on "shaping up" (Ehrenreich and English, 1978; Rich, 1976; Scarf, 1980). In the treatment of breast cancer, both doctors and patients give a great deal of attention and interest to cosmetic reconstruction of the "feminine form," increasing the financial and emotional costs to the patient (Kasper, personal communication, 1984). Finally, surgical hysterectomies (removal of the uterus) are performed with a ruthless indifference to the consequences for women patients (Scully, 1980).

Let us look more closely at this last medical practice as an illustration of men's control over women's bodies. In order to understand the mind set of the (typically male) physician regarding this operation, we will focus on what medical students are taught about hysterectomies. Beliefs are also handed down through textbooks, including beliefs about gender. Scully (1980:143) quotes the 1975 edition of *Novak's Textbook of Gynecology:* "Within the last five years there has been increasing enthusiasm among many gynecologists for hysterectomy, especially vaginal, as an elective method of sterilization." Scully comments:

> The authors of the text then compare hysterectomy with tubal ligation and note that the former involves *greater morbidity and mortality* as well as *longer and more expensive hospitalization.* Nonetheless, they state that hysterectomies are definitely a trend in the country as a whole, adding: "Menstruation is a nuisance to most women, and if this can be abolished without impairing ovarian functions, it would probably be a blessing, to not only the women but to their husbands."

Scully then quotes (1980:144) a 1975 study by Cornell University Medical College which found that 1,700 deaths resulted from the 787,000 hysterectomies performed in 1975. Even more astounding was the finding from the Cornell study that in 22 percent of the cases surgery was unnecessary, resulting in 374 avoidable deaths.

What makes these facts about the increase in hysterectomies a vivid illustration of the belief in patriarchy is that women are not always advised of the relative dangers or complications of the two procedures (hysterectomy versus tubal ligation); as the Health Research Group in Washington, D.C., puts it (in Scully, 1980:145): "What is clear is that in many instances there is little evidence of informed consent by the patient and that these operations have been 'sold' to the public by surgeons in a matter not unlike many other deceptive marketing practices." Conventional women who have been taught that "doctor knows best" will find added enforcement of their subordinate position in an operation directly related to their role in the family as wife and mother. They can correctly assume that doctors who would perform vasectomies without the informed consent of their patients would be subject to strong negative sanctions.

PUBLIC SPACE: INEQUALITY IN WAGE WORK

Because work for pay is the means by which societies like ours ensure the production of necessary goods and services, wage work is at the heart of the economic order. A person who works for a wage has direct access to money, which in turn buys a multitude of goods and services, like food, housing, clothes, health, education, entertainment, vacations, and security in old age. The social location of the conventional woman who is rooted in the home affords her only indirect access to these material resources, and research has shown that the "displaced homemaker," whose marriage for any reason has failed to function as a means of support, ends up in dire economic straits (Bergmann, 1981; Ferber, 1982).

The housewife depends for her livelihood on her husband's check. She considers this an appropriate arrangement because she has internalized the belief that a wife should be economically dependent on her husband, because his destiny is job security and hers is marital security. One of the consequences of this belief is that she sees no alternative but to continue to try to make her marriage work if she finds herself in an unsatisfactory marriage. The belief in different destinies for men and women operates to keep conventional women in their proper place, the home.

"Yes," you might say, "but what about those women who have been entering the work force in greater and greater numbers in the past few years? Surely they are closing the gender gap regarding access to material resources." You may, in fact, point out that so many more women have gone into medicine and law or into other graduate programs that certainly by the 1980s the salaries of men and women in the professions and in managerial and administrative positions are about equal. In addition, of all the women professionals you know, you may not recall any of them ever complaining about wage discrimination. "So," you say, "what's all this fuss about? Hasn't the issue of unequal access to material goods been resolved by now?"

A Statistical Overview

Let us begin by saying that we do not intend to question your own experience. The description of the professional women in your own immediate environment may indeed by quite accurate. At the same time, others could describe situations in which professional women of their acquaintance are, even now, experiencing wage discrimination. But remember that we are taking an aerial view here, and your personal experience or someone else's illuminates only a small part of the national picture. We need to consult national statistics. In Table 5–1, our first aerial-view "photograph," we present data from the Bureau of Labor Statistics, *Current Population Survey* of 1981 (Rytina, 1982:25–31). Before we discuss these data, keep in mind that the total number of workers in this survey was 72,491,000, of which 39.5 percent were female. Because the data in this table are limited to full-time workers, we can make comparisons on salary as well. The overall median[3] weekly earnings, both sexes combined, was $289; but the male salary figure was $347 and the corresponding female figure was $224, $123 lower than males' weekly salary. If you calculate that differential to a yearly figure, the average woman working full-time in 1981 made $11,648; the average man made $18,044, a $6,396 differential.

For readers who have never examined census data before, it may be helpful if we describe some of the major census categories. Professionals, for instance, include engineers, computer specialists, operations and systems researchers and analysts, personnel and labor relations workers,

TABLE 5–1   Median Weekly Earnings of Wage and Salary Workers Employed Full Time in Occupations with Total Employment of 50,000 or More, by Sex, 1981 Annual Averages (Numbers in thousands)

Occupational Group	MEN		WOMEN		Weekly Differ- ential	Percent Female Workers
	Total Employed	Weekly Earnings	Total Employed	Weekly Earnings		
Total	43,888	$347	28,603	$224	$123	39.5%
Professional/ technical	7,358	439	5,512	316	123	42.8
Managers/ administrators*	5,630	466	2,235	283	183	28.4
Salesworkers	2,412	366	1,189	190	176	33.0
Clerical	3,032	328	11,034	220	108	78.4
Craft	9,963	360	595	239	121	5.6
Operatives+	5,775	298	3,664	187	111	38.8
Transport equip- ment operatives	2,656	307	136	237	70	4.9
Nonfarm laborers	2,893	244	335	193	51	10.4
Farmworkers	641	180	88	146	34	12.1
Service workers++	3,475	238	3,515	170	68	50.3
Private house- hold workers	17	—**	298	104	—	94.6

Source: Adapted from Nancy F. Rytina, "Earnings of Men and Women: A Look at Specific Occupations," *Monthly Labor Review* (April 1982), pp. 26-29.

*Except farm.

+Except transport.

++Except private household.

**Dashes indicate earnings not shown where base is less than 50,000.

social scientists, and vocational and educational counselors (as well as the better-known professionals, such as doctors, lawyers, nurses, teachers). Service workers include dental assistants, childcare workers, bartenders, police, firefighters.

Just as the male as chief breadwinner was evident in our aerial photograph of the American family (Figure 5–1), so we can distinguish the pattern of male domination in Table 5–1, where all census categories except professional/technical, clerical, service and private household have less than 39.5 percent female workers, the average of females in the work force. Moreover, typical male salaries are higher in all categories without exception, even among clerical and service workers, which are "female-dominated" categories. In order to see the pattern of male domination more clearly, we have calculated the distribution of men and women in each of these census categories, and we have also designated which of them are white-collar, blue-collar, farm and service occupations (see Table 5–2). We will, in addition, look at those occupations where men and women tend to "cluster" within each census category, and their salaries.

TABLE 5–2 Distribution of Males and Females in Census Occupational Groups, among Salary Workers Employed Full Time in Occupations with Total Employment of 50,000 or More in 1981, by Percentage.

Occupational Group	MEN (Percent Employed)	WOMEN (Percent Employed)
White Collar		
Professional/technical	17.0	19.0
Managers/administrators*	13.0	8.0
Salesworkers	5.0	4.0
Clerical	7.0	39.0
Blue Collar		
Craft	23.0	2.0
Operatives[+]	13.0	13.0
Transport equipment operatives	6.0	0.5
Nonfarm laborers	7.0	1.0
Farmworkers	0.1	0.3
Service workers[++]	8.0	12.0
Private household workers	.03	1.0
Total**	99.13	99.8

Source: Adapted from Rytina (1982:26–29); see Table 5–1.

*Except farm.

[+]Except transport.

[++]Except private household.

**Totals do not add to 100% due to rounding.

Table 5–2 shows a slightly larger proportion of women in the professional/technical category, although as a proportion of the total number of workers, they represent 43 percent (see Table 5–1). However, half the women in professional or technical occupations cluster in two occupational categories: teachers below the college level (30 percent), who make $311 per week, and nurses (20 percent), whose weekly salary is $326. When you think of female "professional," is the image of a nurse or an elementary school teacher the first one that comes to mind? Or do you picture a "professional" as primarily doctor, lawyer, or college professor? The typical female professional, as seen through our overview of the Rytina (1982) data, is more likely to be an elementary school teacher or a nurse, as you may have expected. Eighteen percent of professional women are elementary school teachers (as compared with 3 percent of professional men), and 16 percent are registered nurses (as compared to 0.5 percent of professional men). If we add kindergarten, secondary, and adult education teachers to elementary school teachers, and if we add dieticians and therapists to nurses, we increase the female percentages to approximately *one half* of all professional women. So although your neighborhood may contain a much larger percentage of female doctors, lawyers, and college professors, that is not the true nationwide situation. Across the country, our overview shows (Rytina, 1982) that among all professional women, 2 percent are college professors (compared to 4 percent for men), 1 percent are lawyers (compared to 3 percent for men), and 0.7 percent are physicians (compared to 2 percent for men).

By contrast, males are more evenly distributed throughout occupations labeled as professional/technical; the largest clustering is among male engineers (20 percent), whose weekly salary is $547; other large male clusterings are among accountants ($433), secondary school teachers ($387), and engineering and science technicians ($371). Another white-collar census category where there seems to be nearly equal gender distribution is among salesworkers. However, 52 percent of female salesworkers are salesclerks, with a $154 weekly salary, whereas the largest clustering of males is among sales representatives, with a $407 weekly salary. As you might expect, the largest clustering of female clerical workers (who also represent the largest percentage of all women workers) is among secretaries (29 percent), whose weekly salary is $229. Among male clerical workers, the largest clusterings are among stockclerks and storekeepers ($304) and shipping and receiving clerks ($263).

Among blue-collar workers, craft workers contains the largest percentage of all male workers within the census categories.[4] Male craft workers are predominantly (28 percent) mechanics and repairers, whose weekly salary is $328. The blue-collar category in which Table 5–2 shows an equal distribution of men and women workers is that of operatives. For women, the term operatives translates as primarily sewers and stitchers (20 percent), whose weekly salary is $156; they also cluster among checkers and examiners ($219) and assemblers ($205). Male operatives are primarily machine operators (16 percent), whose weekly salary is $309, and they also cluster among welders and flame cutters ($338) and assemblers ($297).

Female service workers fall primarily into two occupational categories: health services (35 percent), whose salary is $185, and food service (35 percent), with a $148 weekly salary. Male service workers cluster around two different occupational categories: protective service (35 percent), with a $322 weekly salary, and cleaning service workers (32 percent), with a $222 weekly salary.

Gender Inequality Dynamics

One of the dynamics of gender inequality at work in these macrostructural patterns is that jobs typically filled by women are paid less than jobs typically filled by men, even when one employer pays both wages, and the jobs require equivalent amounts of training, and demand equivalent amounts of skill and effort. In many state governments, for example, a secretary is paid less than a truck driver, and registered nurses in government-run organizations are paid less than tree trimmers. Here we have a structural dynamic of inequality so taken for granted that it has only recently been raised as an issue. This issue, which is now labeled "work of comparable worth," is explored more fully in Chapters 8 and 11.

Figure 5–2 summarizes the data from Tables 5–1 and 5–2. Here we have the average American man and woman holding the paychecks they receive weekly for the types of jobs they perform. For sake of simplicity, we collapsed white-collar jobs into two categories. We think it is important to separate out salesworkers and clerical, since there is such a disparity in the weekly salaries. Because there were so few, we eliminated farm workers and added private household workers to service workers.

The most illuminating pattern in Figure 5–2 is found in the different sources of male and female paychecks, which accounts in part for the fact that the average male's paycheck is "fatter" or larger than the average female's. The majority (73 percent) of American women working full time in 1981 are located in sales and clerical, blue-collar, and service occupations, where the weekly salary ranges from $220 to $104. The majority of American men working full time (91 percent) are located in blue-collar, sales/clerical, and professional/technical or administrator/managerial occupations, with weekly salary ranges from $466 to $244. (By now the reader can probably recognize how deceptive it is to compare the 70 percent of women who are in white-collar jobs with the 42 percent of white-collar male workers without also comparing the types of jobs and salaries.)

Another dynamic of gender inequality in the workplace is sexual harassment, which is defined in the *Code of Federal Regulations* (1980, No. 1604.11:925):

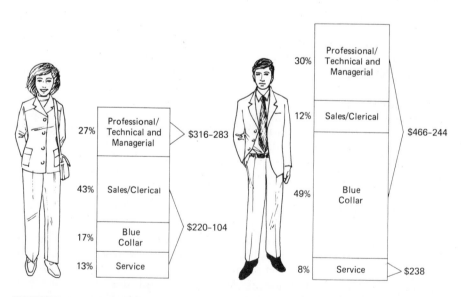

FIGURE 5–2   Average American Female and Male Full-Time Workers with their Weekly Paychecks, 1981
Source: Based on data from Tables 5-1 and 5-2.

Unwelcome sexual advances, requests for sexual favors, and other verbal or physical conduct of a sexual nature constitute sexual harassment when (1) submission to such conduct is made either explicitly or implicitly a term or condition of an individual's employment, (2) submission to or rejection of such conduct by an individual is used as the basis for employment decisions affecting such individual, or (3) such conduct has the purpose or effect of substantially interfering with an individual's work performance or creating an intimidating, hostile or offensive working environment.

The victims of sexual harassment are typically women, in part because, as MacKinnon explains (1979:31): "Few women are in a position to harass men sexually, since they do not control men's employment destinies at work, and female sexual initiative is culturally repressed in this society." Sexual harassment can take many forms, from "verbal sexual suggestions or jokes, constant luring or ogling, brushing against your body 'accidentally,' a friendly pat, squeeze or pinch or arm against you, catching you alone for a quick kiss, the indecent proposition backed by the threat of losing your job, and forced sexual relations" (Working Women United Institute (1975) quoted in MacKinnon, 1979:2).

In Chapter 4 we presented some examples of sexual harassment in the everyday lives of individual female workers; here we take a brief aerial view of the prevalence of this practice in the American workplace. The results of one of the first surveys (Farley, 1978) of working women that focused on sexual harassment were startling; 70 percent of the women reported that they had personally experienced some form of sexual harassment, and 94 percent cited sexual harassment as a serious problem. Similar findings from other research are cited in MacKinnon's *Sexual Harassment of Working Women* (1979:26–27). While we await further research findings to determine the precise extent of this practice, it appears to be a widespread phenomenon.

What are the implications of sexual harassment for American women? Most important, sexual harassment perpetuates the subordinate status of women who are treated as sexual objects. As MacKinnon puts it (1979:235): "A man in the position of authority, whether a supervisor or teacher, uses his hierarchically superordinate role to place conditions of sexual compliance on his female subordinate's access to the benefits of her job or her educational program. The necessity of dealing with sexual pressures that are, by virtue of the man's positon and actions, bound up with the woman's desired goal (getting a job, doing a job, getting an education) burdens and restricts her access to the means of survival, security, and achievement." The findings of ongoing research on sexual harassment may well be the "tip of the iceberg," the unveiling of an oppressive but heretofore hidden practice that has operated as a powerful sanctioning mechanism to keep women in their "proper" place (that is, sexually subordinate), and to remind them of the conventional belief in different destinies for women and men—inferior for women, superior for men. Research has also demonstrated that sexual harassment of female college students is prevalent in American institutions of higher learning. See, for instance, Crocker (1983), Lott et al. (1982), Brandenburg (1982).

The Mechanics of Job Channeling

Now that we have examined recent national data which show gender inequality does indeed persist in our society, we want to step back and make some sense of it. Why these inequalities? Part of the answer is in what we have already seen—that is, that American women typically hold different jobs from men, jobs that are paid less, and this translates into a statistically lower average for women. Why the job channeling, and why the lower salaries for "women's" jobs? Notice in Figure 5–2 that we have pictured our average American female and male workers with smiles on their faces. Given the overwhelming evidence of wage differentials and job channeling in the data we have presented thus far, you may wonder why we picture a smile on the woman's face.

Her smile is, in fact, a key to why these inequalities persist, and it brings us to the second part of our answer. Our smiling woman worker symbolizes the conventional women who have internalized the cultural beliefs that perpetuate these inequalities in the world of work—namely, the belief in natural differences and the belief in different destinies for men and women. Our smiling female figure strongly believes that her job outside the home is secondary to her all-important role as homemaker. She approves of this arrangement, and she accepts it. In fact, these beliefs are sacred to her because they are, in her estimation, the very basis of family life.

The job channeling that placed our smiling female worker in a lower-paying job was not a coincidence, a fluke, or an unlucky break. She was prepared for it by many different people—by her parents and siblings, by her friends in the neighborhood and at school—all of whom reinforced the belief in the different destinies of men and women. And this belief is still being conveyed in the various forms of the mass media as well.

The Mass Media. A recent study of television programs by George Gerbner provides evidence that the message of women's and men's "appropriate places" continues to be communicated. After videotaping and analyzing 1,600 prime-time TV programs over the past 15 years involving more than 15,000 characters, Gerbner and his assistants found (*Newsweek*, December 6, 1982) that TV male prime-time characters outnumber females by 3 to 1. And with only a few exceptions, women are portrayed as weak, passive satellites to powerful and effective men. Females generally are typecast as lovers or mothers, whereas males play a vast variety of roles. Also, less than 20 percent of TV's married women work outside the home, compared to more than 50 percent in real life. Gerbner concludes that TV's distorted depictions of women reinforce stereotypical attitudes and increase sexism. What is important to underline here is that our conventional female worker holding her smaller paycheck who watches these programs is smiling partly because she accepts these images; she does not see them as distorted, because she believes in the different destinies of men and women.

Education. Education is the most important socializing institution for future workers. Both the quality of the guidance and training provided by educational institutions as well as the level of educational achievement are the means by which women and men are located at different places and in different numbers in the workplace. Channeling people into fields of specialization in colleges and universities precedes any job channeling at the workplace. Is there evidence that female students, for instance, are encouraged to shun certain fields of study leading to higher-paying "male" jobs? Even though women received almost half of the bachelor's degrees in 1980, some of the fields of specialization in which they were underrepresented were (Vetter, 1982:39): mathematics (42 percent), physical sciences (24 percent) and engineering (9 percent). At the master's level, where women also received almost 50 percent of the degrees in 1980, they were even less visible in these same fields. The proportion of women receiving M.A. degrees in mathematics was 36 percent, in the physical sciences it was 19 percent, and in engineering 7 percent. Finally, at the Ph.D. level, where women received only 30 pecent of the degrees in 1980, the channeling pattern was even stronger. The proportion of female Ph.D. degrees in mathematics was 13 percent, in the physical sciences it was 12 percent, and in engineering, 3 percent. The belief that schooling is not as important for women as for men, that females do not have to work as hard in school as males because they are not destined to compete for the important and higher-paying jobs, is transmitted quite successfully by the educational institution.

What happens to women who are not "perfectly socialized" and who deviate by attaining college degrees? How does the economy, for instance, sanction them? Macro data showing the payoff on added years of schooling for females help to answer these questions. Waite (1981:4–5) reports that among full-time, year-round workers in 1979, "the average income for women with bachelor's and advanced degrees ($14,735) was *less* than the average for male *high school dropouts* ($14,806)" (emphasis ours). This statistic, showing that women with bachelors' degrees or better are making less than the average male high school dropout, fairly shouts the warning to female college students sacrificing to attain a college degree. These lower salaries are meant to deter women from deviating; that is how social control operates.

There is additional evidence that women who disregard the belief in different destinies for men and women receive negative sanctions. A study published in 1979 (National Research Council:2) found that the percentages of Ph.D.s who were unemployed and seeking employment (another indicator of unequal access to money) were consistently higher for women than for men in all fields of science, engineering, and the humanities. The male range of unemployment was from 1.7 to 0.2 percent, averaging 0.8 percent; the female unemployment was from 7.4 to 0.2 percent, averaging 3.4 percent. The evidence that female unemployment among Ph.D.s is four times that of males indicates not only that gender inequality persists, but that women who go against the belief in different destinies are negatively sanctioned.

Wage Discrimination.   Another form of negative sanctioning, as we pointed out earlier, is wage discrimination. If job channeling does not work to deter women from training for and obtaining "male" jobs, then another form of sanctioning is applied—namely, wage discrimination. We look now at some higher-paying occupations, which typically require additional education and/or training, to see whether inequality in the form of wage discrimination persists. Rytina (1982:30) lists the twenty occupations with the highest median weekly earnings for men employed full time in wage and salary work in 1981; these male earnings range from $619 for aerospace and astronautical engineers to $507 for civil engineers. As you might guess, the range of highest paid occupations for females begins and ends with lower earnings. The highest median weekly female earnings, that of operations and systems researchers and analysts, is $422, and the occupation at the lower end of the range, that of librarian, is $318.

Of the twenty occupations with the highest weekly earnings for men, we can compare salaries only on seven, due to an insufficient number of women workers in occupations like aerospace engineer, stock and bond sales agent, economist, medical and osteopathic physician, college and university administrator, and airplane pilot. We will be able to compare the earnings gap in eighteen of the highest-paid occupations for women, because the male base is insufficient only in the case of registered nurses and librarians. We have compared all the male and female salaries on these occupations with the highest median earnings where the base number was sufficient, and we have ranked these occupations by the size of the differential, with the largest differential listed first. Table 5–3, which resulted from these computations, could be viewed as an index of inequality of access to material goods in the form of wages and salary.

The Example of Education.   Take a look, for example, at the pattern of wage discrimination within the social institution of education to see the extent of the sanctions operating against women there. Across the country, educational administrators at every level are predominantly male, and they are also paid more than their female counterparts at every level. The most dramatic example of wage discrimination is among elementary school teachers who, as we have seen, are predominantly female (82 percent). The typical male elementary school teacher's weekly salary of $379 is higher than that of females at $311 (see Rytina, 1982). Another strong piece of evidence of wage discrimination is salaries of female college professors, whose weekly salary (see Table 5–3) of $389 is not only less than that of male college professors, but is also less than the weekly salary of male elementary and secondary school administrators ($520) and less than that of male vocational and educational counselors ($451). In addition, the female college professors' salary is almost equal to that of male *secondary* teachers ($387), and it is only $10 more per week than male *elementary* school teachers ($379). Thus, females with Ph.D. degrees teaching college students are making only $10 per week more than male high school teachers, who usually have only B.A. degrees, or at most an M.A.

**TABLE 5–3   The Earnings Gap: 1981 Median Weekly Earnings of Highest Paid
Occupations* of Men and Women Full-time Workers, by Gender
Differentials⁺ and Percent Female**

Occupation	WEEKLY MEDIAN SALARY			Percent Female Workers
	Male	Female	Differential	
Bank officers and financial managers	$514	$310	$204	36.5
Health administrators	545	357	188	49.0
Personnel and labor relations workers	514	330	184	48.7
Engineers	547	371	176	4.7
Lawyers	574	407	167	21.5
School administrators, elementary, and secondary	520	363	157	32.4
Life and physical scientists	512	363	149	20.9
Public administration officials, n.e.c.	484	337	147	27.1
Social scientists	522	391	131	34.0
Computer systems analysts	546	420	126	25.1
Computer programmers	447	329	118	28.4
Vocational and educational counselors	451	336	115	50.6
College and university teachers	485	389	96	29.2
Physicians, dentists, and related	495	401	94	23.2
Operations and systems researchers and analysts	515	422	93	24.5
Secondary school teachers	387	321	66	48.9
Editors and reporters	382	324	58	45.6
Ticket, station, and express agents	419	370	49	40.9
Postal clerks	407	382	25	32.8

Source: Adapted from Nancy F. Rytina. "Earnings of Men and Women: A Look at Specific Occupations," *Monthly Labor Review* (April 1982), pp. 26–29.
*These are the highest paid occupations, excluding those where the base is less than 50,000.
⁺In every case, the difference means how much more males make per week than females.

In general, the least deviant female workers, who are in clerical and high school teaching jobs, are sanctioned the least (see Table 5–3 for the four lowest wage differentials). Wage discrimination is operating effectively to keep women out of the higher-paying occupations. Given the costs involved, it is a wonder that there are still as many women "deviants" as there are.

SUMMARY

In summary, the transmission of dualistic value systems by the institutions of education, religion, the family, and the mass media helps to guarantee that men and women will want to conform to social expectations. If, however, socialization is not entirely effective, sanctioning mechanisms provided by the institutions of the economy, the law, and medicine serve to dissuade potential deviants and thus to guarantee that the present set of gender arrangements in the family will be maintained.

We have also demonstrated the pervasiveness of gender inequality in the institution of wage work. That inequality goes a long way to explaining women's subordination in the family. As we have seen, the socializing and sanctioning institutions of society have functioned to perpetuate gender inequality in the workplace in the same manner as we saw them operating in the realm of the family.

We conclude by returning to the question we raised in Chapter 2: Why does gender inequality persist in America? We have shown that the question can be partly answered at the macro level. Our aerial view of the large-scale social institutions has demonstrated that gender inequality has been maintained partly because the law, education, religion, the mass media, and the economy have all reinforced gender conformity both at home and at work. But that is not the whole answer. If we want a full explanation, we must understand what is going on at the micro and subjective levels as well. Why is our happy secretary happy? As we noted in Chapter 3, she fully accepts (internalizes) the beliefs, values, laws, and sanctions of the larger society. She recognizes her unequal situation, but she sees it as *right* and *good*. In Chapter 4 we saw how her friends, family, neighbors, and co-workers reinforce this kind of thinking—that is, how the micro elements do their part as well. The social control model is working so successfully that the secretary can say, "This is wonderful!" about her situation.

Why, on the other hand, is the unhappy secretary unhappy? She has come to criticize the social institutions which she now sees as impinging on her, and she no longer fully accepts (internalizes) the prevailing social values and norms. In particular, she has assessed her own situation as both *unequal* and *wrong*, so she no longer has a conforming conscience. She now perceives the conventional people in her immediate environment, (friends, family, neighbors, and co-workers) as coercive, as pressures rather than reinforcers. In addition, the institutional constraints, such as her lower paycheck, her educational channeling, the sexist TV ads, and all-male bosses, are no longer seen by her as legitimate; in short, she has become aware of her subordinate position. In the case of the unhappy secretary, there is some instability or disequilibrium with regard to the functioning of the social control model. All is *not* running smoothly.

In the first half of the book, we have provided you with the reasons why our happy secretary is happy. In the next part, we will explain why our unhappy secretary wants something done about her situation and what is being done to change it.

NOTES

1. Although it is true that data for census and large-scale surveys are derived from individual human beings, and thus are initiated at the subjective level, these data are quickly quantified and converted into percentages or other statistics. Once grouped in this way, the analysis takes on a national or regional character. Because the view of the individual is lost in

such analysis, and because the focus is on the entire society or on large aggregates in society, we label such data "macro-level."

2. Some of the designated poverty-level incomes for 1980: $5,338 for two persons, $6,539 for three persons, and $8,385 for four-person families.

3. *Median* refers to an average, representing the value of the "middle" case in a rank-ordered set of observations; if the weekly salaries of five people were $104, $229, $239, $326, and $386, the median would be $239.

4. The term *pink collar* is often used to separate female white-collar, blue-collar, and service workers from males in these categories, since females typically cluster in the lower-paid jobs.

Part II:
Social Change

6
THEORETICAL OVERVIEW: SOCIAL CHANGE

We start this section of the book with a mental experiment. Picture yourself in the following situation. As part of a class assignment, you are interviewing families in your neighborhood about how they divide up the work in the home. At one house, the door is opened by an old gray-haired man who ushers you in, explaining, in a confused sort of way, that everyone else is out. As you explain what your task is, he starts to babble away in seemingly greater confusion. Suddenly you recognize him. His picture has been in all the local papers.

"Albert Williams or Rip Van Winkle?" the caption had read. Apparently Mr. Williams had disappeared in 1930, leaving a wife and young son. He had returned only recently to his only living relative, a grandson living in your neighborhood. It appears that following a lapse of memory, he had been institutionalized abroad since the 1930s and had only now, as a result of new therapy, recalled who he was. As you place the 80-year-old man, you realize there's some sense to his apparent babbling. Indeed, what he's saying is relevant to your class assignment. When you introduced yourself to him, you triggered a string of anxious questions, and he seems to expect some answers from you. Here's what he is saying:

You are asking who does what around this house? I'm almost ashamed to tell you how things are around here. They are all crazy, I think, my grandson, Jim, Ann, his wife, and the two children. Ann's out working half the time. Works a big job, same as Jim's, and brings in as much money as he does. Jim's home half the time, cleaning, shopping and cooking, and looking after the kids. What's more, he says he *likes* it! He says he likes "mothering" the kids. Won't put in any more time than he does on his job, even though he could make a lot more money! You should see him, rocking them, playing with them, cooking for them, singing with them. I tell you, in this house, it's impossible to tell who wears the pants. They all seem very happy, it's true, but what's going to happen to those children? What's the poor little boy, Lyn (just look at that name for a boy) going to grow up like? How's he going to learn to be a man? You say you study this sort of thing? Tell me, how could normal, decent, intelligent people get themselves into a mess like this?

In this half of the text we provide you with the materials for answering Rip Van Winkle's questions, as well as for solving the other puzzle that we left you with at the end of Part I, our unhappy secretary and the reasons for her sense of disgruntlement. For in this section of the book we explore the changes currently under way in the American institution of gender.

Our exploration of these changes is divided into two sets of activities. First we give you some conceptual tools for understanding the changes by defining them precisely and by identifying the basic social processes that explain them. This definitional and theoretical effort is presented in this chapter. In the next four chapters, Chapters 7 through 10, we present you with blocks of empirical information about the changes under way in our gender arrangements. In combination, the theoretical framework and the empirical accounts will give you a map of these changes sufficiently detailed to allow you to answer our modern-day Rip Van Winkle.

To dispel any impression of chronology we may unintentionally have perpetrated, let us expand on the sort of description we are really constructing. We are building a description around two models of American gender. The first we call *conventional arrangements;* it was described in Part I. We emphasize in this model the inequalities those arrangements produce. Our second model is the *changing situation;* it will be the focus of Part II. In it we try to isolate and identify trends and processes of change in our conventional arrangements. Both models are what sociologists call *ideal types*—that is, simple, dramatic representations of certain aspects of a real situation. To grasp fully the nature of our present gender arrangements, you must superimpose one of these models on the other. The result depicts our present situation.

Now let us turn to the main task of this chapter: a conceptual and theoretical exploration of the changes occurring in our gender institution. We divide this chapter into two major sections. The first defines what we mean by changes in the American institution of gender and identifies certain general barriers to those changes. The second presents a general explanation of these changes, our theory of social change. Our presentation throughout this chapter is conceptual and theoretical; a fuller presentation of the data is given in Chapters 7 to 10, which are built on the theory presented here.

CHANGE IN GENDER ARRANGEMENTS: ITS NATURE AND LIMITS

"Are they mad?" poor Rip Van Winkle asked you as he described task sharing in his grandson's household, his grandson's positive feelings about "mothering" his children and inhibitions about full commitment to career advancement, his granddaughter-in-law's involvement with her job, and her determination to mix her own mothering activities with some reasonable regard for having a career. From his own memory of family life in 1930, the arrangements in his grandson's family seem to stand on its head everything he had assumed to be normal. He wants you to explain to him how two people could so deviate from "normal" arrangements of family life without bringing down society's wrath.

Any answer would first have to point out that the behavior he was observing in his grandson's family was not peculiar to the two adults involved, but was typical for families in certain sectors of American society today. Second, an answer would have to make the point that the changes that had occurred in the organization of family life for people like his grandchildren are not limited to family routines, but are part of a much wider wave of change that had occurred in the organization of gender in America. Only by giving him a clear understanding of this wider pattern of change could you begin to make the behaviors in the household understandable.

Let us try to identify the main dimensions of the changes that have occurred. To do so, we use some of the analytic guidelines offered earlier when we described conventional gender arrangements.

Public and Private Spheres

One important distinction we have maintained throughout is that between public and private spheres of social experience. *Public sphere* refers to the complex, bureaucratically organized institutions of modern life: the economy, the state, formal education, organized religion, the professions and unions, the mass media of communication and of entertainment. In advanced industrialized societies like ours, the main power centers of the society lie in this public sphere. *Private sphere* refers to the less formal, emotionally more open networks of social relationships that coexist with the public sphere: marriage, family, kin, neighborhood, community, friendship. In advanced industrial societies like our own, the private sphere is perceived as less powerful than the public sphere, and is in fact heavily affected by actions and developments in the public sphere. The private sphere, however, has its own range of distinctive functions, providing a series of practical and emotional "services" for individuals, serving as the wellspring and the anchor of personality, and renewing in the individual those physical and emotional energies that fuel the public sphere.

The hallmark of the conventional gender arrangements is that women have restricted access to the public sphere, while men have restricted participation in the private sphere. In the public sphere women are conventionally limited to low-status, low-power positions, while men occupy almost the entire range of positions, including all the high-status, powerful ones. Women are, conventionally, the principal figures in the private sphere; adult men, partly by choice, partly because of institutional arrangements, occupy a more marginal status in that sphere. Because of the overall relationship between public and private spheres, however, men's position in the private sphere is functionally marginal but in a practical sense powerful, while women are functionally central but practically dependent in that sphere. In the public sphere, women are both marginal and powerless.

Given this summary of our conventional gender situation, the changes that have occurred in them may be summarized in the following propositions:

Proposition 1: Compared to earlier times, women now have considerable access to the public sphere. This is shown by the number of women who now work, their penetration of a series of occupational categories from which they were excluded in 1930, the number of women now holding status-laden, remunerative jobs, the number of women in the whole range of higher educational programs, the role of women's interest groups, of elected women and of women appointees in politics, the participation of women in formal religious organizations and in the mass communication media, as we show in Chapter 9.

Proposition 2: Accompanying the movement of women into the public sphere, there has been a searching and critical review of gender arrangements in the private sphere, and fairly energetic efforts to rework various of those arrangements. This is shown by critiques of the "full-time housewife" role, of the emotional inhibition that conventional arrangements foist on men, of the costs to parenting adults and to children of a situation in which only women "mother." It is also shown by moves toward equal parenting, the sharing of household tasks, the flextime and job-sharing work arrangements. These changes are described in Chapters 8 and 9.

Proposition 2 has two subsidiary propositions: Proposition 2a: There is no simple cause-and-effect relationship between Propositions 1 and 2. The two kinds of changes are intricately interconnected and mutually reinforcing. Proposition 2b: This work of criticism and change was undertaken initially and most forcefully by women on behalf of women. The extension of the critical stance toward conventional male gender roles on behalf of men is a spinoff of the women's movement.

The Tripartite Lens

Linking our description of change to the basic concepts of public and private spheres gives us our first, most general summary of the kinds of changes occurring in American gender arrangements. Let us now take another approach to this particular set of changes, in an effort to make the phenomenon more visible. This second approach uses another cluster of basic concepts introduced earlier: that of macrosocial, microsocial, and subjective phenomena. In attempting to analyze a complex social phenomenon, we have argued that one has to analyze it at all three levels. If we turn this tripartite lens on contemporary changes in gender arrangements, we come to the following conclusion:

Proposition 3: Contemporary changes in gender arrangements are visible in American society in its macrosocial arrangements, in its microsocial systems, and at the level of individual subjectivity. Again, there is no simple cause-and-effect relationship among these different levels of social change. Rather, these different levels of change are intricately interconnected and mutually reinforcing. Later chapters (7–10) will document these multilevel changes. Here we will provide a few illustrations to support our assertion.

Macro-Level Change. Changes in the gender-linked aspects of the large-scale institutions in American society are clearly visible if we compare the situation around 1930 to that in our own time. One illustration of this level of change is the economy. In 1930, female labor force participation was 24.3 percent; in 1980, it was 51.6 percent (Oppenheimer, 1970:3; Bureau of the Census, 1980).

Similar massive changes are perceptible in education, religion, law, political organization, and medicine. We will describe these changes more fully in Chapters 8, 9, and 10. Here we merely want to make the point that the changes in family life which so bothered Rip Van Winkle have, as background, society-wide changes in American social institutions.

Micro-Level Change. At the level of face-to-face relationships, one can also discern changes between 1930 and the 1980s that have major implications for the organization of gender in American society. Some of these changes are direct consequences of the macro changes already noted. In work situations, for example, some people have had to get used to women in positions of authority over them, and legally enforced desegregation has brought males and females together in sports and recreation in a way unknown in the 1930s. Other of these changes express the reorganization of gender in the private sphere. An illustration is the changed division of labor in the family, to which we have already paid attention. Yet other changes are not as easily anticipated from what has been said so far. Conscious efforts at more unisex socialization for children is one such case. Another is the change in styles of address. The term "Ms.," for example, would completely befuddle our Rip Van Winkle, as would the various "person" terms, such as "spokesperson" or "chairperson."

The careful use in written materials of "his or her" in place of merely "his" is another illustration of this. The pressure for nonsexist terminology is dramatically illustrated by the statement in the guidelines to authors issued by our publishers, Prentice-Hall (1975:20):

> In your writing, be certain to treat men and women impersonally in regard to occupation, marital status, physical abilities, attitudes, interests, and so on. . . .
> Men and women should be portrayed as people rather than as male or female. Be careful to avoid sexist language that excludes men or women from any activity or that implies that either sex is superior or dominant in a particular role. Where possible, in referring to people use words that have no sexual connotations; for example: human being, salesperson, supervisor, student, and the like. Try to avoid the use of *he* or *man* in the generic sense.

These changes are alterations in the very quality of communication between people, subtly shaping the images communicated in interpersonal relationships. In Chapters 9 and 10, we review the range of changes of this type now under way in American society.

Changes at the Subjective Level.   Many people's ways of viewing the world, of defining situations, of defining themselves, and of valuing their experiences have changed. The belief by both men and women that it is natural for women to have worthwhile jobs and careers, the choice by increasing numbers of women to limit, delay, or reject childbearing, the growing expression by men of a need to be closely involved in childrearing and domestic routine illustrate these changes. So too do much deeper critiques of all our conventional assumptions, which encourage critical reflection on our taken-for-granted gender identities. The complex of changes of this type is discussed in Chapter 7.

Changes in Gender Inequality

Various key concepts introduced earlier have given us some useful ways of depicting in summary form the changes that have occurred over the past fifty years in American gender arrangements. Using the concepts of public and private spheres, we have been able to capture the qualitative nature of these changes. Using the concepts of macrosocial, microsocial, and subjective, we have been able to grasp something of the depth and range of the change. One other cluster of concepts will be utilized to depict the consequences of these changes. This conceptual cluster centers on the theme of *gender inequality,* explored most fully in Chapter 2. You will recall that we described six dimensions of that concept: categorization, functional differentiation, segregation, unequal access to material goods, differential value, and unequal power. Looking at the trends in gender arrangements over the past fifty years through the lens of this cluster of concepts gives us our fourth and final proposition.

Proposition 4: In terms of all six dimensions or indicators of inequality (categorization, functional differentiation, segregation, unequal access to material goods, differential value, and unequal power), gender inequality has decreased between 1930 and the 1980s. In other words, the sharpness of the difference drawn between females and males has been blurred somewhat, and the experience of subordination has decreased. Change has not occurred at the same pace over all the dimensions of inequality, however, and recently there may even have been some movement back to the patterns of behavior we have been calling conventional. If we could measure the degree of inequality on all six dimensions for the year 1930 and then again for the year 1980, we would be able to draw a precise profile of the change that has occurred. Although this sort of precision is not within our grasp, we will in succeeding chapters return, with concrete blocks of data, to this issue of decreasing levels of inequality. At the moment, we give only an impressionistic profile of what these data suggest.

The most marked area of reduction in inequality has occurred, we think, in general social views about the functional differences between the two genders. Many people, in other words, are less certain than they were in 1900 that there are a whole range of functions only men can perform adequately and another whole range which must be the exclusive province of women. The next most obvious area of change has occurred on the dimension of access to material goods. Women now have greater direct access to money—the key, as we have pointed out, to material well-being. Their growing participation in wage labor explains this. Softening of opinions about the different functions of the two genders and increased access to wage labor are closely interrelated.

In a ranking of the dimensions of inequality on a continuum of greatest to least change, we would next place segregation and differential valuing. Job segregation remains a dramatic feature of our organization of work (Matthaei, 1982). But in other aspects of life, like education or leisure activities, and in the valuing of females, there have been noticeable decreases in inequality.

Least change has occurred on the dimensions of power and categorization. Although material independence does give women greater power than they had in 1930, that power is still less than the material power available to men. Moreover, at the level of political power, women have not yet achieved unity and an unambiguous voice in politics. And apart from some weak trends toward unisex names and unisex dressing of the young (usually in the direction of blurring femaleness rather than maleness), it is still taken for granted that individuals must be typed as female or male, and that they should have attached to them an array of cuing devices for making the process of typing easy. (Thornton, Alwin, and Camburn, 1983).

The Untidy Package: Structural Limits to Change

In sum then, there are visible trends toward greater equality in the recent history of our gender institution, trends that have so altered that institution that anyone catapulted forward in time from, say, 1930 to the 1980s would be surprised and startled. Women participate much more in wage work, and on occasion in the pursuit of active careers; the various dimensions of gender inequality (categorization, functional differentiation, segregation, unequal access to material goods, differential valuing, and differential power) are somewhat less sharply drawn than they were fifty years ago; and these shifts are visible in public attitudes, patterns of interpersonal relations, and in macrosocial trends. But as we said earlier, this description is a formal model of those social processes that highlight shifts to greater equality. It is not the whole picture. In the overall context of American life, trends toward gender equality are muted by the continuity of conventional patterns of inequality. The result, for most people, is the experience of an "untidy package" (Berger, Berger, and Kellner, 1976) of gender arrangements, whose elements do not really mesh together, a package in which relationships and attitudes of gender inequality and of gender equality coexist in an uneasy and untidy "muddle." Those who wish for a situation of even greater equality (as we do) have also to recognize that shifts in that direction are slowed further by structural "limits." We want to pause and identify three of these structural limits to change, each of which may be observed at all three analytic levels.

The Limits of Complexity. Gender arrangements are an extraordinarily complex system, permeating almost every aspect of social life. This system is also, as we have argued before, in many ways so taken for granted that we are blind to it, not even recognizing its existence. As a result, people who set out to change some aspect of this system will often fail to see other areas of it, which then persist because they are simply not tampered with. For example, we may discover that although parents make conscious efforts to socialize both boy and girl children in an identical manner by giving unisex names, toys, and clothes, and by affirming the equal value of both genders, they may unconsciously transmit to the children affirmations of basic difference. Dad is always called on to unload the heavy stuff out of the station wagon, or fix the fuses, or take the business calls coming into the house ("men are stronger, better at mechanical things, and at business matters"). Mom has referred to her all the sewing repairs, all the work relating to kinfolk through gift buying, letter writing, and invitations for holidays, and all the scraped knees that require "kissing and making better" ("women are better at key domestic things, at private sphere relationships, at nurturance and emotional expressiveness"). The complexity of the original system serves to explain the "messiness" of the change process, with unnoticed loose ends hanging out, as it were, all over the place.

The Limits of Interdependence. Not only are our gender arrangements complex, but the various elements are often so interdependent, and so connected to the wider social system, that a desired change in one area may necessitate changes that are not feasible or desired in other areas. For example, the ability of both parents to devote equal time to childrearing means they must be part of that lucky and small minority with the kind of professional careers that give both partners flexibility in job scheduling. Most couples do not have that degree of control over their work time. Few people would openly deny that they would like to see fathers spend more time with their children. But realizing that ideal requires adjustments in the organization of work that many more people are unwilling or unable to effect. Similarly, although many people would agree that women should be given a chance to earn a decent wage, that chance requires adjustments in payment for typical "women's work" that employers cannot or will not make, and systems of state-supported childcare to which our political system cannot or will not make a commitment.

The Limits of Active Resistance. Limits posed by complexity and interdependence result from the organization of social life. An active hostility to gender equality is not necessarily an element in these barriers to change. But developments toward gender equality do generate active hostility and resistance from those who feel a strong commitment to conventional arrangements. A fuller exploration of the reasons for this hostility will be given in Chapter 11; here, we briefly sketch two forms of active resistance. The first is the phenomenon of "swings" in public opinion toward and then away from equality, illustrated by the retreat after World War II of women from wage work to unpaid domestic segregation, and by the trends toward retrenchment that have been visible in the early 1980s, following the gains of the 1970s. These swings seem to be linked to more general shifts in public opinion toward and then away from all forms of liberalization, shifts that undergird the rhythms of our political history.

The second form of active resistance to gender equality is more visible and clear-cut. It is made up of a variety of organized interest groups actively mobilized, whatever the general political mood, to oppose those aspects of the feminist movement which, in the light of their interests and values, they find offensive. This mobilization has defeated the ERA; and it is illustrated in the Right to Life movement and the Moral Majority's affirmation of traditional family values. These interest groups always have a public of sympathizers, and even in moments of liberalization, manage through the political process to set up roadblocks to change. When the general climate of opinion swings away from liberalization, they achieve their maximum influence in the political process. At these moments, one has not mere roadblocks to gender equality, but actual reversals of the trend toward that equality.

Given these kinds of limits to the institutionalization of gender equality, we might wonder how the move toward equality even got under way, and why it has managed to make the headway it has. The next section offers an explanation.

SOCIAL CHANGE: THE THEORETICAL MODEL

The first section of this chapter answered in brief, schematic outline the question, "What changes have occurred in our conventional gender arrangements in recent years?" In this section, we will try to answer the question, "Why these changes?"

Our answer is our theory of social change. Our theory will be general in two ways. First, it will use some general concepts—power, meaning, tension, innovation, diffusion—that can be used to explain many episodes of social change. Second, it will identify a set of general events and developments that in combination produced the changes which concern us here. Our theory of social change is directly analogous in function to the theory of social control presented in Chapter 2. There is also a direct carryover from the content of the theory of social control to that of the theory of social change—namely, our key analytic distinctions of macrosocial (aerial photos), microsocial (home movies), and subjective (X rays). We will use these three approaches again throughout this part of the book. There is, however, one additional analytic exercise we have to use as we look at a process of change at any of the three levels. We have to look at the phenomenon being studied *at different points in time.* That is the only way we can really tell that a situation is changing.

Time Frame

As we said at the beginning of the book, our focus is on contemporary features of the American institution of gender. We are not attempting either a cross-cultural study of that institution or a historical account of the forms it has taken in America. Yet one of our major points about the contemporary institution of gender in America is that it is changing, and to support that claim, we will have to look at the institution over time. In this section of the book, then, we will look at attitudinal factors, interactional dynamics, and macrosocial processes that impinge on our gender institution, but we will look at them in a time perspective. That time perspective is presented in two forms: as a historical account (of developments in feminist thought, or of the organized women's movement, for example), and as trend data (for example, of women's employment or educational experiences).

In choosing to look at a process over time, we come to a crucial choice, that of time frame. This choice is particularly difficult in studying the transformation of our gender institution and the efforts people have made to produce a situation of greater equality. For the institution of gender has been, historically, in a process of constant transformation, though in all this change the fact of gender inequality has held constant. The attempts by people, and particularly by women, to eliminate this inequality are also visible as a constant record stretching back at least four hundred years (Rossi, 1974; Gordon, 1976; Degler, 1980; Spender, 1982). We therefore have made a fairly arbitrary decision. We will focus on the twentieth century, going back no further than 1900, and often looking back only two to three decades. The year 1900 does not represent any particular watershed in the chronicle of gender inequality. For our purpose, however, which is to demonstrate that change is occurring in the contemporary organization of gender in the direction of greater equality between women and men, this time perspective is sufficient. We turn now to a description of our theory of social change.

Conceptual Building Blocks

Meaning. The happy secretary and the unhappy secretary in Chapter 2 *think* differently. Viewed from the outside, the two women are in identical situations. But their interpretations and judgments of that situation are sharply different. The first woman thinks the situation is fair; the second thinks her situation exploitative. The screens of interpretation and judgment they bring to their situations sociologists call their *meaning systems,* the systems of ideas through which they make sense of their experiences.

Each one of us operates out of a meaning system. Before we can act in a situation, or react toward some observed phenomenon in our environment, we almost invariably have decided what that situation is by interpreting it in the light of our meaning system, our general repertoire of knowledge and ideas. Interpretation is often a split-second activity, so much a habit that we do not know we are doing it—as, for example, when we stop at traffic lights[1] (a signal that would be meaningless to someone from a nontechnological society). Interpretation is sometimes a slower, more deliberative process—as, for example, when we "wake up" to the fact that the red light has been red a long time and we try to decide whether it is broken or retimed, whether we should proceed through the intersection or not. The general point is that meaning conferral precedes action and is the prerequisite for action, whether the action is one of willing acquiescence to a situation or of angry mobilization to resist.

In Chapter 3 we described how our happy secretary acquired her meaning system. She was taught it formally, she was taught it informally, she absorbed it "naturally" over the course of her life—from parents, teachers, peers, the media, from husband, neighbors, religious leaders, co-workers, and job supervisors. Living in the conventional system of gender arrangements, she has learned in all the ways just indicated what gender means, what being female means, and she confers meaning from this perspective easily, unreflectively, naturally. In actions and words, she also helps teach others consciously and unselfconsciously her society's meaning system about gender. By these means, the conventional arrangements reproduce themselves.

Our puzzle now is how the unhappy secretary came by her viewpoint. Only when we know the answer to this will we be able to explain *her* actions to change her situation. Posing the question more generally, we ask how new meanings arise, given the powerful dynamics in an established social situation for social control and system reproduction. In the particular case that concerns us in this book, we want to know how new meanings about gender have arisen in our society. With an answer to this question, we will be a long way toward explaining the changes in gender arrangements.

Inherent Tensions: The Wellspring of New Meanings. Social organization contains powerful dynamics for the maintenance and reproduction of meaning. But societies also contain within themselves areas of tension, contradiction, and resistance. These inherent tensions exist at all three of our analytic levels. Four key areas of tension are of particular importance to our theory of change: tension or contradiction within an overarching system of beliefs and values (macrosocial); tension produced when individuals are "imperfectly" taught a conventional meaning system (microsocial); tension arising from an individual's resentment of powerlessness (microsocial); tension produced by the human capacity for reflection (subjective). In combination these centers of tension have made it inevitable that certain individuals would, over and over again, create personal meaning systems that reject our conventional gender arrangements, and over and over again would try to persuade others to their perspective.

Power. The wish to change a situation, however, is generally not enough to produce change. The unhappy secretary is up against some pretty stiff opposition to her attempted rebellion—from her boss, from her co-workers, from her family, and so on. Hanging over her are threatened sanctions of loss of money, approval, and affection. But changes have been effected in the face of opposition.

This fact gets us to the second essential lever for effecting social change, the lever of *social power*. Social power is the ability to have one's way, to impose one's will on others. If the secretary is to effect what she sees as an improvement in her office situation, she will have to exercise power. More generally, when people wish, on the basis of their different meaning systems, to change an established social arrangment, they have to be able to mobilize resources sufficient to override those who try to oppose them. Otherwise, their efforts at change will be abortive.

What resources can people mobilize? *Physical force,* the ability to threaten to hurt or kill or physically immobilize another person, is the image of a power resource that probably comes most immediately to mind. But in the particular change process we are exploring here, the movement toward greater gender equality, physical force has not been a significant power resource for those bent on change. But many other power resources can be used in social situations: *money,* of course, but also the ability to withhold *emotionally significant rewards,* such as affection and approval; *communicative resources,* which allow one to infuse others' perceptions and actions with one's own meanings; and *the ability to organize* large numbers of like-minded people for collective action. Organization of this type requires energy, time, skill, knowledge, and communications media, which are all therefore further power resources.

All these power resources have been mobilized around the effort for greater gender equality—at the microsocial level, in interpersonal negotiations, and at the macrosocial level, in efforts to restructure social institutions. And so, in our effort to explain changes in gender arrangements, we come to the "power puzzle." The power puzzle breaks down into a series of questions: What power resources do those who are changing our conventional gender arrangements use? How did they come by these resources? Or, since the conventional gender situation itself is anchored in a certain power arrangement, we can ask, what changed the power balance in our society, so that those bent on change could be partly effective.

Social Innovation and Shifting Power Balances.

Social Innovation and Shifting Power Balances. Innovation is the creation of a new "thing," new in the sense of novel, different, hitherto unknown. Along with social tension, innovation is an important cause of social change. Over the past hundred years or so, Western societies have responded to and absorbed a series of major scientific, technological, and organizational innovations. Our thesis is that these innovations have had the unanticipated consequence of shifting the power balance in our gender arrangements so that critics of those arrangements have had a better chance for pushing through changes.

Four key clusters of innovation are: (1) the Industrial Revolution of the late nineteenth and early twentieth centuries; (2) the economic developments known as postindustrialism in the late twentieth century; (3)

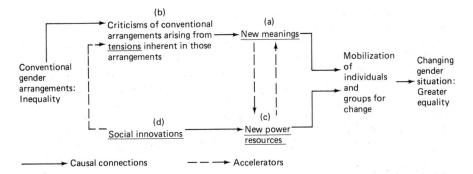

FIGURE 6–1: The General Model of Social Change

contraception; and (4) mass media communication. The impact of these innovations on women's situation has been twofold. First, the process of incorporating these innovations into social life has necessitated certain adjustments in gender arrangements. Second, both the innovations themselves and the adjustments have made available to women new power resources. These include money; new emotional value; leisure, literacy, and education; facilities for disseminating new ideas about gender; and facilities for organization and mobilization. Equipped with these new resources, women have, either individually or collectively, and either systematically or piecemeal, managed to renegotiate some aspects of their gender situation in the direction of greater equality with men.

Our theory of social change is therefore fairly easy to grasp. For social change of the type that interests us in this book to occur, two things have to be simultaneously present: new meaning systems and a shift in the balance of social power. Each of these preconditions for social change is in turn created by an important cluster of social processes: new meanings arise out of a variety of tensions present in any stable social situation, and changes in the balance of social power can result from social innovations which, like the stone in the pond, have an ever-widening ripple effect in a society.[2] Our model is graphically presented in Figure 6–1. As you will see, it shows that the two change levers, meaning and power, and their respective sources, tension and innovation, are closely and intricately interconnected. Not only must each line of factors be simultaneously present for change to occur, but each line of factors feeds the other, acting as an accelerator for the other.

INHERENT TENSIONS AND NEW MEANINGS ABOUT GENDER

Four inherent sources of tension in our conventional gender system lead to criticism of those arrangements and the creation of new viewpoints about gender.

Tension Arising from an Overarching System of Beliefs and Values

Our traditional gender system is founded on an assumption of inequality. It assumes that females are lesser human beings than males, less able to achieve, to make their way independently in the world, to think deeply, to lead effectively, and so on. This belief in woman's innate inferiority justifies and makes acceptable the general subordination of women to men. In effect, it justifies the practice of both protecting women (as a weaker, dependent "species") and of expecting them to serve male needs for mothering, domestic service, sexual gratification, and so on. The assumptions of female inferiority and necessary female subordination are what people mean by the term *sexism*. Sexism is directly analogous to racism, in which we make the same assumptions about another race.

Sexism is in direct contradiction with certain central values that lie at the heart of American culture. These values emphasize the dignity and worth of the individual human being; they stress the rights of all individuals to equal treatment, equal opportunity, equal access to achievement and fulfillment, as well as their democratic rights as individuals to participate fully and equally in the life of the society. These values are so frequently submerged by the realities of inequality in our society that cynics often dismiss them as hypocritical postures, empty of meaning and content. But a great deal of evidence about ordinary people's views shows that these values strike deep chords of meaning and response for Americans (Rossi, 1974; Lerner, 1977; Tarshis, 1979; Shapiro and Shapiro, 1979; Murray, 1982).

The roots of these values are in that amalgam of Judaism, Christianity, Renaissance thought, and Protestantism which we call Western culture. America's particular history of revolution, pioneer settlement, republicanism, democracy, and civil war has heightened this complex of values. A generation ago, a famous writer pointed out that the coexistence in America of this value complex and racist attitudes was an ongoing source of tension in the culture, an "American dilemma" (Myrdal, 1944). Throughout Western society, it might equally be said, the coexistence of these values of individual worth with sexism has proved an ongoing source of tension, a "Western dilemma." Criticism of our conventional gender arrangements has frequently been generated out of this tension. The critics have been both women and men (Mill, 1867/1980; Rossi; 1974; Spender, 1982).

Tension Arising from "Imperfect" Socialization

A perfect consensus on the meanings that undergird our conventional gender arrangements is made difficult because of massive, macrocultural contradictions. A perfect consensus is also rendered nearly impossible because of variations and idiosyncrasies in the complex microsocial processes by which each individual in our society is socialized into our system of gender relations.

Our gender arrangements are not "natural." Nor are they without costs for individuals who live by them. Their persistence depends on socialization; on a complex of processes by which each new member of society is taught gender-relevant meanings, actions, and relationships. A vast array of agents (parents, schools, peers, kinfolk, siblings) teach a vast number of people (every child born into American society) our complex, intricate, and often implicit system of gender ideas and activities. When one considers the complexity of this process, one cannot help being amazed that it works as well as it does. And one is not surprised to discover that there are people who slip through the process without acquiring deeply and fully the total array of gender-relevant beliefs and values.

We have only to think of the variations that may occur in the way a child is socialized by its parents, for example, to get this point. There are children whose parents, for any one of the reasons discussed in this section, do not operate out of a conventional framework; parents who, having several children of the same sex, satisfy their own needs for children of both genders by treating one or more children as though they *were* children of the opposite gender; children raised in one-parent homes; children raised in matriarchal family systems; only children; and so on. There is no need to belabor the point. It is enough to say that at any moment in the recent history of our society, one could encounter in the population women and men whose socialization gave them outlooks on our gender system partially or wholly out of step with conventional attitudes, values, and beliefs.

Clear evidence of this is visible in the biographies of feminist spokespersons. See, for example, the biographies in Rossi (1974), and those of such figures as Virginia Woolf (Bell, 1972), Margaret Fuller (Blanchard, 1978), Aphra Behn (Goreau, 1980), Charlotte Gilman (Hill, 1980). Also see the biographies of unorthodox literary or political women like Olive Schreiner (First and Scott, 1980), Alice James (Strouse, 1980), Eleanor Roosevelt (Lash, 1971).

Tension Arising from Powerlessness

Powerlessness is being unable to do what you want, and being constrained instead to do what someone else wants. The experience of powerlessness is extremely hard to bear. It produces feelings of irritation, frustration, and rage. We all find ourselves in situations where we are powerless, but we put up with experiences of powerlessness because we perceive them to be only part of our total experience, and because we expect that there will also be the more satisfying experience of freedom and power.

Powerlessness becomes a particularly explosive experience, however, for individuals who find themselves in an interlocking system of relationships that keeps them permanently in the situation of powerlessness. Their subordination is structured, long term, or even permanent. Children find themselves in this situation; so do adolescents; so do minority group members and people in jobs in which they take, but do not give orders; so do women. Psychologists and psychiatrists have mapped the effects of the experience of impotence on the developing psyche of children: the evidence of anger exploding outward; of anger turned inward; of guilt, fear, repressed bad feelings; of the curious emotional-cognitive splits the child makes, and of equally curious myths it makes up to make tolerable the experience of powerlessness.[3] Sociologists and political scientists argue that in social life, relationships of super- and subordination are fundamentally unstable because of the tendency of subordinates to resent and resist their subordination. They describe the elaborate sociopolitical myths both parties in the relationship may cling to in an effort to stabilize the situation, to make subordination voluntary. This theme was first introduced by Max Weber, "The Three Types of Legitimate Rule," in Gerth and Mills (1958), and has subsequently been developed by a variety of writers, such as Dahrendorf (1959), Collins (1975), and Bendix (1978).

Women's traditional situation in our society has been one of structurally created, permanent powerlessness. By and large, women have found themselves doing what the men in their lives want them to do, rather than pursuing their own personal ends. This was dramatically so in 1900, which is our earliest time frame, but it persists in decreasing amounts in later decades. This enduring experience of powerlessness has produced many of the same phenomena psychologists, psychiatrists, sociologists, and political scientists have found in studying other powerless people: fervently held, elaborate myths justifying subordination; anger turned inward, with depression and self-destructive behaviors; deep attitudinal-emotional splits or ambivalences; anger banked down and smoldering; anger bursting outward in rage, protest, and resistance. Fueled by the last type of anger, individual women have repeatedly rejected conventional meaning systems in favor of those which promise more freedom and power.[4]

Tension Arising from the Human Capacity for Reflection

We turn now to a source of tension discernible in human subjectivity—namely, the human capacity for reflective thought. Human consciousness has a dual capacity. On the one hand it guides, and is absorbed in, the development of activities and projects. On the other hand, and simultaneously, it is capable of detaching itself from the pure experiencing of those activities and projects and turning its attention on the actor and the activity, becoming aware of them as "things," as "objects." In other words, human consciousness is so constituted that human beings can "catch themselves in the act," "see" themselves and their actions even as they are absorbed in self and action. This ability to detach, to "see" self and activity as objects, is what we all the *ability to reflect*. *Reflection* is the process by which we detach attention from the flow of experiencing and turn that attention analytically to the actor (self) and the act. Philosophers and social scientists say that only human beings have the capacity for reflection (Husserl, 1931; Schutz, 1932, 1967; Mead, 1934; Blumer, 1969; Berger and Luckmann, 1967). And all human beings are capable of reflective thought.

Reflective consciousness is a bomb ticking away in the midst of established social arrangements. It sets in process modes of thought that are the very opposite of that taken-for-granted consciousness which blinds us to the objective characteristics of what we are experiencing. Reflection prompts awareness and self-awareness, analytic and evaluative scrutiny, theoretical understanding, and a systematic grasp of causation. These modes of seeing the everyday established routines of living make possible mobilization for change.

As we said, all people slip back and forth between nonreflective consciousness and some mode of reflective consciousness. Over the course of human existence, most people's experiences of reflection have probably been fleeting, or else caught up with immediate problem-solving efforts centered on the pragmatic details of daily living. But under certain circumstances, reflection can become a sustained activity, and one that moves to higher levels of abstraction such as theoretical or philosophic understanding and critique. These circumstances are leisure, literacy, formal education, and cultural conduciveness.

The subsistence-level peasant whose energies have to be totally mobilized to eke out an existence is least likely to engage in deep reflective activity. Those living in a society and situation sufficiently prosperous to allow them a significant portion of leisure time are more likely to engage in sustained reflection. And highly complex, prosperous societies like those in the West can actually support numerous groups of people—priests, rabbis, professors, researchers, artists, poets, philosophers, intellectuals—wholly for reflective thought, and presumably for the general social benefits that reflection produces (Marx, 1867; Mannheim, 1936; Mills, 1963).

The ability to put one's thoughts on paper and to react to the thoughts of others as they are objectified on paper (literacy) enormously enhances an individual's ability to "see" experience as an object and to deal with it in the various modes of reflective thought. It also enhances the capacities of a social group to engage in extended communication over time and space, and in sustained collective reflection about socially identified problems. The higher the level of literacy both at the individual and the collective level, the higher the potential for sustained, high-level reflective consciousness.[5]

Literacy is obviously the product of formal education. But formal education, at least in its Western form, also directly trains the individual in such reflective skills as systematic description, analysis, scientific and philosophical scrutiny, explanatory rigor, and disciplined critique. The higher the level of formal education, both at the individual and the collective level, the higher the potential for sustained reflective consciousness.

In a social group that places a high value on tradition and stability, the reflective energies of individuals will be directed to those ends, and the activities of individuals in the direction of change will be disregarded and ineffective. According to a famous early sociologist, Max Weber, the complex civilizations of both Confucian China and Hindu India were of this type (Weber, 1916/1964; 1916–1917/1958). Western civilization, in contrast, and American culture in particular, is change-oriented, with predictable consequences both for the direction of reflective activity and for social receptivity to the consequences of that activity. This circumstance is called *cultural conduciveness,* a term introduced by Smelser (1962).

Almost all the variables that foster sustained reflective work have been present in American society for most of its history, and have increased steadily in intensity as we move toward the present. So our conventional social arrangements have always been the object of sustained critical scrutiny, and that dynamic for evaluation and change has increased in intensity over time. As a spinoff of this general situation, the meanings that surround conventional gender arrangements have repeatedly been subjected to analysis and criticism both by Americans and by members of other Western societies (Rossi, 1974; Spender, 1982). That cluster of reflective work has also increased in intensity over time.

INNOVATION AND NEW POWER RESOURCES

In this section we describe four historical events whose consequences, usually unanticipated, have been to shift the power balance that sustained our conventional gender arrangements.

The Industrial Revolution

Historians see the Industrial Revolution as one of the great watersheds in human history, the boundary between a way of life based on agricultural production of a relatively unmechanized type, the human experience for hundreds of centuries, and the mechanized, industrial, urban life style of our own experience. Although the Industrial Revolution occurred primarily in the nineteenth and early twentieth centuries, well outside the time frame for this book, the working out of its consequences for gender are still with us. From one vantage point, the Industrial Revolution created our conventional gender system. From another viewpoint, it put in place in that system the processes for its critique and change. Our focus here is on the latter viewpoint.

The innovations on which the Industrial Revolution was founded are both technological and organizational, and they fundamentally reworked our economic life. Among the long list of inventions, some are particularly important. These include the invention of capacities to use new forms of energy (first coal, and then electricity, oil, and gas) in place of the age-old energy sources of human and animal muscle, water, and wind; the invention of a multitude of machines based on these new energy sources that could perform the crucial economic functions of agricultural production, manufacturing, and transportation with a level of speed and volume hitherto unknown; and the reorganization, around those new technological possibilities, of human relationships into complex bureaucratic forms and extensive and complex networks of association—the factory, the corporation, the modern city, the global trade network. Those innovations had originally appeared in England at the beginning of the nineteenth century (around 1800). By the latter part of that century, they had spread to American society. The years between 1875 and 1910 mark the heyday of the transformation of American society from a traditional agricultural system to a modern industrial one.

How did this economic transformation affect our gender arrangements?[6] First, by subtly increasing the power resources on which women, as individuals, could draw in their efforts to renegotiate their situations. Second, by accelerating the processes that give rise to new meanings about gender. Let us look at each of these consequences in turn.

The Industrial Revolution fundamentally altered the organization and social significance of the family in ways that both increased women's material dependence on their husbands, and gave them new power bases from which to negotiate for new, less oppressive arrangements in their immediate life situations. The Industrial Revolution was a tremendous force for *individuation*, for breaking the ties between individuals and all the groups that had previously constrained them. Individuals were uprooted from the old environment of kin and community, from the constraints of economic survival through household production, from a diffuse complex of social indebtedness based on reciprocated services, from traditional loyalties and obligations.

Individuals now were spatially and socially mobile. They lived in the impersonal changing world of the big city; they supported themselves through individual wage work. And money, that wholly impersonal medium, became the sole means of exchange, the way to buy oneself out of any form of social indebtedness. On the surface, this individuation did not seem to impinge directly on women, who still remained enmeshed in family responsibilities. But increasingly that family was the stripped-down nuclear family of parents and young children, rather than the extensive kinship system of earlier, less mobile times. In that new family form, without the traditional pressures of community and kin, the power relationship between husband and wife became simpler and starker. On the one hand, perhaps, flagrant abuses of power may have been more possible (wife or child abuse unmonitored by community); but certainly, on the other hand, the relationship was more susceptible to negotiation and renegotiation by either of the two adult partners.

The Industrial Revolution also intensified the *dualism* between public and private spheres of social experience. Except for a steadily decreasing number of family-run farms and small businesses, the Industrial Revolution took work for economic subsistence out of the household. One now left the household on a daily basis to procure the wherewithal for subsistence by work in the factory, the business, the bureaucratized office—or one did so, anyway if one were an adult male. The women stayed at home to look after the children and run the house. Even when women went out into the economic world of wage labor, the activities of the home remained their responsibility.

And what were those activities, given that economic subsistence was no longer a household industry? Essentially, women's work was reproducing the work force: of producing and rearing children, of caring for and revitalizing the adult worker. This work was practical and demanding, but unpaid. Much of it was emotional work. For the shrinking of the family's direct productive functions went along with the increasing centrality of the nuclear family as a place of temporary retreat for the working individual, as a center of emotional stabilization and renewal. The consequences of this dualism of putting economic power into the hands of the male wage earner have been much noted, and are very real.

Less commented on is another outcome: the fact that by increasing the emotional significance of the nuclear family to individuals, new emotional power resources came into the hands of the hitherto subordinated members of that social institution. More fathers now cared deeply for their children, female as well as male, and would seek to advance their well-being. More husbands now would feel emotional attachment to their wives, and would be prepared to consider arguments about their wants and needs. It is not that in preindustrial societies particular men did not on occasion come to love their daughters or their wives, but since the Industrial Revolution, the emotional functions of the family and the absence of other structures to fill those needs *structurally* generated those sentiments on a far more general scale. It is no coincidence that the spread of industrialism coincides with the spread of the cults of childhood (Aries, 1960) and of romantic love between adult men and women (Goode, 1959). To phrase it rather dramatically, the new functions of the family made it harder for the majority of men to assume women to be nonhuman (mere chattels, sexual objects, beasts of burden) and increased the probability that they would see them as human, if second-class human. And in any conflict, seeing the essential humanity of one's opponent softens the fierceness of one's will to do battle.

As we can see, there is a seepage between the power outcomes of the Industrial Revolution and the discovery of new meanings about gender. In more direct ways too, the Industrial Revolution accelerated the processes by which new meanings about gender were created. The Industrial Revolution transformed society into a much more complex, *differentiated system*. There were greater densities of people in the new urban centers, many, many more occupations, more social groups with which to affiliate, more products with which to develop an individual life style.

When this is combined with individuation, we find a system in which "slippages" in socialization are much more likely than in traditional agrarian communities. As we noted earlier, that kind of slippage is an endemic source of new meanings in a society, a wellspring of social change. The dualism between public and private worlds also had consequences for the system of gender meanings. On the one hand, the differences between the two worlds—public and private, paid and unpaid labor, technological sophistication and emotional expressiveness—were sharply drawn. It had worked out that the former area was seen as the world of men, the latter as the world of women. On the other hand, by drawing the line so sharply between male and female experience, dualism served to make subordination more clearly visible to the reflective eye.

Moreover, the Industrial Revolution vastly increased the possibilities for reflective thought in the population. Industrialism required literacy and education at some level: for running machines and coordinating factory functions, for maintaining complex business and other bureaucratic forms, for enhancing consumption beyond subsistence needs, for communication within vast human networks, for the ongoing spiral of technological invention on which the system rested. The workers needed a degree of literacy; so did their bosses; and so did the women who raised children to be workers or bosses, or to be companions to workers and bosses, or to be household managers and consumers of a vast complex of products for sale in the marketplace.

The Industrial Revolution created social wealth on a scale hitherto unknown. Some of this wealth was collectively funneled to groups whose job was reflective work in the interests of the whole collectivity: scientists, educators, intelligentsia, literati. Even more of the wealth was absorbed by the privileged upper and middle classes, and bought for them leisure, extended educational opportunities, and the facilities for personal cultivation (books, art, music). The children and the women of these classes shared in these by-products of the new prosperity. Leisure, literacy, education, cultivation of reflective skills—all these were generated by the Industrial Revolution for greater numbers of people than ever before, and for greater numbers of women than ever before. This situation generated increased volumes of critical work on all aspects of taken-for-granted living arrangements, including gender arrangements.

Postindustrialism

Postindustrialism is the label for another wave of economic innovations that has been absorbed by American society since roughly the 1960s. What is meant by *postindustrialism?* Essentially we are talking again about a series of technological and organizational innovations in the American economy, the results of which shifted the primary bases of production and employment away from the pure "factory model" of early twentieth century industrialism toward the economic forms based on "computer age" technology: computers and other information-processing equipment; fully automated machinery; further breakthroughs in energy sources, including atomic power, minute transistorized energy cells, energy "chips," and so on.

Even more significant than technological invention for postindustrialism are the organizational innovations that underlie it. These include the post-Keynesian "invention" of full-blown consumerism as the basis for economic prosperity; the gigantic global structure of multinational business corporations as a formal mechanism in the regulation of production and commerce on an international scale; and the use of big government, which through regulation, military needs, and a vast array of social services has become a full-fledged partner of the economy (Bell, 1973; Habermas, 1975; Toffler, 1970; Barnet and Muller, 1974; Wallerstein, 1976).

Postindustrialism has altered American society in two ways that crucially affect gender arrangements. First, the economy requires that individuals, at a high and ever-accelerating rate, consume an ever-expanding array of goods and services. (By *consume*, we mean purchase either directly in the market, or indirectly through taxes, insurance schemes, and so on.) Our grandparents in the pre-1920s period would be shocked at the abundance of goods and services available to ordinary people, at the careless wastefulness of our patterns of using those goods and services, and at the unremitting pressures we are under from advertising, from peer groups, and from "improvement" groups of all types to avail ourselves of new things. In effect, this produces for people today a constant pressure to maintain a high and expanding level of income. It is a pressure that has intensified in an inflationary economy.

Second, postindustrialism has dramatically altered the pattern of employment in our society. The factory with its smokestacks, symbol of the Industrial Revolution, is now a shrinking employment base for the population, as agriculture was around 1900. With multinational corporate planning, those factories have often been relocated abroad, where labor is cheaper, and their products transported for sale to the American market. The American work force now is increasingly employed in two alternative settings: the high-technology, high-skill, high-automation manufacturing enterprises (electronics, for example, or military hardware), and the rapidly expanding tertiary or service sector.

Between 1973 and 1979, 13 million nonagricultural new jobs were added to the job market, a rapid rate of expansion. The new jobs, however, were concentrated in three employment sectors: state and local government, services, and retail trade. The two latter sectors account for over 70 percent of all the new jobs (Rothschild, 1981). The majority of these jobs in terms of status and wages require workers who will work seasonally or short hours, who will accept relatively dead-end jobs and low wages (salespeople, restaurant staff, fast-food personnel, for example). A significant number of these jobs, in contrast, demand workers with higher levels of literacy and education than that demanded of the production-line factory worker (clerical worker, workers in government services, workers in the new high-skill industries are all examples).

The combined effects of consumerism, inflation, and the new employment patterns have been:

1. To draw women in increasing numbers into the work force (51.6 percent in 1980; 55 percent projected by 1990)
2. To draw not only single but also married women into the work force, generating the new phenomenon of the two-income family (41 percent of all families in 1980)
3. To increase on a societywide scale the amount and quality of education required of workers, both male and female (in 1900 7 percent of the population graduated from high school; in 1940, 50 percent; in 1980, over 80 percent).

These changes have in turn had a major impact on our gender arrangements. At the microsocial level the woman wage earner, armed with the power resource of her own wage-earning capacity, with her awareness of discriminatory treatment in the job market because of her gender, and stressed or angered by the "supermom" expectations on her as both worker and homemaker, has attempted in her family, community, and job setting to renegotiate the terms of her situation (Zillah Eisenstein, 1981b). Collectively, all the resources and pressures just listed, along with the reflective skills produced by a superior education, have made women a mobilizable force for political and social change on the whole range of issues that center on gender arrangements.

Contraception

Industrialism and postindustrialism are best conceptualized as massive, macrosocial changes in our economic life. These macrosocial changes have, in a sort of ripple effect, led to changes in gender arrangements. They have done so essentially by shifting the power balance in the long-standing relationship of super- and subordination of males and females. Industrialism and postindustrialism have made available to women money, economic significance, emotional significance, leisure, literacy, education, and that sense of relative deprivation that fuels social movements. These new power resources have been used to effect macrosocial changes in law, in economy, in polity, and so on. Perhaps more important, they have seeped into the dynamics of male-female interaction and have transformed the patterns of that interaction in the general direction of equality between the genders in both condition and opportunity.

As these changes have been in process, another set of innovations has also been dramatically transforming our gender system. We speak here of what could be called the contraceptive revolution (Gordon, 1976; Reed, 1978; Fee and Wallace, 1979). These changes are best visualized at the microsocial and subjective levels—as innovations in our patterns of interpersonal relationship and of individual consciousness. From one perspective, the contraceptive revolution is based on a series of mechanical and chemical inventions that give women new freedom in their sexual relationships. The stages of this revolution can be linked to a series of dates: 1882, the invention of the diaphragm; the 1950s, the invention of the "pill" and the intrauterine coil; 1973, the Supreme Court decision that made abortion a legally available means of birth control.

From a second perspective, the contraceptive revolution is founded on changes in our general ways of thinking that both undergird and are by-products of industrialism: a practical rationality and acceptance of scientific reasoning reinforced by prosperity, literacy, and education. In the absence of this change in consciousness, the mechanical and chemical innovations that make up the more visible aspects of the contraceptive revolution do not easily "catch on," as many Third World family planning programs have shown. When this consciousness is present, birth control will be attempted with a degree of effectiveness, even in the absence of general unavailability of female contraceptives.

A third factor affecting modern contraceptive and birth control practices is also a spinoff of our urban-industrial life style. Children are an economic asset in agrarian economies, as a work force. In modern industrial societies, they are an economic liability. Rationally, one must limit the number of one's offspring (Folbre, 1983; Scanzoni and Scanzoni, 1981). In combination, these three aspects of contraceptive behavior do in fact produce a revolution. They give women almost complete control over their reproductive behavior, and effectively disentangle the old fusion of sexuality, reproduction, and marriage.

Consider the plight of the nineteenth-century woman: she could choose to remain unmarried, a choice that generally consigned her to an economic and social limbo, and to erotic and emotional deprivation; or she could choose marriage, which gave her economic and social status and a chance at an erotic and emotional life, but which also enslaved her to her own fertility. It was not unusual for a woman to be almost continuously pregnant over a twenty-year span. Pregnancy, miscarriages, and the care of young children locked a majority of women into an endless round of drudgery like that of the subsistence-level peasant. Like that peasant, she had little possibility for a reflective analysis of the causes of her lack of freedom, and consequently little chance of working to change that condition.

In contrast, look at the women of the 1980s. Knowledgeable about and with easy access to an array of birth control techniques, they can now separate erotic need from the decision to marry, and the decision to marry from that to have children. Some will decide not to have children. Almost all the others will time childbearing to fit in with their own life plans. On the average, they will each bear two children (1.8 in 1975), committing between two to six years out of a full work life of something over forty years to the tasks of childbearing and baby care.[7] One cannot overemphasize the significance of the difference between this situation and that of the nineteenth-century woman. Women now have historically unparalleled autonomy from what was their age-old lot, bearing children. The energy and time this autonomy releases undergirds the changing meaning and power systems that have in recent years begun to transform our gender system.

The Media of Mass Communication

Finally, we will look at a cluster of technological and organizational innovations that has transformed a process hitherto conducted at the micro-social level into a mass or macrosocial phenomenon. This cluster of innovation, the revolution in our media of mass communication, has major consequences for the shaping of human subjectivity. Our great-grandparents witnessed the rise of the popular press, the transformation of newspapers from news and opinion with limited distribution to a medium able to reach huge regional populations. By the 1960s, our country had witnessed the revolution in radio communication, the rise of the film industry, and the development of television. People in the 1980s have access to streamlined versions of all these media because of such inventions as transistors, satellite communication, electronically processed opinion polling, and so on. They also are linked in a massive distribution system of books and magazines.

What does this mean? It means that the average individual today has vastly expanded access to information and opinions, and that those people who manage to tap into input points in this communications system, those who write for or get the attention of reporters for TV, or the press, or radio, instantly affect the thinking of a huge audience nationwide or even worldwide. Our concern in this chapter has been with how systems of meaning and power have altered in a way that made the contemporary changes in our gender arrangements possible. The revolution in our means of mass media communication has played an important role in both alterations in gender meaning and alterations in gender power. Those who, because of the social tensions already described, arrive at a new meaning system may get their views heard by an enormous audience. To the extent that those various tensions are experienced by sectors of that audience, these new meaning systems will be heard.

The mass media have therefore served to diffuse alternate meaning systems. This has certainly been true of feminism in the last twenty years. And to the extent that these new meanings persuade a significant sector of the audience, people mobilize either individually or collectively to bring about change. Mobilization to act is one of the most fundamental power resources. Much of the move toward gender equality in recent years has been produced by a social movement of people mobilized, now into association, now into public opinion pressures, now into marches and rallies, now into lobbying and writing campaigns, on behalf of one or another of the issues raised by contemporary feminists. In the mobilization that has shaped this movement, the mass media have played a crucial role.

SUMMARY

A summary of our general argument is given in Figure 6–2. We started by posing a problem: What would you say to old Rip Van Winkle? We have given you an answer. First, that the behaviors he observed were part of a general trend in our gender arrangements toward gender equality. These changes have been in process for a long time, and had begun even when Rip lost his memory, in 1930. They had quickened in recent times, and the changes they produced had become visible on a large scale.

Two crucial change processes together had changed our gender system. First, there was the constant tendency of people to criticize conventional gender arrangements and to suggest new ways of organizing gender, a tendency captured in our description of the unhappy secretary in Chapter 2. This tendency results from a series of permanent tensions in our society, in our culture, and in our nature as human beings. Second, a series of innovations (industrialism, postindustrialism, contraception, and the mass media) had given women a variety of new power resources. In the following chapters we provide empirical evidence for our claim that the gender institution is undergoing a process of significant change.

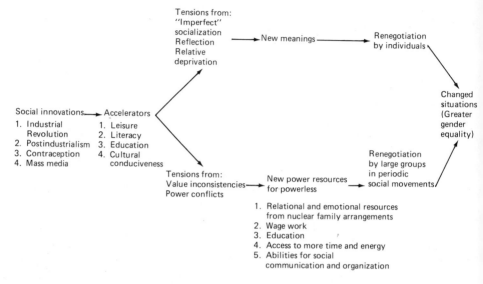

FIGURE 6-2: Causes of the Gender Revolution

NOTES

1. But this habituation is the result of a more self-consciously aware process of learning a meaning—as, for example, when we were learning to drive.

2. Power shifts may result from a number of other factors, such as invasion, the absolute rather than relative diminution of a powerful group's resources, and direct mobilization around new ideas. But innovation is an important change factor and is crucial for explaining the gender changes that are our present concern.

3. See Chodorow (1978) for a review of the clinical, psychological, and psychoanalytic literature on these responses to powerlessness; see also Dinnerstein (1976).

4. This too is evident in the biographies of feminist writers, as well as in their writings. See Rossi (1974) and Spender (1982) for the views of early feminists, and Chapter 7 for contemporary feminism.

5. The thesis of writing as objectivated meaning is presented by Mead (1934), Schutz (1932, 1967), and Berger (1967). A historical account of the macrosocial consequences of printing on our civilization is found in Elizabeth Eisenstein (1979).

6. The account that follows draws on writings of a variety of ideological and theoretical persuasions: see Degler, 1980; Chodorow, 1978; Shorter, 1975; Zaretsky, 1976; Gordon, 1976; Berger, Berger, and Kellner, 1976; The Frankfurt Institute, 1972; Parsons and Bales, 1955; Parsons, 1964; Aries, 1960; Goode, 1959.

7. The range, two to six years, depends on how one calculates the demands of this period. Minimally the three months preceding and following a birth should be factored into the equation; maximally one adds in the period of time until extensive institutional care of the child in nursery school or even kindergarten becomes available.

7
SUBJECTIVITY: NEW BELIEFS ABOUT GENDER

Turn back to Chapter 2 and look at the unhappy secretary again. Why is she unhappy? What is the difference between her and her happy co-worker? According to the analysis, her happiness, and her potential rebellion, result from her views about her situation, from two subjective factors discernible at the X-ray level of analysis. One is a feeling of pure anger, an emotional "gut" rejection of her situation, symbolized in her thinking "This is the pits!" But people in all sorts of circumstances, even when their beliefs are wholly conventional, occasionally feel fed up. Our unhappy secretary also has an "awareness of impoverishment." That is, she operates out of a system of beliefs which is consistent with her anger and which heightens her awareness of the inequities in her situation. What are those beliefs, and how did she come by them?

Our approach to answering these questions is anchored in two key assumptions: that a person's belief system deeply affects her or his actions; and that systems of belief are socially created. Let us look at each of these assumptions in turn.

What people believe, their definition of a situation, is of enormous importance in explaining how they respond to and act in that situation. This proposition is one on which this text is based. It suggests that people's beliefs, usually socially acquired, are a major determinant of whether they accept or reject the gender situation in which they find themselves. At the macrostructural level, this can help significantly to explain whether a pattern of institutionalized behaviors persists or changes.

This is not to imply that people are incapable of personally evaluating their experiences independent of socially acquired beliefs. But socially acquired beliefs will in large measure determine whether one feels one's personal reactions are legitimate or illegitimate, whether one "runs" with them or is ambivalent toward them. For example, someone at the receiving end in an inequitable situation may feel angry and disgruntled, as both the secretaries do. But the unhappy secretary feels that her anger is just, whereas the happy secretary feels guilty and uncomfortable with hers. Along parallel lines, someone may be personally satisfied by a situation socially defined as illegitimate, and consequently will be defensive, unpredictable, and uneasy about the situation. We have only to think of someone we know who is healthy, plump, and happily eating—but who daily confronts our cultural standards of slimness, beauty, and health.

Our unhappy secretary, then, rejects her situation not only because it is one in which she is, objectively speaking, exploited to a sufficient degree that she feels angry, but because she is located in a system of meanings that leads her to perceive her situation as unjust and her anger as legitimate. This leads us to our second basic assumption. Except perhaps in extraordinary instances of genius or prophetic vision, an individual does not construct a global system of interpretation instantaneously and alone, in response to a flare-up of personal rage, and in the face of widely shared, taken-for-granted beliefs about a situation's legitimacy. Certainly a person like our secretary, working hard for her living in a typing pool in the 1980s, does not. New systems of meaning are a social product, the creation of a community of interacting people who then seek to disseminate their ideas more widely into the community. Our secretary's "awareness of impoverishment" is her inheritance from a long tradition of criticism and protest about woman's subordination, the tradition of feminism.

In Chapter 6 we sketched the social conditions that can generate a new, critical system of meaning in the face of massive ideological pressures for conformity. These conditions are structurally produced experiences of powerlessness, inconsistencies in a system of cultural values, "slippages" in socialization to conventional beliefs, the human capacity for reflection, and the social facilitators of leisure, literacy, and extensive formal education. Over more than three hundred years, these conditions have sustained the meaning system of feminism, with its critique of our conventional gender beliefs (Spender, 1982). Periodically the collective action of formulating this critique has entered a phase of intense vitality and expansion. Although it is always difficult to set clear time limits to such periods, some earlier phases of active expansionary feminism include the 1790s (primarily in Europe), the 1850s (in America and Europe), and the 1890s through the 1920s.

For the past twenty-five years, we have lived in one of these phases of intensified feminist critique. Through a variety of channels, this perspective has percolated through to people like our secretary and millions of other women historically so situated (see Chapters 8 and 9) that they are receptive to this way of viewing the world. The first part of this chapter describes the content of contemporary feminism in America. The second part discusses ways in which its elements have been made available to typically situated women. In Chapter 10 we will describe some of the challenges to conventionality that men have begun to articulate with regard to their own circumstances.

CONTEMPORARY AMERICAN FEMINISM AS A SYSTEM OF MEANINGS

This section describes the emergent feminist beliefs that presently challenge America's conventional ideas about gender. Our description here focuses on three aspects of contemporary feminism: its critique of our gender institution; its internal variations in perspective; and its common, unifying themes. It should, however, be noted that the written record shows a continuous tradition of feminist thought over the past three hundred years and that the ideas expressed in earlier periods are remarkably similar to those presently being "discovered." It is interesting to speculate about the social processes that lead repeatedly to a collective forgetting and collective reinvention of feminism (these processes are explored in Spender, 1982.) Contemporary feminists are, then, an extension of this long tradition of protest. They are "emergent," as we put it, only in this particular sense of seeing themselves and appearing to a general public to be (again) a new invention.

Feminism's most immediately apparent feature is its sustained, multidimensional critique of our gender institution. From Friedan's description (1963) of the housewife's experience of meaninglessness, through Millett's exposé (1969) of the blatant contempt for and violence toward women at the core of our conventional beliefs about gender, to Rich's exploration of both motherhood (1976) and heterosexuality (1980) as enforced institutions, contemporary feminists have probed every facet of our gender institution in what must be one of the most stunning displays of sustained intellectual work in recent times.

It is impossible in the short space available to identify all the exploration that has been done by feminist writers in the past twenty-five years. Their work, sometimes empirical, sometimes theoretical, but always critical, has turned a battery of spotlights on the complex system of institutionalized inequality that has been woman's place in our gender institution.

Among other things, we are now keenly aware of women's disadvantages in the wage-work sector (Lloyd, 1975; Kanter, 1977; Hartman, 1979); their exploitation as housewives and as sexual objects (Lopata, 1971; Oakley, 1974; Barry, 1979; Griffin, 1981); their exclusion from political life (Lynn, 1975; Amundsen, 1971); the discrimination against them in our institutions of religion, education, and athletics (Daly, 1968, 1973; Roby, 1972; Selden, 1981); the indifference and brutality toward them of our legal, health, and mental health professions (Chesler, 1972;

Ehrenreich and English, 1978; Scully, 1980); the tyranny of our norms of motherhood and sexuality (Rich, 1976, 1979); the physical violence practiced against women by intimates and strangers (Brownmiller, 1975); the pervasive antiwoman bias in our language and in our philosophical, scientific, and esthetic traditions (Spender, 1980; Daly, 1978; Griffin, 1978); the general silence in our history about their lives, accomplishments, and protests (Spender, 1982; Boulding, 1976); and the deep distortion of the human potential in both women and men that results from this pervasively oppressive system (Chodorow, 1978; Dinnerstein, 1976).

The importance of this work is clearer when we recognize that most people do not go around self-consciously analyzing their daily experiences. Their awareness of the pattern of their lives is at the level of unreflective, taken-for-granted recipes for living. This is particularly true of our conventional gender arrangements, which have until recently been so unreflectively assumed that even social scientists, who are supposed to be on the alert for such things, did not typically include gender in their list of social institutions.

To put it more vividly, people like our happy secretary and her boss do not go around self-consciously aware of themselves as actively compliant with a system of inequality. As they act, they do not think "patriarchy" or "natural differences" or any of the other labels we gave to their conventional beliefs in Chapter 3. To the extent that they think about the differences in their situations, they assume them to be reasonable and natural.

But by and large they do not think about those differences; their mental blindness to gender as a socially created system of human relationships helps to perpetuate that system. Feminism's critique of gender inequality has made whole sectors of our population "see" what they had not previously recognized: that masculinity and femininity are associated with a complex system of social relationships, legitimated by distinctive beliefs, and shot through with what some claim is an oppressively unequal treatment of women. However people respond to these facts and claims, they are at least now aware of them. Indeed, without the new awareness produced by feminism's critique, we would almost certainly have been unable to write this book—and you would not have thought to read it.

COMPETING THEORETICAL CONFIGURATIONS

Contemporary feminist beliefs are accessible to us through the writings and public statements of a large collectivity of spokespersons. The writers listed above are only a tiny selection from this group. This collectivity is united by its condemnation of gender inequality. It appears tremendously diversified, however, in its explanations of that inequality, its views on how society is organized, on what is distinctive about human beings, and in its strategies for improving the human situation.

Trying to see some pattern in this diversity of viewpoints can be difficult for the newcomer who is exploring the burgeoning literature of feminism for the first time. But there is a pattern, and grasping it allows one to move closer to an understanding of the beliefs now challenging our conventions on gender. Table 7-1 presents our interpretation of this patterned diversity. Identified in it are three configurations of feminist thought: the liberal, the Marxist, and the radical positions. Not every feminist spokesperson will fit neatly into one or the other of these categories. But the configurations are internally consistent and quite visible in feminism. In the paragraphs that follow we will explore these three perspectives in an attempt to depict the range of alternative ideas now available.

Liberal Feminism

In America, this is almost certainly the most widely disseminated and accepted version of feminism. There is an easy complementarity between liberal feminism and the general pattern of sociopolitical beliefs in America which explains in large measure its popularity.

Liberal feminism is, minimally, the feminist base on which our unhappy secretary stands and from which she perceives the injustices of her situation. The classic liberal statement is J. S. Mill's *The Subjection of Women*, 1869. Among contemporary feminist writers, the label probably fits Friedan (1963, 1981), Bernard (1981), Janeway (1980), and Rossi (1974, 1977). (Also see the appropriate selections in Jaggar and Struhl, 1978.)

Central to liberal feminism is a rejection of the conventional belief that men and women have innately different natures. They affirm that although individuals may vary somewhat on specific traits and abilities, there is no consistent sex-linked pattern of variation in traits or abilities. Observable differences between females and males are the product of socialization (social learning) to gender-specific roles. To liberals, the most striking human quality is malleability, adaptability to environmental pressures. Intelligence, or aggression, or the ability to nurture are not sex-determined. Women and men will be as aggressive, intelligent, or nurturing as their social environment allows and encourages them to be.

Society, through the lens of liberal feminism, is an arena in which individuals play out normatively defined roles and realize, to the extent that those social roles and other biographical constraints permit, their innate abilities for achievement and caring. Most societies can be seen as organized into two distinct spheres of activity and experience: the public and the private. Most societies develop gender role expectations that restrict women to the activities and experiences of the private sphere, while directing men into the public sphere. In most societies, both females and males are limited in the range of activity and experience open to them, and they therefore develop more narrowly than they potentially could. Restrictions and limitations on human growth are typically more severe on women.

American society is, in the world population of societies, just, open, and democratic. Even American society, though, still contains within itself certain institutionalized barriers to the ideal of equal opportunity for

TABLE 7–1: Three Configurations or Types of Feminism

Views on:	I. Liberal Feminism	II. Marxist Feminism	III. Radical Feminism
Human nature	Females and males potentially equal in abilities and nurturing. Most distinctive trait—malleability. Males and females become different in ability and traits because of socialization to gender roles	Females and males potentially equal in capacity for self-actualization through productive, socially oriented work. Most distinctive traits—ability to create necessities of social life; perhaps a tendency to seek power over others. Women and men are warped and alienated by societal structures.	Female potential for self-actualization and ethically guided actions at least as great, perhaps greater than male. Most distinctive trait—capacity for selfhood and reflective consciousness as guides to development. These are shaped by societal ideology and power, and by personal experience, including experience of the body. Women, because of their particular experiences of these influences, develop different perceptions, values, identities, and consciousness from men.
Organization of American society	Basically just, democratic, and egalitarian, but with certain residual barriers to individual equality of opportunity. Key societal feature, the distinctive spheres of public and private life	Basically exploitative and alienating. Key social structures—techno-economic arrangements and *social class hierarchy.* Economically dominant class controls most power resources and uses these to ensure compliance of subordinate laboring classes.	Basically unequal, exploitative. Key feature—various systems of exploitation/domination (class, race, etc.), of which the primary and most central is patriarchy, male domination and exploitation of women.

Causes of gender inequality	*Sexism*, a tradition of inequality institutionalized in our culture and organizations. Rigid socialization of females and males into different roles, capacities, and spheres of experience.	Extension, natural outgrowth of *class system*, class oppression. Upper-class women are possessions of the men in their class, working class women function to subsidize and reproduce working-class life. Women's oppression arises from men's *alienation* by the class structure.	*Patriarchy*, a structure of relational and ideological inequality in which men dominate women. Patriarchy is anchored in men's interests in controlling women sexually, re-productively, and as a labor and recreational resource.
Strategies for change	Political mobilization for legal change, economic equality of op-portunity, and less rigid socializa-tion to male and female identity. Also individual actions to rene-gotiate in their microenvironments for greater gender equality.	Destruction of class system by mo-bilization, revolution of subordi-nated economic class, including both male and female members.	Affirmation of positive value, love of women, and either (a) separation from patriarchal mainstream; or (b) confrontation with patriarchy and all its dependent systems of domination.

individuals. Racism is one of these, sexism another. To liberal feminists, gender inequality in America results from the carryover of sexism, an outdated pattern of beliefs and prejudices, into our present institutional structures. Because of sexism, females have less access to society's "goods." Females and males are forced into narrowly circumscribed arenas of social experience and into two unsatisfactory characterological molds. Sexism, like racism, serves no useful collective purpose. Rather, it deprives the collectivity of access to the full range of talents available to it, and is an affront to our deepest cultural values, our belief in equality of individual opportunity and in the dignity and worth of each individual. Because of this, sexism is open to reasoned appeal and therefore vulnerable to the challenge feminists are now mounting.

As basic strategies for the obliteration of sexism, liberal feminists urge that political mobilization produce legal changes, equal economic opportunities, and less rigid gender-specific socialization. They also argue that every individual, once alerted to the implications of sexism, has a responsibility to try to destroy it by renegotiating and reorganizing gender beliefs and arrangements in her or his personal milieu. Our unhappy secretary, then, should not only support political action for legal, economic, educational, and mass media change; she should attempt to challenge sexism in her office, her family, and her circle of friends.

The ideal social arrangement for liberals is one in which each individual is free to make an informed choice about her or his gender life style. It is a world where one can be a housewife or househusband, an unmarried careerist or part of a two-paycheck family, in which one can freely decide about having children, and in which heterosexual and homosexual life styles are respected personal choices. With such freedom, America will move even closer to the realization of justice and freedom. In this basic acceptance of American society, and in its emphasis on individualism, choice, freedom, and equality of opportunity, liberal feminism is linked directly to the central values of the American ethos.

Marxist Feminism

If liberal feminism is the most popular version of feminism in America, Marxist feminism is the version most deeply rooted in an established intellectual tradition, the overwhelmingly extensive body of literature which has, since the late nineteenth century, expounded and expanded on Karl Marx's ideas (see Chapter 1). Marxist scholarship is a worldwide activity, more intense in socialist societies and in Third World and Western European societies than in America. In all those areas of intense Marxist specialization, Marxist feminism has not only scholarly but general public appeal greater than it has so far attained in America. A significant group of American feminists, however, are Marxist feminists (Eisenstein, 1979; selected writers in Jaggar and Struhl, 1978; Kuhn and Wolfe, 1978; Hamilton, 1978; MacKinnon, 1982).

Like liberals, Marxist feminists deny that there are innate, natural differences between females and males. All human beings are equal in their potential for growth and self-actualization. To Marxists, realization of this potential comes through productive, unexploited, socially relevant work, work that helps to create the material, social, and cultural goods that sustain a community's life. Unlike liberals, however, Marxist feminists see society not so much as an aggregate of individuals in action, but as a massive arrangement of social structures that potentially may enhance, but in fact almost always inhibit human beings from realizing their full potential. In other words, Marxist feminists are concerned most with the macrostructural approach to society, whereas liberal feminists focus as much attention on individual attitudes and actions as they do on structural dynamics.

To Marxist feminists, the key macrostructural feature of social life is the class system. Almost every society that has ever existed has a class system in which the members of the dominant class control *as their own property* the community's resources for economic production. Control of this key social resource, economic power, gives the dominant class access to all the other sources of social power, including political, legal, and ideological power. These power resources are used to control economically subordinate classes which, lacking economic resources, survive by becoming an economic resource—labor power—and working for a wage or livelihood. Since that wage or livelihood is always less than the productive value of the worker's labor, the subordinate class, the laboring class, is a crucial source of wealth for the dominant class. This is one reason why this class must be controlled and kept docile. Since subordinated classes always at some level maintain an interest in their emancipation, the relationship between dominant and subordinated classes is the central conflict in society.

Marxists describe the evolution of a variety of class-stratified societies in world history: from primitive, unstratified, communal groupings; to early agrarian settlements with the first stages of property and wealth accumulation, and the first classes; through slave societies, feudal societies, early industrial (or capitalist) societies, and late industrial societies of both the monopoly and the state capitalist versions. American society falls into the stage of late monopoly capitalism. To many Western and Third World Marxists, the self-proclaimed "classless" Communist societies are in fact late industrial, state capitalist systems.

Gender inequality is for Marxist feminists an outgrowth of the class system and of the frustration and alienation it produces. Gender inequality may have been the first class system. In the evolution of societies into primitive agrarian accumulation, some men laid claim to communal economic resources as their personal property at the same time as they claimed women as their possessions, their wives. Wives were a primitive labor force, producing wealth for their husbands and owners in exchange for a subsistence livelihood. They also produced male heirs of undisputed paternity to whom a father's property could pass. The husband-owner's control over female labor and reproduction was perhaps the first concrete expression of a class system. Since then, however, class systems have become extensive, elaborate, macrostructural social phenomena. In the later stages of society, gender inequality becomes a peripheral and dependent extension of class inequality.

In American society today, the dominant class is the bourgeoisie, which owns as personal possessions the means of industrial production, of the commercial production of agricultural goods, and the apparatus of national and international commerce. Bourgeois women are not owners of property, but the wives and possessions of bourgeois men, men skilled in the arts of possession. Bourgeois women produce heirs and provide emotional, sexual, and social services in return for an appropriately elegant style of subsistence. Not much different in objective standing from the original wife-slave of primitive agrarianism, they are, in Rosa Luxemburg's phrase: "the parasite of a parasite" (Luxemburg, 1971:220, quoted in MacKinnon, 1982:7).

Women in the subordinate class in America today, in the wage-earning class, both blue and white collar, function unintentionally to perpetuate the class system. As wage earners, they are the most poorly paid and least unionized, an unresisting source of profit for the bourgeoisie. As potential workers, they are a threat that helps keep unionized male wage demands in line. As wives, they subsidize the bourgeoisie by providing unpaid housework and childcare, thus disguising the real costs of maintaining a worker. The wage earner's wife also provides her husband with a tiny experience of tyranny, recompense for his powerlessness in the bigger scale of things. She is, in other words, "the slave of a slave" (MacKinnon, 1982:8).

The solution for gender inequality is, for Marxist feminists, the destruction of the class system. This requires organized revolutionary action by wage earners to destroy the situation in which some people own or control economic production for their personal benefit. Only when economic resources are truly communally owned and managed for the communal good will classes disappear. With the disappearance of classes will disappear all the systems of class alienation, including racial and gender inequality. In the interests of class revolution, working-class women and men must remain unified and mobilized. Any movement that is divisive of working-class solidarity, as racial liberation and women's liberation movements become, are antiprogressive.

To many readers, this viewpoint might appear as strange as liberal feminism appears "reasonable."[1] Which of you, for example, recognizes yourself or the women of your acquaintance as "parasites of parasites" or "slaves of slaves"? Must women wait for the improbable date when capitalism collapses before they assert their claims for a better situation? Are women in the self-proclaimed Communist countries really free from gender inequalities? These are some obvious questions.

But while making these criticisms ourselves, let us try to point out some of the less visible but real strengths of this approach. First, much more than liberal feminism, Marxist feminism sensitizes us to the varieties of inequality, apart from gender inequality, that exist in our society, including the inequalities of race, class, and age. It makes us think of the relatively greater misery of the double or triple minority person (the poor, black, older woman, for example) in comparison with that of the affluent, white, young woman. Marxist feminism, moreover, because of its global, historical, macrosocietal perspective, gives us a much broader view of gender inequality. From that broader vantage point it is easier to accept the argument that there are some women somewhere who are "slaves of slaves" or "parasites of parasites." Finally, Marxist feminism suggests a way to explain in sociocultural terms both the universality of gender inequality and its variations in form. This, as we pointed out at the beginning of this book, is a crucial test of a good social theory of gender. For all its weaknesses, then, and despite its counterintuitive "feel," Marxist feminism has fuller, more systematic explanatory power than liberal feminism.

Radical Feminism[2]

Liberal feminism may be the most widely diffused version of feminism in America. Marxist feminism draws on the most systematically formulated intellectual tradition. Radical feminism, however, in one or other of its many manifestations, is the form of feminism most frequently espoused by the active spokespersons of the American feminist community. Intellectually speaking, radical feminism is both the pulsating life center and the cutting edge of American feminism. Because its activity is one of creating new insights and of forging ahead to answer the new questions suggested by the previous explanations of gender inequality (including its own earlier explanations), radical feminism is difficult to pin down. Its ideas seem constantly to grow and change. In its underlying themes, however, the radical feminist position is amazingly consistent, and has been so over the whole three hundred or more years of feminist thinking (Spender, 1982).

The basic themes in radical feminism are an affirmation of positive valuation and love for woman, and correlatively, a deep sense of grief and rage over the oppression that has always been woman's lot. The assertion of woman's special worth is done in defiance of a whole universe that devalues woman as inferior; the expressions of rage at her oppression are done against a backdrop that catalogs in detail the whole global record of that oppression. In these two basic themes, then, radical feminists resemble the more radical stance of racial and ethnic minority groups, the "black is beautiful" claims of black Americans, the detailed "witnessing" of oppression by Jews. As they develop these two themes in their intellectual work, we are given a fuller picture of radical feminists' views of human nature, social organization, gender inequality, and strategies for change.

The human traits radical feminism values most highly are the capacity for self-actualization or personal fulfillment on the one hand, and the capacity for a humane, caring, ethically guided orientation to one's actions and environment on the other. The essential facilitator for the expression of either or both traits (and they are closely intertwined) is human reflective consciousness, a consciousness that is always affected by and at its best is in touch with the whole range of experiences which impinge on the individual. Included among these experiences are socialization to cultural beliefs, one's situation in the various institutions and hierarchies of domination that constitute society, the context, including the emotional qualities, of one's personal milieu, and the experiencing of one's body and of the partly biological, partly sociocultural functions associated with that body.

For all these reasons, women and men develop different forms of consciousness, different ethical capacities, different selves. Men, because of their control over macrostructural arrangements, can keep more consistency between their personal experiences and the macrostructural mappings of human experience in the culture. Men's consciousness, moral sense, and selfhood are more unified and simplified. Women, because of the discrepancy between personal experience and male-dominated macro-social definitions of their experience, develop a more divided and complex consciousness, moral sense, and selfhood. There is some basis, then, for the claim that men and women are different. But women are at least equal to men in their capacities for reflection, self-actualization, and ethical judgment. There is no basis for a claim to male superiority in any of these areas. Indeed, the male experience of domination probably corrupts men fundamentally, particularly on the issue of ethical judgment. Women's dual experience of subordination, and of bearing and caring for new life, may give them a deeper, fuller ethical sense. Radical feminists not only affirm the equal potential of females and males, as liberals and Marxists do; they go further and imply that in the qualities that matter, females may both potentially and actually be superior to males.

Subordination and Domination: Patriarchy.   Society, for radical feminists, is characterized primarily by its structures of domination and subordination. In this they follow the Marxist viewpoint rather than the liberal. But radicals take the thesis of domination further. Every social institution is to be understood as containing within itself a structure of domination, of persons who control and others who are controlled. At a deeper level within society, coloring the patterns of inequality within institutions, are the basic structures of domination and submission, the structures of class, race, age, and gender inequality.

Of these deeper structures, the most fundamental, the primary form of domination and submission, is that of gender, of male domination and female subordination. This structure radical feminists call *patriarchy*. Radicals differ from Marxists in their insistence that patriarchy, not class, is the basic model of domination. Patriarchy was not only historically the first structure of domination and oppression, as the Marxists sometimes acknowledge; it continues as the most pervasive, most enduring system of inequality, the crucible in which all other forms of inequality are formed. It is by participation in patriarchy that men learn how to hold other human beings in contempt, to dehumanize them, and to control them. It is here that men see and women learn what subordination looks like. Patriarchy produces deep human neuroses like guilt and repression, sadism and masochism, manipulation and deception, all of which prompt men and women to other forms of tyranny. Patriarchy, to radical feminists, is the invisible but socially most significant structure of social inequality.

Gender inequality is the product of patriarchy. Radical feminists explore patriarchy from many angles. Embedded within their explorations, however, is an image of patriarchy as violence, the violence of men and of male-dominated institutions toward women. Violence may not be apparent as physical cruelty. It may be veiled in more complex forms of exploitation, manipulation, and control: in pornography; in standards of fashion and beauty; in tyrannical norms of motherhood, monogamy, chastity, and heterosexuality; in sexual harassment in the workplace; in the practices of gynecology, obstetrics, and psychotherapy; in unpaid housework and underpaid wage work. Violence in fact exists whenever one group controls in its own interest the life chances, the environments, the actions, and the perceptions of another group, as men do women.

But to radical feminists, the vision of patriarchy as institutionalized violence against women is also centrally and crucially that of the practice of physical violence against women: rape, sexual abuse, spouse abuse, incest, sexual molestation of children, hysterectomies and other savagely excessive forms of surgery, and the explicit sadism in pornography are linked to historic and cross-cultural cases of witch burning, the stoning deaths of adultresses, the persecution of lesbians, female infanticide, Chinese footbinding, the forced suicides of Hindu widows (*suttee*), and the savage practice of clitorectomy. Through the radical lens, we have an image of woman, mutilated and bleeding, as the visual representation of what patriarchy does.

Why Patriarchy Persists.   Why then does patriarchy exist as a near universal fact? Because men have needs which women, and in some cases only women, can satisfy. Women satisfy male sexual desire in a uniquely effective way (see Chapter 1; see also MacKinnon, 1982; Rich, 1980). Women's bodies are essential to species reproduction, at least up until now (Firestone, 1970). In these two ways women are an essential means to male ends. Women also provide a useful labor force, as Marxists have noted, for economic production, childrearing, and household management. Women can be pleasant companions, sources of emotional renewal, signs of social status and power. This complex of useful functions that women provide for men explains why men have everywhere sought to impose their interests on women, to keep them compliant. But varying social circumstances provide different rank orderings of the significance of these various functions, and therefore variations in the details of patriarchy from society to society (Mitchell, 1963/1971). Radical feminism, like Marxist feminism, offers a sociocultural explanation for both universal gender inequality and for cross-cultural variations in the pattern of that inequality.

Why then have male interests always prevailed over female interests? Why are there no recorded cases where women have imposed a matriarchy? Why have they always been victims of patriarchy? This issue is only partly worked out by radical feminists. Part of their answer seems to be that men have a greater need of women than vice versa. Men have an interest in controlling women, against which women mobilize only an interest in their own autonomy. The motivational drives for domination are not equal in the two sexes.

Another part of their answer seems to be that, propelled by their interest in domination, men singly or together can muster the most basic resource of all, physical force, to establish control. Once patriarchy is in place, all the other power resources—economic, ideological, political, legal, emotional, communal—can be marshaled to maintain its hold. But physical violence always lurks in the background as the last line of defense. And those defensive strategies have repeatedly been tested. Radicals show that women have constantly resisted patriarchy and sought autonomy. And they have repeatedly been defeated by patriarchy. Only in subterranean ways, in "lies, secrets, and silences" (Rich, 1979) have women kept alive, sometimes alone, sometimes in the company of other women, some sense of an independent existence.

Proposals for Change.   What is to be done to defeat patriarchy? Radicals propose a basic reworking of our consciousness, and affirmation of love (rather than hate) for women. Loving women means many things: knowing them as they really are rather than through the distorting lens of patriarchal ideology; being unified with them (the "sisterhood") so that women trust, support, appreciate, understand, and are loyal to each other; grouping together for mutual defense; delighting in their company, even to the point of seeking erotic and sensual pleasure with women. Beyond this transformation of consciousness, radicals seem to suggest two alternative strategies: separatism, or withdrawal from patriarchy into a world of women-run businesses, women's communities and households, and lesbian love relationships; and critical confrontation with patriarchy, at every point that one encounters it.

How does one evaluate radical feminism? Intuitively it may seem to some of our readers to be excessively strong "medicine" in its portrayal of the oppressiveness of patriarchy, in its insistence that patriarchy is the central social inequality, in its view that American society is as oppressive as any other in this area, and in its depiction of men as ruthless exploiters. Theoretically, though, it is the most sophisticated variant of feminist theory, a systematic "thinking through" of the phenomenon of gender inequality. But radical feminism will seem "strong medicine" to only some of our readers. As Steinem said recently, four things radicalize a woman: getting a job, getting married, being a mother, and getting older (*Washington Post*, July 1983). We expect that our readers will fall along a continuum in their responses to radical feminism. Most men will find it "too far out," and women will find it variably attractive, depending on how many of these four experiences they have had.

Feminism's Common Themes

Let us return for a moment to our unhappy secretary. Assume she has been sampling feminist ideas in a rather haphazard way, following her own inclinations: subscribing to *Ms.* and reading it fairly carefully; picking up a paperback now and then from the local bookstore; keeping an eye on newspaper and TV reports; perhaps settling down to read a couple of serious feminist works on her vacations. What understanding of feminism would she arrive at? Would she find any basic core of agreement behind the barrage of criticism and the variations in viewpoint we have just described? Here we propose four themes on which feminists generally agree: the beliefs that woman's liberation means, variously, equality, power, knowledge, and a new ethic. Although our secretary might not offer the same listing, we think that she and anyone else who has taken a serious look at feminism would agree that feminists share a common core of beliefs, and that our identification of those beliefs does no violence to the evidence.

Liberation Means Equality.   Most feminists believe women and men are equal in their human potential for intelligence, productive work, achievement, nurturance of other human beings, and care of their natural environment. They also assert that only in the exercise of all these capacities can human individuals grow fully. Our system of gender inequality is perceived by feminists as limiting both women and men from growing to their full potential. The destruction of institutionalized gender inequality, the achievement of gender equality, is therefore for all feminists an essential means for human liberation. The different groups of feminists vary, however, in their views on who is most impoverished by gender inequality. To liberals, women are more restricted and limited. To radicals, men, the power wielders, may be more fundamentally blinded and corrupted. To Marxists, working-class women and men are equally stunted and limited by the bigger system of class inequality.

What does equality mean? To liberal feminists, it means legal and constitutional equality; equality of opportunity with regard to society's educational, occupational, and political resources; equal participation in the duties and rewards of both public and private space; and an even-handed or "unisex" socialization, so that each individual can acquire the positive traits of both female and male roles as they are presently constituted in our society. Marxists and radicals accept that equalities of this type are useful, but argue that they will be changes in form rather than substance unless accompanied by bigger structural shifts toward equality. These macrostructural equalities include equal access by all individuals to society's material resources (the Marxists), and ideological and power changes that make women and men equally valued and equally empowered (the radicals). In both these perspectives too, "equality" becomes "equity"—the affirmation that society should not merely provide open opportunity, but should provide "goods" in a way that is responsive to people's needs and differences.

Liberation Means Power.   Most feminists agree that they need a power base in society from which to secure, in a long-term sense, any equalities their present mobilization may bring. Various strategies are advanced for the acquisition of this power base: the political mobilization of women within the American electoral process; class revolution by all working people and a unified sisterhood working at all levels in society to protect women's well-being. In all these ways, feminists advance a claim to social power as power is usually understood: counteractive power; power to have one's way in the world despite the opposition of others; power, in other words, over others.

Some feminists have serious reservations about this claim to power over others. Explaining all the evils of our world in terms of entrenched systems of domination, believing that domination or power over others corrupts the power wielder, they wonder if women will not themselves be corrupted as they grasp the reins of domination along with, or instead of, men. This concern leads them to ask critical questions about our taken-for-granted views about power. Is power always a zero-sum game? Do some people always have it at the expense of others? Could this concept of power itself be a by-product of patriarchy? Such questions lead to an alternative view of power: the power of each individual to choose freely; to create her or his own world rather than to oppress others; to control her or his body, mind, and personal projects; power to be pooled with that of others for communal growth. This alternative image of power is implied in much feminist writing. Whether it is purely utopian or to some extent realizable, and how it relates to the practical, confrontation thesis of power, are open questions.

Liberation Means Knowledge.   The third theme common to much of feminism is that liberation means seeing through patriarchy's ideology and coming to know the experiences and situation of women and men as they really are. Outsiders may claim that people merely relinquish one set of ideological lenses for another, that people will simply move from conventional gender ideology to feminist ideology. But feminists, while acknowledging this possibility, do not believe people must always be blinded by ideology. They claim it is possible to see clearly, to arrive at knowledge more sure than we presently have within the perceptual maze which is patriarchy.

The route away from ideology to knowledge involves using not only the obvious procedures of science, such as empirical observation, measurement, experimentation, and logical reason. It involves using all the other means by which people know: esthetic imagination, intuition, empathy, introspection, confronting human emotions and transcendent systems of value. Above all, it entails a sustained reflective and critical scrutiny of oneself and one's world, and of the processes by which those two structures are created and sustained.

Feminists have used various combinations of these knowledge-producing processes to discover and describe the hitherto hidden inequalities and tyrannies in institutionalized gender; the lives of women, and to a degree also of men, as they actually develop, infused with, buried beneath, and yet to a degree independent of that institution; the perceptions, interests, and values women and men have in the face of inequality, particularly of gender inequality. Only with such knowledge, they claim, can people really see inequality as it is and work for equality. Only armed with this knowledge can people be empowered in the conventional sense of knowing the enemy, and in the deeper sense of knowing the projects and values through which they must seek to realize themselves individually and collectively.

Liberation Means a New Ethic. Both implied and explicit in feminism is the theme that the movement against gender inequality may introject into society a new set of ethical principles which will make the world a safer, more humane place for all humankind. The emphasis of this new ethic is on wholeness, on bringing together what has been forced apart, on healing. Feminism in its most ambitious voice seeks to bring together into a renewed wholeness all the classic dichotomies: reason and emotion, mind and body, humanity and nature, fact and value, science and art, public and private, achievement and nurturance, male and female.

Feminists argue that patriarchy requires and works to perpetuate this tearing apart, in thought and in practice, of what is in fact whole cloth, the tapestry of life itself. While this tearing apart has produced whole systems of mastery, hierarchy, and control, and secured humankind its place in nature, it has been done at a terrible price. That price includes human pain and neurosis, the destruction of nature, and technology and aggression now running out of control. Deep in woman's experience of her body, her sexuality, her procreative function, her motherhood and sisterhood, her way of being in the social and natural world, lies an alternative vision. That vision affirms the creation and nurturing of life; the interconnectedness of humanity and nature; of body and mind; of reason, value, and emotion; and the interdependencies of human collectivities. Only if human societies can be infused with these new values can people pull back from the brink of destruction on which they now stand. This vital new vision, women's vision, will affect society only if women affirm themselves in the world.

THE DIFFUSION OF NEW MEANINGS

Feminist ideas spread from the intellectual circles in which they are formulated out to sectors of the general public, sectors including people like our fictional unhappy secretary. But with all the talk of backlash these days (see Chapter 11), some of you may be wondering whether that character is just wishful thinking on our part. So before we describe the diffusion of feminist ideas, let us present some evidence that public attitudes are shifting in a feminist direction.

Attitude Shifts

Several studies published in the last ten years have described people's attitudes toward issues having to do with gender equality (Cherlin and Walters, 1981; Herzog and Bachman, 1982; Lipman-Blumen and Tickamyer, 1975; Mason and Bumpass, 1975; Mason et al. 1976; Ransford and Miller, 1983; Schreiber, 1978; Spitze and White, 1980; Thornton and

Camburn, 1979; Thornton and Freedman, 1979). We will report on two of the most recent. Both studies look only at white women. For a comparison of men and women, black and white, see Ransford and Miller (1983).

A 1981 report by Bers and Mezey describes the attitudes of 219 women who hold leadership positions in conventional community women's associations: League of Women Voters, PTA organizations, garden clubs, and the women's clubs of Catholic and Protestant churches. These women live in three suburban communities near Chicago. They are, typically, in their forties, married, with children, not engaged in wage work, fairly affluent, and Republican—women one might expect to be fairly conservative in their attitudes toward feminism. And at one level, they are. Over 70 percent of them claimed they were not feminists. Yet when asked about specific issues having to do with gender, they came out strongly, as Table 7–2 indicates, in favor of the nontraditional position typically advanced by feminists.

We would venture to affirm with considerable certainty that twenty years ago very few of these women would have supported the idea of community-run centers for rape victims and battered wives, or after-school day-care programs; very few would have been opposed to sex-role stereotyping in school books; almost none would have thought of having separate charge accounts, of the unfairness of paying male breadwinners more for the same job than women, and of giving boys, but not girls, career educations. The same thing could be said for each of the issues listed in Table 7–2. By one means or another, the questions and opinions feminists have introjected into public debate have influenced the thinking of these women.

An even more recent study by Thornton, Alwin, and Camburn (1983) actually charts the shift in attitudes toward a feminist position that has occurred in the eighteen-year period between 1962, the year before Friedan's *The Feminine Mystique* triggered the latest round of feminist critique (see Chapter 8), and 1980, a year in which the backlash against feminism was a much heralded political "fact" (see Chapter 11). At intervals over this period, a group of about 1,000 married women in the Detroit area, women who had had a child in 1962, were asked for their views on issues of gender equality. Questions touched on such topics as whether husbands should make the important family decisions, whether a wife should expect help with housework from her husband at the end of his workday, whether a woman can have a full-time job and still be a good mother, and whether a wife should put her husband's career first. These women come from a greater range of socioeconomic backgrounds than the community leaders of the Bers and Mezey study, and many more do wage work part- or full-time. In 1980, their 18-year-old children were also interviewed.

The data reported in this study show a steady shift toward nontraditional, egalitarian views on gender arrangements, with no significant slackening of pace in 1980, the year of the so-called retreat from feminism. For example, in 1962, 32.5 percent of the group felt that husbands and wives should participate equally in making important family

TABLE 7–2 Attitudes toward Feminist Issues among Women Community Leaders

	Percent Agree	Percent Disagree	N
Most men are better suited emotionally for politics than women.	18.0	82.0	217
Women who succeed in politics have to sacrifice their femininity to get there.	13.3	86.7	218
Career education for boys should have a higher priority than career education for girls.	7.8	92.2	217
Local community organizations should sponsor rape crisis centers.	83.6	16.4	214
Women should be able to get charge accounts in their own names without their husbands' permission.	88.0	12.0	217
In groups with both male and female members, it is appropriate that top leadership positions be held by males.	10.7	89.3	214
In deciding on raises and promotions employers should consider whether the employee is supporting a family.	18.4	81.6	212
Local community organizations should sponsor temporary residences and counseling for battered wives.	81.6	18.4	212
School boards should remove textbooks that use examples of sex-role stereotyping which portray women in unfavorable images.	59.7	40.3	211
It is wrong for women to work in typically male jobs such as prison guard, coal miner, or construction worker.	34.6	65.4	217
Affirmative action for women is a form of discrimination against qualified males.	31.0	69.0	213
Local community organizations should sponsor programs to provide education and training for displaced homemakers.	65.3	34.7	213
Women should be legally entitled to half their husbands' income.	58.8	41.2	211
Local school and/or park districts should sponsor after school day-care programs for which parents pay.	69.8	30.2	215

Source: Trudy Haffron Bers and Susan Gluck Mezey, "Support for Feminist Goals among Leaders of Women's Community Groups," *Signs: Journal of Women in Culture and Society,* 6, no. 4 (Summer 1981), 742.

decisions, while in 1980, 71.3 percent had this expectation; in 1962, 47.4 percent expected their husbands to help with housework and in 1980, 69.2 percent did so; in 1977, 65 percent believed a working woman could be a good mother, and in 1980, 78.3 percent did so; in 1977, 49.2 percent felt that a wife's career was as important as her husband's, and in 1980, 54.4 percent felt this way. The last two questions were added to the study in 1977. It is interesting to think about the percentage who would have had nontraditional views on these questions in 1962.

In this study, as in many others, family level of education and the woman's wage work experience were positively related to a tendency to nontraditional gender views. Also of interest is the fact that nontraditional mothers were very likely to have nontraditional children. Daughters of nontraditional mothers in fact were more egalitarian than their mothers, sons somewhat less so. In other words, our unhappy secretary is empirically plausible. She could be one of the working mothers in this study, or the daughter of one of these women. And she may be active in her local PTA or church, as the Bers and Mezey study suggests.

Why have her attitudes, and the attitudes of the women in the studies just described, become increasingly nontraditional and feminist? Feminist thinkers argue that women's experience of subordination can lead them to be spontaneously critical of conventional gender beliefs. The Thornton study certainly provides some evidence for this. A significant minority of the sample were nontraditional in 1962, before the present women's movement became a visible public phenomenon. The bigger social context in which these women live has also been changing in the last eighteen years, with steady trends toward women's participation in wage work and higher education, and an increasing precariousness of marriage, as evidenced in divorce rates (see Chapter 9). These changing circumstances may make conventional attitudes seem increasingly irrelevant. But a third reason for these attitudinal shifts is the diffusion of the feminist beliefs described earlier out into the American public. People have been offered, quite explicitly, an alternative way of thinking about gender, and many of them have been persuaded. It is this last process of attitudinal change that we will now describe.

A Diffusion Model

In Figure 7–1 we present a model of the diffusion of feminist beliefs. The innermost circle represents the spokespersons[3] of feminism, those thinkers and political activists formally and systematically developing theories, policies, and strategies. These people form a community in which individuals are linked together directly or indirectly through various interactional networks. In the second ring of the diagram are the big societal-level social structures that serve as channels for disseminating the ideas of the inner circle. We identify four macrostructural channels: the publishing industry, an array of special interest groups in politics and the professions, higher education, and the mass media. The outermost circle represents the general public, whose ideas, as we have seen, are changing. In Chapter 8 we will be looking again at some of the elements of this model, such as the "new woman" journals of the publishing industry and women's studies programs in higher education. Our interest there is in the new social support systems that help women who decide to break with convention. Here we factor them in as part of the diffusion process that changes women's (and men's) beliefs about gender so that they get to the point where they want to act in nontraditional ways.

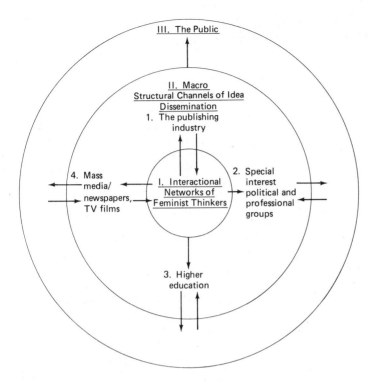

FIGURE 7–1   The Diffusion of Feminist Meanings

The Community of Feminist Thinkers

The point we want to make in this section is that the feminist ideas described in the first part of this chapter are the joint creation of a collectivity of thinkers who communicate and interact. We think this point important for two reasons. First, it helps us to see a meaning system like feminism as a social product, rather than as some sort of disembodied construct, or as the work of a few isolated individuals who scribble away in a study, or even an attic, somewhere. Second, we will discover that some of the interactions and communications which help to create feminism are also the processes which begin to disseminate it. We have not been able to discover any systematic study of the links among contemporary feminist thinkers, but we have been able to piece together bits of evidence to support our claim that they do communicate in at least three distinct ways.

First, they read and draw on one another's published works. Most major theoretical statements by feminists are heavily referenced and foot-noted, and even the most casual look at these references and footnotes will show the complex pattern of reciprocal intellectual indebtedness among these writers. You might want to test our claim by leafing through the articles in an issue of *Signs*, the leading journal for women's studies scholarship, or by glancing at a contemporary classic like Bernard's *The Female World* (1981), or Daly's *Gyn/Ecology* (1978), or MacKinnon's "Feminism, Marxism, Method, and the State: An Agenda for Theory" (1982). These published statements are of course not only a form of indirect interaction between major feminist thinkers. They are also a key channel for making ideas accessible to a more general public.

Second, feminist thinkers are also visible members of the leadership of that sociopolitical phenomenon, the women's movement (see Chapter 8). As such, they encounter one another and other leadership people frequently at the various activities and events that spring out of that movement. They help to administer some of its key pressure groups (see Table 7–3). They serve on the editorial boards of feminist journals. They attend major conferences together, such as meetings of the National Women's Studies Association (Morgan, 1968; Boxer, 1981), the 1977 National Women's Conference in Houston (Evans, 1980), and the famous "gender gap" meeting of the National Women's Political Caucus at San Antonio in 1983.

They are active in special interest activities of the movement: lesbian and gay rights meetings (Morgan, 1968; Dworkin, 1976; Rich, 1979); women's health meetings; Women and the Law Conferences (*Off Our Backs*, 1983). They attend the meetings of professional associations and serve on discussion panels together at, for example, the meetings of the American Sociological Association (*Signs*, 1979), the Modern Language Association (Rich, 1981), the International Congress of Learned Societies in the Field of Religion (Daly, 1973). Through this continuous process of intellectual-political relating, key feminist thinkers become acquainted and share their ideas. In these settings, too, their ideas are disseminated more widely, both to movement members and to casual observers.

Third, feminist thinkers work together during the actual process of formulating their ideas. A good illustration of this is to be found in the "Acknowledgment" section of Adrienne Rich's *Of Woman Born* (1976), which acknowledges inspiration from, conversations with, and extended critical commentary from a long list of feminists, including thinkers such as Barbara Gelpi, Robin Morgan, Mary Daly, Susan Griffin, Tillie Olsen, Alice Rossi, and Kathleen Barry. A cross-check of these other writers shows that many of them describe a similarly deep indebtedness to Rich. Feminist thinkers then form what Rich describes as "a working community." Within that community, there are networks of close intellectual cooperation as well as more attenuated lines of communication. But the intensely vital life of this community may be conceptualized as the center of a system of meaning that reaches out in ways which eventually transform the consciousness of ordinary women and men.

Macrostructural Channels: The Publishing Industry

The ideas of this inner circle of thinkers are most directly and effectively disseminated when they are published as books or journal articles and distributed through the sales networks of the publishing industry. We have not yet found a systematic study of the publishing industry's role in

TABLE 7–3 Interlocking Directorates among Feminist Groups (1978)

	WLDF[1]	NOW-LDEF[2]	NWPC[3]	ACLU[4]	CWPS[5]	WEAL[6]	CLASP[7]	NARAL[8]
Barbara Bergmann						*	*	
Jessie Bernard					*	*	*	
Margaret Gates		**			*	*		
Ruth B. Ginsburg				*		*		*
Krysten Horbal			*					*
Margaret Kohn	*						*	
Odessa Komer	*		*				*	
Brooksley Landau	*						*	
Sylvia Law	*	*		*				
Judith Lichtman	*			*		*		
Margaret Moses				*		*		
Harriet Pilpel				*				*
Bernice "Bunny" Sandler†				*		*		
Diana Steele				*		*		
Gloria Steinem			*			*		*

Source: Annual reports and personal interviews, Gelb and Palley, (1982:62).
1. Women's Legal Defense Fund
2. National Organization for Women—Legal Defense and Education Fund
3. National Women's Political Caucus
4. American Civil Liberties Union
5. Center for Women's Policy Studies
6. Women's Equity Action League
7. Center for Law and Social Policy—Women's Rights Project
8. National Abortion Rights Action League

** Once director.

† Director, Project on the Status and Education of Women of the American Association of Colleges.

feminism's diffusion. Our own preliminary research, however, shows extensive involvement in the production and marketing of feminist and women's studies writings.[4] Our description of this involvement is organized to depict the various publics reached by sectors of the publishing industry. There is, of course, some overlap between our categories.

Publications for a Primarily Feminist Audience. There are, at the latest count, 92 women's presses and publishers, usually women-owned and run, and dedicated to the distribution of feminist books (Women's Institute for Freedom of the Press, 1983). Examples of these presses are The Feminist Press, Virago, Eden, Diana, KNOW, Inc., Links, and Out and Out Books. These companies are typically small and financially precarious. Some of their products may be finding their way out to more general audiences. Virago's reissues in paperback of earlier feminist writings are, for example, finding their way into university and "serious" bookstores. But these publishers primarily reach people already fairly deeply committed to feminism: feminist writers, the leadership of the women's movement, and those who think and act out of feminism and draw inspiration from the feminist writers.

There are also, at latest count, 279 periodicals, the majority devoted primarily to feminist and women's studies issues (Women's Institute for Freedom of the Press, 1983). Some of these publications have a fairly restricted reach, are financially fragile like most feminist presses, and appeal to sectors of the public already converted to feminism. Others are more established, widely distributed publications that may reach not only feminists, but also academics and the more highly educated sectors of the general reading public. Also included is *Ms.*, a feminist publication reaching all parts of the public. We will pay special attention to *Ms.* at the end of this discussion of the publishing industry.

Publications Reaching a Primarily Academic Audience. We refer here to books published by the university presses and to the disciplinary journals such as the *American Sociological Review*, the *American Political Science Quarterly*, the *American Journal of Psychology*, *College English*, and so on. Our preliminary research shows almost every university press now publishing a list of titles in the general area of women's studies. Most scholarly journals, especially in the humanities and social sciences, now regularly feature articles in the same general area.

The authors of these publications may not be drawn from the central circle of feminist theorists, though many of this group do publish through this medium. The authors are often members of the academic community persuaded by the feminist appeal. Books and journals of this type are sold primarily to members of the academic community, who subscribe to disciplinary journals, frequent university bookstores, and order books in response to journal advertisements, booksellers' displays at scholarly meetings, and direct mailing to academics by academic publishers. This audience includes feminists in academia, people curious about the issues raised by feminists, and casual browsers. This university public, though numerically small, is nevertheless a strategic "gatekeeper" for the transmission of ideas. As we shall see below, they teach the huge population of college students, a population that includes prospective teachers in elementary and secondary schools.

Publications Reaching the Educated Sectors of the General Reading Public.   Included here are intellectual journals like *Daedalus, Harper's, The Atlantic Monthly,* and the *New York Review of Books,* and fairly serious books published through major commercial publishing houses like Macmillan, McGraw-Hill, Harper & Row, Basic Books, Harcourt Brace Jovanovich, and Prentice-Hall. Journals in this category carry an occasional article on feminist questions, usually by a leading feminist thinker. Our research on the commercial book presses shows all the major publishing houses now carry a list, of variable length, dealing with feminist and women's studies issues. Many of the books by leading feminists are produced and marketed through this medium.

The journals are bought by educated people with intellectual inclinations. The books are bought by those who frequent university and "serious" bookstores, or who order books after reading book reviews, or in response to advertisements in the intellectual journals, the disciplinary journals, and the established feminist journals. Through this channel, the more serious reading public encounters feminist ideas.

Publications Reaching a Mass Audience.   This category includes mass-marketed paperback books produced by companies like Pocket Books, Bantam, Dell, Doubleday, and Anchor Books. These publications are marketed not only through the channels already discussed, but also find their way to popular bookstores, and sometimes to the bookstands of drugstores, supermarkets, and airport terminals, where they will be bought, almost on impulse, by people engaged in some other errand. All these companies have funneled aspects of feminism to a mass public, including sometimes key feminist statements. Pocket Books, for example, recently mass marketed a popularized feminist statement on female dependency, Dowling's *The Cinderella Complex;* Dell sold Friday's *My Mother, My Self.* Crucial feminist statements have been marketed by Bantam (Rich's *Of Woman Born* and Rossi's *The Feminist Papers*) and Doubleday (Millet's *Sexual Politics*).

In this category we include mass-marketed "new woman" magazines like *New Woman, Working Woman,* and *Working Mother,* which reach an audience similar to that of the books just discussed. The version of feminism disseminated through this channel is highly qualified by popularization and commercialization.

One magazine also marketed in this way is *Ms. Ms.* is an anomaly among popular "new woman" journals. Founded by a leading feminist, Gloria Steinem, it includes a large group of influential feminists and women's studies specialists on its advisory editorial board, and at one time or another has published serious statements by almost all the leading feminist thinkers. Yet *Ms.* uses a format so light in other respects and advertisements so absolutely typical of other mass-marketed magazines that it is a popular and at the same time significant conduit for feminism. Founded in 1972, by 1978 its circulation was close to 400,000 (Phillips, in Tuchman et al., 1978). In 1983 its circulation was close to half a million.

Why would publishers publish feminist writings? We can think of only three reasons: because of a feminist commitment (our first publication category); because of feminist pressure on editorial structures (an element in the university-oriented publishing world); and because they make money. This last reason, the fact that there is an important market for such publications, is surely the major reason for the involvement of the commercial and mass marketing presses.

Macrostructural Channels:
Political and Professional Interest Groups

As we saw above, the intellectuals who are formulating feminist ideas are often visibly active in the social and political activities of the women's movement. But that movement's organized leadership consists not only of feminist writers, but also of a much larger number of people whose work is primarily that of political action. This political work is done through a number of organized interest groups that attempt to influence our political process. The most signficant of these are listed here in alphabetical order (the list is from Gelb and Palley, 1982):

> A.C.L.U.'s Reproductive Freedom Project
> Center for Law and Social Policy—Women's Rights Project
> Center for Women's Policy Studies
> National Organization of Women
> NOW's Legal Defense and Education Fund
> National Women's Political Caucus
> Women's Equity Action League
> Women's Legal Defense Fund

In Chapter 8 we discuss the political work of some of these groups. Here we want to consider their function in disseminating feminist ideas.

Both the writers and the political action people in the leadership of the women's movement are feminists in the deepest sense. They share a common perspective. Political action people absorb feminist beliefs through their reading and through their interaction with feminist theorists. Political action people probably also affect the ideas of the feminist theorists in this same interaction. Most important, the political action leadership, by actions in society, disseminates feminist beliefs. Groups like the ones just listed mount campaigns in pursuit of feminist goals; they organize write-in movements, collect signatures, have fund drives, distribute literature, organize marches and rallies, lobby politicians, bring legal action suits, call for legislation, appear before congressional committees, and make speeches. All this activity serves to make feminist views visible to the political community and to the general public.

On a smaller scale, this process of interest group organizations oc-curs within the major professional associations, the formal organizational structures of the academic and service professions.[5] One writer has called the seventies the "decade of the caucuses" (Briscoe, 1978), meaning that this was a time when movement leaders and those persuaded to feminism by their reading organized within the professional associations in special groups whose purpose was to look at their professions through a feminist lens. *Caucuses,* as these groups were called, were organized in almost all the associations of the humanities and social sciences. In sociology, this caucusing process is embodied in Sociologists for Women in Society (SWS), a very active and intellectually lively organization with both a national and local chapters. The natural sciences have responded more slowly, but here too the process is well under way, as Table 7–4 shows.

Women's caucuses monitor discriminatory practices in their profes-sions. They link feminists in the profession into a support network. They attempt to get feminists and their supporters elected to office within their organizations and to have research on gender issues incorporated into the programs of association meetings and the publications of the profession. Though their degree of effectiveness varies, the overall impact of these caucuses is significant. They have made the academic disciplines and the major professions somewhat sensitive to the sexism so long unconfronted within them, and brought about a reorientation of academic interest to-ward feminist-tinged gender issues.[6] This reorientation of academic inter-est has affected the publishing industry, and has had a major impact on our third channel of dissemination, higher education.

Macrostructural Channels: Higher Education

People who teach and do research in our colleges and universities, as a significant sector of the population of "serious" readers and as members of professional associations with their special women's caucuses, are a "public" so situated as to be significantly influenced by feminist beliefs.

One consequence of this is that a significant percentage of academics have begun to direct their work toward gender issues. Academics are structurally under pressure to discover, teach, research, and write about topics that, in the context of existing scholarly work, appear to be novel. The effect of the feminist perspective has been to open up a hitherto unrecognized but now seemingly inexhaustible treasure trove of new, researchable topics. This new research, while still housed primarily in academic departments, is on occasion carried out in special research centers for women's issues, such as those at Wellesley, Radcliffe, and Stanford. Book-length and article-length reports of this research now flow into the publishing industry, increasing the amount of feminist lit-erature which that industry makes available to the public.

One category of book produced by academics on gender issues is the textbook. This particular form of writing leads us to the most significant role of higher education as a channel for disseminating feminism's new meanings: the communication that goes on between college and university faculty and students. Thirty-two percent of whites, 19 percent of blacks,

TABLE 7–4 Caucuses of Women in the Natural Sciences

Name and date established	Scientific society
Committee on the Status of Women in Physics (1971)	American Physical Society
Caucus of Women Biophysicists and Committee on Professional Opportunities for Women (1972)	Biophysical Society
Committee on Professional Opportunities for Women (1972)	Institute for Electrical and Electronic Engineers
Women Geoscientists Committee (1973)	American Geological Institute
Women's Caucus of the Endocrine Society (1976)	Endocrine Society
Committee on the Status of Women Microbiologists (1970)	American Society for Microbiology
Women in Cell Biology (1971)	American Society for Cell Biology
Women Chemists Committee (1927)	American Chemical Society
Professional Opportunities for Women Committee (1975)	American Institute of Chemists
Committee on Women in Biochemistry (1972)	American Society of Biological Chemists
Committee for Women in Statistics (1970)	American Statistical Association
Women's Caucus (1971)	American Association for the Advancement of Science
Task Force on Women in Physiology (1973)	American Physiological Society
Association for Women in Mathematics (1971)	None
Caucus for Women in Statistics (1970)	None
Women in Science and Engineering (1971)	None
Society of Women Engineers (1950)	None
Society of Women Geographers (1925)	None
Federation of Organizations for Professional Women (1972)	None
Association for Women in Science (1971)	None
Women in Science Committee (1975)	New York Academy of Sciences

Source: Adapted from Anne M. Briscoe, "Phenomenon of the Seventies: The Women's Caucuses," *Signs: Journal of Women in Culture and Society,* 4, (1978), 152–158.

and 16 percent of Hispanics in the United States in 1979 received some college education (Bureau of Labor Statistics). This population includes almost everyone who goes on to teach in secondary and elementary schools. Both directly and indirectly, then, communication between faculty and college students can channel feminist ideas to an enormous public. There is good evidence that this conduit for feminist ideas is in fact in place.

An objective measure of this process is to be found in program and curriculum changes occurring in higher education. (Boxer, 1982). The first courses on women began to appear in college curricula in 1967, shortly after feminism entered its contemporary phase of expansion. In 1969 the syllabi of sixteen such courses were published in *Female Studies I,* and in 1970 the first integrated women's studies program, consisting of ten courses, was established at San Diego State. Since then the growth of course offerings and programs has been phenomenal, one of the major "growth industries" (Boxer, 1981) of higher education. In 1979, there were 30,000 courses on women and gender issues in place in college and university curricula, and 300 women's studies programs, of which 24 were offering graduate degrees. In 1982, 450 women's studies programs were in place (*Women's Studies Newsletter,* Fall 1982). Boxer (1982) shows that students in these courses and programs were fairly consistently exposed to a basic core of feminist writings.

These programs and courses introduce large sectors of the college student population to elements of the feminist belief system. Even for those who never take one (probably still the large majority of students), the presence in listings of courses like "Women and Literature," "Women in History," and "Gender Role Socialization" suggests the existence of an orientation to which students of a generation ago were oblivious. That sensitization may well make such students stop to read a popular news-magazine or newspaper article on gender, or buy a paperback at the bookstore, and so become more aware of feminist beliefs.

Macrostructural Channels: The Mass Media

We come finally to the mass media, the dissemination channel that probably came first to mind. We mean by the mass media films, television, radio, newspapers, news magazines like *Newsweek* or *Time,* and widely circulated popular magazines like *Family Circle.* Objectively speaking, these media jointly constitute an idea-disseminating structure with the widest reach in our society, a reach that directly affects the consciousness of almost every American. Many of you will remember seeing an item about the women's movement in a TV newscast, or listening to a talk show exploration of a feminist issue like job discrimination or battered wives, or you have noted a special issue of a news magazine devoted to women's "decade of progress," or seen a movie like *Tootsie* or *Kramer vs. Kramer,* which address gender issues. Surely, you will say, this is *the* way people learn new ways of thinking about gender.

Perhaps. But if so, they are being taught by a medium that is highly selective, biased, and distorting of feminist interests. Social scientists who study the media give us pretty conclusive evidence that little has changed in terms of presentation of gender (Tuchman, 1979; Goffman, 1979). While conventional family magazines like *Family Circle* do now discuss the problems of working mothers, magazine fiction, TV entertainment, and advertising generally still depict women as a numerical minority, as outside the wage sector, and as dependent on men for advice, love, and protection. Newspapers and newsmagazines pay scant attention to major "movement" events, or relegate such news to the "women's page" along with fashion news, recipes, and advice on etiquette.

Our point is that people whose contact with feminist viewpoints comes solely through the mass media are getting elements of that perspective in an unsystematic and distorted way, elements moreover embedded within a deeper structure of very conventional images and ideas about gender. Unless an individual relates highly selectively to these messages, it is unlikely that the media will function to transform her or his views. That capacity for selectivity will most probably be generated by contact with one of the three other channels of dissemination.

The Public: "Getting the Message"

At the beginning of the second part of this chapter, we gave you evidence that attitudes among the general public are changing in a feminist direction. We have just described four macrosocial channels that serve to disseminate feminist ideas. Is there any way we can prove a link between the channels and the changing attitudes? In the next three chapters we will describe patterns of action that are transforming our gender system, and which are frequently prompted by these beliefs. We want to end this chapter by presenting four individual cases of changing beliefs. In each of them you will be able to detect the role of various idea-disseminating structures. We will not comment on the relationship of these individual cases to the question we just raised; we think they speak for themselves.

Case 1, reported on by Ed Bruske in The Washington Post, July 18, 1982. The writer tells how his mother, after an absolutely conventional middle-class suburban life as wife, housewife, and mother, had at the age of 52 just graduated at the top of her class from college, and was on her way to graduate school. He says this about her:

> My mother was never a revolutionary. We never had to deal with a mother who wanted to be more than we are used to, a Mom. . . . There must be thousands who, like her, never ventured out on their own, but followed the women's movement alone with a cup of coffee in their suburban kitchen, reading and digesting the new ideas. There must be thousands who felt empty and now recall, as my mother does, that until then "I thought I was the only one who felt that way."

Her friends were incredulous when in middle age she started going to college, but she "found conversation and support in academe."

Case 2, reported in Evans (1980:227–228). A suburban housewife, Jan Schakowsky, talks about how isolated she felt in the late sixties, with few female friends and two babies "in diapers." She started to hear about the women's movement and "I started reading, you know, even women's magazines, and watching talk shows . . . I knew that if I ever met Gloria Steinem we would be best friends . . . *Ms.* magazine, I read it totally uncritically . . . it was my magazine." She and her friends began a consumer group where "we talked about the problems that we faced related directly to the fact that we were women." Jan Schakowsky went on to play a major role in the Citizen Action Program in Chicago and then in the Illinois Public Action Council.

Case 3, reported in Evans (1980: 229–230). Darlene Stille worked her way through college, then got a job in an insurance company. The work was crowded, "noisy . . . uncomfortable . . . gloomy . . . depressing. I just couldn't believe that after all those years of effort, this is what it had come to." She was angry because she felt so "stuck." She was even angrier when she was rejected for a promotion because of her gender. Nevertheless, she avoided the women's movement until the mid-seventies, when some friends talked her into attending a NOW meeting about job discrimination. "I came away from that meeting feeling something could be done." Two days later she was picketing for equal treatment for women. Later, Stille became chairperson of Women Employed, the association that organized a nationally televised demonstration on behalf of a secretary who was fired because she refused to make coffee. The secretary was rehired.

Case 4, reported by Carla Hall in The Washington Post, July 21, 1983. Kathy Wilson at age 22 got a sales job in Kansas City, Missouri, where she did well and was pretty satisfied, until she discovered that two men whom she had trained were making $100 more a month than she was. " 'They're getting more money because they are men,' my boss told me . . . I didn't know about the [Equal Employment Opportunity Commission]." She quit her job. "I was just sort of outraged. [My husband and I] just had endless discussions about it. Endless. I *couldn't* believe it. I *could* not believe it." Kathy Wilson joined the local chapter of the National Women's Political Caucus. Kathy Wilson, now 33, is just beginning her second term as president of the National Women's Political Caucus.

NOTES

1. Marxists, of course, would say that liberalism generally, and liberal feminism in particular, is not in any absolute sense "reasonable." It merely appears reasonable because as an ideological system that masks and advances the interests of a dominant group, it is heavily disseminated through all our socialization structures and unreflectively taken for granted in our society.

2. For radical feminist statements, see Atkinson (1974), Barry (1979), Daly (1973, 1978), Firestone (1970), Greer (1971), Griffin (1978, 1981), MacKinnon (1982), Morgan

(1970, 1982), Millett (1969), Rich (1976, 1980, 1981), and Rowbotham (1972). See also the selection of papers in Jaggar and Struhl (1978).

3. Only our concern with nonsexist language makes us use the term spokespersons. Feminist theorists in the contemporary women's movement are, almost without exception, women.

4. "Preliminary" is the only term for this research. It consists of (i) noting the publishers of our collection of feminist and women's studies literature; (ii) studying the references in this literature for the publishers of other feminist works; (iii) systematically studying advertisements in *Signs*. By this means we compiled a list of hundreds of publishing enterprises involved in marketing gender-related writings.

5. By "service professions" we mean primarily lawyers, doctors and related health professionals, and social workers.

6. *Signs* systematically reviews the various academic disciplines in an attempt to chart this reorientation (see all the issues of *Signs* since its first issue, Summer 1974).

8
SOCIAL STRUCTURES PROMOTING GENDER EQUALITY*

Chapter 7 described new beliefs about gender and the processes by which those beliefs are disseminated. Chapters 8 and 9 analyze how social structures make possible both new subjective understandings affirming gender equality and new access to power resources for implementing that equality. For purposes of analysis, we hypothesize two types of structures: Chapter 8 examines those structures actors intentionally create or adapt for promoting gender equality; Chapter 9, those changes in social structure that lead to gender equality as an unintended by-product.

Social structures are collectively created patterns or channels for relationship. They are not the relationship itself, for a relationship is the actual process by which actors take account of each other subjectively and behaviorally. Social structures are the arrangements in society which (1) prescribe how a relationship should proceed; and (2) affect the probability that the relationship will occur at all. In the case history given at the end of the last chapter of the woman who, having earned a college degree, could not break out of a series of clerical jobs, we saw how the present structure of American occupational life channels women into less desirable workplace situations than it does men with the same qualifications.

This chapter looks at two levels of social structure that people in our society today are using to promote gender equality, the macro and the micro. Our analysis of macrostructures will focus on the contemporary

*By Ruth Wallace, Patricia Lengermann, and Jill Brantley.

women's movement. Our exploration of microstructures will look at consciousness raising, networks, and friendship. Our particular focus is on how women have adapted or invented social structures to promote gender equality.

MACROSTRUCTURES: THE WOMEN'S MOVEMENT

This section explores how the ideas presented in Chapter 7 have been translated into organized acts of power at the macro level to help promote gender equality. We look, in other words, at the contemporary women's movement, the organizational extension of feminism. Our discussion has four parts. First, we describe the type of social structure a social movement is. Second, we outline the development of the contemporary women's movement. Third, we look at the organization of the movement, at the particular way that it is a mobilization of power in the cause of gender equality. Fourth, we explore the ways in which the women's movement has brought power to bear on government as a means of moving society in the direction of gender equality.

The Women's Movement as a Social Structure

A social movement is one of the more extensive and visible ways in which large numbers of people mobilize to produce change in a society. This mobilization is guided by a shared system of intensely held values and beliefs that set goals for and pattern the actions of movement members. Minimally these beliefs and values identify basic wrongs in society and describe what ought to be the proper organization of society. A movement's belief system also offers explanations for why the wrongs exist and strategies for setting them right. On these latter issues, however, there is typically less consensus and, indeed, significant friction.

The belief system guiding the contemporary women's movement is feminism, which we described in Chapter 7. Certain aspects of that description are pertinent here. First, we saw that feminism at the most general level is a unified viewpoint, intensely infused with values and anchored in certain general themes about women's situation in society. Second, below this level of generality there are competing perspectives: the liberal, Marxist, and radical. Third, people vary in the degree to which they espouse feminism as a coherent and centrally meaningful belief system. Many people do stand within feminism as their essential, systematically patterned view of the world. Others are affected only by elements of this perspective disseminated to them in diluted forms by the various communications media. All these features—an overarching consensus, internal variations in perspective, and in intensity and coherence of belief—are general features of a social movement. They help produce both its cohesion and its internal differentiation.

A social movement is a structure patterning the relationships of large numbers of otherwise unrelated people, typically dispersed over a wide geographic area, and drawn from a diversity of social backgrounds. Any effective movement contains within itself organizations for linking its membership together; visible centers of leadership; communication among members; means for articulating and elaborating the movement's belief system; and channels for mobilizing and pooling the resources that members can bring to their shared goal. All these organizational structures are marked by a high degree of fluidity and change. For a movement is above all a structure characterized by broad-based, intense participation.

That degree of participation produces, over most of the life of a movement, invention and experimentation in organizational forms. Individual movements, moreover, vary on many of the criteria raised in this paragraph: size, diversity, and dispersal of members; the particular pattern of organizational forms; intensity of participation; and degree of experimentation and change in organizational structures. Below, we will explore the distinctive patterns of these variables in the contemporary women's movement.

In attempting to produce social change, a social movement brings power to bear on those institutions that function in legitimate ways to change society: government, law, economy, mass media, and the idea-shaping community of intellectuals, researchers, and scholars. The power resources internal to a movement are on the one hand the mobilization of its members, and on the other the effectiveness of its organization. A movement may translate these resources into a variety of power relations with the key change-producing institutions: *influence,* which brings the public or the personnel of those institutions around to the movement's view of the world; *domination,* which threatens the material well-being of those structures with economic, political, or legal sanctions; *coercion* through the use of physical violence; or the establishment of its own *legitimacy* as a structure of change.

This last base for power can be produced by leadership that is appealing to a general public; by direct appeals to the community's traditions or to its constitutional and philosophical principles; or by claims to special expertise, such as an exclusive knowledge of a particular constituency. Each social movement assembles its own distinctive package of power strategies for effecting change.

The Development of the Contemporary Women's Movement

An organized social movement by and on behalf of women has been part of American political life for the past hundred and fifty years. Speaking very generally, three major phases are visible in the history of the women's movement: 1848–1920; 1921–1959; and 1960 to the present. Throughout the first phase, women remained highly organized and mobilized. They pursued with considerable effectiveness such goals as access to higher education and birth control, improved working conditions, and the right to own property, control their own wages, and unionize. Their rallying cry, however, was for the right to vote, which they achieved in 1920 by securing passage of the Nineteenth Amendment to the Constitution (Flexner, 1971; Rossi, 1974).

During the second phase the movement lost momentum, dwindled in size, and shrank to only a few groups like the tiny, radical Women's Party and the multipartisan League of Women Voters, which emphasized education of voters but avoided ideological stances. One cause of this decline was the movement's failure to find a new rallying cry to replace that of women's suffrage. A second was class division within the movement. A third and perhaps the most significant cause was the impact of the Great Depression and World War II, and of protracted periods of political conservatism in the 1920s and 1950s, on the movement's membership and organizations. By the end of the fifties it must have appeared to feminists that the work of building a women's movement would almost have to begin again from scratch (Deckard, 1979).

Nevertheless, during the 1960s that renewal and revitalization did occur. By the end of the sixties, the women's movement had entered a phase of intense, perhaps unparalleled, mobilization. This period, which we label "the contemporary women's movement," is our focus in this chapter.

Four factors produced the new phase of intense mobilization by women that has been our recent history. First, as we will see in Chapter 9, women's participation in the paid work force and in higher education, which had grown steadily all through the century, increased sharply from the sixties on, while discrimination continued in all institutional areas. Here lay the potentially mobilizable base of the movement. Second, as we saw in Chapter 7, feminism as a belief system entered a new phase of elaboration and dissemination, beginning with Friedan's best-selling critique, *The Feminine Mystique,* in 1963. This development helped and continues to help sharpen women's understanding of their discontent. Third, once the movement got into high gear both ideologically and organizationally, publicity by the technologically sophisticated mass media enormously expanded its reach (see Chapter 6). Fourth, the course of American politics during the sixties led women along a variety of avenues to organization on their own behalf. It is this last factor we now describe more fully.

Two strands in American political life during the sixties gave women political experiences they would use to create organizational structures for the women's movement: a turn toward political reform in government and intensified political activism. Let us look at these in turn.

In 1960, mainstream American politics signaled its shift toward a new period of reform with the election of President John F. Kennedy. Kennedy, apparently to repay the women who had worked in his campaign, and despite his own fairly traditional views on women's issues, established a Presidential Commission on the Status of Women in 1961. The commission served as a stimulus for the establishment of similar state-level organizations. An important structure for connecting people interested in women's issues had officially been called into being. It also raised hopes that official action on behalf of women would follow (Deckard, 1979; Peterson, 1983; Rawalt, 1983).

The hopes were soon dashed. In 1963, the Presidential Commission issued a cautious, nonmilitant report. The inaction of the commission was buried in the public mind by the growing pressures of the black civil rights movement. This movement was to have important consequences for women as well; one was the passage of the 1964 Civil Rights Act. As a ploy to ridicule this legislation, its opponents extended the clause barring discrimination in employment, Title VII, to include a prohibition of discrimination by sex. The act passed, but in 1965, when it went into effect, the Equal Employment Opportunity Commission (EEOC) would not implement the clause on women's employment, calling it a "fluke."

In 1966 a National Conference of States Commissions on Women refused to act against EEOC's recalcitrance. Spurred by this inaction, a group of feminists came together on the conference's last day to found the National Organization for Women (NOW), whose declared purpose was to act as a multipurpose lobbying and pressure group working for gender equality. NOW would become the spearhead for women's activism of a basically moderate form. In the wake of NOW's formation came a number of other moderate or liberal women's groups, including the Women's Equity Action League (WEAL), Federally Employed Women (FEW), and Human Rights for Women, Inc., all founded in 1968 (Deckard, 1979:346–349).

At the same time, in the society at large the civil rights movement on behalf of blacks and the New Left movement against the Vietnam war drew women into politics. But once in, women found that they were the object of extreme sexist attitudes and that their critiques of sexism were dismissed as trivial (Deckard, 1979; Evans, 1980). These women were typically ideologically much more radical than those who were the moving force in NOW and WEAL. They too felt the need to organize solely on women's issues. From 1967 onward they began to splinter away from the civil rights and New Left movements to form feminist groups. The Woman's Radical Action Project, the Westside Group, Radical Women in New York, Redstockings, and the Feminists are some of the key organizations they created. All this organization, by both moderates and radicals, occurred in the glare of often exploitative media publicity. It reached an audience of women angered by their experience of discrimination and already aroused by the growing flood of feminist writings to a conceptual grasp of their situation in society. A new phase of the women's movement began.

Organizational Forms of the Contemporary Women's Movement

There are many instances when an organizational plan is superimposed by a group of experts on an essentially unresponsive population. Examples include development planners trying to create participatory village councils in certain rural areas, and a department's faculty working to produce a majors' society within its student body. This, however, is not the situation with the contemporary women's movement. There a large, diverse population of believers, galvanized into action by processes and events, began autonomously generating its own organizations for communication, participation, leadership, and change.

This effort did involve reaching out to the visible organizations of experts on the political landscape, groups like NOW and WEAL. These organizations were in turn actively working to link up with their constituencies. Data on NOW's membership illustrate the effectiveness of this process of mutual attraction. In 1966 NOW had 300 members; in 1971, somewhere between 5,000 and 10,000; in 1973, 30,000 (Deckard, 1979:349); in 1978, 125,000 (Gelb and Palley, 1982:28); in 1984, 250,000 (personal communication with NOW, January 1984).

Much more of this work of organizing for change was undertaken by women acting with extraordinary enthusiasm and independent of the intellectuals and organizers the media identified as leaders of the movement. The result has been an organizational structure which is decentralized, consisting of innumerable groups varying in size, scope, and project, but which coheres through a loose, flexible dynamic of associational links and shared concerns (Taylor, 1981, in Richardson and Taylor, 1983).

At the organizational base of the movement, forming one of its fundamental supports, is an uncountable number of spontaneously formed small groups. The membership of such groups is typically drawn from a single locality: a small town, a suburb or neighborhood, a college campus, office, or apartment building. The founding members are usually friends or acquaintances drawn together by a project. Other members will be recruited by word of mouth or by notices on bulletin boards or in small local publications. The purposes of such groups vary: self-understanding, such as occurs in consciousness-raising groups; self-expression, through women's poetry or art or music collectives; or provision of a service, such as counseling for incest and rape victims, shelters for battered and homeless women, childcare cooperatives for working mothers, women's bookstores and presses, and multipurpose women's centers.

Procedurally, these groups tend to be nonbureaucratic and informal. Individually, they may be precarious and ephemeral. But aggregatively, these grassroots associations persist as a constant and significant feature of the movement, the precise and vital point of intersection between feminist believers and the emergence of movement organization (Taylor, 1981, in Richardson and Taylor, 1983; Deckard, 1979; Evans, 1979; McDonough, 1980; Cassell, 1977).

A huge number of larger, more visible associations coexist or interact with these small, grassroots organizations for communication, mobilization, and leadership. Varying in size from a single study or research center to a mass organization with hundreds of thousands of members, most of these associations differ from the grassroots groups in that they are more formal in organization, procedure, and recruitment methods; have a wider geographic reach; pursue women's issues on a bigger scale; and are more securely funded, typically by membership fees, but sometimes by foundation money (Gelb and Palley, 1982). They are consequently more durable. Descriptions of the range of this type of association follow.

Traditional Women's Associations.   Included here are groups like the American Association of University Women, the League of Women Voters, and the National Federation of Business and Professional Women's Clubs. These groups were all founded prior to the start of the present phase of the women's movement. Activists in the present wave of feminist mobilization see them as cautious, establishment-oriented, and conservative. Yet these groups have provided important support for such key movement programs as ratification of the Equal Rights Amendment and equal education opportunities for women (Rawalt, 1983; Millsap, 1983), for they are organizations with large memberships and large budgets (Gelb and Palley, 1982).

Multi-Issue, Mass-Based Associations.   The most powerful of these groups is NOW, with 250,000 members, over 700 local chapters, a multimillion-dollar annual budget, a large permanent staff, and an elaborate structure of task forces and lobbying activities over most of the range of women's issues. NOW tries to be ideologically broad in its relation to feminism, but has often been accused by the radical wing of the movement of excessive caution and conservatism (Gelb and Palley, 1982; Deckard, 1979). The Women's Equity Action League (WEAL) is a similar but much smaller association.

Single-Issue Groups.   Included here is a long list of associations, each of which exists primarily to pursue some specific goal. Influential organizations in this category include the National Abortion Rights Action League (NARAL), with over 90,000 members and a multimillion-dollar budget (Gelb and Palley, 1982); the National Coalition for Women and Girls in Education, a federation of over fifty national associations (Millsap, 1983); Wider Opportunities for Women, which focuses on employment issues; ERAmerica; and the Women and Health Network.

Marxist and Radical Groups.   The associations described above typically are guided by the liberal version of feminism. Marxist feminists and radical feminists have also formed associations to promote their ideals of social change. Visible Marxist-Socialist groups have included such associations as the New American Movement and the Chicago Women's Liberation Union (Deckard, 1979). On p. 167 we mention several radical groups that helped shape this latest phase of the women's movement.

Socialist and radical feminist groups differ from the liberal associations in basic organizational form. They tend toward small, locally centered, self-contained groupings, which evolve and change their structure and names rapidly, and which are linked together in loose coalitions by common speakers, writers, and movement events. Both their own ideological commitments and the sociopolitical culture in which they seek to survive help to explain this more fluid and elusive form.

None of this should, however, lead us to underestimate the significance of the socialist and radical groups in the movement. For one thing, their views and organizational skills directly affect many of the grassroots and special constituency organizations. For another, the line between these groups and the intellectual community of feminists is highly permeable. The activities of these groups feed directly into the process of idea creation and dissemination that mobilizes the women's movement and sustains its critical analysis of society.

Groups Representing Special Constituencies. In Chapter 7 we described how women's studies programs and professional caucuses have drawn the academic community into the women's movement. A variety of other organizations have developed or reoriented to link other special constituencies with the movement. Examples include Nine to Five, which mobilizes secretaries and clerical workers; the Coalition of Labor Union Women; Older Women's Liberation; organizations with a religious constituency like Mormons for ERA and the Catholic Women's Ordination Conference; and organizations with a lesbian or homosexual constituency, such as Daughters of Bilitis, the Furies, and the National Gay Task Force.

Electoral Campaign Groups. Finally a number of groups have come into being to help women obtain political office. These include the National Women's Education Fund, which trains women for campaign work and for political office; the Women's Campaign Fund, which raises money for candidates in national-level politics; and the National Women's Political Caucus (NWPC), which works to increase women's participation in party politics and their election or appointment to political office (Fraser, 1983). Of these groups, the NWPC is the oldest and most influential. Founded in 1971, the organization is multipartisan, and has as its primary aims the political mobilization of women and increasing the involvement of women in practical politics at all levels.

Factors in Movement Cohesion

At the beginning of this chapter, we defined social structure as a collectively created system of social arrangements patterning and channeling human relationships. This section has looked at the contemporary women's movement as a structure that patterns and channels the relationships of people mobilized by the goal of gender equality. What we have found is a structure which is complex, diversified, decentralized, and subject to considerable experimentation and change. One might logically raise the question of what processes hold this structure together. Our search of the literature suggests that the following six factors are crucial to the movement's cohesion:

1. *The overarching belief system of feminism.*
2. *Shared interests* in a more equitable situation for women, produced by women's common location in such key institutions as work, family, and education.
3. *Overlapping memberships* in movement organizations.

4. *Cross-cutting linkages of friendship and acquaintance* that create an informal but effective medium for intraorganizational communication.
5. *Formal cooperation in support of policies advancing gender equality.* In its most striking form, this occurs through massive coalitions of dozens of organizations.
6. *Participation in major movement events.* People from the whole spectrum of the movement participate in marches and demonstrations such as those protesting rape or supporting the Equal Rights Amendment; in annual meetings on special topics like the Women and the Law Conference and those of the National and Regional Women's Studies Association; annual cultural events like the Michigan Womyn's Music Festival; and such major movement displays of solidarity as the International Women's Year Conference in Mexico City, 1975, the First National Women's Conference in Houston, 1977, and the San Antonio "gender gap" meetings of the Women's National Political Caucus in 1983.

These various ties, though loose and flexible, have made the women's movement into a significant force in American politics. We turn now to an exploration of the movement's impact on our governmental processes.

The Impact of the Contemporary Movement

Any comprehensive assessment of the impact of the women's movement would have to look at women's changing sense of self, at shifts in public attitudes about gender equality, and at the restructuring of gender-specific meanings, relationships, and power in such institutions as family, economy, politics, education, and the mass media. Such an assessment is beyond the scope of this book; we focus instead on the ways in which the women's movement, in pursuit of its goal of gender equality, has brought power to bear on the state. We look first at changes that have been achieved through this means, and second at the power processes used by the movement in its interaction with government.

ERA.   Any account of the political activities of the contemporary women's movement must begin with the drive to obtain a constitutional amendment that would make illegal all discrimination on the basis of sex. This proposed amendment is known as the Equal Rights Amendment or ERA. Over the whole period 1960 to the present, the ERA has functioned symbolically and practically as the movement's central project. A major portion of its power resources has been committed to obtaining passage of the ERA. The record of that effort shows a mix of success and failure.

The ERA was first proposed as a movement project in the twenties, after passage of the Nineteenth Amendment gave women the vote. At first only a demand by the most radical groups in the movement, by the late fifties it had become an important goal. When Kennedy's Presidential Commission on the Status of Women failed to endorse the project, the movement adopted ERA as its rallying cry. In March 1972, after years of intense political maneuvering, the movement won a major victory. Congress approved the amendment and sent it to the states for ratification (Rawalt, 1983).

The story of the ratification struggle is presented in Chapter 11. Over a ten-year period, ERA gained approval by thirty-five states, three states short of the number needed. Over all this period, the movement waged an intense struggle on behalf of the amendment. At the present time the leadership, still committed to that struggle, has begun the process all over again and is once more trying to move an equal rights amendment through Congress.

A constitutional amendment against sex discrimination is not only symbolically important; it is of enormous practical value. Without it, gender equality has to be fought for on an issue-by-issue basis. Over the whole of the contemporary period, even as the struggle for the amendment went on, movement members have continued to fight sex discrimination issue by issue. They have had considerable success. Let us look at some of the changes produced in the areas of economy, education, and family.

The Economy. In the area of economic life, the movement's goal has been to increase women's access to the material goods that can sustain them in independent well-being. Although, as we show in Chapters 5 and 9, marked inequality still persists in this institution, over the past twenty years the government has, under pressure from activists, moved to ensure women equality with regard to hiring practices, salaries, promotions, pension plans, and access to credit (Fleming, 1983). Pregnancy can no longer be a basis for discrimination in employment, and must be covered by an employer's health and disability benefits (Gelb and Palley, 1982).

Employers have begun, here and there, modest experiments with flexible work schedules and childcare facilities, and some monitoring of sexual harassment in the workplace (MacKinnon, 1979). Childcare tax deductions have been made available to working mothers. And in recent years government has given somewhat more attention to the arguments of women's activists on the issue of "comparable worth"; that is, that an employer should not pay markedly higher salaries for "men's jobs" than for "women's jobs" when those jobs require equivalent amounts of training, effort, and skill.

Education. The cause of equal treatment in education has also been pressed actively and effectively (Gelb and Palley, 1982; Millsap, 1983). It is now illegal to discriminate by sex in education. This applies to all levels of education, including vocational training; to all educational facilities, including athletic programs; and to both the students and the employees of educational organizations. However, a February 1984 decision by the Supreme Court seriously weakens these efforts (see Chapter 11). Government funds have also been made available for "counseling and other services to encourage women to enter fields of study long denied them" (Millsap, 1983:96). Sexual harassment in educational organizations is now open to official sanction.

The Family. Obviously, many of the changes just described affect women's status in the family. Increased earning power, job protection during pregnancy, independent access to loans and credit, and the somewhat greater availability of flextime schedules and childcare all increase women's independence in relation to marriage and within the family. The women's movement has worked in many other ways to enhance that independence.

It has turned official attention to issues of spouse abuse and marital rape (Zeitlin, 1983), argued effectively that a wife who supports her husband's education and is subsequently divorced has claims on his enhanced earning power, and begun to get official pressure on fathers who default on child support. The movement has forced government agencies to research the health hazards of various contraceptives, keeping some off the market and getting clear warnings attached to others (Lear, 1983; Kasper, 1983). It has worked to have abortion made legal (Gelb and Palley, 1982). This last gain has given rise to a major political struggle described in Chapter 11.

Exerting Power on Government

To produce these changes the women's movement has brought power to bear on all three branches of the federal government.

The Legislative Branch. The Congress passed the ERA in 1972, and extended its ratification period, in 1978, from seven to ten and a half years (Rawalt, 1983:69). Congress has also passed several significant pieces of legislation bearing directly on gender equality. Examples include Title VII of the Civil Rights Act of 1964, prohibiting discrimination by sex in employment; Title IX of the Educational Amendments of 1972, banning sex discrimination in education;[1] the Equal Credit Opportunity Act of 1974, making credit discrimination on the basis of sex illegal; the Women's Educational Equity Acts of 1974 and 1978, which fund educational programs facilitating gender equality; and the Pregnancy Disability Act of 1978, prohibiting discrimination against pregnant women in the paid work force in such areas as hiring, promotion, and insurance.

Movement activists were only marginal actors in shaping some of this legislation. Title VII, as we saw earlier, was a ploy by opponents of black civil rights. Title IX, which made sex discrimination in education illegal, was the work of one congresswoman, Edith Green (Gelb and Palley, 1982; Millsap, 1983). Sectors of the movement were, however, major initiators of legislation like the Equal Credit Opportunity Act and the Pregnancy Disability Act, and of congressional passage of the ERA (Gelb and Palley, 1982; Rawalt, 1983).

The women's movement has exerted power of the following types on legislatures:

1. Influencing the views of legislators directly through testimony at hearings and intense lobbying, and indirectly by affecting public opinion with media messages, conferences, and public lectures.

2. Domination—that is, the use or threat of political sanctions. This is done with grassroots pressure such as write-ins and demonstrations, or by organizational pressure from influential supporters. A massive coalition of over 120 major organizations, for example, rallied around the ERA.
3. Direct access to the legislative process by means of legislators who are movement members or sympathizers. The activity of Congresswoman Green on Title IX illustrates the effectiveness of this type of power. Movement organizations like the National Women's Political Caucus exist primarily for the purpose of increasing this power base.

The Executive Branch.   This branch of government has also functioned for the women's movement as a means to social change. For example, the Food and Drug Administration has issued guidelines or actually prevented contraceptive products from reaching the public, and it was an amendment to an executive order (11246), by President Johnson in 1967, which required all government contractors to refrain from discriminatory practices in employment.

Much more awesome is the power of the executive branch with regard to the implementation of legislation. It is the federal bureaucracy that translates general legislative statements into a complex of compliance guidelines; takes responsibility for monitoring compliance; and punishes noncompliance. The executive branch puts the teeth into legislation. On occasion, as for example with Title VII of the Civil Rights Act, whole sectors of Title IX of the Educational Amendments, and across the board in the recent "backlash" years of the Reagan administration (see Chapter 11), it may refuse to bite, or may merely nibble, at the discriminatory practices prohibited by law.

Exerting power on the executive branch of government is probably a more demanding task for the women's movement than the task of dealing with the legislature. The latter actively requires periodic intense mobilization around a particular piece of legislation, but the former demands constant monitoring of an enormously complex system and steady, unremitting pressure. In this task the movement uses some of the same tactics as those used with Congress: influence through testimony and lobbying; the threat or use of political sanctions either from grassroots or high-level organizational pressure; and attempts to obtain direct access to these structures through the election of executive leaders or through influencing executive appointments. Additionally, the movement uses an elaborate monitoring process involving a complex of organizations like the National Coalition for Women and Girls in Education, which involves over fifty major educational associations. To deal with extensive administrative resistance, the movement also uses legal sanctions.

The Courts.   The courts have acted against gender inequality in three ways: initiating policies; protecting gains made and subsequently threatened; and enforcing legislation. The most striking example of the first function is the Supreme Court ruling in 1973, in the case of *Roe* v. *Wade,* which extended the constitutional right to privacy to a woman's choice on abortion (Gelb and Palley, 1982). Other examples are the prohibition of marital rape, initial profeminist rulings on comparable worth, and the ruling against sex discrimination in retirement plans.

An illustration of the use of the courts to protect threatened gains is to be seen in the current fight over abortion, much of which is being waged through the courts. The enforcement of legislation has occurred when movement members have fought an inactive administration on the enforcement of Title VII of the Civil Rights Act or Title IX of the Educational Amendments (Rawalt, 1983; Millsap, 1983; Beard and Greenberger, 1983).

The tactics used by the women's movement to exert power with the judiciary differ considerably from those used with Congress and the administration. Neither influence nor the threat of sanctions will work in this relationship. What is required, first, is a skillful appeal to laws, constitutional principles, and judicial precedents. The second requirement is manipulative control over the details of court procedure. This calls for a highly mobilized and skilled community of feminist lawyers; a flow of information to this community, alerting it to possibilities for legal initiatives; and the availability of good case material—that is, of individuals whose circumstances provide a clear, unqualified basis for an argument in favor of gender equality.

To this end, feminists have created not only close networks of lawyers across the country, but also special legal associations like the Women's Legal Defense Fund and the National Women's Law Center, which function solely to monitor issues of women's equality. Wider coalitions of women's groups, like the National Coalition for Women and Girls in Education, channel information to these groups of lawyers. Interaction among these wider networks and the legal groups to a large extent makes possible the availability of good cases (Beard and Greenberger, 1983).

Overall, then, the women's movement has built up a structure of power relations with government consisting of influence, legitimacy claims based on constitutional principle and special expertise, and the threat or use of political and legal sanctions. Overall there has been little recourse to economic sanctions, violence, or either charismatic or traditional legitimacy. The structure of the American gender institution itself explains the relative neglect of these strategies. Even without them, the movement has proved itself a powerful political structure, which has functioned with considerable effectiveness to promote gender equality. Ultimately its power resources are the size and diversity of its membership, the intensity of its mobilization, and the strength, variety, and effectiveness of its organizational structures.

MICROSTRUCTURES

This part of the chapter explores how women have invented, adapted, and imitated social structures at the micro level as ways of gaining gender equality. An invention is an assembling of existing sociocultural elements into a new form; an adaptation is an adjustment of an existing structure to meet new demands; and an imitation is a copying of the behavior of another group. Feminists have invented one major new microsocial structure, the consciousness-raising group. Under the impact of changing gender arrangements, women have adapted the social structure with which they have perhaps always been most successful, friendship, and imitated the basically male microstructure, the network. In our analyses of consciousness raising, friendship, and networks as social structures helping women effect gender equality, we look at the content of each as an arrangement of meaning, organization, and power; the probability of participation by women within each structure; and how women have used the structure to promote an ideology of gender equality and to gain new power resources.

Consciousness-Raising Groups

The consciousness-raising group is the great social structural invention of the women's movement—one that has been adapted and imitated by other social movements, including men's liberation groups (see Chapter 10). The consciousness-raising group is the social structure that has done most to effect the growth of a feminist consciousness at the grassroots level, to change the way average American women see themselves and their relation to feminism. As an invention, consciousness-raising groups constitute a new assembling of existing meaning (the value of reflection), existing organizational forms, (the small group), and existing types of power, influence, and knowledge. The following sections explain the content of consciousness-raising groups as a social structure, discuss the possibilities for women's participation within this structure, and analyze how this structure aids in the quest for gender equality.

Structure: Content. The meaning system for consciousness-raising groups is value-based, and its primary value is reflection. Reflection is valuable because it helps us analyze why we see things as we do. We can look or intend toward things in many ways; but as the philosopher Martin Heidegger maintains, we never see things in themselves; we always see things as *some*things (Jones, 1975:297–299). Usually we see things in terms of their "use" value. Thus, this printed piece of paper is probably for you at this moment "a page in an assigned text." In another context, it might be the place you hid $10 or placed a flower to be pressed. How you intend toward a phenomenon depends on your social situation. Reflection helps you think about why you see things as you do, why things and people are the *some*things and *some*people they are to you.

From this basic value of reflection, consciousness-raising groups draw their two main activities. First, they help members to reflect on the ways they are aware of or intend toward the world around them and why they see that world and themselves as they do. Because consciousness-raising groups exist as a structure for social change, members tend to focus on the oppressive aspects of the status quo and how those oppressive aspects hurt their self-images. This first task of reflecting on how one interprets the world clears the way for the second task of consciousness raising, which is changing consciousness—helping group members direct their consciousness toward certain phenomena in certain ways. This action often involves having members not only see new things, but see familiar things in new ways. In *A Group Called Women,* Joan Cassell (1977:18–19) characterizes the act of consciousness-raising as a "transformation where the individual switches worlds." Often group members have been socialized to see the world as a place where they have no real right to significance. The groups encourage members to see the world in a way that affirms their right to be and to be significant.

The value of reflection shapes the organization and power arrangements of the consciousness-raising group. Interaction within a group is egalitarian and cooperative, emphasizing respect for what each individual can contribute and can learn by reflection. The way the group cooperates is typified by Patricia McDonough (1980) as having four stages: opening up, sharing, analyzing, and abstracting.

In opening up, people establish "a positive atmosphere of support" in which they can begin to talk about what they see as oppressions. How long this process takes depends on the group. Cassell (1977:36) notes that women in real crisis sometimes open up very quickly and intimately even among strangers. Gabrielle Burton, in her account of her own transformation via a consciousness-raising group, *I'm Running Away from Home, But I'm Not Allowed to Cross the Street* (1972:35), described her group's first weeks as "tedious." The opening up stage is often difficult because group members have responded to the hurt of oppression by burying it.

But as the hurt is acknowledged, group members start to share their experiences about being oppressed. This sharing is important, because it confirms the *social* reality of what the individual members have been broaching. As Pamela Allen has written in *Free Space: A Perspective on the Small Group in Women's Liberation,* "Through experiencing the common discussion comes the understanding that many of the situations are not . . . based on individual inadequacies, but rather have a root in the social order" (cited in McDonough, 1980:32).

In the analytic stage, members try to understand the causes for the effects they have been describing; they try to explain why they have experienced oppression. The final stage, abstraction, translates the analysis into a general theory to be used to deal with new situations and to generate ideas for changing what is defined as oppressive in the present system.

All this activity occurs within an egalitarian distribution of power. For the most part, consciousness-raising groups proceed without formal leaders (Cassell, 1977:35). The sources of power are the influence and knowledge that come from systematic, articulated reflection. Group members do not try to use influence or knowledge to have someone else do what they wish; they use their power to develop understanding of the present and a sense of the possibilities for change. Within the group, at moments, one member will exercise influence over the others through her contributions. The purpose, however, is never to "win" an argument, but rather to achieve a critical understanding of one's present and one's capacity to change.

Structure: Participation. The participatory structure of consciousness-raising groups embodies the women's movement principle of respect for the individual's subjective, private, personal, lived experience. Consciousness-raising groups are not therapy requiring a leader, chapters of some parent organization requiring some bureaucratic procedures, accrediting institutions accountable to outside agencies, or profit-making. These negative strengths all contribute to the positive capacity of consciousness-raising groups to reach people where they are—geographically, economically, ethnically, emotionally. This flexibility well serves women bound by commitments to children, dependence on male heads of household, or limited economic resources.

Anyone potentially can join or start a consciousness-raising group. The main requirement is 4 to 15 persons interested in reflecting on shared life experience. Joining is facilitated by knowing someone in such a group, and it is certainly made easier by living in an area, like Manhattan in the early 1970s, where many groups exist. Joining may be precipitated by some moment of personal crisis (see Cassell, 1977: chap. 3, and her comments on Newton and Walton, 1971). Gabrielle Burton traces her joining to a conjunction of factors: a local church sponsoring a discussion of women's liberation at a time when she was plagued by "constant guilt over daytime sleeping" that left her fearing she was sleeping her life away, and her desire for something better for her daughters.

To attend and participate, women must be committed to valuing their own and others' experiences. There are no experts, and the woman who sees herself as "just a housewife" is valued as highly as any woman working in the public sphere. The tolerance of members for each other's reflections sometimes causes groups to bog down in the ruminations of a disturbed member. But students of consciousness raising are quick to emphasize that these groups attract no more disturbed persons than any other social movement and that the vast majority of members function very adequately in society by any number of social science measures (Cassell, 1977:26, and Newton and Walton, 1971, cited in Cassell).

Members' tolerance, moreover, does appear to have a limit. As the members move into the analytic and abstracting stages, they usually must confront and accept the "ideological assertion of the 'oppression of women,'" which Cassell (1977:36) finds some are unable to do. These women either leave or are dropped by the group.

Absence of formal structure means that groups both form and dissolve easily, making quantification a problem. But lack of clear statistics should not lessen our sense of the impact these groups have had on the participants and the families and friends of participants.

Structure: Gender Equality. The consciousness-raising group has been the primary microstructure for mobilizing women to stand for gender equality. It is, as we have suggested, a structure that both promotes and issues from feminist consciousness, a "feminist method," as Catharine MacKinnon (1982:21) names it. Its accomplishments are so deep and so broad as to defy cataloging. Here we emphasize three major ways consciousness raising helps women in the struggle for gender equality:

1. It increases women's self-esteem as individuals and as members of a disadvantaged but worthy group.
2. It helps women identify, confront, and articulate the source of their oppression.
3. It helps women work out their own theory of feminism, which lets them return to the world better prepared to cope with and to change the unequal system of gender.

Consciousness-raising groups contribute immediately to members' esteem by asserting the importance of women's subjective experience—of how women feel about life as they live it. Raised and living in a male-dominated society, women are socialized to believe the significant world is the world of the public, the expert, the external, a world from which they are excluded or in which they are second-class citizens. Within the consciousness-raising group there are no experts; the external world of achievement yields to the internal world of beliefs and understandings; and the experiences of the private sphere are valued in themselves.

But as MacKinnon (1982:27–28) sees, there is an even deeper sense in which the valuing of the subjective is essential to women's self-esteem. Women in American society are the ultimate object. One of the primary lessons of the adolescent girl is that her great "achievement" is not to achieve, not to be a doer, a subject, a shaper, but to become the object of, the reward for, some male's doing, shaping, and achieving. The woman learns to look at herself as a product, which some male may wish to possess. Consciousness raising puts her back as the subject or center of action and of being.

As they move to the analytic stage of consciousness raising, women confront the causes of their oppression and objectification. The group experience becomes essential in this confrontation for two reasons. First, by seeing that her experience is shared by other women, the individual woman can realize that her feelings and her situation are, to reassert C. Wright Mills' famous distinction, "social issues" not "private problems" (this distinction is cited in Carden, 1974, and McDonough, 1980). Until she defines the causes of her oppression as social rather than personal, the woman cannot find solutions because she habitually looks in the wrong place, turning inward, seeking therapy, believing the world is well but she is sick.

The group experience affirms her worth as an individual and as a member of a disadvantaged group that has survived and achieved despite its oppression. She knows that the problem is social, not personal. Burton (1972:36–38) describes reaching this conclusion:

> However, one quickly realizes that there are no personal "solutions" possible. This is because it is not a personal "problem."

> Massive social change must occur: establishment of daycare centers, equal pay for equal work, re-education of children, etc. Thus the personal group becomes of necessity a political action. This is what is meant by the current maxim: The personal is political.

Repeatedly the consciousness-raising group leads women to the same conclusion as sociologists and feminist scholars and theorists: the arrangements of personal, private life are not separate from the power arrangements of society, but are shaped by these power ("political") arrangements.

The group experience is equally important in empowering the woman to face this understanding of her situation. The woman in the consciousness-raising group sees that she is oppressed by a patriarchal system because she is a woman. This vision involves a series of potentially dangerous admissions and rejections. It acknowledges that the males the woman has been trained to look to for protection are also oppressors— are, indeed, protectors because they are first part of the oppressive system of patriarchy. Acknowledging the male as oppressor, in turn, threatens a key identity for most women, the relation to some male. The relation does not have to be abandoned, but it cannot be continued in its conventional form once this confrontation has occurred.

At this critical stage, the group support of other women seems absolutely necessary, because if, as most sociologists believe, "identities are socially bestowed, . . . [t]hey must also be socially sustained and fairly steadily so. One cannot be human all by oneself, and apparently one cannot hold on to any particular identity all by oneself" (Berger, 1967:100). This principle is confirmed by Cassell's reports of interviews with women who found they needed the support of the consciousness-raising group or some part of the women's movement in order to hold onto the new image of self as woman in a larger society that genuinely does not believe in the absolute equality of men and women.

The consciousness-raising group, then, is the feminist social structure that allows women to see themselves in a new way, as equal beings, with equal rights to the world's resources, with equal rights to choose, with equal rights to have the world before them. But that consistent repetition of the theme of equal rights to choose and to be makes women with raised consciousness deeply aware that they can claim no more than equal rights—as women, as members of a race, a class, a religion, a nation. And it is this vision that makes feminism such a potent force for human liberation.

Friendship

Friendship is the conventional social structure probably most amenable to women's needs, but under the impact of the movement, women have come to reassert and redefine friendship in general and friendship with other women in particular as central relations in their lives. We say "reassert" and "redefine," because throughout women's history, friendships between women have been regarded as the central relationship of life by many women. But this vision has always had to compete with the male definition of heterosexual love as the key relation in a woman's life. Women today, while not necessarily rejecting heterosexuality and friendships with men, are again affirming the absolute value of friendships with other women. We will see why friendship is so significant for women's liberation as we look at the content and participatory structure of friendship and at how women have used friendship to promote gender equality.

Structure: Content. The content of friendship as a social structure has encouraged it as a relationship for women. We can say that friendship involves two main meaning systems, values and emotional expression. The distinction between "friend" and other similar relations, such as "colleague," "acquaintance," or "support network member," is that these others may have a rational-goal meaning system at their core; the people in them come together to exchange aid. But in friendship persons are drawn together by a mutually voluntary recognition of emotional attachment, usually based on some perception of the value (as a form of "the good," not as "usefulness") of the other.

Power in a friendship, then, tends to be equal because each person's main resource is the expression of liking or the threat of the withdrawal of such expression. Even in instances where people stand in unequal power relations in other social structures, if they are friends, within that relationship their power is equal.

Within the structure of friendship, one defines the other and expects to be defined as a particular individual. Ascribed statuses are accepted as simply part of the makeup of the friend. One is expected to value the collective experience of the friendship above oneself and to be willing to sacrifice for a friend. The ideal typical interaction of friendship is cooperation, which may take two main forms: friends embarking on joint projects or one friend taking as her project the aiding of another in reaching the other's goal. This cooperative interaction covers both concrete activities of aid and the subtler but equally important task of sharing in the social construction of reality through intimate conversation.

Structure: Participation. Women, under current gender arrangements, have a greater probability of fulfilling the structural demands of friendship than do men. As noted in Chapters 3 and 4, women's gender-role socialization prepares them to be more expressive, more supportive, and more nurturant than men. Further, women's experience of powerlessness in most areas of social life makes them value more and be more at ease in an essentially egalitarian structure in which one must seek consensus (see the discussion of Gilligan, 1982, in Chapter 4). And left by traditional gender arrangements to the organization of the private sphere of life, women have found friendship as primary a social structure as men seem to have found business networks.

Contemporary studies suggest that women's use of friendship as a social structure is much greater than men's. Lillian Rubin (1983b:24), reporting the results of "interviews about friendship with over 200 men and women—married, divorced, and single—[ranging] in age from 30 to 55 and [coming] from all walks of life," found that "over two thirds of the single men couldn't name a best friend, and those who could were much more likely to name a woman than a man. By contrast over three fourths of the single women had no problem in identifying a best friend, and almost always that person was a woman." Rubin further found that among the married persons, many more men than women named their spouse as their best friend; the married women, even when they named their husband as best friend, almost always included the name of one or more women friends to whom they also felt they could turn in distress.

Structure: Gender Equality. Friendship in America today is an increasingly important social structure in the promotion of gender equality. On the one hand, friendship between women is (1) a positive assertion of the essential worth of the female, (2) a source for constructing a meaningful social reality in which males need not dominate, and (3) a support in the process of thinking through change. On the other hand, as the traditional family diminishes in numbers and the concept of "friends as family" gains currency in people's thinking, women's ability to create and maintain friendships becomes an increasingly important social resource for both women and men.

Because women live in a world in which their self-worth is often determined by males—husbands, teachers, employers—the selection of another woman as a close or best friend becomes an important positive assertion about oneself. In selecting another woman as a friend, a woman is affirming that women can be people of value and that friendship between women can be rewarding in itself and does not need the sanction of a male presence. A woman respondent in Robert Bell's *Worlds of Friendship* (1981:20) explained:

> There is a special quality of friendship that I feel for my woman friends that I don't feel for men. It's the shared experience of having grown up as females, of knowing we share many common experiences. Because the man has always had it a bit better you often feel somewhat second class in friendships with men. If it's not sexual then it often seems to be that you are a bit patronized in the relationship.

Women seeking to make changes or having changes thrust upon them may see friendships with other women as significant social supports, making it possible to construct a personal reality in which a male does not have to play the dominant role. There are varieties of evidence that women are choosing to construct these new personal realities. For instance, Bell (1981:70) explains that the majority of men who divorce in their forties and fifties remarry, but the majority of women do not:

> The number of women not remarrying may be a reflection of the low number of available men for remarriage. But probably more important is the option not to remarry. There is some evidence that that option is strongly supported by friendship networks of women of similar age and

marital status. The friends provide the means for a social and interpersonal life without a husband. It also seems clear that women are better able to adapt to not having a husband than is the man to not having a wife.

What these women find in their relationships with female friends is summed up by a 45-year-old female attorney (Bell, 1981:64):

> I have four close women friends. I can be completely honest and self-revealing because they know everything about me. I can talk about all kinds of personal things. I think that friendships are more important than marriage. To have no friends would be worse than to have no marriage.

Friendships with other women are repeatedly reported as important supports in the process of change. Friends help one to articulate and confirm one's sense of reality. Cassell (1977:32) describes how one woman was helped by "her new women's liberation friends [who] had terms to describe the behavior of [her] husband . . . 'sexist' or 'oppressive.' " Naturally, friends' support need not always be critical of another. And even women who are not seeking change can be supportive of women friends who are.

Women's social power, and hence gender equality, may be advanced by the emerging social structure of "friends as family," people forming groups to serve many traditional functions of the conventional family bound by friendship rather than kinship. This trend seems an understandable outcome of a variety of changes in American life: half the couples married since 1970 are now divorced; the average American moves once every three years; over the last decade, the number of males living alone has doubled and the number of females living alone has increased by 60 percent; and the number of unmarried couples living together has more than tripled (Lindsey, 1981). It is estimated that by 1990 only half the households in the United States will consist of husband, wife, and young children—a decline of three-fourths from 1960 (Masnick and Bane, 1980). These statistics make obvious the difficulty of maintaining the traditional family unit as the center for celebration and support.

Networks

If friendship seems the social structure to which women's gender socialization leads them, networking seems an alien structure. In developing networks, women have quite consciously imitated what men in American society seem to have more or less unconsciously evolved.

Structure: Content.   A network operates in a rational-goal meaning system. The purpose for knowing other people in the network is that they may serve some end, often career advancement. This open rationalism stands in opposition to the meaning system of friendship, in which one voluntarily values the other and the relationship as an end in itself. In networks, one is there to use and to be used. This use is not necessarily manipulative; it may be simple influence—one is hired because one is most qualified for the position, but one learns about the position *via* the network.

But the network can also play the power game folk wisdom identifies as "not-what-but-who-you-know." Within the network, the individual is recognized primarily as a member of the collectivity, the network. Often persons move into the network via a prep school or college connection (hence, the pun on "old school tie"). The basic form of interaction is cooperation. But the form of cooperation is based on exchange: You recommend me and I'll recommend you.

Structure: Participation. Women's participation within conventional business and academic networks has been difficult for several reasons. Often the woman lacked the appropriate entry vehicle of proper school attendance or military service or athletic achievement. And even if she met the basic entry requirement, those who could have introduced her did not perceive her as a serious candidate for professional life. When women did gain admittance, it was usually on the terms "judge me as an individual," which meant that women within networks could not help other women the way men helped other men. An additional barrier is that most women are not psychologically comfortable in a structure in which it is all right to use people (Gilligan, 1982). Women are socialized to value relationships more than outcomes; networks value relationships because they produce outcomes.

Structure: Gender Equality. To overcome these disabilities, women have consciously imitated male networks and formed their own all-female networks. As women have returned to the public work sphere, they have increasingly formed spontaneous networks at home and on the job to help handle the dual demands of career and home. Networks have also been formed among older college students returning to college. Some women also speak of developing "networks for emotional support." Professional and business women have formed career networks, with regular meetings designed for exchange of information about jobs, courses, and possible opportunities. A newspaper reporter described one such meeting:

> Business cards and resumes fly furiously at their monthly luncheon meetings. . . . Members announce job openings and receive a membership directory, listing each woman's training, interests and current career title. At the end of the meeting, there is a "business card drop" where each woman puts her card into a pile and draws one out. Each woman contacts the woman whose card she's drawn and meets her for lunch. (Krucoff: The Washington Post, January 21, 1980)

Finally, networks of feminists and coalitions of women's groups function as a basic power resource in the drive for gender equality.

The very conscious sense of design behind the growth of these women's networks is captured in the title and purpose of Mary Scott Welch's how-to book, *Networking: The Great New Way for Women to Get Ahead* (1980). Welch's goal is to explain how networks have developed and how contacts made in these networks have been used for information, advice, ideas, and moral support. Welch describes groups like Women's Forum, Inc., in New York City, which includes among its 155 members Bella Abzug, Barbara Walters, and Erica Jong, and the "River Oaks Breakfast Club," a gathering of professional women in Houston, Texas. She notes that there are music networks, sports networks (a basketball league of female attorneys), and support networks (battered wives discussion groups). In her appendix, Welch presents sample by-laws and organization plans and a directory of networking groups in the United States and Canada, with names, addresses, phone numbers, and contact persons.

The growth of networks makes clear that women are able to build relationships along the rational model of the network structure. These networks help women achieve greater gender equality by giving them access to inside information on jobs, educational programs, changing jobs, functioning successfully in traditional all-male preserves, asking for promotions, etc. And they can provide support when women encounter discrimination arising out of traditional gender arrangements.

SUMMARY

This chapter has described the structures feminists use to promote gender equality. The most significant of all these structures is the contemporary women's movement, which has had effects on both the larger society and on microstructures. The most important conclusion that can be drawn from an analysis of this movement is that the drive toward gender equality in America today springs from a variety of sources and manifests itself in a multiplicity of forms. The women's movement, in its widest sense, is not the work of a small group of leaders, but an extensive grassroots mobilization, using the term "grass roots" in its basic sense to refer to an uncountable aggregate of ordinary individuals that serves to anchor and nurture a movement. The question of whether this movement can be reversed will be addressed in Chapters 11 and 12.

NOTE

1. See Chapter 11 regarding the recent watering down of Title IX.

9
SOCIAL INSTITUTIONS: NEW ARRANGEMENTS FOR WOMEN*

The changes in meaning and social structure described in Chapters 7 and 8 occurred within a context of societal transformation of which gender equality is an unintended by-product. The largest social structures in the society, institutions such as the economy, education, and the family, have not intentionally functioned to foster gender equality. But changes within them have provided possibilities for increased gender equality. Here we examine how changes in three institutional areas in this century, patterns of employment, education, and family life, provide part of the answer to the question of what has happened to meaning and power arrangements between men and women in the 1980s.

A social institution is a particular type of social structure. It is the structure most sociologists see as the largest building block of society. An institution is distinguished from other social structures, such as formal macro organizations like the women's movement or more informal micro groups like friendships, in that an institution patterns all aspects of an area of life which the society feels concerns all members and in which the society attempts to regulate the behavior of all members. For instance, how you raise your children can have a direct impact on the well-being of others. If children are not properly socialized, they may become destructive of other people's rights and may not be able to provide for themselves as adults. Because of these concerns, the society collectively attempts to

*By Ruth Wallace and Jill Brantley.

regulate marriage and family. This same principle of collective concern explains the institutionalization of education and the economy.

A social institution is further distinguished from other social structures by its past. When we speak about something being institutionalized, we mean not only that it patterns an area of collective concern, but that it has done so for some time. This principle is important when we consider the process of change. An institution usually has persisted through several generations; this persistence over time means that children have been socialized to the institution as a part of their everyday taken-for-granted reality. Further, adults in the course of socializing children have themselves often come to believe more firmly in the institution, because in order to explain and justify it to children, the adults have created or repeated a variety of legitimations. Legitimations are the after-the-fact reasons people give for why an institution is the way it is. In Chapter 3, when we described conventional beliefs we were describing the legitimations for our institutions of gender.

Institutions, thus, are the social structures most resistant to fluctuation, because they are so widespread, involve so many people, affect nearly all aspects of life within the sphere they pattern, and have been part of most people's social reality from birth. Change within institutions tends to be gradual or evolutionary rather than immediate or revolutionary. Sudden institutional change often confronts people with conditions of disorientation such as "future shock," in Alvin Toffler's (1970) popular phrase.

The changes we will be looking at in this chapter in economy, education, and family occurred over a period of time extending from at least 1900—and that date is really only a socially conventional cutoff. The rate of these changes has accelerated over the last twenty-five years, with important consequences for the movement toward gender equality. For the slow, massive patterns of institutional change have resulted in (1) women's increased participation in the labor force; (2) women's increased involvement in higher education; and (3) women's transformed position in the family, with increased control over the reproductive process and the re-patterning of family roles. This chapter focuses on these institutional changes, describing them, explaining them, and drawing out their implications for gender equality.

There are two qualifications to everything we are about to say. First, the institutional trends we describe are incomplete, leaving a great deal still to be done if full equality is ever to be realized. Often too, they have generated new problems, such as sharp patterns of occupational segregation and a growing problem of sexual harassment at work and in higher education. We will note these issues of continuing inequality, but our interest is in change *toward* equality, and our account will focus on that.

The second qualification relates to the fact that we treat the changes described in this chapter as products of forces other than the women's movement. Yet none of these changes can in fact be wholly divorced from the women's movement. As we have repeatedly emphasized, that movement has shaped both the pace and direction of change by disseminating ideas and providing new power resources; it has enabled women to enter the labor force in greater numbers, to enter traditionally all-male professions, to return to school, to take control of their reproductive capacities. But we must understand the context in which these accomplishments have been possible. The women's movement has been a factor in Western history for four hundred years, feminist scholars argue. In this chapter we try to think concretely (as we thought theoretically in Chapter 6) about the institutional changes that have given the women's movement, in contemporary times, its quite considerable degree of success.

FEMALE PARTICIPATION IN THE LABOR FORCE

Many sociologists regard the economy as the basic institution of society (the family is the other contender for this position). The economy is the institution that patterns the production and distribution of goods and services and thus determines the distribution of the necessities of biological existence. As we stressed in Chapter 6, not to participate directly as a wage earner in a capitalist economy is to be dependent on others for one's subsistence. The condition of not being a direct wage earner or having a direct personal source of income is one that women and children shared within capitalism. It is a condition that has changed dramatically in the past twenty-five years. In this section we describe, explain, and discuss the significance for gender equality of two major changes in the economy:

1. Women's increased participation in the labor force
2. The evolution of the types of jobs women hold.

Increased Participation

Descriptors of Participation. Census data in 1980 reported that women represented 43 percent of the total work force in America and that 52 percent of working-age women held paid jobs. This was the first time in American history that census data have shown the majority of women of working age in the labor force. Further, as we can see from Figure 9–1, much of this increase in female participation has occurred since 1960. Between 1960 and 1980, female participation increased 17 percent from 34.5 to 51.6, compared to an increase between 1940 and 1960 of 9.1 percent. And predictions for 1990 of the percentage of working-age women in the work force vary from 54 to 61 percent, and for 1995, from 58 to 65 percent (Waite, 1981:35). If the most extreme of these predictions is correct, two-thirds of all working-age women will be employed in paid jobs by 1995.

Significance. These changes in labor-force participation are tremendously significant for the movement toward gender equality. They provide women with new power resources and also the possibility of new ideas through contact with other women in the workplace and through reflection on their own workplace experience.

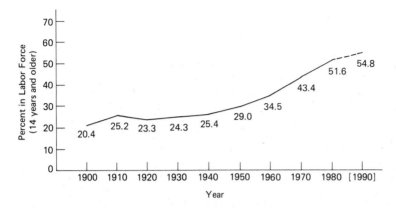

FIGURE 9–1   Female Labor Force Participation: 1900–1990
    Sources: For 1900 to 1960, U.S. Bureau of the Census, in Oppenheimer
    (1970:3). For 1970, *Employment and Training Report of the President, 1981:*
    Table A-1. For 1980, U.S. Bureau of the Census, *Current Population Reports,*
    Series 60-127:5. For projected 1990 percentage, Smith (1979:13–15).

The fact that women are earning money and thus directly supplying
at least some of their own material needs increases their sense of power in
two vital areas. First, the women experience an immediate gain in their
sense of the power of work, sociologically understood as the ability to
change the environment by the effort of one's body. The woman who
works at home—and as one bumper sticker has noted, "Every mother is a
working mother"—is certainly using her body to change her environment.
But she is given no sense in terms of power of the worth of those efforts.

In joining the paid labor force, the woman discovers that her work
can increase her power of domination. Domination is the control of
scarce, necessary resources. In a capitalist economy, for the wage earner,
money is the vital resource. The woman who joins the paid labor force
experiences an immediate increase in her sense of control over a necessary resource. No matter how small the wage and how much that wage
may already be committed to the paying of the family expenses, the
woman now knows that she can provide in part for her and her family's
subsistence. She is no longer dependent on a male who "goes to work"
and is the "breadwinner."

In a capitalist system, the sense that one can support oneself, can do
something for which others will give money, is an extraordinarily important element in self-esteem. The woman who has never held a job or has
not held one for years has doubts about her ability to work, to move into
that public sphere where the male daily "fights" to "win" a living. Once
the woman has successfully moved into the employment system, she can
reflect on her abilities with a new sense of confidence. She may also begin
to reflect on certain inequities between male and female workers in that
system. And given the nature of work today, she will have other women
with whom to share her experience.

As more women move into the labor force, all women's visions potentially change what constitutes the proper sphere for female activity. Isabel Sawhill, former director of the National Commission for Manpower, sees the difference greater female participation in the labor force makes as follows: "To me these trends suggest a whole new set of social expectations among the younger generation and indeed we have evidence of a marked shift in attitude about 'women's place,' especially among the young and well-educated" (Waite, 1981:3). More females in the labor force mean that for increasing numbers of women, the public sphere of paid employment is a proper sphere for female activity.

Causes.   There is much debate about what has caused the increased female participation in the labor force. We have hypothesized (in Chapter 6) that this increase is due to the transformation of the American economy from one based on the production of goods to one based on the production of services. These services range from increased health and welfare benefits such as insurance companies, therapy programs, and medical care, to increased leisure activities such as courses in sports, dancing, and art, to increased conveniences such as retail sales and fast foods. The distinctive difference between an economy based on the production of goods and one based on the production of services is that goods-based production requires heavy amounts of machinery, whereas service-based production requires many workers—that is, it is "labor-intensive." Goods-based production can, up to a point, reduce costs by improving machinery. Service-based production finds most of its costs in labor and therefore seeks cheap labor. One ready source of cheap labor has been women returning to the work force part-time or to provide a second income (Rothschild, 1981).

Many social scientists are now concerned over where the economy will move next, and how long and how fully a service economy can be self-sustaining. You may have heard indications of this concern in discussions about the continuing deficit in international trade with countries like Japan, which have become more efficient factory-based producers of goods. From the standpoint of workers, especially female workers, a concern must be that a labor-intensive economy can increase profits only by serving more or by cutting wages. In either instance, as public school teachers are already discovering, this means pressure on the worker in the form of loss of wages or increased working hours. And either of these developments would threaten the precarious power base women have established in the labor force.

The Evolution of the Jobs Women Hold

Descriptors of Job Change.   We need to look at two types of changes here: (1) the movement of women into occupations normally dominated by males; and (2) changes in the types of occupations dominated by females. We describe these changes by the use of Tables 9–1 and 9–2, and Figures 9–2, 9–3, and 9–4.

Table 9–1   Occupational Distribution of Women in the Labor Force: 1900, 1920, 1940, 1960, 1980

Major Occupation Group	PERCENT DISTRIBUTION				
	1900	1920	1940	1960	1980
Professional/technical	8	12	13	12	19
Managers/officials	1	2	3	4	8
Clerical	4	19	22	29	39
Sales	4	6	7	8	4
Craft	1	1	1	1	2
Operatives	24	20	20	16	14
Nonfarm laborers	3	2	1	1	1
Private household	29	16	18	8	1
Service	7	8	11	13	12
Farm workers	19	14	4	2	.3
Total	100%	100%	100%	94%*	100.3%+

Sources: For 1900, 1940, 1960, Bancroft, *The American Labor Force,* and U.S. Bureau of the Census, in Oppenheimer (1970:149). For 1920, Mandle (1979:47). For 1980, Rytina (1982:25–31).
*The 1960 percentages do not add up to 100 because 5.8 percent of the women had no occupation listed.
+The 1980 percentages do not add up to 100 because of rounding.

   Table 9–1 reveals the distribution of women in the census occupational categories at five points in time: 1900, 1920, 1940, 1960, and 1980. We can see that the percentages have at least doubled since 1900 in the following occupational groupings: professional/technical, managers/officials, clerical, and craft. Occupational groups that show female decreases by at least one-half are nonfarm laborers, farm workers, and private household. Note that the two groupings showing a slow but steady increase from 1900 to 1960 and an accelerated increase between 1960 and 1980 are in the professional/technical and managerial categories. This might suggest a movement into formerly "male" occupations, but we know from our examination of the gender distribution within these categories in Chapter 5 that female professionals, for example, are still primarily nurses and elementary school teachers in the 1980 data.

   Let us summarize the changes in the way women are now distributed in the work force compared to their distribution in 1900. Some occupations are virtually disappearing, such as female farmworkers, private household workers, and nonfarm laborers. Although there has been an overall decrease of women in the blue-collar and service categories since 1900, a potentially significant shift is hidden in these data— namely, the large influx of women into the skilled trades (craft and kindred). Though the increase is only 1 percent, this represents a doubling of women in the craft categories in the last twenty years. The number of female machinists, for instance, has almost tripled, from 6,700 in 1960 to 19,000 in 1980, and the numbers of female electricians

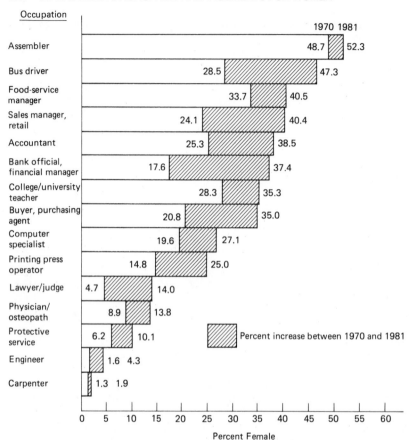

FIGURE 9-2 Percentage of Females Employed in Selected Occupations, 1970 and 1981
Source: Janet L. Norwood, *The Female-Male Earnings Gap: A Review of Employment and Earnings Issues,* Bureau of Labor Statistics Report 673 (Washington, D.C.: U.S. Department of Labor, 1982), p. 8.

and tool and die makers have quadrupled, from 2,500 in 1960 to 10,000 in 1980, and from 1,100 in 1960 to 5,000 in 1980.

Women are being found in other new locations in the work force. In Figure 9–2 we present the increases between 1970 and 1981 in the percentages of females employed in some traditionally male occupations. Assemblers have become predominantly female, with women constituting slightly over half of this occupational group by 1981. In three of the occupations—bank and financial managers, lawyers and judges, and engineers—female workers have more than doubled in percentage over the past decade. Other traditionally male occupations in which females have increased over 10 percent since 1970 are bus drivers (18.8 percent), sales managers, retail (16.3 percent), buyers/purchasing agents

(14.2 percent), accountants (13.2 percent), and printing press operators (10.2 percent).

Six of the occupations in Figure 9–2 are in the professional-technical category: accountants, college/university teachers, computer specialists, lawyers/judges, physicians/osteopaths, and engineers. Four are managerial-administrative: food service managers, sales managers (retail), bank officials/financial managers, and buyers/purchasing agents. Two are craft: printing press operators and carpenters. Two are operatives: assemblers and bus drivers. The remaining occupations are in the protective service sector: police, guards, firefighters.

Obviously some of these jobs—like bus drivers, police, physicians, lawyers, and college teachers—are more visible to the general public than others. But, in fact, only 10 percent of police were women in 1981 and only 14 percent lawyers and physicians. This may seem surprising, because you are seeing more female police officers, lawyers, and professors. This new visibility is a result of former paucity—there seem to be many more because we notice women in these fields. Your own world may indeed include a higher percentage of many of these women, but keep in mind that Figure 9–2 depicts the national scene.

Politics is another occupation that is becoming a new location for American women. While females have always been active in politics as secretaries and unpaid campaign helpers, they have only recently been winning elections to office themselves. Only able to vote since 1920, when the Nineteenth Amendment passed, women are latecomers to the political scene and are only beginning to exercise their political power.[1]

As you can see in Figure 9–3, women are most visible in the state legislatures, where their proportion has increased slowly but steadily and significantly, from 5 percent in 1971 to 13 percent in 1983. Representation in some states is better than others, of course. There were seven states where the proportion of women legislators was over 20 percent in 1982: New Hampshire (29 percent), West Virginia (24 percent), Colorado and Maine (23 percent), and Connecticut, Oregon, and Vermont (22 percent). And there were six states where women made up less than 5 percent of the legislators in 1982: Alabama, Arkansas, Pennsylvania, and Tennessee (4 percent), and Louisiana and Mississippi (1 percent) (National Women's Political Caucus, 1982). Because experience in state legislatures facilitates the movement to other political positions, organizations like the National Women's Political Caucus are focusing on the support of female candidates for state legislatures in the 1980s. (Personal communication with staff at Washington, D.C., office of the National Women's Political Caucus, March 1983).

Figure 9–3 also shows an increase in female mayors from only 1 percent in 1971 to 8 percent in 1983, the greatest increase in the figure, since women mayors increased eight times whereas female state legislators only doubled. The percentages on mayors include cities of over 30,000, so the base number of mayors has increased from 695 in 1971 to 854 in 1983 (National Women's Political Caucus, 1982). There has also been a minuscule 1 percent increase of females in the U.S. Congress since 1971.

FIGURE 9–3 Women Mayors and Women in the United States Congress and State Legislatures, 1971–1983
Sources: Municipal Yearbooks, 1971–1981, and National Women's Political Caucus, *1982 National Directory of Women Elected Officials.*

Of the elected women officials, the least visible are those in Congress. Women constitute only 2 out of 100 senators and 21 out of 435 representatives, although women are 52 percent of the population.[2]

We have been discussing occupations that provide women with qualitatively new experiences. But there have also been changes in the traditionally female occupations. Table 9–2 depicts the rank ordering of the ten leading female occupations from the census years 1900, 1920, 1940, 1960, and 1980. As we can see, there has been quite a turnover of the top ten occupations since 1900. The top ten female occupations around 1900 were chiefly farm and home-related. For most of the women workers of 1900 the workplace was in the home, with the exception of teachers and saleswomen. The decline of agriculture, the growth of service industries, and other shifts in the industrial composition of American society are reflected in the top ten occupations of 1920 and 1940. By 1940, farm occupations had disappeared from the top ten list, and women workers began to move out into the urban wage sector. Women in the work force in 1940 had a qualitatively different experience than female workers of 1900.

By 1980, the female move into the public sphere had accelerated, private household occupations had disappeared from the top ten list, and increased reliance on technology and bureaucratic organization was evident among women workers. Four of the top ten occupations were cleri-

TABLE 9–2 The Ten Leading Occupations of Women Workers: 1900, 1920, 1940, 1960, 1980*

Rank	1900	1920	1940	1960	1980
1	Servants	Other servants	Servants (private family)	Steno-graphers, typists, and secretaries	Secretaries
2	Farm laborers (family members)	Teachers (school)	Steno-graphers, typists, and secretaries	Other clerical workers	Book-keepers
3	Dress-makers	Farm laborers (home farm)	Teachers (n.e.c.)	Private household workers	Teachers (elementary school)
4	Teachers	Steno-graphers and typists	Clerical and kindred (n.e.c.)	Sales-women	Nurses, registered
5	Laundry work (hand)	Other clerks (except in stores)	Sales-women (n.e.c.)	Teachers (elementary school)	Miscel-laneous clerical
6	Farmers and planters	Laundresses (not in laundry)	Operators, apparel and accessories	Book-keepers	Typists
7	Farm and plantation laborers	Sales-women (stores)	Bookkeepers, accountants and cashiers	Waitresses	Managers and adminis-trators (n.e.c.)
8	Sales-women	Bookkeepers and cashiers	Waitresses (except private family)	Miscellan-eous operators	Sewers and stitchers
9	House-keepers and stewards	Cooks	House-keepers (private family)	Nurses, registered	Nursing aides, orderlies, and at-tendants
10	Seam-stresses	Farmers (general farms)	Trained nurses and student nurses	Other ser-vice work-ers (except private household)	Sales-clerks (retail)

Sources: U.S. Bureau of the Census: for 1900, 1920, 1940, and 1960, in Berch (1982:12–13); for 1980, in Rytina (1982:25–31).

*Categories are given in order of size and according to each census, regardless of changes in definition.

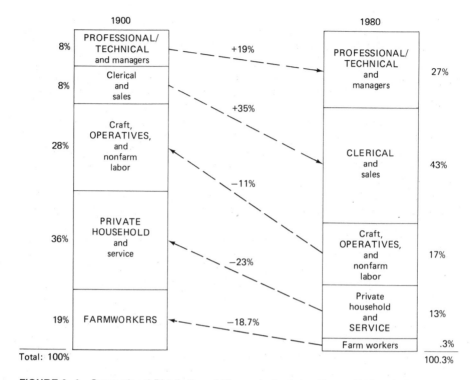

FIGURE 9–4   Occupational Distribution of Women in the Labor Force, 1900 and 1980 (based on Table 9–1)
Where categories have been collapsed, we used capital letters to show which category is predominant.

cal (secretaries, bookkeepers, miscellaneous clerical, and typists). There is also evidence of increasing professionalization in the 1980 census data, as two of the top four occupations are teachers and nurses; in addition, a managerial category appeared for the first time.

One way to summarize the changes in the distribution of females in the work force since 1900 is to compare the 1900 with the 1980 data. By collapsing some of the categories from Table 9–1, we can provide a picture of the shifts over the past eighty years (see Figure 9–4). The most dramatic changes are the 35 percent increase in female clerical and sales workers, and the 23 percent decrease in private household and service workers. As we noted earlier, the experience of females as farm workers has virtually disappeared. While the 19 percent increase in female professional/technical and managerial workers may also seem to change the configuration of the female work force, we should keep in mind that most of the professional increases are among elementary school teachers and registered nurses. Nonetheless, as depicted by the direction of the arrows in Figure 9–4, the dramatic increases of women in white-collar categories have been accompanied by large decreases in the blue-collar, private household, service, and farm worker categories.

These rather substantial changes in the way women are distributed in the work force do indeed represent new experiences for women workers. But the changes in distribution cannot be interpreted as a massive retreat from women's jobs. Women are located in the public sphere of work, but most of them are located primarily in low-paying "women's" occupations; there is still gender job segregation.

Significance. These changes in areas of employment have helped increase gender equality. The fact that women can now look for jobs in a wide variety of occupations means that women's chances of finding employment are more nearly equal to men's—though there is still definitely a gender gap in employment opportunity. The possibility of movement into traditionally male occupations has improved many women workers' self-esteem, as these jobs are often more highly regarded, simply by virtue of being seen as "men's work," and nearly always better paid than corresponding women's work.

There are indications that the new experiences these women are having in nontraditional jobs have led to power shifts and to a receptivity to new meanings. Walshok's book on blue-collar women (1981) is replete with such evidence. She describes the women in skilled jobs whom she interviewed thus (1981:151–152): "They had high levels of satisfaction, defined their work as interesting and challenging, and reported increasing levels of competence and self-confidence as a result of their experiences." One of Walshok's subjects, a young woman working as a cable splicer for a telephone company, put it this way (Walshok, 1981:151): "I always lacked self-confidence in myself, and this is helping a lot because it is something that I want real bad. I'm pushing myself a lot on it, and I'm showing myself I can do things that I didn't think I could do."

Another woman described the challenge of her work as an auto mechanic this way (Walshok, 1981:144–145):

> I found what I really liked when I was working in the shop was that my body felt better, I was getting exercise, and I need exercise really bad because I'm so out of shape, and that was really important to me, that my job wasn't a sit-down job, I liked that. It got hard at times, you know, where your body was pooped out, but then it feels good because you felt you had exercised so you had more energy in the long run. And doing something with your hands was kind of cool, because you could see what you were doing. Actually see the results—when you fixed a car it ran—the immediate satisfaction, and that's something I never have had on a job. In a factory you don't see where it's going or anything, so that's cool, plus you know that you did it. It's like solving a puzzle—when you get the answer—yeah!

On the other hand, negative experience in the workplace may also play a part in increasing a demand for gender equality among women employed in traditionally female jobs. As we have seen, the jobs dominated by females have changed dramatically within this century, from private services such as servants and seamstresses, to clerical workers. This change, as noted earlier, is a result of transformations within the economy. Nevertheless, the woman who moves into an office position finds herself part of a bureaucracy that claims to select the most qualified persons for its positions and to provide clear statements of what each position entails. The woman in this work situation can make a better evaluation of her own skills relative to other workers than might have been possible for a woman in private employment as a housekeeper or seamstress. Women doing clerical work in large offices have a first-hand opportunity to see how well they perform and how well others, perhaps often male supervisors, perform, and who is really doing what work. This experience has produced the impetus for the movement for equal pay for comparable work.

The bureaucratic emphasis on clearly stated job descriptions has helped women workers distinguish and substantiate differences between exploitation as "office wife" and employment in the duties in their job description. Awareness of discrepancies between actual tasks and stated position duties has led women into protests, like the one described in Chapter 7 for the secretary who refused to make coffee. The secretary who refuses to make coffee may be emerging as a sort of mythic figure symbolically representing all the women workers who are willing to do what their job demands, but are unwilling to be exploited as "chief nurturer" of workplace males simply because they are the same gender as these males' original primary caregivers.

Further, this change in employment does for women what Marx saw clearly the factory system did for workers in the nineteenth century: the bringing together of many women workers in one place provides, however unintentionally, the opportunity for feminine/feminist definition of conditions in that place to emerge. Not only are women able to talk together, but they become acquainted with other working women, in both traditional and nontraditional occupations, they can find new role models and mentors, and they can form networks for career advancement.

Causes of the Change.   The transformation of American society and of the global economy in the postindustrial age has changed the types of labor and the types of occupations most in need of workers. Even job categories that have retained the same title may now refer to a very different type of work. For instance, the category of "assembler" no longer necessarily refers to someone involved in putting together large machinery or automobiles on an assembly line; it also refers to the worker engaged in the detail-oriented work of assembling small transistorized parts for electronic appliances. This is work to which women, socialized to attend to detail and often to do close work with their hands, are particularly well suited.

This postindustrial age is characterized by a bureaucratic form of organization in nearly all major institutions of life; the economy, education, health and welfare, and even religion, as well as government, are conducted according to bureaucratic principles of clear job descriptions, hierarchical arrangements, and written records. This last requirement has called into being huge numbers of clerical workers, many of whom are women because our conventional gender arrangements make it possible for employers to pay them less.

FEMALE PARTICIPATION IN EDUCATION

Education is the institution that patterns the distribution of knowledge, just as the economy patterns the distribution of goods and services. And education is in many ways as closely tied to patterns of stratification and segregation as the economy. The right to possess and the actual possession of various types of knowledge are ways persons are stratified and segregated by educational experience. In this section, as we explore the significance for gender equality of the increased participation of women in higher education and the movement of women into traditionally male-dominated academic fields, we again seek to understand why women have made this movement at this time.

Description of Women's Participation

Table 9–3 is an aerial view of the proportion of B.A., M.A., and Ph.D. degrees awarded to women in 1900, 1930, 1960, and 1980. The overall trend is toward increasing proportions of college degrees being awarded to women. This trend is comparable to the trend we discussed in the previous section regarding women's participation in the labor force. There has been a dramatic increase in the proportion of degrees going to women overall, from 17 percent in 1900 to 49 percent in 1980, a 32 percent rise. In general, then, we can say that the institution of higher education has become a new location for women, just as the work force has. However, if we examine the various levels of higher education, we see that the female location is primarily on the lower rungs of the higher education ladder, at the bachelor's and master's levels. Female doctoral recipients, who were barely visible in 1900, have steadily increased, from 6 percent in 1900 to 30 percent in 1980.

While the bulk of bachelor's, master's, and doctoral degrees con-

TABLE 9–3   Proportion of Degrees Awarded to Women: 1900, 1930, 1960, 1980

| Year | All Degrees | DEGREE | | |
		Bachelor's	Master's	Doctorate
1900	16.9%	19.7%	19.1%	6.0%
1930	39.5	39.9	40.4	15.4
1960	34.2	35.3	35.1	10.5
1980	48.8	49.2	49.5	29.7

Source: Betty M. Vetter, Eleanor L. Baber, and Susan Jensen-Fisher, *Professional Women and Minorities: A Manpower Data Resource Service* (Washington, D.C.:Scientific Manpower Commission, 1982), p. 27.

ferred on women are still in education, the humanities, and psychology, there has been a slow but steady increase in math, the biological sciences, and the social sciences, and even a slight increase in the physical sciences and engineering (Vetter, 1982:39). In engineering, the most heavily male field, women's degrees have gone from less than 1 percent in 1950 to 9 percent of B.A.s, 7 percent of M.A.s, and 3 percent of Ph.D.s in 1980.

Table 9–4 shows that in 1950, the only "female" fields (those in which over 50 percent of the degrees were conferred on women) were education (65 percent) and humanities (57 percent) at the bachelor's level. By 1980 these two disciplines were "feminized" at the master's level as well, and they were joined by psychology at both levels. (We have designated this by the dotted lines in Table 9–4.) In addition, by 1980 women received close to half (42 and 43 percent) of the B.A. degrees in the "male" fields of mathematics, biological science, and social sciences. In most of these disciplines, the "peak" year for degrees awarded to women was the latest one, 1980. But that is not true for the traditionally feminine fields of education and humanities at the bachelor's level, where the peak year for education (76 percent) was 1965; for humanities (68 percent) it was 1966 (see Vetter, 1982:39). Since then there has been a downward trend in the percentage of female degrees in these two disciplines (though this does not show in Table 9–4 because we are looking at only two points in time), a trend we might label as a "slight defeminization" trend. Giele (1978:267) points out that the people in the most "masculine" fields, like engineering, mathematics, and the physical sciences, enjoy the highest prestige and financial reward; it is not surprising that the movement of women into these fields is both recent and slow.

If, over the next thirty years, the percentage increase remains the same, the only "masculine" fields in 2010 will be engineering and the physical sciences, and on the doctoral level only, mathematics. The data in Table 9–4 indicate that women are receiving more degrees in formerly

TABLE 9–4   Percent of Degrees Granted to Women in Selected Fields, 1950 and 1980

	BACHELOR'S			MASTER's			DOCTORATES		
	1950	1980	Increase	1950	1980	Increase	1950	1980	Increase
All Fields	33%	49%	16%	32%	49%	17%	9%	30%	21%
Education	65	73	8	42	70	28	16	45	29
Humanities	56	62	6	38	58	20	18	39	21
Psychology	44	66	22	25	56	31	14	43	29
Mathematics	22	42	20	19	36	17	6	13	7
Biosciences	28	42	14	22	38	16	11	28	17
Social Sciences	22	43	21	23	35	12	8	27	19
Physical Sciences	11	24	13	8	19	11	5	12	7
Engineering	0.5	9	8.5	1	7	6	0.5	3	2.5

Source: Vetter et al. (1982:39).

"masculine" fields at the bachelor's level, and there is slow but steady penetration into male disciplines at the M.A. and Ph.D. levels as well.

More recent (1981) data from the United States Department of Education (1983:78) show mixed results regarding women's greater educational opportunities. Between 1980 and 1981, there have been small increases in percentages of women receiving Ph.D. degrees in some "male" fields. For instance, the female percentage increased from 13 to 15.6 percent in mathematics and from 3 to 4.1 percent in engineering; however, there was virtually no change between 1980 and 1981 in biological sciences (28 to 28.3 percent); and in physical sciences the female percentage of Ph.D. degrees remained the same, 12 percent.

Before concluding this section on educational opportunities for women, we want to take a look at the changes over time with regard to dentistry, medicine, and law. Table 9–5 depicts these changes. In 1950 there were only 18 women in the entire country receiving degrees in dentistry, less than 300 in law, and close to 600 in medicine. The numbers of female degree recipients in all three fields remained small in 1960 and 1970, but as we can see in Table 9–5, there were significant changes in the percentage of women receiving degrees in dentistry, medicine, and law in the 1970s, in the wake of the women's movement. The greatest increase between 1970 and 1980 was in law (24.8 percent), followed by medicine and dentistry, with increases of 15 and 12.4 percent respectively.

By 1981 women were approximately one-third of those receiving law degrees, and one-seventh receiving degrees in dentistry. The percentage of degrees conferred in any field, however, is not the same as the percentage of those who are working full time in those fields. If we turn back to Figure 9–2, we can see that women were only 14 percent of lawyers and physicians working full time in 1981, for instance.

Significance for Gender Equality

Increased participation in education, like increased participation in the economy, provides women with both new power bases and the possibility for new meaning systems.

The chief types of power gained through education are influence, domination, and rational-legal authority. Knowledge presumably makes it possible for the possessor to mount a better argument, to do a particular type of work more effectively. Certainly the feeling that one possesses knowledge gives one greater confidence in presenting an argument. Thus, women with college educations potentially expand their influence both because they do in fact know more than persons without advanced education and because they believe they know more. A part of this "knowing more" should include knowing how to find out what one does not know. Learning how to do research and gaining confidence that they can learn what they need to also increases the possibilities for women to act influentially.

Further, if women acquire particular skills through education, they can use those skills as a scarce resource. The type of policing of member-

TABLE 9–5 Numbers and Percentage of First Professional Degrees Conferred on Women in Dentistry, Medicine, and Law: 1950, 1960, 1970, 1980, 1981

Year	Dentistry*	Medicine[†]	Law[‡]
1950	0.7%	10.4%	3.5% (in 1955)**
	(18)	(584)	(288)
1960	0.8%	5.5%	2.5%
	(26)	(387)	(230)
1970	0.9%	8.4%	5.4%
	(34)	(699)	(801)
1980	13.3%	23.4%	30.2%
	(700)	(3,486)	(10,754)
1981	14.4%	24.7%	32.4%
	(788)	(3,833)	(11,768)

Source: U.S. Department of Education, National Center for Educational Statistics, "Surveys of Earned Degrees Conferred," in Digest of Educational Statistics, 1983 edition.

*D.D.S. or D.M.D.

[†]M.D.

[‡]LL.B. or J.D.

**Data prior to 1955 not shown because they lack comparability with the figures for subsequent years. Number in parentheses is actual number of women.

ship by various professional organizations such as the American Medical Association and the American Bar Association are ways of ensuring that this domination continues. Only persons who have given evidence of successful mastery of a level of education by courses taken and by examinations passed are allowed to practice in the professions.

The possession of a degree thus places the woman within a professional social structure and gives her institutional authority—be it as a doctor, a lawyer, a certified public accountant, a social worker, a registered nurse, or an architect. The woman is now institutionally empowered to do. And the woman who is so institutionally empowered has more power than a man who has not met these educational requirements. Men as well as women find themselves seeking the services of the professional woman.

Besides providing access to new power resources, education also systematically provides the opportunity for reflection. As we noted in Chapter 6, for an individual woman to make changes, she must have an occasion and a reason for reflecting on her present situation. The woman in higher education is given both. At nearly all schools, no matter how technical and narrowly circumscribed the major, general education requirements—in writing, in literature, in history, and in social science—offer both the occasion and the reason for reflection.

Causes of Increased Participation

Again, of course, the women's movement has played a significant role. But let us focus here on the context in which that role has been played.

When a society self-consciously defines itself as an "advanced technological society," a society in which there are vast amounts of "know-how" to be had, education as an institution assumes enormous importance and becomes at once a right and a reward. This has been the situation in the United States in the twentieth century generally and especially since World War II. At the end of World War II, one of the ways a grateful society thanked returning servicemen was through the so-called G.I. Bill, which gave veterans handsome educational benefits. This produced a generation of workers who probably valued education more than any age cohort in American history—valued it perhaps because it was one of the chips they had to play in the game of getting a job and earning a living. Anyone who has a degree has a vested interest in believing that degree stands for a body of knowledge and skill the marketplace should reward. As people earned degrees and entered the economy, they tended to define possession of a degree as necessary for those entering after them. This emphasis on education led, in turn, to a tremendous growth in the numbers of persons going into teaching and in the numbers and size of American colleges and universities. This growth meant that a great many workers had an interest in people continuing to go to school.

The "postwar baby boom"—a period of rather remarkable fertility that ran from roughly the mid-1940s to the mid-1950s—helped ensure use of this expanded educational system, as did Korean war veterans using their G.I. Bill. But as both groups of potential students diminished, an expanded educational system needed to look for new students. One ready source was women, many of whom had perhaps had a little college and then dropped out to marry and raise a family.

Further, in the 1950s and 1960s, as Americans enjoyed unparalled prosperity, they began to extend the benefits of higher education to all their children. Not just the brightest son, but all sons and all daughters were to have a college education. This parental goal was understandably applauded by educators as American colleges and universities experienced the greatest growth in world history.

Thus, a faith in education led to an expanded educational system, which in turn led to a greater emphasis on education, promoting further expansion of the system and leading in the end to a need for new students. One need only listen to college admissions officers today discussing the quest for and impact of the nontraditional student on higher education to see that women moved into a market ready to receive them.

ADJUSTMENTS IN THE FAMILY OF PROCREATION

The family is the institution that patterns the private sphere of life in American society; it is expected to produce from that private sphere an individual capable of contributing in the public sphere. This means that the family must nurture its members materially and emotionally; see that they are clothed, fed, sheltered, educated; pay bills; and run interference between individual members and the outside world of economy, education, and government. Sociologists sometimes divide families in terms of an individual's position in them. The family you are born into is called your "family of orientation," since its function from your standpoint is to socialize you for life in society. The family you create with your marriage partner is your "family of procreation," and in it you socialize your children (who experience your family as the family of orientation).

From the standpoint of women's experience, the major change in family structure is within the family of procreation. In this section we will look at two major changes within that family structure: (1) the trend toward smaller family size, marked by women's assuming more control over reproduction and procreating less; (2) the change in women's duties within that family as they have increasingly become contributors of a second paycheck or sole breadwinners. We will first describe the phenomenon, then consider its significance for gender equality, and then its cause.

The Trend Toward Smaller Family Size

Descriptors of the Trend. At the beginning of the twentieth century, the birth rate was 30 per thousand, as you can see in Figure 9–5, but by 1940 it had dropped to 19.4. In 1945, the beginning of what has been called the "baby boom" period, it increased to 20.4 and remained in the 20s until 1965, which is the beginning of what has been labeled the "baby bust." At that point (1965), the birth rate fell to 19.4 and continued to decrease until 1980, when, as you can see, there was a slight upturn. We include the 1981 figure to show that the 1980s may include a series of downs as well as ups. But at the present, the birth rate is well below the "baby boom" level.

An interesting phenomenon recently, and one that is related to the contraceptive revolution, is the rise in the number of older mothers. In 1980 the greatest increase in fertility was for women between the ages of 30 and 34. There were 131,205 women in that age group who gave birth in 1980, and many of them were mothers for the first time. In fact, the number of births for women between 30 and 34 was up 94 percent over 1975, a rather astounding increase for a five-year interval (National Center for Health Statistics, cited in *Newsweek*, January 17, 1983). Postponing the first child until her career is established means, among other things, that a woman can better afford to buy good childcare, is less likely to drop out of the work force, and therefore is in a more powerful position to negotiate for time and energy expenditures both at home and at work.

One reason why some women are beginning to have their first children later in life is that they postponed marriage in the first place. Since 1960, age at first marriage has been increasing for both sexes in the United States. The median age at first marriage for women, which had been 22.0 in 1890 and 21.3 in 1930, fell to 20.3 in 1960 and then increased to 22.5 in 1982; for men it had been 26.1 in 1890 and 24.3 in 1930, and it dropped to 22.8 in 1960 and then increased to 25.2 in 1982 (National Center for Health Statistics in *Newsweek*, January 17, 1983, and U.S. Census Bureau in

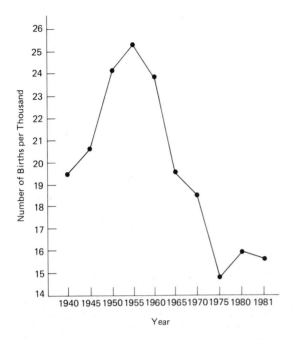

FIGURE 9-5 United States Birth Rates, 1940–1981
Sources: Statistical Abstracts (1981:58), and National Center for Health Statistics, cited in *Newsweek,* January 13, 1983, p. 25.

Washington Post, July 1, 1983). The trend for the last twenty years is toward postponement of first marriages, which allows more time on the job or in school before taking on the responsibilities of marriage and parenthood. Some evidence that occupational aspirations and higher educational attainment leads to postponement of marriage for women was found in a study of 1957 high school graduates. For the females in this study (but not for the males), high occupational aspirations in high school were associated with postponement of marriage, and for both sexes higher educational attainment was associated with later marriage.[3]

Smaller Family Size and Gender Equality. From the standpoint of the mother, the capacity to limit family size brings with it the capacity to plan one's own life without the sense that those plans could always be interrupted by an unexpected pregnancy. This ability to plan makes it feasible to think about a career. Further, the emphasis on smaller families is usually accompanied by a desire to provide more benefits for these fewer children. This desire may serve as an impetus to women to return to the work force.

The control of reproduction that has made smaller family size possible has also made postponing marriage more feasible because sexual activity is no longer tied to marriage and procreation. Postponing marriage almost automatically forces a woman into the work force, where she may begin to map out plans for a career like her male colleagues. The woman who postpones marriage and defers childbirth until later usually has launched a career and is probably committed to the idea that a woman should work in the public as well as the private sphere. These attitudes, studies suggest (Thornton et al., 1983), are conveyed to her children.

Causes of the Trend.   Although it is tempting to look to the invention of the birth control pill as the main cause, in fact the limitation of family size appears to accompany improvements in community health and prenatal and infant care. Infant mortality rates decrease, and parents can concentrate on providing well for the children they do have rather than having as many children as possible in order to ensure some survivors. As we pointed out in Chapter 6, limiting family size is also the result of changes in our economic organization that make children not an economic asset, as they are in agricultural systems, but an expense or liability. With this desire for smaller, better-cared-for families, the contraceptive pill becomes a major means for achieving the goal. But it is important to remember that the contraceptive pill was not the result of research in birth control, but of research in infertility. It resulted from the attempt to help couples have children. We stress this to make our point again, that all the changes we have outlined in Chapters 7 and 8 have taken place in the context of societal changes that were often unintended.

The Changing Duties of the Woman within the Family of Procreation

Descriptors of the Trend.   Current descriptors of the duties performed by the wife or mother in a family suggest that she has assumed new duties in the public sphere as partial or full-time breadwinner, without relinquishing duties in the private sphere as housekeeper and prime nurturer.

You will recall that the issue of the two-paycheck family was the most troublesome one for our Rip Van Winkle, who disappeared in 1930. In his earlier "life" in the United States, married women were only a minority of the work force. Although it is true that females, both married and unmarried, participated in the labor force in large numbers during World War II, there was a female exodus away from the workplace once the war was over. By 1947 things were getting back to "normal," with only 20 percent of married women in the work force (Bureau of Labor Statistics, cited in Odendahl and Smith, 1978:2). Since then, however, each decade has experienced approximately a 10 percent increase in married women working for pay, and by 1980 slightly more than half of married women were in the labor force.

Table 9–6 depicts the trends regarding marital status and female labor force participation in 1890, 1920, 1940, 1950, 1960, and 1980. The makeup of the female labor force has changed radically during the twentieth century. At the turn of the century, two-thirds of the female labor

TABLE 9–6   Marital Status and Female Labor-Force Participation: 1890, 1920, 1940, 1950, 1960, 1980

Year	Married	Single	Other*	Total
1890	14%	68%	18%	100%
1920	23	77	+	100
1940	36	49	15	100
1950	53	32	15	100
1960	60	24	16	100
1980	56	25	19	100

Sources: For 1890, 1920, 1940, 1950, and 1960, Historical Statistics, in Mandle (1979:48); for 1980, Waite (1981:3).
*Includes divorced or widowed women.
+Data not available.

force was composed of single women; only a minority, one-seventh, were married. But there was such an influx of married women after World War II that married women became the majority group. By 1980, the married-single ratio was almost reversed, with over half the female labor force composed of married women and only one-fourth of single. However, if we add the percentage of divorced and widowed women to the single category in Table 9–6, we could say that among females in the labor force in 1980, 56 percent were married and 44 percent were single, divorced, or widowed. The participation of wives, facilitated by the contraceptive revolution, has dramatically changed the makeup of the female labor force.

In order to understand better the impact on the family as a whole, we need to know what portion of those wives in the labor force are mothers, especially mothers of young children. Figure 9–6 shows that increasing proportions of married women with or without children under age 18 have entered the work force in the last thirty years. In particular, we can see that the pace of increase in the percentage of mothers with children under 6 years old accelerated to approximately 45 percent by 1980, almost equal to those with no children under 18 years of age (46 percent). However, among married women in the labor force, the participation rate is highest for those with children 6 to 17 years of age (62 percent), and it has also accelerated during the 1970s. In 1980, however, divorced mothers had the highest rates of labor-force participation in all three categories. For divorced women with children under 6 years old, the rate was 68 percent; with no children under 18 years old, the rate was 71 percent; and with children 6 to 17 years of age, the rate was the highest of all, 82 percent (Waite, 1981:20).

The "new experience" of mothers of young children who are in the labor force is complex, especially for those who are divorced and whose households depend entirely on their salary. A nationwide study found that 79 percent of divorced fathers in America do not make child support payments (The Washington Post, June 11, 1983). The child support pay-

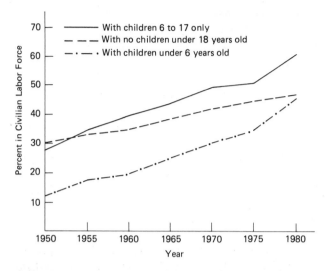

FIGURE 9-6 Labor Force Participation Rates of Married Women by Presence and Age of Children: 1950–1980
Sources: For 1950 to 1974, U.S. Department of Labor, Bureau of Labor Statistics, *U.S. Working Women: A Chartbook,* Bureau of Labor Statistics Bulletin 1880, in Scanzoni and Scanzoni (1981:341). For 1980, Bureau of Labor Statistics, in Waite (1981:20).

ments that are received average less than $2,500 a year. As a recent newspaper article put it (*The Washington Post,* June 16, 1983): "Contrary to popular belief, many of these delinquent fathers have substantial incomes. A California study showed, moreover, that a year after divorce, while the wife's income typically dropped by 73 percent, the husband's rose by 42 percent" (See Weitzman, 1981). Divorced mothers represent single-paycheck families, for the most part.

But the married working woman has led to a significant economic group, the two-paycheck family. In Figure 9–7 we can see how much greater the economic power of the two-paycheck family is compared to all other family types (Oppenheimer, 1977; Rapoport and Rapoport, 1977; Aldous, 1982). The wife's paycheck, in fact, may make the difference between subsistence living and comfortable living. Among married couples, those with a wife in the paid labor force had an annual family income in 1980 higher by $8,000 than those in which the wife was a full-time homemaker. White families had the largest proportion of two-paycheck households in 1980, 42 percent, compared to blacks with 32 percent and Hispanic families with 34 percent (see Figure 5–2). Table 9-7 gives us a sense of when this shift to two-paycheck families occurred.

Wives in the two-paycheck families and women heads of household continue to perform unsalaried work in the home. What are the trends regarding what has been termed the "Superwoman" syndrome? Are there any changes in the amount of time salaried wives are spending on home-

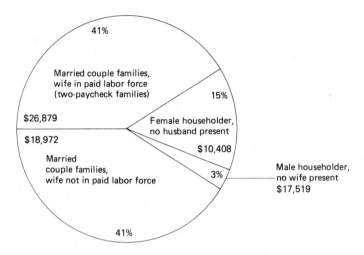

FIGURE 9–7 Type of Family and Median Family Income, 1980: All Races
Source: U.S. Bureau of the Census, *Current Population Reports,* 60-127:7.

making duties? Are their hours of housework decreasing? We rely on three studies that provide data on hours per week (in Smith, 1979:194) and one study on minutes per day (in Waite, 1981:10–11) spent in work at home. Two studies in the mid-sixties found wives spending an average of 34 hours per week in housework, but a study in the mid-seventies found that the hours of housework had decreased to 27 hours per week (in Smith, 1979:194).

The married men in these studies increased their time spent in housework from the mid-sixties to the mid-seventies by one hour, from 13 to 14 hours per week. In a recent research report, Pleck and Rustad (1980) suggest that most of the decline in women's family work took place in routine cleaning. Economist Frank Stafford's study (in Waite, 1981:10–11) provides data regarding average minutes per day spent in 1965 and

TABLE 9–7 Percentage of Wives Gainfully Employed: 1900–1980

Year	Wives Gainfully Employed
1900	5.6%
1910	10.7
1920	9.0
1947	20.0
1968	45.0
1980	52.0

Sources: For 1900, 1910, 1920, 1968, and 1980, Hayghe, in Aldous (1982:28–29). For 1947, Smith et al. (1979:4).

1975. He found that salaried wives spent 181 minutes or 3 hours per day on work at home in 1965 and 2.4 hours per day in 1975. Although there was a decrease of 38 minutes per day from 1965 to 1975, this study found salaried husbands increasing their time spent on housework by a scant 2 minutes, from 23 to 25 minutes per day. As Smith summarizes this phenomenon (1975:115):

> Thus, when a wife goes out to work, she usually continues to do most of the work that gets done at home. Wives who work full time make up most of their housework on weekends, thereby cutting down what had been their free time. The result, certainly, is overload for wives.

Significance for Gender Equality.   We have already discussed the gains the woman achieves in terms of gender equality in going into the paid work force. But reflection on the "Superwoman" syndrome shows some loss of gender equality. To the degree that the woman is working in essence at two full-time jobs, salaried worker and mother-housekeeper, she is ultimately finding her most valuable power resource, her own capacities to change her environment by reflection and by work, diminished. She is being denied time to reflect on her situation and on ways to improve it. She is being worked to the point of being chronically tired and hence unable to act effectively on ideas she may have for improving her situation.[4]

Causes of the Change in Duties.   Women have returned to work for a variety of reasons: economic need, the desire to achieve certain dreams for self and children, and shifts in popular perceptions.

One reason is genuine economic necessity. Using 1975 figures, the Bureau of Labor Statistics reported (in Smith, 1979:69) that 25 percent of the women in the labor force were married to men who earned less than $10,000 per year. Economist Nancy Barrett (in Smith, 1979:69) elaborates on the theme of economic necessity:

> Of the nearly 37 million women in the labor force in 1975, 8.5 million were single (never married); 6.9 million were widowed, divorced or separated; and 9.5 million were married to husbands who earned less than $10,000 per year. (The Bureau of Labor Statistics estimates that it took $9,838 for a family of four to maintain a low standard of living in 1975.) These figures total 24.9 million women—68 percent of the female labor force—who are clearly working because of necessity.

Another reason may lie in the determination to do more for fewer children and to the faith in education that makes college a part of that "more." College tuition costs from the 1960s on have grown at a rate far exceeding other areas of the economy. This growth in tuition costs can perhaps be explained by the increasingly technical nature of a college education. The emphasis on technology forced colleges to make heavy investments in expensive scientific and technical equipment, which often became outmoded before it could be paid for. Further, rising prices of energy have affected all large institutions that must maintain buildings in almost constant use.

Part of the drive of the two-paycheck family may have resulted from the desire to meet the demands of rising college costs. In addition, spiraling costs of housing have made wives working a necessity for middle-income families seeking to own their own homes. Further, the wife's wages have become, for many families in the inflationary 1980s, a form of unemployment insurance, as unemployment rates have been rising, particularly in the construction and manufacturing industries, which are heavily male. The 1980s have seen a proliferation of newspaper stories giving statements from unemployed husbands, all of them attesting to the fact that without the wife's job (low-paying though it is in most cases), it would have been difficult to keep bread on the table. Wives in clerical or service jobs, which are still in demand during inflationary times, have in fact become the sole breadwinners when the two-paycheck family becomes a one-paycheck family because one spouse is fired or "let go."[5]

Economic necessity and the power of "facticity" seem to have altered attitudes toward married women in the paid labor force over the past fifty years. Oppenheimer (1970:44–55) analyzes a series of national polls, from 1936 to 1960, that help to answer this question. In reply to a statement about married women with full-time jobs outside the home, the percent approving in 1936, 1937, and 1938 were, respectively, 15, 18 and 22.[6] In 1942, one year after the United States entered World War II, to the question phrased thus: "As things are now, do you think married women should work in war industry?" 60 percent approved. After the war was over, the original question was asked again in 1945, and the approval rate decreased to 18 percent. It almost doubled fifteen years later, when 34 percent approved of wives working in 1960.

A more recent Harris poll (Harris, 1981:22) showed that twenty years later, in 1981, a solid majority, 85 percent, approved of the statement: "Even if they do have families, women should be given opportunities equal to men to work and have careers outside the home." Over the past fifty years, there has been a dramatic change with regard to attitudes toward working wives, from 15 to 85 percent approval.

CONCLUSION

In this, the third and final chapter in which our focus has been almost exclusively on women, we have described changes in the social institutions of the economy, education, and the family since the beginning of the twentieth century that have resulted in new experiences for American women. Our social change theory argues that these changes have been brought about by the combined forces of postindustrialism, contraception, and the contemporary women's movement. Over the past eighty years, our trend data have shown that women have been moving to new locations in the public sphere, both into the labor force (primarily in female-dominated occupations) and into higher education (primarily as students).

Some family changes, such as a lower birth rate and the postponement of marriage, have facilitated the female movement into the public sphere; however, until there is more restructuring of the family as an institution, the "new experience" for the typical female who is in the labor force will continue to be a double burden, an overload. In the next chapter, we will look at the new experiences of American males and the new social arrangements that make it possible or force them to renegotiate their positions to participate more fully in the private sphere of the home and participate in a different way in the public sphere.

NOTES

1. Black men were allowed to vote when the Fifteenth Amendment was passed in 1870, but not black women. It was not until fifty years later that women, black and white, were given the right to vote.

2. Even women who have been elected to Congress are often "not seen," as illustrated in an anecdote about Colorado Representative Patricia Schroeder (*Newsweek*, November 1, 1982). It seems that when she arrived in Washington in 1973, the then Speaker Carl Albert "greeted her cordially—and turned to her husband to ask what committee assignment he would like."

3. Paul Voss, "Social Determinants of Age at First Marriage in the United States," in Smith (1979:108).

4. Using data from a national sample of married couples, Ross et al. (1983:821) found that the amount of housework done by the husband has a direct negative effect on the wife's depression.

5. Although we have been emphasizing the greater economic rewards of the two-paycheck family, we realize that one of the costs involved is the absence of a traditional homemaker (usually a wife) to perform the socioemotional functions in the everyday life of the family. This dilemma will be discussed in the final chapter. (See Hunt and Hunt, in Kahn-Hut, Daniels, and Colvard, 1982:181–191; also, see Andre's *Homemakers: The Forgotten Workers*, 1981.)

6. The question in 1937, 1938, and 1945 added: "if she has a husband capable of supporting her."

10
CHANGING VIEWPOINTS AND NEW ARRANGEMENTS FOR MEN

We turn our attention in this chapter to the evidence of some changes that have been taking place in contemporary America in men's relationships to the workplace and to home and family. To see more clearly what has been happening, we will again use all three analytical approaches: an aerial view of changes in the social structure, a home-movie view of new arrangements at home and at work, and an X-ray view of men's changing viewpoints about gender equality.

Contemporary American males vary in the degree of their commitment to gender equality. The majority are reluctantly making room for women in the workplace, involuntarily bowing to laws that now prohibit them from discrimination on account of sex. On the home front, however, these same men expect and want no alteration of the conventional situation. As James Doyle argues in the conclusion of his book, *The Male Experience* (1983:290):

> We find little evidence that a large number of men are supportive of any real or significant changes in the power structures that dominate our patriarchal society. As for a ground swell of men pushing for liberation from their restrictive images of masculinity or the traditional elements of the male sex role, the evidence is weak at best in some male circles and nonexistent in most others.

In other words, what most men think about the proper place for men and women has not changed. That is why they are dragging their feet when structural changes dictate different behavior in the workplace (see Chapter 11). Other men in our society, a tiny but growing minority, no longer subscribe to conventional gender arrangements. They have redefined both men's and women's places, and are voluntarily beginning to act out their belief in gender equality at home as well as at work. These men are accepting women in the workplace as equals and even as superordinates. At the same time, they are taking responsibilities at home, sharing equally in both childrearing and housekeeping tasks. In short, these men, like our unhappy secretary, have said "This is the PITS!" to the conventional definition of their situations, and have their feet firmly planted in both the public and private spheres. It is these change-oriented men who are the focus of this chapter.

At this point, we would like to add a note of caution. One cannot categorize all American males (or females, for that matter) as either traditional or nontraditional on the matter of gender equality. In fact, many are somewhere in the middle of the painful process of reconstructing their social worlds. For such men, the change is a slow and piecemeal process. Some men, for instance, have changed their thinking and behavior with respect to certain gender issues, like equal work for equal pay, but remain traditional with respect to other issues, like the acceptance of women in managerial positions. Because we are concentrating on men's changing viewpoints and new arrangements with regard to gender, we will focus here primarily on one end of the continuum, where we find profeminist males.

Figure 10–1 presents a model for explaining why this small group of men has rejected all aspects of our conventional gender situation, and why a much larger number of men find themselves caught up in a process of piecemeal change toward gender equality. The basic elements of this model are by now familiar to you, for we have used them consistently throughout the second half of this book. The model identifies *new meanings* and *new power relations* as the basic causes of the changes that interest us here. By "new meanings," we refer to beliefs in gender equality. "New power relations" refers to a reduction in male dominance and a shift toward greater power sharing between the genders.

In Figure 10-1 we identify the two most general historical causes of new meanings and new power relations: the postindustrial restructuring of the American economy, and the political and ideological impact of the contemporary women's movement. In this chapter we focus on the more immediate structural and situational developments that funnel the effects of postindustrialism and the women's movement into men's experiences of gender. These developments include the macrosocial factors of legislation, occupational shifts, educational changes, the mass media, and the men's liberation movement. They also include such micro phenomena as the effect of working wives and on-the-job changes, the role of friends, consciousness-raising groups, and changes in family life style. We look first at legislation, occupational shifts, and the effects of working wives

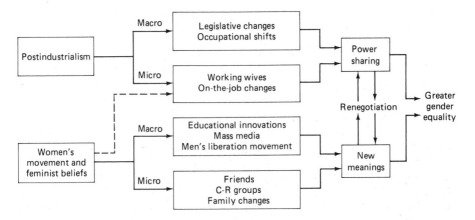

FIGURE 10-1   Greater Gender Equality: Processes Moving Men Toward Power Sharing and New Meanings

and of on-the-job changes. These changes shift the power balance between women and men. We then turn to education, the mass media, the men's liberation movement, friends, consciousness-raising groups, and family dynamics, which we treat primarily as forces reworking men's beliefs about gender.

MACRO PRESSURES FOR POWER SHARING

Power sharing costs men more at work. It may cost women more at home. Homemaking and childcare are the woman's responsibility in the family, and it may cost her to give up some of the control she exercises in this domain. In the workplace, power sharing means that men give up some of their control and prestige to women, that they surrender their monopoly of the dominant positions in the public sphere. Why would men give up some of their power? First of all, they avoid legal sanctions created by the legislation on equal treatment for women (Chapter 8). Secondly, they may be faced with unalterable changes in the organization of work (Chapter 9), changes that begin to suggest new job possibilities. In this section we will look at the legal changes that have pushed men to share their power at work and those that have enabled men to have more equal opportunity in the home. We will then look at occupational changes.

Legislative Changes

When we discussed legislative changes in Chapter 8, we looked at laws and regulations prohibiting discrimination in hiring, salaries, benefits, training, and education, on the basis of sex. We pictured these legislative changes as the basis for female equality. Once in place, these laws can (and have) open(ed) many doors for women in the public sphere. Once inside, the males with whom they work discover the women can do men's work as well or better than they themselves can. So while these laws have given more women the opportunity to work in areas that were predominantly male domains, they have also given men a working experience with women that has challenged their thinking about men being better at certain jobs than women.

The legislative changes that have directly affected men's opportunities on the home front are those regarding divorce and custody. As Chambers (1982:1) puts it, "Today the idea that women are better suited than men for taking care of children seems to many people outdated and calls for new legal presumptions in custody cases. Most states have adopted a single standard of the 'best interests of the child,' and expressly repealed all preferences based on a person's gender." The latest trend, in fact, is a preference for joint custody; over half the states have joint custody provisions on the books, and others have bills pending in their legislatures.[1]

As we have pointed out again and again in this book, people are not born with nurturing traits; they acquire them, and many men are more gentle, warm, sympathetic and altruistic than many women. In addition, as Chambers points out (1982:5), "Human beings have an amazing capacity to respond to the demands of new situations, especially those in which they have voluntarily placed themselves. Thus, fathers may acquire 'nurturing traits' in father-custody situations." These changes in child custody laws may, therefore, result in a slight shift of power in family organization, giving to some men a larger share of childrearing power.

Occupational Shifts

The other side of the picture of the phenomenal growth in the numbers of women participating in the labor force is, of course, the proportional decrease in the numbers of men as a percentage of the labor force. In 1947 (Strober, 1976:134), shortly after World War II, men were 72 percent of the labor force; in 1950, they were 70 percent. The percentage of men continued to decrease; in 1960 it was 67 percent, in 1970, 62 percent, and by 1980 it was down to 57 percent. Thus, the proportion of men as a percentage of the total labor force has slowly but steadily declined by 15 percent in the past 33 years. If women continue to enter the labor force at about the same rate, there could be an equal number of men and women in the labor force by 1990, or shortly thereafter.

Why this decline in the numbers of male workers? Strober (1976: 124, 135) argues that it is due to three factors: (1) an increased percentage of young men staying in school, made possible by the higher incomes of their parents (and wives) and by the educational benefits of the GI bills; this training was encouraged by the increased job opportunities for male college and professional school graduates; (2) an increased percentage of older men retiring because of increased eligibility for social security and private pension benefits, as well as an increase in mandatory retirement rules in companies and institutions; (3) the expansion of occupations that were already heavily female.

Accompanying this reduction in the overall percentages of men in the labor force is a slight decrease in the percentage of men in male occupations and a small, though almost imperceptible, shift into some of the women's jobs. If you turn back to Figure 9–2 showing the percentage of females in selected male-dominated occupations, you can see that the largest male decrease was among male bank officials and financial managers, 20 percent from 1970 to 1981. Other decreases of 10 percent or more were: bus drivers, 18 percent; sales managers, 16 percent; buyers and purchasing agents, 15 percent; accountants, 13 percent; and printing press operators, 10 percent. All these are still predominantly male occupations, but less so. This could mean some sharing of power in these ocupations with women. The fact that the men in these occupations are working as peers with so many more women makes work a qualitatively different experience. This different experience is shared with all others with whom these women in male occupations come in contact on an everyday basis—the commuters who ride the buses, the customers who interact with female sales managers, buyers, and purchasing agents, and so on. For men, this contact can change the meaning of the work situation. We would not be surprised to see some of these men beginning to encourage their sisters, wives, aunts, and mothers to aspire to occupations that offer more economic power than most female occupations.

Two of the female-dominated occupations that show small increases in male participation are nurses and teachers (except college and university). In 1970 there were 2.6 percent male registered nurses; in 1981 there were 3.2 percent, and in 1982 male registered nurses had increased to 4.2 percent (Norwood, 1982:8, and Rytina, 1982:26). Berch (1982:204), looking at data from 1972 to 1978, states: "the number of male secretaries rose 24%, the number of male telephone operators increased 38% and the number of male nurses increased 94%." Among teachers below the college level, males represented 29.6 percent in 1970, and 32.9 percent in 1982 (Norwood, 1982:8, and Rytina, 1982:26). Interestingly enough, these two occupations require nurturing skills. We can anticipate a continuation of the shift of males into these occupations, if more schools and more parents socialize children in a different, more androgynous way. But the most important impetus to these occupational shifts is postindustrialism. In addition, Berch argues (1982:204) that more men will move into service-sector jobs as traditional male blue-collar jobs decrease and the economy continues to shift toward service work.

MICRO PRESSURES FOR POWER SHARING

Although legislative changes and occupational shifts have encouraged or pushed men to share their economic and social power with women in the public sphere, two resources have facilitated power sharing on the home front and pulled men into the home to share homemaking and nurturing responsibilities: working wives and on-the-job changes.

Working Wives

When we discussed female labor-force participation as a power resource for greater gender equality in Chapter 9, we alluded to the economic necessity of wives working for pay. Table 9-7 shows that over half of the wives in married couple families are now working, and Figure 9-7 shows that the two-paycheck families have a substantially higher median annual income—$8,000 more annually than married-couple families where the wife is not in the paid labor force. For some families, the wives' income has meant economic survival, and even a form of unemployment insurance. For others, it has meant the possibility of buying a home and/or sending children to college.

We also indicated a change in attitude among the general public about working wives that has made the climate more favorable for them. Over the past twenty years, the proportion of working wives has increased by 20 percent (Norwood, 1982:6). In 1960, 30 percent of wives were in the paid labor force; in 1970, it was 40 percent; and in 1980, 50 percent. Mothers with children between 6 and 17 have higher rates of labor-force participation than all other categories of working wives, and their participation rates have grown steadily from 39 percent in 1960, to 49 percent in 1970, to 62 percent in 1980. Mothers with children under 6 years of age have lower but also increasing rates: for 1960, 1970, and 1980, their rates moved from 19 to 30 to 45 percent (see Figure 9-6).

What has all this increase meant for men, in particular for the husbands of these women? First of all, it means that the percentage of husbands with working wives has also increased, so another way of stating these increases is to say that by 1980 half of all American husbands had wives who were in the paid labor force. The sheer number of working wives is, in and of itself, a dramatic change for the American family. But if we look deeper into this changed situation, we can detect an even more revolutionary mechanism—the wife's work experiences as they affect the husband.

The following statements from two males who were equal parenting are illustrative:

> Maybe I don't do as much as I should, but I help out some—you know, with the kids and the housework. I even learned how to cook a little because she comes home later than me two days a week and everybody gets hungry. So I get the meal started those nights. It's only fair, isn't it? She helps out in her way, so I do in mine. (Rubin, 1983a:35)

> I started out scared of what would happen to us, but it's been great. I've gotten to know my kids—really know them—and that may be the biggest gift of all. At first, Beth wasn't making enough money to make much difference. But now . . . what a relief! I never knew it felt like such a big load to support the family until I found out it wasn't all mine anymore. It's like when you know it's safe to feel something, you let it happen. Well, that's the way it was. All of a sudden I understood that a lot of the time when I was behaving like a damn *macho* bastard, I was just mad as hell at having to take care of them all. (Rubin, 1983a:18)

Another effect turns on the fact that 80 percent of working women are in low-paid occupations, and vast numbers of them are more highly educated than their male co-workers. We would assume that wives relate their daily work experiences to their husbands, that these same husbands are directly affected by the low paychecks their wives are receiving. This is just one of the reasons why some husbands are not detached listeners. In fact, it could be argued that no other subordinate group has had such an intimate relationship with the dominant group. The revolutionary potential of working wives' influence surpasses that of consciousness-raising groups, friendships, and the men's liberation movement for the countless husbands who have neither time nor inclination for these extrafamilial influences, but who interact on a daily basis with their wives. Working wives' rage may be beginning to penetrate the consciousness of these husbands, if our daily conversations with and readings about such husbands are any indication.

One word we could use to characterize husbands of working wives is ambivalence. On the one hand, husbands receive a reward in the relief they experience from a wife's economic support. No matter how small a contribution, her paycheck softens the blow of family expenses, and of course this is doubly true during an inflationary period. Her paycheck can also provide freedom for the husband to decline overtime work, to refuse a job transfer, to take time out to seek a better job, to enroll in classes preparing him for a second career, or to start a business. In general, a working wife's paycheck can relieve some of the stress and strain of his own job, thus improving his health.[2] On the other hand, a husband loses some prerogatives in the form of service, emotional support, and some influence in decision making at home when his wife receives a paycheck. Researchers have found (in Smith et al., 1979:121) that a wife, in going out of the house to work for pay, is expanding her role to one of a higher status than homemaker. A husband who assumes homemaking functions is correlatively adopting a role of lower status. The husband's costs and rewards balance out, and the net effect is positive when his wife works by choice, however. As Smith et al. put it (1979:122): "The one study that looks at the overall balance of satisfactions and tensions finds that husbands as well as wives are more satisfied if the wife is working by choice than they are if she is working out of necessity or if she is a full-time housewife."

Since a key issue for marital happiness is whether or not the wife wants to work, we need to reflect on the factors which make this choice possible. It goes without saying that a husband's attitude is a necessary but not sufficient condition. His positive attitude depends on his own job constraints.

On-the-job Changes

Men and women who believe in the goals of egalitarian marriages and of equal parenting recognize the need to demand on-the-job changes at the male's job location, for few companies pay more than lip service to the idea of paternal participation. As one day-care consultant put it (*News-*

week, October 30, 1981:97), "We talk about working mothers, but not working fathers."

Working men tend to agree that such on-the-job changes are necessary. Harris (1981:30) found 84 percent of working fathers agreeing that it would be a good thing if "employers made it easier for working parents to arrange their jobs and careers around their children." In particular, Harris (1981:54) found over 60 percent of working men responding that it would help their families "a great deal" or "somewhat" if there were some form of flextime schedule at their job locations, schedules such as "choice between a 7 to 3, 8 to 4, or 9 to 5 workday"; "freedom to set a work schedule, as long as you work 70 hours every two weeks"; "work schedules that allow one day to work at home"; and "a four-day workweek with longer hours each day but a three-day break." A finding by Presser and Cain (1983) underlines the need for these on-the-job changes. Using 1980 Bureau of Labor Statistics data, they found that a third of working couples with children are working staggered hours, often not overlapping at all, as a way of sharing childcare.

The man who will receive the greatest gain from such changes is the single parent; he is the man in the greatest need of such resources. But other groups favor part-time work as well. Meltz, Reid, and Swartz (1981) indicate that young men (and women) single and under 25 prefer part-time work if they are pursuing further education or training, and older workers over 55 also tend to favor part-time work or job sharing as they near retirement age.

The extra time with children will be a benefit for the father with a working wife as well as the father whose wife is home fulltime. In addition, such changes as flextime, childcare facilities, job sharing, and part-time work give full-time housewives the freedom to choose whether or not they leave home to work or to obtain training or further education. Also, older males (and females) who desire to retire earlier and more gradually benefit by job-sharing and part-time opportunities. These on-the-job changes, especially at the male's job location, are still visible in only a minority of job settings. We see them as the key ingredient for the second stage of the movement toward greater gender equality.

MACRO SOURCES OF NEW MEANINGS

In this section we attempt to understand how some American males are able to "take the role of the other," that "other" being the change-oriented women we have been describing, and how these men subsequently adopt an egalitarian attitude toward gender arrangements. One writer (Katz in Pleck and Sawyer, 1974:155) suggests that the two major means for men to unlearn society's expectations are: (1) recognizing and unlearning the underlying contempt most men feel for women, and (2) questioning the male hierarchy of values.

In large measure, men's redefinition of their own situations has been affected by women's redefinition of theirs, the latter being essentially a product of the reborn women's movement. As Robert Fein puts it (in Pleck and Sawyer, 1974:56): "Men, spurred by wives, sisters, and female friends who have come to view themselves through feminist lenses, are examining the nature of masculinity—and finding society's image of the 'real' man to be wanting." In this section, we will look at the macro-level influences that foster the male's redefinition of self and gender relationships. We begin with educational innovations.

Educational Innovations

Some of the changes various educational institutions have initiated over the past fifty years have influenced the changing American male to reinterpret gender arrangements. At the high school level, the growing phenomenon of the desegregation of high school courses like "auto-shop" and "home economics" has helped to break down sexist stereotypes. Some of these courses have required a new description like "gourmet cooking," to attract males. Nonetheless, they have learned that as males they can be good at cooking and kitchen management and also enjoy it. For example, the Future Homemakers of America, founded in 1945 for junior high and high school students of home economics, has changed its image and broadened its program to include not only cooking, childcare, and checkbook balancing, but also programs on leadership, decision making, and problem solving, as well as the study of teenage pregnancy, alcoholism, and nutrition. A *Newsweek* (July 27, 1981) report on the FHA membership states that the membership is now 7 percent male, and that boys are an "increasingly common sight at its meetings," a sign that homemaking is beginning to be taken seriously by at least some young men.

Male college students certainly have a lot more female classmates now, many of whom perform academically as well as or better than they do. Look back for a moment at Table 9–3. We can see that in 1900 men were awarded approximately 80 percent of the B.A.s and M.A.s. By 1980, this had decreased to 50 percent. By 1980, there were an equal number of men and women B.A. and M.A. students in the commencement procession. In 1900, men were awarded 94 percent of the Ph.D.s; by 1980, it was 70 percent. Another way of saying this is that one of every three people in the Ph.D. commencement procession was a female in 1980. This fact was certainly a qualitatively different experience for the males involved, and it could not help but affect their thinking about women's intellectual inferiority.[3]

Of course the changes differ by major fields, as a reexamination of Table 9–4 will show. Although males were still awarded 97 percent of the engineering doctorates in 1980, there has been a rather substantial decrease (almost 20 percent) in male doctorates between 1950 and 1980 in the biological and social sciences. How well men are adjusting to the experience of having more than just a few token women Ph.D. students is an open question. What we do know is that they are having to make room for these women.

What about college curriculums? Some of the new courses males could be exposed to in the 1980s, like Women in History, Women in

Literature, and/or Sex and Gender Roles (see Chapter 7), may also be a vehicle bringing males to a new and critical consciousness about gender arrangements.[4] Whether males enroll in such courses or not is only part of the issue. One of the important functions of educational institutions is a more diffuse dissemination of knowledge and values. That these courses exist and that students affected by them are raising critical questions about gender equality, that approximately half of all college students are female, and that they are a significant presence in many formerly male fields all create a climate in educational institutions more conducive to greater equality.

Mass Media Changes

The mass media, as a forum where critical views on gender equality are heard and aired, can affect the thinking and beliefs of men as well as women, and can be for both a resource for new meanings. The emergence of writers like Ellen Goodman and Mary McGrory in the daily newspapers can affect a man's thinking about woman's place. But where can he find a new view of his own place? Nontraditional men are beginning to find role models in the media like Alan Alda who, in 1980 and 1981, was awarded "Favorite Performer on TV" and "Favorite All-Around Male Entertainer" in all media (*Washington Post*, July 13, 1981:C5). In contrast to more conventional actors and past award winners like John Wayne and Bob Hope, Alda, who refers to himself publicly as a feminist, has made his top political priority the passage of the Equal Rights Amendment, and he acts out his beliefs by turning down roles in major films that are biased against women.

A glance at popular men's magazines such as *Esquire* and *Sports Illustrated* will also reveal indicators of some new meanings. For instance, the November 1982 issue of *Esquire* featured an article by Anthony Brandt entitled "Father Love" on pains and joys a man feels for his children. The February 28, 1983, issue of *Sports Illustrated* included a lengthy article on Lousiana Tech's women's basketball team with photographs of one of the star players, a sign that women's sports are finally beginning to be taken seriously. The fact that these topics—a father's emotional rewards and women's sports—are given space and prominent display in these traditional men's magazines is a small breakthrough for a change in the meaning of gender arrangements.[5] Thus far, there are no widely circulated counterparts of *Ms.* or *Working Women*, but some magazines for the changing male are beginning to appear—for example, *Achilles Heel: A Magazine of Men's Politics; Changing Men;* and *M: Gentle Men for Gender Justice.* (Pleck, 1981: 175–181 gives a comprehensive listing of media resources.)

Movies of the 1980s like "Kramer vs. Kramer" and "Tootsie" are also indicators of the nontraditional messages being conveyed to males. "Kramer vs. Kramer," a story of the joys and pains of a single father's relationship with his son, is not a depiction of an isolated incident in our society. Census figures for 1980 show that over a million children are being raised exclusively by their fathers, a 65 percent increase since 1970

(*Newsweek,* November 30, 1981:93). Indeed, the growing phenomenon of fathers winning custody of children in divorce settlements has been referred to as "Kramerization." In "Tootsie," Dustin Hoffman's role reversal, in which he plays the part of a female hospital administrator who stands up for her own and other women's rights in a TV series, was a lesson in female devaluation for the movie audience and a consciousness-raising experience for Hoffman, as he attests in an interview (*New York Times,* December 21, 1982:C11).

The "new male" can take courage from the fact that the small number of nontraditional films depicting males as caring and nurturing persons that are being produced are, by and large, box office successes. Pressure for change of the male image in the media will come from the growth and strength of the next resource, the men's liberation movement.

The Men's Liberation Movement

Inspired by the women's liberation movement, some nontraditional men have begun to question their own impoverishment, to criticize the values they have internalized as male or masculine values. Jack Nichols, author of *Men's Liberation* (1978:317–318), singles out the following values from which the members of the men's movement are attempting to free themselves:

> A saner society will flower when men liberate themselves from contrived, socially fabricated prohibitions, cultural straitjackets, and mental stereotypes that control and inhibit behavior through arbitrary definitions of what it means to be a man. When it is clear that the *worship of the intellect* is destructive, as are the *idolization of competition, admiration for what is big,* and the resort to *violence as remedy,* men will react differently to one another, with different expectations, priorities, purposes, and awarenesses. Instead of admiring top dogs, domineering masters and bosses, and instead of supporting power coups, they will regard such persons and their activities as anachronistic and counterproductive. (Emphasis ours.)

Basically, Nichols sees the men's liberation movement as a revolution in values, a revolution against worship of the intellect, idolization of competition, bigness, and violence.[6] He views these values as dangerous in a nuclear age, and he sees the men's movement as a search for the alternatives that will emphasize more humane values like emotional fulfillment, cooperation, a belief that "small is beautiful," and a commitment to nonviolence. Pleck (1980:425) points out that the traditional masculine values are part and parcel of partriarchal sexual politics, which sets up a division between straight and gay men, between "real men" and "those who are not." He draws on illustrations from a men's movement documentary film entitled "Men's Lives," in which a high school male studying modern dance explains that others have labeled him gay because he is a dancer. "When asked why, he gives three reasons: because dancers are 'free and loose,' because they are 'not big like football players,' and because 'you're not trying to kill anybody.'" (This is an almost perfect echo of the values listed by Nichols.)

One way of undercutting the men's movement and its nontraditional, nonviolent values is to label it as "gay" and dismiss it as irrelevant, and thus reassert the higher privilege and greater power of conventional, presumably straight men. At its core, the men's liberation movement is a challenge to male patriarchy, a radical change in the male definition of self-worth. Elise Boulding underlines the importance of the men's liberation movement when she states (1976a:116):

> The men's liberation movement in setting out to destroy both the image and the reality of sex-linked dominance behavior, may in the end be the most significant social movement of the twentieth century. By liberating the potential for tenderness in men, it undercuts much of the rationale for sex-linked dominance and sets the stage for a new kind of involvement of men with children.

The male liberation movement has had a dual orientation, one personal and the other political. The primary goal of the personal orientation is to relieve the stress and other health problems that contribute to the male's shorter life span. Allied to this goal is a search for deeper personal relationships with others, with men *and* women, with fathers *and* mothers, with brothers *and* sisters, sons *and* daughters. While the primary orientation of the men's movement is on the personal level, the secondary goal is more political. It includes the pressure to change the occupational structure to make it more flexible and family-oriented, to press for changes like flextime, childcare, job sharing, and so on. In addition, the men's movement is determined to stop male discrimination and to promote greater gender equality by pushing for changes in such areas as child custody laws, the draft, auto insurance, and alimony.

As a national movement, this movement is still in its incipient stages. At present it could best be described as a growing number of men's organizations scattered throughout the country, groups like Free Men and Men's Rights. There is currently no male counterpart to the National Organization for Women. Because the history of the men's movement thus far has yet to be written, we will draw on an analysis by James Yenckel, who followed the men's movement through 1981 and 1982 in a series of newspaper articles in *The Washington Post*.

As Yenckel describes it, the men's movement "is developing along two divergent paths." Those on one path, calling themselves feminist men, see the male sex as responsible for the oppression of women. Their function is to "help men shed the role of oppressor of women." They have been gathering annually since 1975 at Men and Masculinity Conferences, drawing approximately 600 representatives from over thirty men's centers across the country. There have been some efforts to bring the local groups under a national organization with an elected council to spur the formation of more groups, but they have not as yet succeeded. Feminist men have also strengthened efforts aimed at "counseling men who batter women to end their urges for violence," exemplified by groups like AMEND (Abusing Men Exploring New Directions), or MESA (Men to End Spouse Abuse), which are among the 60 or more organizations which have sprung up nationwide to offer counseling and therapy to batterers. Feminist men welcome homosexuals to their national conferences, which include a number of workshops directed to homosexuals.

The second segment of the men's movement, known as men's rights advocates, while supporting the goal of gender equality, sees society as the oppressor of women, and its priorities as men's issues. These include working to end economic discrimination against the under-25 male who pays more for automobile insurance and attempting to increase the life span of the American male. Men's rights advocates also mobilize on issues like statutory rape laws, which "view all men as aggressive and all women as passive"; alimony laws "requiring an unemployed male to pay support to a wage-earning ex-wife"; abortion, when men have "no say over whether the pregnancy should have been aborted"; and child custody and divorce reforms. Men's rights advocates do not usually include gay topics on their agendas because, as one organizer put it (Yenckel, 1982:C-5): "If we're going to reach a cross-section of males, we have to be careful in the beginning stages to present as broad a picture as possible."

In June 1981, 100 representatives of men's rights groups from twenty-one states, the District of Columbia, and Canada met at Houston, Texas, to form the National Congress for Men, which officially endorsed the Equal Rights Amendment. This was followed by a second national meeting in 1982 in Detroit, Michigan.

While the two segments of the men's movement overlap on many issues, in particular on consciousness-raising efforts to free men's emotions and on the divorce reform issue, there has been little or no effort to set up a dialog between the two divisions. Given their different ideological positions, perhaps this is neither possible nor feasible. Nonetheless, even at this stage, the men's movement has, for a small but growing number of men, encouraged them in their efforts to build a new world of meaning that will give them a new self-identity, with rights and responsibilities as loving parents and cooperative workers willing to share and to work toward collective goals.[7]

MICRO SOURCES OF NEW MEANINGS

Friendships

Conversion to a new identity, to a new belief system, often comes about through the personal influence of a significant other (Wallace, 1975). We often adopt new beliefs after listening to and becoming convinced by close friends and relatives, those whose approval and affection confer meaning on our lives. Statistical data illustrating gender inequality may never be convincing to us, for instance, when they come from sources beyond our own world. We can always say that such data do not apply to our experiences. Such problems as drug use, mental retardation, divorce, suicide, or sexual harassment may have been of little concern to you until somehow they touched you, in the person of a friend whose child was cruelly raped or who was arrested for possession of cocaine, or someone who suffered the pain of a divorce or suicide in the family. By intimate conversation with a close friend, you may have come to empathize with that friend's pain and anxiety. Often empathetic experience changes our way of making sense of a situation.

In the case of a change-oriented male, "taking the role" of his closest female friend (wife, lover, sister, mother, aunt, or classmate) can change him because it can bring him face to face with a situation which, as that person perceives it, is not fulfilling, not normal, not right, and in a real sense, inhuman. We do not have "hard data" that would tell us how many men have been converted to the basic feminist belief in the dignity of all individuals because a female friend shared her experiences of degradation and/or discrimination, and her subsequent feelings of shame and loss of self-esteem. But we do know that this can change a person's way of thinking (Doyle, 1983:14).

On the other hand, a man may not realize his own impoverishment in the conventional gender situation at home until he vicariously experiences something like an equal-parenting situation through deep conversations with his best male friend. With regard to increased participation at home, males need male role models, just as females need them in the workplace. Giving up some power or letting go in either world can be facilitated by a female role model at home and a male role model at work, each of whom has successfully begun the power-sharing process in the respective sphere. Because power sharing is a sensitive and troublesome process, a close friend is especially important as a catalyst for change.

Having said all this, where can we look for data with which to test our hypotheses about friendship? Unfortunately, the data are hard to come by because the phenomenon of male friendship is so rare. One could marshal evidence about "golfing buddies," Friday night poker game groups, and barhopping pals, but none of these is the type of friendship that demands intimate sharing, or what one sociologist (Collins, 1981) calls "reciprocal revelations." Pleck (1981:149) states that not only are boys less articulate about the nature and meaning of friendship and think it less important than girls do, but they also report reacting less strongly than girls to the loss of a friendship. Pleck cites studies by Caldwell and Peplau (1981) and by Booth (1972) which confirm that men's friendships are less intimate and less spontaneous than women's. The average American male shuns intimate sharing with both males and females (unless the latter is his wife) for fear that the relationship will result in homosexuality in the first case or in a divorce in the second. The following quote from one American male describing how he feels about the lack of intimate friends in his life is illustrative (Engel, 1982:13):

> I've always been amazed at the nurturing emotional support that my wife can seek and return with her close female friends. Often the intimate and intense problems are shared and therefore diminished through empathy. Her three-hour talks with friends refresh and renew her far more than my 3-mile jogs restore me. . . .
> Six years ago, on the evening before we moved across the country, my wife's best friend came over for the final good-bye. Their last hugs were so

painful to witness that I finally had to turn away and leave the room. It was then I began wondering why men so rarely share such poignant relationships, and I came to a number of conclusions regarding the problems inherent in close male friendships.

Engel explains that such friendships "must ignore the dictates of American culture," which require the male to stand alone (the John Wayne type) or to stand with others as a team (football players). The latter relationship is based on competition, ensuring that, as he puts it, "the relationship will never deepen into intimacy but rather stay at a superficial and guarded level," because lurking in the background of intimate male relationships is the fear of a homosexual relationship. Similarly, Hartley (forthcoming, 1985) found her younger male respondents reporting that the only way they met male friends was through sports, and that sports events were the main activities they shared, an activity hardly conducive to intimacy.

One of the respondents in Bell's (1981:81–82) study, *Worlds of Friendship*, a 38-year-old advertising executive, put it this way:

> I have three close friends I have known since we were boys and they live here in the city. There are some things I wouldn't tell them. For example, I wouldn't tell them about my work because we have always been highly competitive. I certainly wouldn't tell them about my feelings of any uncertainties with life or various things I do. And I wouldn't talk about any problems I have with my wife or in fact anything about my marriage and sex life. But other than that I would tell them anything. (After a brief pause he laughed and said:) That doesn't leave a hell of a lot, does it?

Excluding so many items for discussion eliminates or at least plays down the notion of trust, which is at the core of a friendship relationship. It would also be difficult to label the friends described above as intimate friends. Intimate friendships, which have been important resources and facilitators for change-oriented women, are a rare phenomenon in the lives of most American men. Only those men who have been imperfectly socialized and who have been somehow deaf to the dictates against intimacy in friendships have been able to tap this resource. As one of Hartley's (forthcoming, 1985) male respondents put it, friendships are harder for men to come by because "men have to posture and put up a front."

Consciousness-Raising Groups

One of the consequences of the women's movement has been a proliferation (though still on a small scale) of male consciousness-raising groups. Warren Farrell, in his book *The Liberated Man* (1974:217), defines such a group as "a group of persons meeting regularly to develop each other's awareness of alternative ways of overcoming the limitations on our lives that evolved from our view of ourselves as masculine and feminine. The consciousness-raising group creates a subculture which encourages questioning and experimenting in ways that are applicable to one's personal life." Some of these groups are directly linked to the men's liberation movement, and some are more spontaneous.

Chafetz (1978:240) estimates that these groups of men are about the size of their female counterparts of about a decade ago. In a novel based on his own experiences as a member of a men's club in Berkeley, California, Leonard Michaels (1981) describes a consciousness-raising session in which the men in the group gave each other "permission" to be vulnerable in the process of telling their life stories. This book affords the reader a home-movie view of the kind of intimate sharing that takes place in such groups. As Michaels explains in an interview (*Washington Post*, May 26, 1981:B3), "I couldn't even have conceived it (i.e., his book) without the cultural changes brought about by the woman's movement." Michaels firmly believes that such groups are modeled on what women were doing, that these male groups are an offshoot of the female consciousness-raising groups.

What are some of the new meanings emerging from these men's groups? Donald H. Bell, author of *Being a Man: The Paradox of Masculinity*, said, in an interview about his book (*Washington Post*, June 26, 1982):

> "Real" men are more flexible than they used to be. It's more gratifying to be ourselves, the way we want to be.
>
> For the last 200 years there was a ready-made mold and we had to fit ourselves into it at the expense of denying other parts of ourselves, and that was very tragic, having capabilities that we could never express or use.
>
> The woman's movement both forced and helped us to break the traditional male mold. What the mold is now is up to each of us.
>
> I was talking with my barber when I was getting a haircut, the day after the Cooney-Holmes fight, and do you know what we talked about? Not the fight, but about the baby he and his wife had just had. Caring for it and that sort of thing. That's not the sort of thing that would have happened a few years ago.

Another example is an excerpt from the Berkeley Men's Center Manifesto, which sums up the new values adopted in male consciousness-raising groups (in Pleck and Sawyer, 1974:173):

> We, as men, want to take back our full humanity. We no longer want to strain to compete to live up to an impossible oppressive masculine image—strong, silent, cool, handsome, unemotional, successful, master of women, leader of men, wealthy, brilliant, athletic, and "heavy." . . . We want to relate to both women and men in more human ways—with warmth, sensitivity, emotion, and honesty. We want to share our feelings with one another to break down the walls and grow closer. We want to be equal with women and end destructive competitive relationships between men.

These consciousness-raising groups have, for some men, been the source of their first close male friendships (Pleck and Sawyer, 1974:155). In addition to talking about these new definitions of "manhood" and widening the spectrum of tolerable behavior and feelings for men, these groups have also become a forum for discussing the daily renegotiating processes that are taking place in their families. This has made it more possible for some men to relocate themselves so they can participate to a wider and deeper degree in the world of home and neighborhood. We now turn to a discussion of just this issue, the male location in the family.

Family Changes

Two changes that have been taking place on the family front, but only slowly and gradually, are the phenomena of males as single parents and males as homemakers (or "househusbands" as they are sometimes called). If we look back at the data presented in Chapter 9 on types of households and concentrate this time on the single-male head households, we can see that there are fewer single-male head households than female (3 percent compared to 15 percent), but that the median income for the male-head household is higher by $7,000 more yearly. Actually, single-male head households, with a $17,519 yearly income, are almost comparable to the married-couple family with full-time housewife ($18,972). But the significant difference between these two types of households is the number of unpaid services performed by the wife, all of which must be taken care of by the single male householder.[8] Neither male nor female single-parent families have a built-in cook, housekeeper, chauffeur, and babysitter, unless they pay someone to perform these services.

Keep in mind that male single parents are heading families without a wife, that they are performing the dual roles of father and mother as well as breadwinner, that they are indeed the counterpart of the single female parent. Since only 3 percent of the households in this country belong to the category of "male householder, no wife present," it is not surprising that many people do not personally know a family headed by a single male.

The male-female comparison regarding single parents looks different when cross-tabulated by race. If we turn back for a moment to Figure 5–2, we can see that the single householder is far more prevalent among black and Spanish-origin families, but the male proportion is about the same (3 percent for whites and 5 percent for black and Spanish-origin households). The basic differential in median yearly income of approximately $6,000 between white and nonwhite males alerts us to the greater difficulty that nonwhite single males have in fulfilling the role of provider for their families.

A male who is a single parent must have one foot rooted in each of the two worlds of family and work if the family is to survive. In many cases the redefinition of himself as a homemaker came abruptly, as a result of a sudden unexpected death, a separation, or a divorce. Rosenthal and Keshet (1981:307) estimate that the number of children who live with their divorced father is about one-tenth the number who live with their divorced mother. In their study of 127 separated or divorced fathers, they described the conflicts of single fathers as "role overloads" and found their respondents constantly coordinating and juggling work schedules with childcare schedules to meet the expectations of autonomy and independence that are part and parcel of the structure of the male occupational role. As they put it (1981:309): "Women may resist the demands of occupational socialization by the legitimacy of their participation in the family. Men, on the other hand, find little support in rejecting the demands of the work world on behalf of family functions." One of their respondents, a single male parent, said: "My boss is old-fashioned, he does not care what work I actually do, but he must see me there from nine to five. It is very inconvenient for me, and I knew I could get as much work done on a more flexible schedule, but he would not hear of it."

Males have been socialized for career performance, so when they are catapulted into homemaking and nurturing roles, they learn a lot about a hitherto unknown world. Whatever the cause—death of spouse, divorce, or adoption of a child as a single parent—the single males who are heads of households have, with respect to nurturing and homemaking, experience in what it means to be a daily caretaker, what it means to be a mother in addition to being a father.

Another type of family change we will mention, even though the numbers of such family arrangements are minuscule, is the phenomenon of the male homemaker. When this topic is discussed, it is generally assumed that the male in question is a full-time homemaker, that he is not engaged in "work outside the home" or paid work, and that, in fact, the wife is the sole breadwinner in this situation. A separate and more prevalent phenomenon is equal parenting, where both husband and wife share equally in homemaking and nurturing responsibilities. For an X-ray view of the world of such a household, see Roache (1972), "Confessions of a Househusband," in Richardson and Taylor (1983:399–401). To emphasize how unusual the male homemaker phenomenon is, note that the census categories actually rule out the possibility of counting these households.

For the vast majority of Americans, the image of a male homemaker is, as some sociologists would put it (Garfinkel, 1967), a "violation of the scene," a phenomenon that calls into question taken-for-granted assumptions about everyday reality, and to which people respond in a variety of ways. Some males who were the only men in an otherwise all-female situation, one that required a "parent," like PTA luncheons, bake sales at church or school, and class outings or field trips, found that they were virtually ignored and thus made "invisible" by the women. When faced with such an anomaly, people can (and do) respond to it by simply denying the fact of its existence or ignoring it altogether.

Househusbands, however, are rarely the reverse of housewives who give priority to facilitating husbands' careers and tending family needs. Most househusbands feel constrained to take up a money-making project like carpentry, art work, or writing to produce something that has a market value, so they can at least partially fulfill their expectations about their provider role. A case in point is Daniel Pisner, the father of quintuplets born on June 21, 1983, who decided to stay home and raise the babies while his wife returned to her job because, as he puts it (*Washington Post*, June 29, 1983): "It's an experience few fathers have." Unemployed since he was laid off in 1982 from a management consulting firm, Pisner has rejected a number of job offers so that he could take on the role of househusband. However, Pisner stated that, in addition to looking after the children, he hopes to supplement the family income by "working up marketable programs on a home computer" and "investigating several other business opportunities."

The positive experiences of these full or part-time househusbands, if disseminated widely enough, could ease the stress and alienation now suffered by men when they are laid off or when they retire from full-time work. Perhaps new technology will provide men with new avenues for creativity and new meanings.

SUMMARY

Greater gender equality means giving men equal responsibility for the childrearing, nurturing, and homemaking tasks essential for a family's survival. In order to do this, the male transfers some of his time and energy to the home base, thereby possibly relinquishing a portion of his monetary rewards. What does he gain from these new arrangements? His reward lies in the emotional fulfillment that results from caregiving. Given the present 9-to-5 work structure, with its inflexible demands, most full-time workers (male *and* female) have difficulty finding time and energy to fulfill their home responsibilities.

In this chapter we have looked at pressures for male power sharing in the home and at the workplace that are the result of postindustrialism and the women's movement: legislative changes, occupational shifts, working wives, and on-the-job changes. We have also discussed the sources available to men for new definitions of gender arrangements resulting from the contemporary women's movement: educational and mass media innovations, the male liberation movement, friendships, consciousness-raising groups, and family changes. Although we see men's changing viewpoints and the new gender arrangements as currently in the incipient stage, the changes we have discussed can facilitate a movement away from (and beyond) the male mystique, the super-masculine expectations of aggression, force, power, strength, dominance, and competitiveness, and a corresponding movement toward a more equitable and more truly human situation for both men and women in our society. This shift, if it does come about, will be far from smooth, as we will see in the next chapter.

NOTES

1. Judges' courtroom practices tend to change more slowly, however, As Weiss (1979:327, in Scanzoni and Scanzoni, 1981:655) notes: "If present practice continues, the custody of over 90 percent of these children will be entrusted to their mother."

2. Ross et al. (1983), in a national survey of United States households, found the lowest depression levels occurring among men whose wives are employed and who approve of it.

3. This too is a mixed bag. Komarovsky (1976) found the majority of male college students reporting that they preferred intellectual women, but they did not want their dates to outshine them intellectually.

4. One of our male students who now describes himself as a feminist said that the course he took on the sociology of gender helped him to realize that if he ever had a daughter, he would not want her to be treated like a second-class citizen. He subsequently worked as a volunteer to help with the passage of ERA.

5. A content analysis of some men's magazines over a period of twenty or thirty years for nontraditional approaches to gender could be an eye-opener.

6. See, for instance, Marc Fasteau's discussion of the cult of toughness as a masculine ideal of policy makers in *The Male Machine* (1974), or the male childhood scripts described in Chapter 4.

7. We should also note that men who have joined professional groups for women, like male sociologists who are members of the Sociologists for Women in Society (SWS), have discovered another resource for new meanings.

8. A new magazine, *Single Dad's Lifestyle*, advises its readers about a variety of household and parenting skills, from "removing gum from children's hair to explaining menstruation" (*Newsweek*, November 30, 1981:96).

11
RESISTANCE
TO CHANGE

This chapter explores the resistance presently being offered by sectors of our society to changes in our gender institution. "Resistance to change" means something quite specific—perception of change as a threat and the attempt to exert power in the world in order to prevent or reverse that change. Put differently, resistance to change means purposive, deliberate action in defense of what is institutionalized. In this chapter we are not concerned with those who, in a habituated nonreflective way, act out their gender roles along conventional lines. We are concerned with those who take deliberate action to resist gender equality.

To set the stage for our exploration of active resistance to change, however, we must repeat one point. The sequence in this book does not depict a chronology in which conventional gender behaviors occurred in the past, followed by the more egalitarian situation described in Part II. Rather, Parts I and II constitute an analytical breakout of processes all contemporaneously visible in the American institution of gender. Put concretely, you can observe in America today huge numbers of people playing conventional gender roles, and many other people venturing into new behaviors. At the intersection of these two categories of behavior, one finds what we described in Chapters 8 and 10, social movements for gender equality, and what we will be looking at in this chapter, active resistance to change.

This chapter's organization is quite straightforward. It first tries to explain *why* some people perceive the transformation of our gender institution as a threat. Second, it describes *how* these people have mobilized in defense of traditional gender mores. Third, it explores *what* this mobilized resistance has effected.

Behind this straightforward approach are two of the basic conceptual strategies of the text: the interplay of meaning and power in a process of social change, and the three levels of sociological analysis (macrosocial, microsocial, and subjective). In answering the question "Why resistance?" we return to the concept of meaning systems. In describing how that resistance takes form, we in fact look at power mobilization. In describing what has been achieved by traditionalists, we look at the social product of a particular interaction between meaning and power. Throughout all of this, we remain sensitive to the threefold nature of sociological analysis. Each of the sections that follow discusses the particular interaction between macrosocial, microsocial, and subjective processes that makes understandable the issue at hand.

MEANING SYSTEMS AND RESISTANCE TO CHANGE

This section describes the motives, perceptions, and beliefs that lead people to oppose and reject the transformation of our gender institution. This focus on meanings should not, however, lead to the conclusion that subjective factors alone explain the phenomenon of resistance to change. As we have demonstrated throughout this book, subjective factors are intricately interrelated with macrosocial and microsocial factors. Here we will see how much the motives that prompt people to resist change are shaped by the structural and interactional settings in which those people are located. In later sections we will see how these motives interact with people's circumstances.

Since there has been, to date, no systematic investigation of the patterns of meaning in this resistance, our description weaves together the findings of a few fairly narrowly focused attitudinal studies with statements by spokespersons of the traditionalist movement, and with deductions about motives drawn from the actions of movement members or from what social scientists know about human subjectivity.

The data on the patterns of meaning in the movement against gender equality show that it is fueled by a diversity of motives. To depict that diversity, we use a typology suggested by one of the most influential of early sociologists, Max Weber (see Chapter 1). Four types of motives may be identified within the opposition to gender change: rational, valuational, traditional, and emotional. In practice, of course, there is considerable overlap between these different motivations. Weber, however, was attempting an analytical distinction.

Rational Systems

A rational orientation to action is one that seems to the actor and to the observer to be "reasonable" in a pragmatic, commonsense way. Those who act out of this type of meaning system pursue personal interests and goals that make sense given their life circumstances. People may make personal sense of their life circumstances or have that sense given to them by such social structures as the mass media, mass advertising backed by particular economic interests, or political rhetoric advancing the interests of influential groups. In any case, rationally motivated people respond to particular events in ways that are a practical extension of their interests and goals. Someone who resists the transformation of our gender institution on rational grounds, then, is someone who has practical, situationally produced reasons for fearing such change, someone who concludes quite pragmatically that such change will not advance her or his interests.

Given the present pattern of American life, a variety of situations may lead people whose typical orientation to life is rational to resist changes. We will look here at three institutions that produce such resistance: the economy, the traditional family, and our system of class, race, and ethnic stratification.

The Economy. Our system of gender inequality is profitable for a large number of business interests and economic ventures. A shift toward equality can prove costly to those enterprises, whose decision makers may, if their dominant meaning system is a rational one, decide to oppose the change. Let us look at a few examples.

In 1972 the Congress passed Title IX of the Educational Amendments, which made gender discrimination illegal in all educational establishments. Many American colleges, however, invest heavily in certain all-male, revenue-producing athletics, the big spectator sports like football and basketball. Title IX requires either an equally large investment in women's athletics, or a reduction of the investment in male football and basketball to the low level of the outlay colleges typically commit to women's athletics. Either option means a loss of profit. Accordingly, the educational establishment, and even more, the very well-financed National Collegiate Athletic Association, has lobbied heavily against implementation of Title IX. The result: More than a decade after its enactment its implementation remains piecemeal and slow (Gelb and Palley, 1982; Huber, 1981).

In 1978 Congress passed the Pregnancy Disability Act, outlawing discrimination against pregnant women in all areas of employment, and requiring that employers who offer health insurance and temporary disability plans extend that coverage to pregnancy and childbirth. The major opponents of this bill were opponents of abortion rights, whose motivations are shaped by a different system of meaning. But major business groups opposed the bill because of what it would cost them. Among these groups were the U.S. Chamber of Commerce, the National Association of Manufacturers, the National Retail Merchants Association, the American Retail Federation, and some insurance companies (Gelb and Palley, 1982).

The insurance community was even more fully mobilized during the early eighties against the extension of the principle of gender equality to individual retirement plans. The American work force and its employers pour billions of dollars annually into employee retirement plans. Companies who offer this form of insurance have calculated their profits on the assumption that women pay higher premiums, or more commonly, receive lower annuity payments than men because women as a "class" live longer than men. Feminists, however, pointing out that individual women may not live longer than individual men, have labeled this practice discriminatory, and have argued in the courts that gender be factored out of the calculus of retirement insurance, as race and religion, factors that also affect longevity, already are. The insurance community responded with a barrage of publicity seeking to rally public support for its position. In 1983 the Supreme Court ruled in favor of the feminist position, but legislation may still reverse this situation. Undoubtedly, the insurance community remains mobilized in favor of that reversal.

Another major battle looms between those pressing for gender equality and the business community resisting that demand, this time over the issue of jobs of "comparable worth" (see Chapter 8). This is an attempt to use legislation to reduce the wage gap between the jobs staffed primarily by men and those staffed primarily by women when it can be shown that those jobs require roughly equivalent amounts of training and effort and contribute equally to the public good. The costs of such a measure for the business community will be enormous, and it is presently effectively mobilized to dampen any significant discussion of this issue.

The Family. At the more microinteractional level of family dynamics, it has been plausibly argued that both men and women who have long played roles in traditional family systems may develop practical interests in preserving that system. One recent study, for example, has found high levels of psychological distress among men whose wives return to wage work. Despite the obvious financial advantages of this change, the family role system is affected by it in ways that decrease male convenience and prestige (Kessler and MacRae, 1982). It is those family-generated interests that produce male unease with the "working wife" phenomenon.

One provocative study analyzing women's high participation in such traditionalist efforts as the STOP ERA movement has argued that housewives in very practical ways see the "women's revolution" as a personal threat. Such women have invested a lifetime in housework and childcare in the expectation of a measure of social and economic security. They now find themselves demeaned and jeopardized by such changes as liberalized sexuality, high divorce rates, the new viewpoint that a job is essential to a woman's full identity, the trend that makes "Ms." more fashionable than "Mrs.," and the reduction of the once-proud claim to being a "housewife" to the apologetic "just a housewife" (Hacker, 1980). Viewing the erosion of a lifetime investment, such women have made a practical decision to try to stop and perhaps even reverse the transformation of our gender institution.

The Class System. Finally, although significant proportions of the working class and of the racial and ethnic minorities in America have supported the move toward gender equality, a majority of each of these groups still remains lukewarm or even hostile to that trend (Harding, 1981; Rubin, 1976; Davis, 1983; Ransford and Miller, 1983; Dowdall, 1974). This is true for both women and men, despite the fact that women from these strata have traditionally been much more likely to work outside the home than middle-class women. There are a number of reasons for this resistance: the very different family form of these groups, with its implications for personality; the perception by these groups that feminism has often been elitist and racist; above all, their very different strategies for economic survival.

All these groups experience much greater economic marginality than the white, middle-class groups that form the base of the contemporary women's movement. These circumstances require that the family, in nuclear or extended form, function as a unit to protect the economic survival of all its members. The sharp sexual division of labor within that kind of family also seem to make economic sense. Although family unity may in fact be shattered by economic stress (Rubin, 1976), to threaten that unity willfully in pursuit of gender equality seems irresponsible and foolhardy. For working-class or minority women worried at the most basic level about making ends meet, and about the threat of unemployment to them, their husbands, and their sons and daughters, loyalty to family, class, racial, or ethnic group seems a more practical survival strategy than unity with more privileged women.

Valuational Systems

In contrast to the focus on practical interests in the rational system, people who act out of a valuational system focus on general values. They act out of a commitment to those values even when their actions are irrelevant, or even detrimental, to personal interests. Many men, for example, have supported women's claims to equality because they deeply believe in the general value of equality, even though in practical ways they gain nothing and even lose something from the equalization of women's status. Indeed, it has often been valuationally guided action by the American public and the American polity that has made women's dream for equality realizable.

In this section, though, we will look at people whose value commitments place them in opposition to gender equality. We focus in particular on opposition that develops out of religious commitment, and in particular out of a commitment to Christian beliefs.

America is in certain ways an unusually religious society. In terms of professed religious commitment, it is outranked only by India, for 90 percent of all Americans believe in "God or a universal spirit" (Robertson, 1981:421). Forty percent of the population attends religious services on a weekly basis—in contrast with, for example, Great Britain, where the figure is 15 percent. Ninety percent of the population is Christian, 27 percent of that faith being Roman Catholic (Robertson, 1981:419). It is estimated that 50 million Americans belong to the fundamentalist or evangelical Protestant sects (Petchesky, 1981).

Organized religion makes available to believers a system of beliefs and values about the basic issues of human existence. Although there are other routes to such values—through, for example, philosophy, ideology, or art—and although many pressures other than a quest for values bring Americans to religion, it is still true that the primary route to basic values for most Americans is through organized religion. Within the majority religion, Christianity, there are deep undercurrents of faith that support movements toward equality. Most important, there is the Christian belief in the equal value of each human soul, a spiritual equality that transcends variations in worldly status. This belief has prompted egalitarian social movements since the earliest days of the faith. Under its influence, Christians have worked mightily in our own society against slavery and poverty and for the equal treatment of racial minorities. In contemporary times, significant sectors of the various Christian denominations have appealed to this same belief in arguing for gender equality. Groups like Priests for Equality, The Catholic Women's Ordination Conference, and Mormons for ERA have pursued equality both within the churches and in society.

There are however very specific and important values within Christianity that put it at odds with feminist goals. We will look here at three such value clusters: Christian attitudes toward sexuality, toward authority, and toward the human soul.

Attitudes toward Sexuality. At the very center of Christianity is a tangled association of the themes of sin, death, and sexuality, an association that for two thousand years has deeply affected our social and cultural life (Warner, 1976). It is humankind's falling into spiritual defilement, or sin, that is supposed to have made the ultimate terror, death, our unavoidable fate. Both at the level of doctrine and of popular belief, sexual desire is held to be the embodiment of humankind's fall into sin. Christians believe that Christ came to offer a path away from the inevitability of sin and death, a path that requires not only an active commitment to a Christlike life, but also a more passive avoidance of sexual temptation and pollution. Chastity, virginity, and celibacy are, within Christianity, highly valued. For the frailer majority of believers who cannot live in such a state, sexuality must be sanctified by the church in the sacrament of marriage. Only Christian marriage, with its commitment to the bearing of children, legitimates sexuality.

Much of contemporary feminism flies in the face of these beliefs. Operating on a very difficult set of values (Chapter 7), feminists affirm women's active sexual nature, and women's right to sex education, contraception, and birth control. They criticize conventional patterns of heterosexuality, marriage, and mothering as oppressive of women and are tolerant of sexual relations that depart from the orthodoxy of heterosexual marriage. To Christians, these demands are another manifestation of Satan's working in the world.

Attitudes toward Authority. Within Christianity too, there is a deep reverence for relationships of authority—that is for a relationship between a responsible and caring superordinate and a dutifully submissive subordinate. This is supposed to be the relationship between God and the human individual, whose joyful obedience to God's will is in keeping with Christ's behavior on earth. Several human relationships are supposed to conform to this ideal pattern of authority: the relationship between priest and layperson, between parent and child, and between husband and wife. By uncomplainingly playing one's appointed role in these relationships, one manifests God's transcendent design for the world, and one acts out in daily life a divinely inspired form of relationship. To people who hold these values, feminism's claims for women's equality, its critique of patriarchy and of the traditional arrangements in marriage and family seem to call the divine plan into question.

Attitudes toward the Human Soul.   Christians believe that every human being possesses a soul, the divine spark within each of us. The soul is present from the moment life begins; it is the miracle behind each human conception. Moreover, until the soul is born into the social world, it remains unsullied by worldly sin and pride. The fetus then possesses a pure soul, and abortion, which destroys this soul, is the very worst form of murder. Feminist demands that women be given control over their own bodies and their reproductive functions, by abortion if necessary, produce a deep, value-based revulsion in those who hold this item of Christian faith.

In the next section we will look at the mobilization of major Christian constituencies around the traditional family and against gender equality. Many factors other than value conflict help explain this mobilization: political opportunism, very practical and patriarchical self-interest, a conservative rejection of change, and protection of privilege. But it would be wrong to explain the mobilization away wholly in terms of these other factors. A genuine value-based rejection of gender equality, even by women who clearly perceive the practical benefits for themselves of such change, is one basic motivational dynamic in the resistance to gender equality.

Traditional Systems

To act on the basis of a traditional meaning system can imply two things. First, it may mean unreflective, habitual behavior along conventional lines, such as we described in earlier chapters. Such behavior, however, does not constitute active resistance to change. Second, traditional behavior can sometimes be pursued with more self-conscious assertiveness, as when people claim that their actions are deliberately traditional because they value tradition. Our behavior at such holidays as Thanksgiving, Passover, Christmas, and Independence Day will often be justified in this way.

In their everyday lives, though, Americans tend to affirm change rather than tradition. This trait distinguishes our culture from many others. It is therefore rather unusual to hear Americans defend such taken-for-granted institutions as gender purely by an appeal to tradition. Instead, when forced to reflect on or defend the conventional, Americans typically appeal to one of the meaning systems already discussed. They claim practical interest or fundamental value. It is therefore hard to come by evidence of resistance motivated primarily by the sense that what is traditional is valuable.

Yet we probably all feel pretty sure that a traditional meaning system helps fuel any large-scale pattern of opposition to change. For example, the psychological distress discovered by Kessler and MacRae among the husbands of working women is partly, the researchers feel, the result of a deep unease over the departure from conventional marital role expectations represented by the wage-earning wife. The religious involvement of many Americans and its spillover to attitudes about gender equality is often traditionally rather than valuationally motivated.

There is one particularly striking example of traditional meanings in place in the movement against gender change—namely, the frequently heard rallying cry that erosion of the traditional family, with its patriarchical authority and its nonworking mother-wife, will bring about the destruction of all that is sound and good in the American way of life. What this claim implies is that if we accept the transformation of our gender system to one of greater equality, we risk losing our political freedoms, our material affluence, and our collective moral and social conscience.

To those who work for gender equality, this claim seems nonsensical. It is like arguing that we put the American way of life in jeopardy if we extend our principles of equality and freedom to racial minorities.[1] They look for some elaboration of the claim, some specification of the stages by which one moves logically from "the traditional family" to "the American way of life." In the absence of that specification, they dismiss the whole thing as hypocritical bigotry. People anchored in a traditional mentality, however, find this unelaborated claim about the relationship between our family patterns and our general way of life genuinely acceptable. For one hallmark of traditionalism is the assumption that all the established features of a culture are interconnected. To the traditionalist, an age-old system of social arrangements is one fabric, and attempting to alter any part of those arrangements puts the whole pattern at risk. People who think this way need no elaboration of the cry "Protect the traditional family and the American way of life." As the movement against gender change shows, that cry can galvanize whole sectors of our society into political action.

Emotional Systems

We turn now to a consideration of people who act out of systems of motivation and perception fueled primarily by powerful emotional drives: by, for example, rage or generosity, security or insecurity. On this issue, social scientists since Freud have been particularly curious about emotions so deeply buried in the psyche that they are unrecognized by those who act them out. Given what we learned in Chapter 4 about primary socialization to gender, it is easy to see that many such emotions may be at work in the movement against gender equality: preverbally acquired rage against woman-mother, deep insecurities about one's own gender identity, and the terror of chaos and nothingness produced by a challenge to one's primary map of reality.

In this section, we focus on one particular configuration of emotions that appears very strikingly in the opposition to gender equality, the generalized rage and hate associated with what social scientists have called the authoritarian personality. One observer of the reaction against gender change has graphically captured this element of hostility in the movement:

> What is remarkable about all of Schlafly's books is the amount of pure hostility in them. One is struck most . . . by the vehemence of her attacks on her enemies: Nelson Rockefeller, Bella Abzug, Henry Kissinger. . . . In her eyes these people have no shred of legitimacy and no right to exist; they are beyond the moral universe. . . . The hostility is . . . characteristic of the political expressions of the New Right. Richard Viguerie. . . . tells us that one of the most important things about New Right organizers is that they are fighters . . . Jerry Falwell, for his part, is always going on about war . . . Terry Dolan calls (NCPAC) a "gut-cutting" organization. . . . [T]hose who think they are fighting wars, as opposed to electoral campaigns, are likely to feel justified in using extraordinary measures. (Fitzgerald, 1981:25)

Such generalized hostility is part of the syndrome of authoritarianism, a syndrome that may be present in the spokespersons mentioned above or only in the audience to whom they try to appeal. Authoritarianism results from a particular form of childrearing, one that is severely punitive, rigidly assertive of parental and adult power, and insistent on docility, obedience, and emotional self-control on the part of the child. The result for the child is pent-up, volcanic rage that is carried over into adulthood.

This rage can never be expressed openly against those who directly wield power in one's life, but instead spills over into an irrational hatred of powerless groups in one's environment, and of very distant powers that are not directly affected by one's hostility. Authoritarianism may fuel extremist politics of both a left-wing and a right-wing variety. In America, the dynamics for right-wing authoritarianism have been identified in the regional subcultures of the South and Southwest, in the religious subcultures of many of the fundamentalist Protestant sects, and in the class-anchored subcultures of certain economically marginal groups. Repeatedly in our history, authoritarianism, with its resultant generalized hostility and rage, has fueled reactionary political movements.

On the American political scene, the kind of anger we are talking about gets directed in a massive, undifferentiated way against the distant powers of "communism" and "the Eastern Establishment," and against the closer but relatively powerless groups of Blacks, Jews, Catholics, women, and homosexuals. People studying the current movement against gender change have identified within it this old litany of hate (Brady and Tedin, 1979; Dworkin, 1982; Fitzgerald, 1981). Indeed, one of the curious features of the current movement is its venomous, destructive hostility toward homosexuals, an intensity of feeling that makes little sense if we think of the reaction to gender equality as motivated only by pragmatic self-interest, fundamental values, and loyalty to tradition. This particular feature of the movement can be explained in terms of the emotionally generated system of meanings we have been describing, especially when it is recognized that that meaning system now operates in a sociopolitical climate which makes the other traditional scapegoats—Blacks, Jews, Catholics, and women—somewhat more powerful than they have hitherto been. This feature of the mobilization against gender change helps to support our thesis about the emotional element in that movement.

POWER MOBILIZATION AND RESISTANCE TO CHANGE

In this section, we look at the organization of opposition to changes in our gender institution. As we will see, many of those who participate in this organized opposition do so because they hold beliefs of the type described above. Others have become involved in organized opposition first, and have been led by that experience to beliefs that reject gender change and gender equality. We will even discover a few people who are actively mobilized in opposition to the transformation of our gender mores, although they never arrive at any strong beliefs which oppose that change. We can envisage the people discussed above, those subjectively opposed to gender change, and those discussed here, those actively opposing change, as two partially intersecting, dynamically interdependent circles, the former larger than the latter. To a degree, the people in the two circles are the same—but not entirely. To a degree, the existence of each group helps to sustain and enlarge the other.

The organized attempt to use our political and judicial processes to stop liberalization of our gender mores is the work of a coalition of special interest groups. The most important of these are the organizationally unified, single-issue STOP ERA association, the organizationally complex but single-issue Right to Life movement, and the multi-issue, complex political confederation calling itself the New Right. All these groups were born in the period 1972–1974. By 1978, they had converged into a single political movement around the distinctive label "pro-family." This movement is now the most formidable conservative force in American politics, with interests that extend well beyond issues of gender. Later we will trace its impact on the process of gender equality. Here we look at how its three most important strands took form and converged.

Stop ERA

In 1972 Congress passed the Equal Rights Amendment and sent it to the states for ratification. The Equal Rights Amendment (ERA) reads simply: "Equality of rights under the law shall not be denied or abridged by the United States or by any state on account of sex." It seemed to most people at the time noncontroversial enough (see Chapter 8). Despite rumblings from such conservatives as Senator Sam Ervin of North Carolina and from the John Birch Society, warning of unisex bathrooms, homosexual marriages, and women in combat, even the opponents of ERA expected it would obtain ratification. At the state level, resistance was shown only by small, scattered groups of women expressing a preference for "women's privileges" (O'Reilly 1983). By the end of 1972, 22 states had voted for ERA, and the additional 16 states were expected to follow in 1973

(Hacker, 1980). It was at that point that a major, nationwide effort began to oppose the trend toward ratification. That opposition was the work of a national organization calling itself STOP ERA, an organization formed almost single-handedly in 1972 by Phyllis Schlafly.

Schlafly had to that point displayed no deep primary motivational commitment to traditional gender mores, and seems to have arrived at her STOP ERA role almost accidentally.[2] A conservative ideologue of the orthodox style, deeply anti-communist, anti-big government and for a tough defense policy, she has long aspired to a conventional political career (Fitzgerald, 1981). In the late sixties, she had hoped to become president of the National Federation of Republican Women (O'Reilly, 1983), and in 1980 she had expected an appointment by Reagan to the Defense Department (Dworkin, 1982). In both these hopes she was disappointed.

Partly to assuage the disappointment, she founded in the late sixties her own conservative organization, which was incorporated in 1972 and named the Eagle Forum. This organization produced a twice-monthly newsletter that eventually reached 30,000 readers (Fitzgerald, 1981) and arranged annual training conferences for 300 to 400 potential women leaders (O'Reilly, 1983). It was this organization that brought the ERA to her attention. In 1972 she devoted an issue of the newsletter to criticizing it. She received in response such a flood of supportive mail that in 1972 she founded STOP ERA. That response was prompted by all the meanings we have discussed. The mix of motives would provide Schlafly, though she may not have realized it at the time, with the issue that would fulfill her political drive.

For the first few years Schlafly ran STOP ERA out of her house in Alton, Illinois, building it into a network of state-level and local chapters, with thousands of members and grassroots links to a general public of supporters. Its members, though initially inexperienced, soon became an effective lobbying machine that could produce mile-long lists of signatures, impressive mail-in campaigns, and rallies of its supporters in state and federal capitals. Through it all, Schlafly was very visible, giving countless presentations on the lecture circuit and in the media. A cool, sophisticated presence, she became one of the better-known figures on the American political scene, evoking hatred and adoration from different constituencies. In 1978 Schlafly joined her organization and her efforts to the broader umbrella coalition of the New Right (Fitzgerald, 1981).

The Right to Life Movement

In 1973, one year after Congress had passed the ERA, the Supreme Court, in the historic *Roe* v. *Wade* decision, in effect legalized abortion during the first trimester of pregnancy. To feminists, this signified that women had gained a significant grant of autonomy. Religious opposition formed immediately. The first mobilization came from the Catholic Church, whose religious doctrine holds that abortion is equivalent to murder. The National Conference of Catholic Bishops established the Pro-Life Affairs Committee, in effect initiating the Right to Life movement. Since then, the sophisticated, well-financed organization of the Catholic Church has used moral exhortation, meetings of believers, special church collections, telephone campaigns, and a flood of printed materials in an attempt to reverse the legalization of abortion. The strategy has been to fight at the polls for the defeat of pro-abortion legislators and for the election of pro-life candidates, with the long-term aim of amending the Constitution to extend "personhood" to the fetus. Abortion would then legally be murder (Petchesky, 1981).

Opposition also came from the Protestants, particularly from the fundamentalist or evangelical churches. These denominations number some 50 million members whose support can be tapped not only from the Sunday pulpit, but on a daily basis through the radio and television broadcasts of fundamentalist preachers. The fundamentalist Christian constituency has long been a source of conservative action in American politics. Its members view not only abortion, but ERA and all other efforts to liberalize women's status as a violation of biblical precept and divine will. Opposition to abortion, however, made possible a formidable alliance between them and the Catholic Church, their traditional "enemy." Geared from the outset for political action, this alliance has an enormous base and a very effective communication system. By the late seventies, however, the Right to Life movement, like STOP ERA, had been drawn into the New Right Coalition (Petchesky, 1981).

The New Right

In 1974, Gerald Ford selected Nelson Rockefeller as his vice-president, scandalizing conservatives in the Republican party.[3] One conservative who took action was Richard A. Viguerie, head of the Richard A. Viguerie Company (RAVCO). RAVCO is a direct mail business that raises money for its clients—politicians, religious and special interest groups—by making a direct appeal to citizens known to be likely to respond to a particular cause. One secret of RAVCO's success (it was grossing $15 million by the late seventies) is its use of sophisticated computer technology for the assembling and reassembling of lists of donors from stored data banks of people's subscription and donation patterns. Viguerie has increasingly tended to take only customers whose causes mesh with his own conservative beliefs: Conservative Books for Christian Leaders, No Amnesty for Deserters, the National Rifle Association.

In 1974, Viguerie called together a group of young, conservative, politically talented backroom organizers, whose joint purpose was to "create a conservative movement outside the Republican Party" (Fitzgerald, 1981:20). In 1975, the group invented a label for itself, the New Right. Over the next few years, the New Right mastered the art of coalition politics for conservative ends. They linked up single- and multi-issue groups, established foundations and research groups, and organized political action committees (PACs). They drew not only STOP ERA and the National Right to Life Committee into their movement, but also leading fundamentalist media preachers like Jerry Falwell and James Robinson. In addition, the New Right coalition includes such groups as the Moral

Majority, Religious Roundtable, Christian Voice, American Family Forum, the Right to Life PAC, the American Life Lobby, the National Pro-Family Coalition, the Library Court Group, the Heritage Foundation, the Eagle Forum, the Committee for Responsible Youth Politics, and the National Political Action Committee (Fitzgerald, 1981; Petchesky, 1981). In 1980, Viguerie formed the Council on National Policy from key members of this coalition. The council is to function as the steering committee for the whole movement.

STOP ERA brought to the New Right a grassroots lobbying movement. The National Right to Life Committee brought the organization and membership of the churches, as well as the tactic of targeting liberal legislators for electoral defeat. Viguerie's New Right group has the widest political vision, and through RAVCO the capacity to mobilize its now vastly expanded publics for financial support and political action.

Viguerie, like Schlafly, is an orthodox conservative motivated much more by anti-communism and anti-big government beliefs than by a primary commitment to traditional family values. His stand on traditional family issues—against homosexuality, abortion, sex education, contraception, women's rights, and liberalized sexual mores, and for parental and religious control of the schools—while compatible with his general beliefs, has been made central in his platform for reasons of political expediency. These views, which his movement in the late seventies labeled "pro-family," are, for the reasons discussed above, appealing to a huge constituency.

While centering on "pro-family" issues, however, the New Right has incorporated into its program a variety of other themes. It supports such regimes as the South African and the Taiwanese, and is aggressively anti-communist. It is against social welfare, conservation, and regulation of big business, and for big defense budgets and nuclear power. As Petchesky (1981) points out, this expanding framework of beliefs builds potential fissures into the coalition. Feminists against abortion, for example, may have a hard time with a pro-nuclear stance. Middle-class Midwestern and Western women who oppose ERA may also be for protection of the natural environment. Blue-collar urban ethnics who oppose abortion will also oppose any major dismantling of public welfare services, or of the restraints on big business vis-à-vis labor and consumers. So far, however, the New Right coalition has held by mobilizing and centering on "pro-family" issues; on resisting, in other words, the liberalization and transformation of our gender institution.

EFFECTS OF THE MOBILIZATION

A steady flow of accounts in the press bears witness to the fact that the attitudes and organizations described in the preceding sections have led at the microsocial and organizational levels to active opposition to gender equality. At a Pennsylvania college, for example, a female student is deluged with hate mail and has rocks thrown at her windows by groups of male students because in campus politics she has campaigned for the Equal Rights Amendment, for use of the title Ms., and for more women faculty (*Ms.*, April 1983:44). At California State University, Long Beach, the director and several instructors in the women's studies program are fired for teaching materials contrary to "American family values" after "pro-family" groups lobby the university administration (*Feminist Studies*, 9, 2, Summer 1983:387–393).

In Florida, two abortion clinics are firebombed and the director of a third kidnapped by a small terrorist group which demands that he renounce and President Reagan condemn abortion (*Ms.*, November 1982: 19). In Illinois, a teacher with an impeccable work record is suspended without pay and legally charged as immoral because, though unmarried, she has a baby that she refuses to give up for adoption (*Ms.*, April 1983: 23). *The Wall Street Journal* reports that employers "believe a man who would leave the work force to raise children is a 'poor risk' because he might do it again" (*NOW Times*, June 1981), while in Chicago a judge awards custody of two children to a working father rather than a working, and occasionally traveling, mother because "the children are entitled to a stable environment" (*The Washington Post*, October 29, 1980). In Boston, *The Christian Science Monitor* fires an employee because she is a lesbian (*Ms.*, "Gazette," May 1983:29), and in South Carolina three U.S. Rangers stomp a male homosexual to death and are subsequently charged with a misdemeanor (*The Washington Post*, November 4, 1983).

Each of these incidents shows people using whatever power resources they have to protect the traditional organization of gender against those who in some way challenge it. In this section we will focus on resistance to gender equality that occurs in the national political system. For it is on this institution that the organized opposition to gender equality has focused—understanding full well, as feminists do, that action initiated there affects the whole society. Moreover, in the arena of national politics, the interests that seek to protect the traditional family have not been ineffective. We will trace their influence on five major political issues: the elections of 1980; the Laxalt Family Protection Act; the Equal Rights Amendment; the legal status of abortion; and the equal rights–affirmative action policies of the Reagan administration in the first four years of the eighties.

The 1980 Elections

In the chronicle of the latest wave of feminist activity, the early seventies, with, among other things, congressional approval of the ERA, the enactment of Title IX, and the legalization of abortion, mark the cresting of the legal movement for women's rights. That period of accelerated liberalization immediately generated its countermovement, the so-called "pro-family" coalition. At the level of national politics, attempts to brake the pace of change were visible by the late seventies (Eisenstein, 1981 a), but it was covert resistance, inconspicuous and unacknowledged. Formally, official Washington supported the move towards equality. The election of

1980 was significant in that it ushered in a period of more explicit and open political resistance to gender equality.

In the 1980 electoral campaign, the debate on gender equality was perhaps the major issue on which the two major parties differed. The parties were similar in their espousal of neoconservative economic policies, their retreat from Great Society ideals, and their hostility to "big government." On the complex issue of gender, however, party platforms were sharply opposed. The Republicans declared:

> We support equal rights and equal opportunities for women without taking away traditional rights of women such as exemption from military draft . . . . We oppose any move which would give the Federal government more power over families. . . . We reaffirm our belief in the traditional role and values of the family in our society. . . . We affirm our support of a constitutional amendment to restore protection of the right for unborn children. . . . (quoted in Eisenstein, 1981a:194)

In contrast, the Democrats affirmed:

> The Democratic Party commits itself to a Constitution, economy and society open to women on an equal basis with men. The primary route to that new horizon is ratification of the equal rights amendment . . . . The Democratic Party shall withhold financial and technical campaign assistance from candidates who do not support the E.R.A. The Democratic Party supports the 1973 Supreme Court decision on abortion rights as the law of the land and opposes any constitutional amendment to restrict or overturn that decision. . . . We therefore oppose government interference in the reproductive decisions of Americans, especially those government programs or legislative restrictions that deny poor Americans their right to privacy . . . of reproductive choices. . . . (quoted in Eisenstein, 1981a:194)

It was the mobilization of the New Right and its sympathizers within the Republican party that led to the Republican party's stand on women's rights. Both the pressure of pro-rights women's groups and the Democratic party's wish to contrast with the Republicans in the elections led to the Democrats' strong pro-women's rights stand (Eisenstein, 1981a). With the lines thus clearly drawn, the Republicans won the White House from an incumbent Democratic president, at the same time capturing the Senate by defeating many experienced liberal and pro-feminist senators and replacing them with relatively unknown, conservative, and "pro-family" candidates. The "pro-family" movement claimed a major popular victory, and some liberals, like McGovern, agreed (Eisenstein, 1981a).

But was it? Did the 1980 election demonstrate a massive outpouring of sentiment against gender equality and women's rights? Strictly speaking, the evidence does not support this claim. The 1980 elections were marked by low voter turnout. Only 53 percent of the electorate voted, the remaining 47 percent registering no opinion on anything, not even women's rights. Of those voting, 27 percent voted for the Republican presidential candidate, Reagan; 22 percent for the incumbent Carter. Of those voting for Reagan, opinion studies show that by a 4:1 margin they were voting *against* Carter's record on economic and foreign affairs, rather than *for* Reagan's conservatism (including his pro-family stance).

In other words, only a small fraction of the total voting-age public actively registered a pro-family viewpoint as their primary stance. There was no "popular mandate" against gender equality (Eisenstein, 1981a). In American politics, however, electoral outcomes are often determined by relatively small margins at the polls. This was the case in 1980, when the organized "pro-family" minority constituency made a critical difference.

The Laxalt Family Protection Act

The "pro-family" movement is mobilized to protect a certain family form against the multiplicity of changes and challenges that presently seem to threaten it. The type of family the "pro-family" movement sees as traditional and typical of American society is that of a God-fearing, heterosexual married couple, authoritatively in control of its minor children, for whom economic support is provided by a "breadwinning male head of household" and household services, childcare, and emotional maintenance by a nonworking wife-mother-housewife. Threats to this institution include working women, two-paycheck families, househusbands, equal parenting, premarital and extramarital sex, deferred marriage and childbearing, birth control, gay rights, and divorce.

At the level of national politics, this general position on the family has been most fully advanced in the Family Protection Act, or the Laxalt bill. It was introduced by a major spokesperson for the "pro-family" lobby, Senator Paul Laxalt (Republican–Montana), who was reputed to be one of President Reagan's closest personal friends in Washington. This bill seeks to buttress the traditional family form in the following ways:

1. *Nonworking wives.* Special tax benefits for married couples filing joint returns, and a childcare deduction for nonworking married women engaged in "volunteer," "charity," or "religious" work (Title IV, Secs 401-403) (Petchesky 1981:244).

2. *Marriage.* A $1,000 tax exemption for *married couples only* in the year in which a child is born or adopted (Petchesky 1981:245). Also see (1) above.

3. *Male authority.* Restrictions on the federal government's powers to interfere in cases of wife abuse.

4. *Parental authority, especially over children's sexuality.*—Restrictions on the federal government's power to intervene in cases of child abuse; notification of parents before providing birth control, abortion, or venereal disease treatment to adolescents; authorization of parents to review any textbooks used in the public schools; tax credits for private and parochial school tuition, schools in which parental influence can be more direct.

5. *Direct opposition to criticism.* Denial of federal funds to any educational program that includes "educational materials or studies [which] tend to denigrate . . . or . . . deny the role differences between the sexes as it has been historically understood in the United States (Title I, Sec. 101, quoted in Petchesky, 1981:245); withholding of federal funds from any individual or group engaged in "homosexual advocacy."

6. *Reinstatement of gender segregation.* Withholding of federal funds from any school authority that prohibits sex segregation of "sports and other school-related activities" on affirmative action grounds (Petchesky, 1981:245).

At the moment, the Family Protection Act is stalled in committee and, barring a major shift to the right in Congress, it appears unlikely that it will be enacted. Even if enacted, many of its features will run up against judicial opposition because of unconstitutionality. The bill's significance is not so much in its likelihood of enactment, but rather in the comprehensive sense it gives us of the "pro-family" lobby's legislative program. As we will see, elements of this program have found their way into the executive policies of the Reagan administration.

Defeat of the Equal Rights Amendment

In 1982 the ERA, first approved by Congress and sent to the states for ratification in 1972, went down in defeat, an enormous symbolic victory for the "pro-family" movement. "Defeat of the ERA" means that the proposal, which would have made discrimination on the grounds of sex illegal, failed to obtain the 38-state ratification necessary to effect a constitutional amendment. In 1982, despite repeated extensions of the ratification period by Congress, the clock ran out on the ERA. It was three states short of ratification. Holdout states were Alabama, Arkansas, Arizona, Florida, Georgia, Illinois, Louisiana, Mississippi, Missouri, Nevada, North Carolina, Oklahoma, South Carolina, Utah, and Virginia. (Hacker, 1980).

Why was the ERA defeated? As we pointed out above, in 1972 even its opponents had expected speedy ratification. The proposed amendment, sent to the states by Congress in 1972, had been ratified by 22 states at the end of that year, and another 16 were expected to follow suit rapidly in 1973. Additionally, over the ensuing decade opinion polls repeatedly showed that a majority of the population favored the amendment. ERA's defeat must be attributed to the effective pressure-group political opposition of Schlafly's STOP ERA organization.

STOP ERA used a variety of tactics—write-in campaigns, lobbying, rallies at the state house, petitions, and advocacy via the lecture and media circuits—to demonstrate to the state legislature, where ratification had to be given, that there was popular opposition to the amendment. ERA supporters responded in kind, but were slower off the mark. They also had to work by and large against the prejudices of legislators, in contrast to the STOP ERA lobbyists (O'Reilly 1983).

STOP ERA's major effect, as O'Reilly points out, was to make politicians grow cautious about ERA and anxious to put some distance between themselves and a now-controversial issue. By 1980, ERA's fate had been determined. The Republican party's veiled opposition was a recognition of this fact (Hacker, 1980). Nevertheless, an executive and Senate essentially opposed to the amendment added one more factor to the equation against its passage. Moreover, the new coalition between the executive and the pro-family movement could engage in mutual congratulations at the amendment's defeat in 1982.

ERA supporters have sworn to continue the fight. Pointing out that the battle for women's suffrage took seventy years, they are seeking to reintroduce an equal rights amendment in Congress, in effect beginning the process all over again. At the moment of writing, that effort has been stopped, at least temporarily, by a narrow defeat in the House of Representatives.

The Struggle over Abortion Rights

As we saw above, organized opposition to abortion rights, like organized opposition to ERA, took form in the early seventies. Unlike the chronicle of ERA, however, there has been no definitive outcome so far in the struggle between pro-choice and pro-life groups. Because of this, the 1980 elections were more meaningful for the abortion issue than for ERA.

Prior to 1980, the most significant gain of the anti-abortion coalition′ was to bring about an end to federal subsidies of abortions for Medicaid recipients. This restriction on liberalized abortion is generally known as the Hyde Amendment, for it has been annually introduced, ever since 1974, by Representative Henry J. Hyde (Republican–Illinois) as an amendment to the appropriations bill for the Labor and HEW (HHS) departments. Congress first approved the Hyde Amendment in 1976, and has done so annually ever since. Pro-choice groups have challenged the amendment in the courts, but the Supreme Court has upheld its constitutionality. By 1980 a woman's right to abortion still stood, but the principle had been established that the federal government need not support this right financially. Poor women were deprived of their right to abortion, unless they could find other means of paying for the procedure (Gelb and Palley, 1982).

The 1980 elections brought in an administration pledged to oppose abortion, and a much more conservative legislature. The opposition became much more open and militant, essentially mounting a three-pronged attack on a woman's right to legal abortion. The first part of this attack was initiated directly by the new administration, which sought to restrict the practice of abortion in all the administrative areas where it could legitimately do so. In the face of judicial challenges from pro-choice groups, the executive sought to cut off federal funds from any Public Health Service program that provides abortion or abortion-related services; to prohibit federal funding of abortion in the District of Columbia, the Peace Corps, and in health benefits programs for federal employees and for military and other defense personnel; and to forbid funding of abortion research in any population planning program (Lewis et al. 1983).

The second prong of the attack on abortion rights has been implemented through the legislative arm of government. There are before Congress at any moment a variety of initiatives against abortion: proposed legislation to limit the powers of the federal courts on this issue; attempts to initiate a constitutional amendment that would grant "personhood" and therefore the constitutional right to life to the fetus; attempts to extend this right by statute, or to make abortion illegal by statute. A number of legislators have been active in this effort, the most prominent and visible of whom is Senator Jesse Helms of North Carolina. Moreover, President Reagan made it known that he would react favorably to any anti-abortion legislation that crossed his desk. So far the pro-choice groups have managed to protect a woman's right to abortion, but only barely. In 1983 Senator Helm's latest attempt to legislate personhood for the fetus was defeated in the Senate by a vote of 47 to 46 (Lewis et al., 1983; Caudle 1983).

The final line of attack on abortion rights is through the courts, again with the initiative coming from the executive. The Justice Department has presented the Supreme Court with a carefully selected set of test cases aimed at obstructing or delegitimizing abortion rights. Pro-life groups' hopes were fueled by the perception of a conservative shift in the Court on this issue with the appointment of Sandra Day O'Connor. So far, however, this line of attack has failed. In 1983 the Supreme Court ruled firmly, by a 6 to 3 margin, in favor of the present liberal status quo on abortion (Copelon, 1983).

Administrative Policies, 1980-1984

The 1980 elections brought to power an administration committed to protecting the traditional family. The Reagan administration also claims a commitment to gender equality. In fulfillment of this claim, it has set up a variety of task forces and liaison groups relating to women's issues and has appointed a large number of women to high-ranking government positions. These facts must be measured against the policies actually followed by the administration. We have already traced that administration's efforts to circumscribe abortion rights. In this section, we present a sampling of other executive actions that have important implications for the issue of gender equality.

Budgetary Priorities. The Reagan administration was pledged to heavy defense spending, to revitalization of the economy by reducing the tax burden on business, and to bringing relief to the American family by reducing the tax burden on individuals. In order to balance the budget under these constraints, the administration was also committed to reducing "the costs of big government." What this amounted to was an attempt, largely effective, to slash welfare programs. The consequences of these cuts were borne disproportionately by women (Coalition of Women on the Budget, 1983).

This is partly the indirect result of the fact that women constitute 70 percent of that section of our population that lives below the poverty line. Slashes in Aid to Families with Dependent Children, in social security payments to older people, in Medicaid, Medicare, food stamps, housing and energy supplements, job training programs for the unemployed, and nutritional programs for school children all press particularly hard on women, increasing their struggles and reducing their hopes of an escape from poverty. Budgetary cuts, however, also directly reduced services intended for women, such as family planning services, battered wives' and rape victims' centers, and childcare facilities. These cuts also affected "watchdog" government agencies charged with protecting women's civil rights.

Affirmative Action in Employment. Prior to 1980, any employer with more than 50 employees and more than $50,000 in government contracts had to file an affirmative action plan with the Office of Federal Contract Compliance. Under the Reagan administration, only employers with over 250 employees and at least one government contract of over $1 million were required to file such a plan. A contractor was now exempt even if she or he received several millions in government funds, so long as no single contract was in excess of $1 million. This change in policy released 75 percent of all government contractors from affirmative action monitoring. Moreover, the Justice Department has sought, so far unsuccessfully, a Supreme Court reversal of the Weber ruling, which upholds the use of quotas and goals as an affirmative action measure. The government, in effect, backed away from much of its commitment to prevent discriminatory employment practices (Huber, 1981).

Eroding Title IX. Title IX of the Educational Amendments, as we saw above, was enacted in 1972 to outlaw sex discrimination in elementary, secondary, and postsecondary education. Implementation of this law has always been less than fully effective, partly because of active opposition from education groups, and partly because of the complexity of monitoring our large, multilayered educational establishment (Gelb and Palley, 1982).

In the early eighties the Reagan administration took far more drastic steps to limit the effectiveness of Title IX. It suggested that restrictions on sex discrimination, under this law, referred only to sex discrimination against students, and not to the employment practices of educational organizations. It put under review existing guidelines for sexual harassment. It clearly signaled a softening of its watchdog role against sex discrimination in athletic programs. Most significantly of all, the Justice Department under Reagan sought through the courts to reverse the policy of previous administrations whereby Title IX is interpreted as meaning that an educational institution that accepts federal funds for some of its programs cannot discriminate on grounds of sex in any of its programs. The Reagan administration has argued that only the programs that receive federal money are debarred from sex discrimination practices. As an example, a university research program that is federally funded cannot legally practice sex discrimination, but that university's athletic programs, so long as they are not directly funded by the government, need no longer be scrutinized for sex discrimination. In February 1984 the Supreme Court ruled in favor of the Justice Department's position, handing the Reagan administration a major victory and in effect all but killing Title IX.

Prosecuting on Behalf of Discrimination Victims. Even with the changes described above, complaints about discrimination may produce an investigation by government agencies. Under Reagan's administration, however, the Justice Department announced that it would file suit on behalf of individual victims of discrimination, but that it would no longer file class action suits. For example, it would file on behalf of a particular clerk who has experienced job discrimination, but not on behalf of the whole group of clerks in that particular employment setting.

This meant that any individual claiming discrimination had to be prepared to bear the pressure of standing alone before her or his employer through the long process of investigation, and that the benefits of any decision in her or his favor would not extend to other similarly situated employees. Further, the Justice Department would no longer seek back-pay redress for such individuals. A promise to rectify the situation as of the present moment would suffice (Huber, 1981).

Weakening the Enforcement Agencies. Finally, we need to note the effect of budgetary cuts and of administrative opposition to key "watchdog" agencies like the Women's Bureau, the Equal Employment Opportunities Commission, the Office of Federal Contract Compliance, and the Civil Rights Commission. Reduced budgets, in many cases disproportionate to overall patterns in the federal government, led to staff reductions, which in turn produced caseload backlogs extending back over several years. And as this is being written, the administration has moved to create a compliant Civil Rights Commission by firing some of its more independent members and replacing them with "more congenial" appointees.

SUMMARY

This whole book has focused on the contemporary American phase in the history of gender change and of women's struggle for equality. It is useful to remember, however, that this struggle against a constrictive gender system has been waged fairly constantly, and primarily by women, for at least four hundred years (Spender, 1982). At each of the moments when that struggle has swelled into a major social movement (See Chapters 6, 7, and 8), forces in favor of the status quo have mobilized in opposition. The outcome of those struggles between liberationalists and traditionalists has, at worst, been a defeat for the former group, and at best, a serious modification of their demands.

What will be the outcome of the present contest between those who seek to change our gender institution and those who resist that change? In Chapter 12, we attempt to make such a prognosis. At this point, it is important to note two factors that are vital to any attempt at such a prediction, factors closely linked to the account given in this chapter. The first is the role of women's groups that keep a watchful eye on political attempts to circumscribe newly gained rights, and who fight constantly against such attempts (Tinker, 1983). These are some of the unsung resistance fighters of the contemporary women's movement. The second is the question of the durability of the conservative victory in 1980. At the moment of writing, the battle for the 1984 elections is taking form, with both "pro-family" groups and feminists actively marshaling their resources. The outcome will determine whether the events of recent years were merely a moment in history or whether they mark the beginning of a major trend, the latest phase of reversing women's liberation.

NOTES

1. Most feminists in fact deny the basic premise of this claim, the assertion that a move to gender equality will destroy our institution of the family. Distinguishing between the "traditional family," with its hierarchical and patriarchical features, and the general ideal of family life and experience, most feminists affirm the general idea of family. While allowing for alternative life styles, feminists seek to strengthen family life by obtaining for it a more egalitarian form.

2. Schlafly's personal life, indeed, is almost a model of that of the "new woman." A brilliant student with an M.A. in government, she has, in addition to raising six children, written nine books, run for Congress twice, been a delegate to almost every Republican convention since the fifties, earned a law degree when in her mid-fifties, and organized the national STOP ERA organization and her own multi-issue lobbying group, the Eagle Forum (Fitzgerald, 1981).

3. The description here is heavily in debt to Fitzgerald (1981). Rockefeller was seen by conservatives as the enemy of their hero, Goldwater, and as a corrupt member of the liberal-leaning "Eastern Establishment."

12
A CONCLUDING NOTE: LOOKING TOWARD THE FUTURE*

In this book we have sketched four ideals for gender arrangements that significant groups of Americans hold today: the conservative, the liberal feminist, the Marxist feminist, and the radical feminist. This brief concluding chapter looks at the probability each of these ideals has of becoming a reality in the remaining years of this century. Our estimation of these probabilities rests on an analysis of present structures and trends.

Let us first briefly review the four ideals. The conservative viewpoint was presented in all we said about conventional gender arrangements and in our analysis of the backlash against feminism in Chapter 11. Anchored in a belief in the natural differences between men and women, differences many conventional people see as divinely ordained, the conservative ideal for gender is one centering on preservation of the traditional family. In this family, the husband brings in a livelihood and is the authoritative power figure. The wife stays home to raise the children, run the home, and furnish her working husband with a comfortable, caring environment. Parents exercise effective control over minor children. In this ideal world, religion is a central inspiration in people's lives, and such sinful practices as premarital and extramarital sex, abortion, and homosexuality have been effectively banished. The conservative viewpoint accepts gender inequality. Since a challenge to that inequality is the hallmark of feminism, it is clearly antifeminist.

*By Ruth Wallace, Patricia Lengermann, and Jill Brantley.

The three feminist ideals for gender were described in Chapter 7. Liberal feminism affirms the equal potential for growth of all individuals and the basic rightness of our American democratic order. It is, however, fiercely critical of barriers to equal opportunity in our society, seeing them as the product of prejudices like sexism and racism, and of socialization processes that in a multiplicity of ways serve to reproduce those inequalities. In the ideal liberal world, men and women have equal chances of participating in and reaping the benefits of public and private life. Families are egalitarian, children are raised in an atmosphere free of sexist stereotypes, laws and education have opened the possibility of career success equally to males and females, and sexism has become past history.

Marxist feminists believe that the source of all social oppression is class inequality under capitalism, a system which produces the pathologies of oppressed classes, oppressed races, and oppressed women. In the ideal society of Marxist feminists, a revolution by all oppressed groups has destroyed capitalism, producing a world in which all work is equally valued and the variable needs of individuals are humanely met. Social organizations of a variety of types freely provide services that reduce the drudgery in domestic life. Men and women, freed of the anxieties and alienation generated by class and capitalism, relate as equals in creating their personal lives.

Radical feminists argue that the primary model for all social inequality is patriarchy, a system in which male power exploits, abuses, and devalues women. They argue that even a revolution against capitalism will leave this structure intact, as will the gradual and accommodating strategies of the liberals. In the ideal world of the radicals, all patriarchal structures, including our most basic assumptions about nature, human beings, and power, have been critically confronted and dismantled. The divisions produced by patriarchy—nature vs. humanity, reason vs. emotion, public vs. private, superordinate vs. subordinate—have been woven together in people's vision of life. Society and culture affirm woman, her strengths, viewpoint, and sisterhood, as primary values. In this society and culture, all people develop in a humane and supportive environment; they are able to develop fully, and to pattern their personal lives freely.

Let us now attempt to assess the probabilities for any of these ideals becoming a reality. As we demonstrated in Chapter 9, women have in recent years made significant gains in the occupational and educational institutions of our society. Chapter 7 shows that the attitudes of both women and men in our society have shifted steadily toward an acceptance of gender egalitarianism in both public and private spheres. If both trends continue, the liberal ideal for gender seems the most likely to achieve partial realization, particularly on the issues of women moving into the public sphere and of the establishment in the public mind of the principle of gender equality.

But even these fairly modest gains are built on alloyed foundations. First, they depend on two paychecks being better than one. That indisputable "fact" is, in terms of quality of life and real monetary value, only as solid· as the economy is inflationary and as government tax policies are nondiscriminatory against two-income households. The latter point is often an area of bitter debate in tax policy. As we saw in Chapter 11, there are proposals to shift government economic policies to encourage women to stay home. Second, these modest liberal feminist gains depend on government continuing to fund higher education at a sufficient level to guarantee that women can afford to return to school; that women are not forced to choose between educating themselves or their children; and that families are not forced to choose between educating one child (often the male, if conventional scripts hold) rather than another.

Moreover, even if these trends toward work-force participation, educational attainment, and egalitarian attitudes continue, several aspects of the liberal feminist ideal may still fall short of realization. For example, women are still segregated in lower-paying jobs and in college majors that at best lead to mid-level positions. At home, as Chapter 9 showed, women still do the bulk of the work. Changing attitudes have not yet led the majority of men to accept responsibilities in the private sphere as a duty, not a favor. Indeed, many women enter the paid labor force with a sense that they should contribute as a breadwinner and still be the main homemaker. They find themselves in the position of feeling perpetually grateful to the male for any tasks performed at home. In all these areas, the women's movement will have to remain mobilized to effect change if the liberal feminist dream is to be realized.

The conservative vision of gender arrangements will continue to be a significant structure for many women and men, especially among churchgoers of a fundamentalist persuasion and in certain geographic areas such as the rural South. A real transformation of the society in a conservative direction would, however, probably require a severe downturn in the economy, heavy mobilization by the ideological leaders of the New Right, and their effective control over the policies of the state. All this is possible but doubtful in the degree necessary to effect a complete change. And certainly such attempts at conservative change have not and would not go unopposed.

There seems to be far less likelihood that the Marxist and radical ideals will significantly alter the organization of our society and our institution of gender. The Marxist vision would require a revolutionary restructuring of our institutions of political power and economy. That type of restructuring, it appears right now, could only occur after a major disruption of our economic life and a change in political policies on a scale surpassing that of the Great Depression of the 1930s. The radical feminist ideal would require that radical feminists attain major bases of social power in our society on a scale sufficient to produce a cultural revolution. Both in terms of the present organization of our society and of the variable viewpoints within the women's movement itself, such an outcome seems unlikely.

The Marxist and radical ideals will, however, continue to shape and pattern people's actions within the women's movement itself, if we construe that movement in its broadest sense as the interaction between a large number of woman-oriented organizations on the one hand, and a large sympathetic public on the other (see Chapter 8). A permanent question within that movement is whether it will center on the interests of white, middle-class women or whether it will both organizationally and in terms of its values and goals include working-class and minority women. To the extent that the movement maintains momentum in the latter direction, the Marxist feminist ideal will continue as a visible part of our social world. As for the radical critique of patriarchy, that view, as we argued in Chapter 7, lies at the creative center of feminism. As such, it will become visible in the way sectors of the movement pattern their own lives. Even more significantly perhaps, it will function as a constant source of ferment and intellectual growth within the movement.

In our attempt to envisage the future we come finally to the question of whether the women's movement will continue at all, and if so, on what scale. To answer this, we need first to point out again, as we have done in earlier chapters, that for at least three hundred years there has been a tradition of feminist protest, and for at least one hundred and fifty years a women's movement in our society. Given that the structural conditions which produced this protest have not radically altered, the women's movement will continue to be part of our social, political, and intellectual life. As to its scale in the next fifteen years, it would seem that it will be an extensive and highly visible movement rather than a small, marginal one. We base this assertion on our earlier analysis of future trends in women's work-force participation and experience, and of their movement into higher education; on the continuing pressure in their lives in all institutional areas, particularly in family life; on the structural limits to a full-fledged conservative victory; and on the continuing mobilization and vitality of the movement's organizations.

In sum then, for persons devoted to the cause of gender equality, the next fifteen years may be confronted with a cautious optimism that must be untinged by even the slightest complacency. American society will continue to move toward greater gender equality only to the degree that those who believe in that ideal continue to work for it.

REFERENCES

AGONITO, ROSEMARY (ed.). *History of Ideas on Woman.* New York: Putnam, 1977.

ALDOUS, JOAN (ed.). *Two Paychecks: Life in Dual-Earner Families.* Beverly Hills, Calif.: Sage, 1982.

ALPERN, M. "Research on Vision Physiology, Reflective Error, and Related Ocular Abnormalities," *Vision and Its Disorders,* NINDB Monograph no. 4. Washington, D.C.: U.S. Department of Health, Education, and Welfare, National Institute of Neurological Diseases and Blindness, 1967.

AMUNDESEN, KIRSTEN. *The Silenced Majority: Women and American Democracy.* Englewood Cliffs, N.J.: Prentice-Hall, 1971

ANDERSEN, MARGARET L. *Thinking about Women.* New York: Macmillan, 1983.

ANDRE, RAE. *Homemakers: The Forgotten Workers.* Chicago: University of Chicago Press, 1981.

ARIES, PHILIPPE. *Centuries of Childhood: A Social History of Family Life.* New York: Vintage Press, 1960.

ATKINSON, TI-GRACE. *Amazon Odyssey.* New York: Links Books, 1974.

BABCOCK, NORTON, AND ROSS FRIEDMAN. *Sex Discrimination and the Law.* Boston: Little, Brown, 1975.

BAKER, MARY ANNE, ET AL. *Women Today: A Multidisciplinary Approach to Women's Studies.* Monterey, Calif.: Brooks/Cole, 1980.

BANNER, LOIS. *American Beauty.* New York: Knopf, 1983.

BARNET, RICHARD, AND RONALD MULLER. *Global Reach: Power and the Multinational Corporations* New York: Simon and Schuster, 1974.

BARRY, KATHLEEN. *Female Sexual Slavery.* Englewood Cliffs, N.J.: Prentice Hall, 1979.

BARUCH, G. K. "Maternal Influences upon College Women's Attitudes toward Women and Work," *Developmental Psychology,* 6 (1972): 32–37.

BAYER, L. M., AND N. BAYLEY. *Growth Diagnosis: Selected Method for Interpreting and Predicting Physical Growth.* Chicago: University of Chicago Press, 1959.

BEARD, JANE, AND MARCIA D. GREENBERGER. "Women and the Law." In Irene Tinker (ed.), *Women in Washington.* Beverly Hills, Calif.: Sage, 1983.

BELL, DANIEL. *The Coming of Postindustrial Society.* New York: Basic Books, 1973.

BELL, DONALD H. *Being a Man: The Paradox of Masculinity.* Brattleboro, Vt.: Lewis, 1982.

BELL, QUENTIN. *Virginia Woolf: A Biography.* New York: Harcourt Brace Jovanovich, 1972.

BELL, ROBERT R. *Worlds of Friendship.* Beverly Hills, Calif.: Sage, 1981.

BEM, SANDRA LIPSITZ. "Gender Scheme Theory and Its Implications for Child Development: Raising Gender A-Schematic Children in a Gender-Schematic Society," *Signs: Journal of Woman in Culture and Society*, 8, 4 (Summer 1983), 598–616.

BENDIX, REINHARD *Kings or People*. Berkeley: University of California Press, 1978.

BENSON, HELENE A. *Women and Private Pensions*. Washington, D.C.: U.S. Dept. of Labor, Labor-Management Services Administration, 1980.

BERCH, BETTINA. *The Endless Day: The Political Economy of Women and Work*. New York: Harcourt Brace Jovanovich, 1982.

BERGER, PETER, BRIGITTE BERGER, AND HANSFRIED KELLNER. *The Homeless Mind*. New York: Random House, 1976.

———, AND HANSFRIED KELLNER "Marriage and the Social Construction of Reality," *Diogenes*, 46 (1964). Reprinted in Peter Dreitzel, *Recent Sociology, no. 2: Patterns of Communicative Behavior*. New York: Macmillan, 1970.

——— AND ———. *Sociology Reinterpreted: An Essay on Method and Vocation*. Garden City, N.Y.: Anchor, 1981.

———, AND THOMAS LUCKMANN. *The Social Construction of Reality*. New York: Anchor, 1967.

BERGMANN, BARBARA. "The Economic Risks of Being a Housewife," *American Economic Review*, 71, 2 (May 1981), 81–86.

BERNARD, JESSIE. *The Female World*. New York: Free Press, 1981.

———. *The Future of Motherhood*. New York: Bantam, 1972.

———. *Women and the Public Interest*. Chicago: Aldine, 1971.

BERS, TRUDY HAFFRON, AND SUSAN GLUCK MEZEY. "Support for Feminist Goals among Leaders of Women's Community Groups," *Signs: Journal of Women in Culture and Society*, 6, 4 (Summer 1981).

BEST, RAPHAELA. *We've All Got Scars: What Boys and Girls Learn in Elementary School*. Bloomington: University of Indiana Press, 1983.

BIRD, CAROLINE. *The Two Paycheck Family*. New York: Rawson, Wade, 1979.

BLANCHARD, PAULA. *Margaret Fuller: From Transcendentalism to Revolution*. New York: Delta, 1978.

BLUMER, HERBERT. *Symbolic Interaction: Perspective and Method*. Englewood Cliffs, N.J.: Prentice-Hall, 1969.

BLUMSTEIN, PHILLIP, AND PEPPER SCHWARTZ. *American Couples*. New York: Morrow, 1983.

BOGART, KAREN, *Technical Manual for the Institutional Self-Study Guide on Sex Equity*. Washington, D.C.: American Institutes for Research, 1981.

BOOTH, ALAN. "Sex and Social Participation," *American Sociological Review*, 37 (1972), 183–192.

BOSWELL, SALLY L. "Study on Women's Career Choice and Academic Achievement," *Association for Women in Mathematics Newsletter*, 9 (1979), 14–15.

BOULDING, ELISE. "Familial Constraints on Women's Work Roles," *Signs*, 1 (Spring 1976), 59–117 (a).

———. *The Underside of History*. Boulder, Colorado: Westview Press, 1976 (b).

BOXER, MARILYN J. "For and about Women: The Theory and Practice of Women's Studies in the United States," *Signs: Journal of Women in Culture and Society*, 7, 3 (Spring 1982), 661–695.

BRADY, DAVID, AND KENT TEDIN. "Ladies in Pink: Religious and Political Ideology in the Anti-ERA Movement," *Social Science Quarterly*, 56 (1979) 564–575.

BRANDENBURG, JUDITH BERMAN. "Sexual Harassment in the University: Guidelines for Establishing a Grievance Procedure," *Signs: Journal of Women in Culture and Society*, 8, 2 (Winter 1982), 320–336.

BREINES, WINI, AND LINDA GORDON. "The New Scholarship on Family Violence," *Signs: Journal of Women in Culture and Society*, 8, 3 (Spring 1983), 490–532.

BRISCOE, ANNE M. "Phenomenon of the Seventies: The Women's Caucuses," *Signs: Journal of Women in Culture and Society*, 4, 1 (1978), 152–158.

BROWNMILLER, SUSAN. *Against Our Will: Men, Women and Rape*. New York: Simon and Schuster, 1975.

BRYANT ANITA. *Bless This House*. New York: Bantam, 1976.

———. *Mine Eyes Have Seen the Glory*. Old Tappan, N.Y.: Fleming H. Revell, 1970.

BUFFERY, A. W. H., AND J. A. GRAY. "Sex Differences in the Development of Spatial and Linguistic Skills." In C. Ounsted and D. D. Taylor (eds.), *Gender Differences; Their Ontogeny and Significance*. Edinburgh, Scotland: Churchill Livingstone, 1972.

BURTON, GABRIELLE. *I'm Running Away from Home, But I'm Not Allowed to Cross the Street*. New York: Avon, 1972.

CALDWELL, M., AND L. PEPLAU. "Sex Differences in Same-Sex Friendships," *Sex Roles* 8 (1982): 721–732.

CAPLOW, THEODORE. "Christmas Gifts and Kin Networks," *American Sociological Review*, 47 (June 1982): 383–392.

CARDEN, MAREN LOCKWOOD. *The New Feminist Movement*. New York: Russell Sage Foundation, 1974.

CASSELL, JOAN. *A Group Called Women: Sisterhood and Symbolism in the Feminist Movement*. New York: McKay, 1977.

CATER, LIBBY, ANNE SCOTT, AND WENDY MARTYNA. *Women and Men: Changing Roles, Relationships and Perceptions*. New York: Aspen Institute for Humanistic Studies, 1976.

CAUDLE, SHELIA. "Abortion Rights Rescued: The Triumph of Coalition Politics," *MS*, January 1983, 40.

CHAFETZ, JANET SALTZMAN. *Masculine/Feminine or Human? An Overview of the Sociology of the Gender Roles*. Itasca, Ill.: Peacock Publishers, 1978.

CHAMBERS, DAVID. "Child Custody," *The Committee for Gender Research*, University of Michigan, Ann Arbor, no. 2 (Fall 1982), 1–5.

CHERLIN, ANDREW, AND PAMELA BARNHOUSE WALTERS. "Trends in United States Men's and Women's Sex Role Attitudes, 1972–1978," *American Sociological Review*, 46 (1981), 453–460.

CHERNIN, KIM. *The Obsession: Reflections on the Tyranny of Slenderness*. New York: Harper, 1981.

CHESLER, PHYLLIS. *Women and Madness*. Garden City, N. Y.: Doubleday, 1972.

CHODOROW, NANCY. *The Reproduction of Mothering: Psychoanalysis and the Sociology of Gender*. Berkeley: University of California Press, 1978.

Coalition on Women and the Budget. *Inequality of Sacrifice: The Impact of the Reagan Budget on Women*. Washington, D.C., March 1983.

COLLINS, RANDALL. "On the Micro-foundations of Macrosociology," *American Journal of Sociology*, 86, (1981) 984-1014.

———. *Conflict Sociology: Towards an Explanatory Science*. New York: Academic Press, 1975.

Committee on the Status of Women in Sociology. "Sexist Biases in Sociological Research: Problems and Issues," *American Sociological Association Footnotes*, 8, 1 (January 1980), 8–9.

COPELON, RHONDA. "Abortion Rights: Where Do We Go From Here?" *Ms*. (October 1983), 146.

CORSO, J. F. "Age and Sex Differences in Pure Tone Thresholds: Survey of

Hearing Differences from 18 to 65 Years," *Archives of Otolaryngology,* 77 (1963), 385–405.

CROCKER, PHYLLIS. "An Analysis of University Definitions of Sexual Harassment," *Signs: Journal of Women in Culture and Society,* 8, 4 (Summer 1983), 696–707.

DAHRENDORF, RALF. *Class and Class Conflict in Industrial Society.* Stanford, Calif.: Stanford University Press, 1959.

DALY, MARY. *Gyn/Ecology: The Metaethics of Radical Feminism.* Boston: Beacon Press, 1978.

———. *Beyond God the Father: Towards a Philosophy of Women's Liberation.* Boston: Beacon Press, 1973.

———. *The Church and the Second Sex.* New York: Harper & Row, 1968.

DAVID, DEBORAH S., AND ROBERT BRANNON (eds.) *The Forty-Nine Percent Majority: The Male Sex Role.* Reading, Mass.: Addison-Wesley, 1976.

DAVIS, ANGELA Y. *Women, Race and Class.* New York: Vintage, 1983.

DE BEAUVOIR, SIMONE. *The Second Sex.* New York: Knopf, 1952.

DECKARD, BARBARA SINCLAIR. *The Women's Movement: Political, Socioeconomic and Psychological Issues.* New York: Harper & Row, 1979.

DEGLER, CARL N. *At Odds: Women and the Family in America from the Revolution to the Present.* New York: Oxford University Press, 1980.

DE GOOYER, JANICE, AND FARFALLAH BORAH. *What's Wrong with This Picture? A Look at Working Women in Television.* Washington, D.C.: National Commission on Working Women, 1982.

DINNERSTEIN, DOROTHY. *The Mermaid and the Minotaur.* New York: Harper & Row, 1976.

DOWDALL, JEAN. "Women's Attitudes towards Employment and Family Roles," *Sociological Analysis,* 35, 4 (Winter 1974): 251–262.

DOWLING, COLETTE. *The Cinderella Complex.* New York: Summit Books, 1981.

DOYLE, JAMES A. *The Male Experience.* Dubuque, Iowa: Brown, 1983.

DWORKIN, ANDREA *Right Wing Women.* New York: Perigree Books, 1982.

———. *Our Blood: Prophecies and Discourses on Sexual Politics.* New York: Perigree Books, 1976.

EHRENREICH, BARBARA. "An Agenda for Economic Recovery: Barbara Ehrenreich Interviews Frances Fox Piven." *Ms.* (January 1983), 42.

———, AND DEIDRE ENGLISH. *For Her Own Good: One Hundred and Fifty Years of the Expert's Advice to Women.* Garden City, N.Y.: Anchor-Doubleday, 1978.

EISENSTEIN, ELIZABETH L. *The Printing Press as an Agent of Change.* Cambridge, Eng.: Cambridge University Press, 1979.

EISENSTEIN, ZILLAH. "Antifeminism in the Politics and Election of 1980," *Feminist Studies,* 7, 2 (Summer 1981), 187–205 (a).

———. *The Radical Future of Liberal Feminism.* New York: Longman, 1981 (b).

———. "The Sexual Politics of the New Right: Understanding the Crisis in Liberalism in the 1980's." In Nanerl O. Keohane, Michelle Z. Rosaldo, and Barbara C. Gelpi (eds.), *Feminist Theory: A Critique of Ideology.* Chicago: University of Chicago Press, 1981, 77–98 (c).

——— (ed.). *Capitalist Patriarchy and the Case for Socialist Feminism.* New York: Monthly Review Press, 1979.

ELLIOT, ELIZABETH. *Let Me Be A Woman.* London: Hodder and Stoughton, 1976.

ELSHTAIN, JEAN BETCHKE. "Feminism, Family and Community," *Dissent* (Fall 1982), 442–449.

ENGEL, ELIOT. "Of Male Bondage," *Newsweek,* June 21, 1982, 13.

ENGELS, FREDERICK. *The Origin of the Family, Private Property and the State.* New York: International Publishers, 1942/1970.

Epstein, Cynthia Fuchs, *Women in Law*. New York: Basic Books, 1981.

Evans, Sara. *Personal Politics: The Roots of the Women's Liberation Movement in the Civil Rights Movement and the New Left*. New York: Vintage 1980.

Farley, Lin. *Sexual Shakedown*. New York: Warner Books, 1978.

Farrell, Warren. *The Liberated Man*. New York: Random House, 1974.

Fasteau, Marc. *The Male Machine*. New York: McGraw-Hill, 1974.

Fee, Elizabeth (ed.) *Women and Health: The Politics of Sex in Medicine*. Farmingdale, N.Y.: Bay Wood, 1983.

———, and Michael Wallace, "The History and Politics of Birth Control: A Review Essay," *Feminist Studies*, 5,1 (Spring 1979), 201–15.

Felsenthal, Carol. *The Sweetheart of the Silent Majority: The Biography of Phyllis Schlafly*, Garden City, N.Y.: Doubleday, 1981.

Ferber, Marianne A. "Women and Work: Issues of the 1980's," *Signs: Journal of Women in Culture and Society*, 8, 2 (Winter 1982), 273–296.

Firestone, Shulamith. *The Dialectic of Sex: The Case for a Feminist Revolution*. New York: Bantam, 1970.

First, Ruth, and Ann Scott. *Olive Schreiner*. New York: Schocken, 1980.

Fitzgerald, Frances. "The Triumphs of the New Right," *The New York Review of Books*, November 19, 1981, 19–26.

Fleming, Jane P. "Wider Opportunities for Women: The Search for Equal Employment." In Irene Tinker (ed.), *Women in Washington*. Beverly Hills, Calif.: Sage, 1983.

Flexner, Eleanor. *Century of Struggle*. New York: Atheneum, 1971.

Folbre, Nancy. "Of Patriarchy Born: The Political Economy of Fertility Decisions," *Feminist Studies*, 9, 2 (Summer 1983), 223–234.

The Frankfurt Institute of Social Research, *Aspects of Sociology*. Boston: Beacon Press, 1972.

Franklin, Phyllis, et al. *Sexual and Gender Harrassment in the Academy: A Guide for Faculty, Students and Administrators*, New York: The Modern Language Association, 1981.

Fraser, Arvonne S. "Insiders and Outsiders: Women in the Political Arena." In Irene Tinker (ed.), *Women in Washington*. Beverly Hills. Calif.: Sage, 1983.

Friedan, Betty. *The Second Stage*. New York: Summit Books, 1981.

———. *The Feminine Mystique*. New York: Dell, 1963.

Friday, Nancy. *My Mother, My Self*. New York: Dell, 1977.

Gagnon, I., and W. Simon. *Sexual Conduct: The Social Sources of Human Sexuality*. Chicago: Aldine, 1973.

Garfinkel, Harold. *Studies in Ethnomethodology*. Englewood Cliffs, N.J.: Prentice-Hall, 1967.

Gelb, Joyce, and Marian Lief Palley. *Women and Public Policies*. Princeton, N.J.: Princeton University Press, 1982.

Gelles, Richard J. *Family Violence*. Beverly Hills, Calif.: Sage, 1979.

Gerth, Hans, and C. W. Mills (eds.). *From Max Weber*. New York: Oxford University Press, 1958.

Giele, Janet. *Women and the Future*. New York: Free Press, 1978.

Gilligan, Carol. *In a Different Voice: Psychological Theory and Women's Development*. Cambridge, Mass.: Harvard University Press, 1982.

Gilman, Charlotte Perkins. *Herland*. New York: Pantheon, 1979.

Glaser, Nona Y. "Housework," *Signs: Journal of Women in Culture and Society*, 1 (1976), 905–922.

Glennon, Lynda M. *Women and Dualism*. New York: Longman, 1979.

Glubka, Sharon. "Out of the Stream: An Essay on Unconventional Motherhood," *Feminist Studies*, 9, 2 (1983), 223–234.

GOFFMAN, ERVING. "The Interaction Order," *American Sociological Review*, 48, 1 (February 1983), 1–17.

———. *Gender Advertisements*. New York: Harper & Row, 1979.

———. "The Arrangement between the Sexes," *Theory and Society*, 40, 3 (1977), 301–332.

GOLDBERG, STEVEN. *The Inevitability of Patriarchy*. New York: Morrow, 1974.

GOODE, WILLIAM J. "The Theoretical Importance of Love," *American Sociological Review*, 24, (1959), 38–47.

GORDON, LINDA. *Woman's Body, Woman's Right: A Social History of Birth Control in America*. New York: Grossman, 1976.

GOREAU, ANGELINE. *Reconstructing Aphra: A Social Biography of Aphra Behn*. New York: Dial Press, 1980.

GREER, GERMAINE. *The Female Eunuch*. New York: McGraw-Hill, 1971

GRIFFIN, SUSAN. *Pornography as Silence: Culture's Revenge Against Nature*. New York: Harper & Row, 1981.

———. "Rape: The All-American Crime." In Susan Griffin, *The Politics of Rape*. (New York: Harper & Row, 1979). Reprinted in Laurel Richardson and Verta Taylor (eds.), *Feminist Frontiers*, Reading, Mass.: Addison-Wesley, 1983, 159–168.

———. *Woman and Nature: The Roaring Within Her*. New York: Harper & Row, 1978.

GRONAU, REUBEN. "Leisure, Home Production, and Work: The Theory of the Allocation of Time Revisited," *Journal of Political Economy*, 85, 6 (December 1977), 1099–1123.

GROSSMAN, MICHAEL. "Who Gets the Child? Custody, Guardianship, and the Rise of a Judicial Patriarchy in Nineteenth Century America," *Feminist Studies*, 9, 2 (Summer 1983), 235–260.

HABERMAS, JURGEN. *Legitimation Crisis*. Boston: Beacon Press, 1975.

HACKER, ANDREW "Who Killed ERA? Women or Men," *The Washington Post*, Outlook Section, September 14, 1980.

HALL, ROBERT M., AND BERNICE R. SANDLER. *The Classroom Climate: A Chilly One for Women?* Project on the Status and Education of Women, Washington, D.C.: Association of American Colleges, 1982.

HAMILTON, ROBERTA. *The Liberation of Women: A Study of Patriarchy and Capitalism*. London: Allen and Unwin, 1978.

HARDING, SUSAN. "Family Reform Movements: Recent Feminism and Its Opposition," *Feminist Studies*, 7, 1 (Spring 1981), 57–75.

HARRIS, LOUIS, AND ASSOCIATES. *The General Mills American Family Report, 1980–81: Families: Strengths and Strains at Work*. Minneapolis: General Mills, Inc., 1981.

HARTLEY, SHIRLEY FOSTER. "Components and Characteristics of Friends and Friendship," unpublished ms.

HARTMAN, HEIDI. "Capitalism, Patriarchy, and Job Segregation by Sex." In Zillah R. Eisenstein (ed.), *Capitalist Patriarchy and the Case for Socialist Feminism*. New York: Monthly Review Press, 1979.

HERZOG, A. REGINA, AND JERALD G. BACHMAN. *Sex Role Attitudes among High School Seniors: Views about Work and Family Roles*. Ann Arbor, Mich.: Institute for Social Research, 1982.

HILL, MARY A. *Charlotte Perkins Gillman*. Philadelphia: Temple University Press, 1980.

HITE, SHERE. *The Hite Report: A Nationwide Study of Female Sexuality*. New York: Dell, 1976.

HOWE, FLORENCE, SUZANNE HOWARD, AND MARY JO BOEHM STRAUSS (eds.).

Everywoman's Guide to Colleges and Universities. Westbury, N.Y.: The Feminist Press, 1982.

HUBER, BETTINA. "Gutting Affirmative Action—New Policy in Action," *American Sociological Association Footnotes,* 9, 9 (December 1981), 2–3.

HUBER, JOAN. "Sociology," *Signs: Journal of Women in Culture and Society,* 1, 3 part 1 (Spring 1976), 685–697.

HURN, CHRISTOPHER. *The Limits and Possibilities of Schooling.* Boston: Allyn and Bacon, 1978.

HUSSERL, EDMUND. *Ideas.* London: Allen and Unwin, 1931.

ILLICH, IVAN, *Gender.* New York: Pantheon, 1982.

JAGGAR, ALISON M., AND PAULA ROTHENBERG STRUHL (eds.). *Feminist Frameworks.* New York: McGraw-Hill, 1978.

JANEWAY, ELIZABETH. *Powers of the Weak.* New York: Morrow Quill, 1981.

JONES, W. T. *A History of Western Philosophy: The Twentieth Century to Wittgenstein and Sartre* (2nd ed.), New York: Harcourt Brace Jovanovich, 1975.

KAHN-HUT, RACHEL, ARLENE KAPLAN DANIELS, AND RICHARD COLVARD. *Women and Work: Problems and Perspectives.* New York: Oxford University Press, 1982.

KANTER, ROSABETH MOSS. *Men and Women of the Corporation.* New York: Basic Books, 1977.

KASPER, ANNE, Health Editor for *New Directions for Women,* personal communication, January 1984.

———. "Women's Health and the FDA: A Case of Consumer Lobbying." In Irene Tinker (ed.), *Women in Washington: Advocates for Public Policy,* Beverly Hills, Calif.: Sage, 1983.

KAUFMAN, DEBRA R. "Associational Ties in Academe: Some Male and Female Differences," *Sex Roles,* 4 (1978), 9–21.

———, AND BARBARA L. RICHARDSON, *Achievement and Women: Challenging the Assumptions.* New York: Free Press, 1982.

KENSHALO, D. R. "The Temperature Sensitivity." In W. D. Neff (ed.), *Contributions to Sensory Physiology.* New York: Academic Press, 1970.

KESSLER, RONALD C., AND JAMES A. MACRAE, JR. "The Effect of Wives' Employment on the Mental Health of Married Men and Women," *American Sociological Review,* 47, 2 (April 1982), 216–226.

KINSEY, ALFRED C., ET AL. *Sexual Behavior in the Human Female.* Philadelphia: Saunders, 1953.

———. *Sexual Behavior in the Human Male.* Philadelphia: Saunders, 1948.

KOHLBERG, LAWRENCE. "A Cognitive-Developmental Analysis of Children's Sex Role Concepts and Attitudes." In Eleanor Maccoby (ed.), *The Development of Sex Differences.* Stanford, Calif.: Stanford University Press, 1966.

KOMAROVSKY, MIRRA. *Dilemmas of Masculinity: A Study of College Youth.* New York: Norton, 1976.

KRUCOFF, CAROL. "Careers: Catching on to 'New Girl' Networks," *The Washington Post,* January 21, 1980.

KUHN, ANNETTE, AND ANN MARIE WOLFE. *Feminism and Materialism.* London: Routledge and Kegan Paul, 1978.

LASH, JOSEPH. *Eleanor and Franklin.* New York: Signet, 1971.

LAWS, JUDITH LONG, AND PEPPER SCHWARTZ. *Sexual Scripts: The Social Construction of Female Sexuality.* Hinsdale, Ill.: Dryden, 1977.

LEAR, JULIA GRAHAM. "Women's Health and Public Policy: 1976–82." In Irene Tinker (ed.), *Women in Washington.* Beverly Hills, Calif.: Sage, 1983.

LEIFER, MYRA. "Review Essay: Pregnancy," *Signs: Journal of Women in Culture and Society,* 5, 4 (Summer 1980), 754–765.

LENGERMANN, PATRICIA M., KATHERINE M. MARCONI, AND RUTH A. WALLACE. "Sociological Theory in Teaching Sex Roles: Marxism, Functionalism, and Phenomenology," *Women's Studies International Quarterly*, 1, 4 (1978), 375–385.

LERNER, GERDA (ed.). *The Female Experience: An American Documentary.* Indianapolis: Bobbs-Merrill, 1977.

LEVER, JANET. "Sex Differences in the Complexity of Children's Play and Games," *American Sociological Review*," 43 (1978): 471–483.

LEWIS, KAREN J., MORTON ROSENBERG, AND ALLISON I. PORTER. *Abortion: Judicial and Legislative Control,* Issue Brief 1B74019. Washington, D.C.: Library of Congress Congressional Research Service, March 1983.

LEWIS, ROBERT A. (ed.). *Men in Difficult Times: Masculinity Today and Tomorrow.* Englewood Cliffs, N.J.: Prentice-Hall, 1981.

LEWONTIN, R. C. "Darwin's Revolution," *New York Review of Books,* June 16, 1983, 21–27.

LINDSEY, KAREN. *Friends as Family.* Boston: Beacon Press, 1981.

LIPMAN-BLUMEN, JEAN, AND ANN R. TICKAMYER. "Sex Roles in Transition: A Ten Year Perspective," *Annual Review of Sociology* (1975), 297–335.

LITEWKA, JACK. "The Socialized Penis," *Liberation Magazine,* 18 (March-April 1974). Reprinted in Evelyn Shapiro and Barry Shapiro, *The Women Say, The Men Say.* New York: Delta, 1979.

LITTLE, MALCOLM *The Autobiography of Malcolm X.* New York: Grove Press, 1966.

LLOYD, CYNTHIA B. (ed.). *Sex Discrimination and the Division of Labor.* New York: Columbia University Press, 1975.

LOPATA, HELENA Z. *Women as Widows.* New York: Elsevier, 1979.

————. *Occupation Housewife.* New York: Oxford University Press, 1971.

LOTT, BERNICE, MARY ELLEN REILLY, AND DALE R. HOWARD. "Sexual Assault and Harassment: A Campus Community Case Study," *Signs: Journal of Women in Culture and Society,* 8, 2 (Winter 1982), 296–319.

LOVETT, RAYMOND E. "Private Lives: Working at Home," *Washington Post,* January 23, 1980, p. E5.

LURIE, ALISON. *The Language of Clothes.* New York: Random House, 1982.

LUXEMBURG, ROSA. "Women's Suffrage and Class Struggle." In Dick Howard, (ed.), *Selected Political Writings,* New York: Monthly Review Press, 1971, 219–220.

LYNN, NAOMI. "Women in American Politics: An Overview." In Jo Freeman (ed.), *Women: A Feminist Perspective.* Palo Alto, Calif.: Mayfield 1975, 364–385.

MACCOBY, E. E. AND C. N. JACKLIN. *The Psychology of Sex Differences.* Stanford, Calif.: Stanford University Press, 1974.

MACKINNON, CATHARINE A. "Feminism, Marxism, Method, and the State: An Agenda for Theory." In Nanerl O. Keohane et al. (eds.), *Feminist Theory: A Critique of Ideology.* Chicago: University of Chicago Press, 1981, 1982, 1–30.

————. *Sexual Harassment of Working Women.* New Haven, Conn.: Yale University Press, 1979.

MAHOWALD, MARY BRODY (ed.). *Philosophy of Woman.* Indianapolis: Hackett, 1978.

MANDLE, JOAN D. *Women and Social Change in America.* Princeton, N.J.: Princeton Book Co., 1979.

MANNHEIM, KARL. *Ideology and Utopia.* New York: Harcourt, 1936.

MARX, KARL. *Capital: A Critique of Political Economy,* vol. 1. New York: International Publishers, 1867/1967.

————. *The Economic and Philosophic Manuscripts of 1844,* ed. Dirk J. Struik. New York: International Publishers, 1932/1964.

MASLOW, ABRAHAM H. *Motivation and Personality*. New York: Harper & Row, 1954.

MASNICK, GEORGE, AND MARY JO BANE. *The Nation's Families: 1960–1990*. Boston: Auburn House, 1980.

MASON, KAREN O., AND LARRY L. BUMPASS. "U.S. Women's Sex-Role Ideology, 1970," *American Journal of Sociology*, 80 (1975), 1212–1219.

MASON, KAREN O., JOHN L. CZAJKA, AND SARA ARBER. "Change in Women's Sex Role Attitudes, 1964–1974," *American Sociological Review*, 81 (1976), 573–596.

MASTERS, W., AND V. JOHNSON. *Human Sexual Response*. Boston: Little, Brown, 1966.

MATTHAEI, JULIE A. *An Economic History of Women in America*. New York: Schocken Books, 1982.

McDONOUGH, PATRICIA, M. "Consciousness-Raising: A Method for Communication." Unpublished M.A. final paper, George Washington University, Washington, D.C., 1980.

MEAD, GEORGE HERBERT. *Mind, Self and Society*. Chicago: University of Chicago Press, 1934.

MEISELMAN, H. L. AND E. DZENDOLET. "Variability in Gustatory Quality Identification," *Perception and Psychophysics*, 2 (1967), 496–498.

MELTZ, NOAH M., FRANK REID, AND GERALD S. SWARTZ. *Sharing the Work: An Analysis of the Issues in Worksharing and Jobsharing*. Toronto: University of Toronto Press, 1981.

MERTON, ROBERT K. *Social Theory and Social Structure* (enlarged edition). New York: Free Press, 1968.

MEZIROW, JACK, AND VICTORIA MARSICK. "Education for Perspective Transformation: Women's Re-entry Programs in Community Colleges." ERIC ED166367, 1978.

MICHAELS, LEONARD. *The Men's Club*. New York: Farrar, Straus and Giroux, 1981.

MILL, JOHN STUART. *The Subjection of Women*, ed. Sue Mansfield. Arlington Heights, Ill.: AHM Publishing Company, 1867/1980.

MILLER, CASEY, AND KATE SWIFT. *Words and Women: New Language in New Times*. Garden City, N.Y.: Anchor/Doubleday, 1977.

MILLER, JEAN BAKER. *Towards a New Psychology of Women*. Boston: Beacon Press, 1976.

——— (ed.). *Psychoanalysis and Women*. New York: Penguin, 1973.

MILLETT, KATE. *Sexual Politics*. Garden City, N.Y.: Doubleday, 1969/1970.

MILLMAN, MARCIA. *Such a Pretty Face: Being Fat in America*. New York: Berkley Books, 1980.

MILLS, C. WRIGHT. *Power, Politics and People*, Irving L. Horowitz, (ed.). New York: Ballentine, 1963.

MILLSAP, MARY ANN. "Sex Equity in Education." In Irene Tinker (ed.), *Women in Washington*. Beverly Hills, Calif.: Sage, 1983.

MITCHELL, JULIET. *Psychoanalysis and Feminism*. New York: Pantheon, 1974.

———. *Women's Estate*. New York: Vintage, 1971.

MODLESKI, TANIA. "The Disappearing Act: A Study of Harlequin Romances," *Signs: Journal of Women in Culture and Society*, 5, 3 (1980), 435–448.

MONEY, JOHN, AND PATRICIA TUCKER. *Sexual Signatures: On Being a Man or a Woman*. Boston: Little, Brown, 1975.

MORGAN, MARABEL. *The Total Woman*. New York: Pocket Books, 1975.

MORGAN, ROBIN. *The Anatomy of Freedom: Feminism, Physics and Global Politics*. Garden City, N.Y.: Anchor/Doubleday, 1982.

————. *Going Too Far: The Personal Chronicle of a Feminist.* New York: Random House, 1968.

———— (ed.). *Sisterhood Is Powerful.* New York: Vintage, 1970.

MORRISON, ELEANOR, ET AL. *Growing Up Sexual.* New York: Van Nostrand, 1980.

MURRAY, JANET (ed.) *Strong Minded Women and Other Lost Voices from Nineteenth Century England.* New York: Pantheon, 1982.

MYRDAL, GUNNAR. *An American Dilemma.* New York: Harper & Row, 1944.

National Advisory Council on Women's Educational Programs. *Title IX: The Half Full, Half Empty Glass.* Washington, D.C.: U.S. Department of Education, 1981.

National Commission on Working Women. *A Few Facts about Working Women.* Washington, D.C.: National Commission on Working Women, 1979.

National Research Council. *1979 Survey of Doctorate Requirements.* Washington, D.C.: Commission on Human Resources, 1979.

National Women's Political Caucus. *National Directory of Women Elected Officials.* Washington, D.C., 1982.

NICHOLS, JACK. *Men's Liberation: A New Definition of Masculinity.* New York: Penguin Books, 1978.

NIEVA, VERONICA F., AND BARBARA A. GUTEK. "Sex Effects on Evaluation," *The Academy of Management Review,* 5, 2 (1980), 267–276.

NORWOOD, JANET L. *The Female-Male Earnings Gap: A Review of Employment and Earnings Issues.* Washington, D.C., United States Department of Labor, Bureau of Labor Statistics Report 673, September 1982.

OAKLEY, ANN. *Subject Women.* New York: Pantheon, 1981.

————. *The Sociology of Housework.* New York: Pantheon, 1974.

————. *Women's Work: The Housewife, Past and Present.* New York: Random House, 1974.

ODENDAHL, TERESA J., AND LESLIE E. SMITH. "Women's Employment," *Comment,* September 1978, 1–2.

OPPENHEIMER, VALERIE KINCADE. "The Sociology of the Woman's Economic Role in the Family," *American Sociological Review,* 4, 3 (June 1977), 387–406.

————. *The Female Labor Force in the United States.* Westport, Conn.: Greenwood Press, 1970.

O'REILLY, JANE. "Watch on the Right: The Big Time Players behind the Small Town Image," *Ms.,* January 1983, 37.

PAIGE, KAREN ERICKSEN, AND JEFFREY PAIGE. *The Politics of Reproduction Ritual.* Berkeley: University of California Press, 1981.

PARELIUS, ANN P., AND ROBERT J. PARELIUS. *The Sociology of Education.* Englewood Cliffs, N.J.: Prentice-Hall, 1978.

PARSONS, TALCOTT. *Societies: Evolutionary and Comparative Perspectives.* Englewood Cliffs, N.J.: Prentice-Hall, 1966.

————. *Social Structure and Personality.* New York: Free Press, 1964.

————. "Age and Sex in the Social Structure of the United States." In Parsons, *Essays in Sociological Theory.* New York: Free Press, 1954.

————. *The Social System.* New York: Free Press, 1951.

————. *The Structure of Social Action.* New York: McGraw-Hill, 1937.

————, AND ROBERT BALES. *Family Socialization, and Interaction Process.* New York: Free Press, 1955.

PEARCE, DIANA, AND HARRIETTE MCADOO. *Women and Children: Alone and in Poverty.* Washington, D.C., National Advisory Council on Economic Opportunity, 1981.

PETCHESKY, ROSALIND POLLACK. "Antiabortion, Antifeminism, and the Rise of the New Right," *Feminist Studies,* 7, 2 (Summer 1981), 206–246.

————. "Reproductive Freedom: Beyond 'A Woman's Right to Choose.' " In Catherine R. Stimpson and Ethel Spector Person (eds.), *Women: Sex and Sexuality*. Chicago: University of Chicago Press, 1980, 92–116.

PETERSON, ESTHER. "The Kennedy Commission." In Irene Tinker (ed.), *Women in Washington*. Beverly Hills, Calif.: Sage, 1983.

PHILLIPS, E. BARBARA. "Magazine Heroines: Is *Ms.* Just Another Member of Family Circle?" In Gaye Tuchman et al., (eds.), *Hearth and Home*. New York: Oxford University Press, 1978.

PLECK, ELIZABETH H., AND JOSEPH H. PLECK. *The American Man*. Englewood Cliffs, N.J.: Prentice-Hall, 1980.

PLECK, JOSEPH H. *The Myth of Masculinity*. Cambridge, Mass.: The M.I.T Press, 1981.

————, AND MICHAEL RUSTAD. *Husbands' and Wives' Time in Family Work and Paid Work in the 1975–76 Study of Time Use*, Center Working Paper No. 63. Wellesley, Mass.: Wellesley College Center for Research on Women, 1980.

————, AND JACK SAWYER (eds.). *Men and Masculinity*. Englewood Cliffs, N.J.: Prentice-Hall, 1974.

POLOMA, MARGARET M. *Contemporary Sociological Theory*. New York: Macmillan, 1979.

POMEROY, SARAH B. *Goddesses, Whores, Wives, and Slaves: Women in Classical Antiquity*. New York: Schocken Books, 1975.

Prentice-Hall Author's Guide. Englewood Cliffs, N.J.: Prentice-Hall, 1975.

PRESSER, HARRIET B., AND WENDY BALDWIN. "Child Care as a Constraint on Employment: Prevalence, Correlates, and Bearing on the Work and Fertility Nexus," *American Journal of Sociology*, 85 (March 1980), 1202–1213.

PRESSER, HARRIET B., AND VIRGINIA CAIN. "Shift Work among Dual-Earner Couples with Children," *Science*, February 18, 1983.

RADWAY, JANICE A. "Women Read the Romance: The Interaction of Text and Context," *Feminist Studies*, 9, 1 (Spring 1983), 53–79.

RANSFORD, H. EDWARD, AND JON MILLER. "Race, Sex and the Feminist Outlooks," *American Sociological Review*, 48, 1 (February 1983), 46–59.

RAPOPORT, RHONA, AND ROBERT RAPOPORT. *Dual-Career Families Re-Examined*. New York: Harper & Row, 1977.

RAWALT, MARGUERITE. "The Equal Rights Amendment." In Irene Tinker (ed.), *Women in Washington*. Beverly Hills, Calif.: Sage, 1983.

REED, JAMES. *From Private Vice to Public Virtue: The Birth Control Movement in American Society since 1830*. New York: Basic Books, 1978.

REILLY, MICHAEL D. "Working Wives and Convenience Consumption," *Journal of Consumer Research*, 8, 4 (March 1982), 407–418.

RICH, ADRIENNE. "Compulsory Heterosexuality and Lesbian Experience." In Catherine R. Stimpson and Ethel Spector Person (eds.), *Women: Sex and Sexuality*. Chicago: University of Chicago Press, 1980, 62–91.

————. *On Lies, Secrets and Silences: Selected Prose 1966–1978*. New York: Norton, 1979.

————. *Of Woman Born: Motherhood as Experience and Institution*. New York: Bantam, 1976.

RICHARDSON, LAUREL, AND VERTA TAYLOR. *Feminist Frontiers: Rethinking Sex, Gender and Society*. Reading, Mass.: Addison-Wesley, 1983.

RICHMOND-ABBOTT, MARIE. *Masculine and Feminine: Sex Roles over the Life Cycle*. Reading, Mass.: Addison-Wesley, 1983.

RITZER, GEORGE. *Sociology: A Multiple Paradigm Science*. Boston: Allyn and Bacon, 1975.

RIVERS, CARYL, ROSALIND BARNETT, AND GRACE BARUCH. *Beyond Sugar and Spice: How Women Grow, Learn and Thrive.* New York: Ballantine Books, 1979.

ROACHE, JOEL. "Confessions of a Househusband," *Ms.,* November 1972, 25–27.

ROBERTS, HELEN (ed.) *Women, Health and Reproduction.* London: Routledge and Kegan Paul, 1981.

ROBERTSON, IAN. *Sociology.* New York: Worth, 1981.

ROBY, PAMELA. "Women and American Higher Education," *The Annals of the American Academy of Political and Social Science,* 404 (November 1972), 118–139.

ROSENTHAL, KRISTINE, AND HARRY F. KESHET. "Childcare Responsibilities of Part-time and Single Fathers." In Peter J. Stein (ed.), *Single Life: Unmarried Adults in Social Context.* New York: St. Martin's Press, 1981, 306–324.

ROSS, CATHERINE E., JOHN MIROWSKY, AND JOAN HUBER. "Dividing Work, Sharing Work, and In-Between; Marriage Patterns and Depression," *American Sociological Review,* 48 (December 1983), 809–823.

ROSS, HEATHER, AND ISABEL SAWHILL (with the assistance of Anita MacIntosh). *Time of Transition: The Growth of Families Headed by Women.* Washington, D.C.: Urban Institute, 1975.

ROSSI, ALICE. "A Biosocial Perspective on Parenting," *Daedalus,* 106, 2, (1977), 1–31.

———— (ed.). *The Feminist Papers: From Adams to de Beauvoir.* New York: Bantam, 1974.

ROTHSCHILD, EMMA. "Reagan and the Real America," *New York Review of Books,* February 5, 1981, 12–18.

ROWBOTHAM, SHEILA. *Women, Resistance and Revolution.* New York: Vintage, 1972.

RUBIN, GAYLE. "The Traffic in Women: Notes on the Political Economy of Sex." In Reyna Reiter (ed.), *Towards an Anthropology of Women.* New York: Monthly Review Press, 1975.

RUBIN, LILLIAN BRESLOW. *Intimate Strangers: Men and Women Together.* New York: Harper & Row, 1983 (a).

————. "Why He Needs You More than He Can Admit," *McCalls,* 60, 8: (1983b) 20–24 and 148–149.

————. *Women of a Certain Age: The Midlife Search for Self.* New York: Harper & Row, 1979.

————. *Worlds of Pain: Life in the Working Class Family.* New York: Basic Books, 1976.

RUDDICK, SARA, AND PAMELA DANIELS, (eds.). *Working It Out: 23 Women, Writers, Artists, Scientists and Scholars Talk about Their Lives and Work.* New York: Pantheon, 1977.

RYTINA, NANCY F. "Earnings of Men and Women: A Look at Specific Occupations," *Monthly Labor Review* (April 1982), 25–31.

SANDAY, PEGGY REEVES. *Female Power and Male Dominance: On the Origins of Sexual Inequality.* Cambridge, Eng.: Cambridge University Press, 1981.

SAWHILL, ISABEL. "Discrimination and Poverty among Women Who Head Families," In Martha Blaxall and Barbara Reagan (eds.), *Women and the Workplace.* Chicago: University of Chicago Press, 1976, 201–211.

SCANZONI, LETHA DAWSON, AND JOHN SCANZONI. *Men, Women, and Change: A Sociology of Marriage and Family.* New York: McGraw-Hill, 1981

SCARF, MAGGIE. *Unfinished Business: Pressure Points in the Lives of Women.* New York: Ballantine Books, 1980.

SCHAEFER, L. *Women and Sex: Sexual Experiences and Reactions of a Group of Thirty Women as Told to a Female Psychotherapist.* New York: Pantheon, 1973.

SCHREIBER, E. M. "Education and Change in American Opinion on a Woman for President," *Public Opinion Quarterly*, 42 (1978), 171–182.

SCHLAFLY, PHYLLIS. *The Power of the Postive Woman.* New Rochelle, N.Y.: Arlington House, 1977.

SCHUTZ, ALFRED. *The Phenomenology of the Social World.* Evanston, Ill.: Northwestern University Press, 1932, 1967.

SCIMECCA, JOSEPH. *Education and Society.* New York: Holt, Rinehart and Winston, 1980.

SCULLY, DIANA. *Men Who Control Women's Health: The Miseducation of Obstetrician–Gynecologists.* Boston: Houghton Mifflin, 1980.

SELDEN, GARY. "Frailty, Thy Name's Been Changed: What Sports Medicine Is Discovering about Women's Bodies." In Laurel Richardson and Verter Taylor (eds.), *Feminist Frontiers.* Reading, Mass.: Addison-Wesley, 1983.

SELLS, LUCY. "Mathematics—A Critical Filter," *The Science Teacher.* (February 1978), 28–29.

SEXTON, PATRICIA CAYO. *The Feminized Male.* New York: Random House, 1969.

SHAPIRO, EVELYN, AND BARRY SHAPIRO, (eds.). *The Women Say, The Men Say.* New York: Delta, 1979.

SHORTER, EDWARD. *The Making of the Modern Family.* New York: Basic Books, 1975.

SMELSER, NEIL J. *The Theory of Collective Behavior.* New York: Free Press, 1962.

SMITH, RALPH E. (ed.). *The Subtle Revolution.* Washington, D.C.: The Urban Institute, 1979.

SMITH-ROSENBERG, CARROLL. "The Female World of Love and Ritual: Relations between Women in Nineteenth-Century America," *Signs: Journal of Women and Culture in Society* (Autumn 1975), 1–29.

Sociologists for Women in Society. "Panel Review of the Rossi Thesis," *Signs: Journal of Women in Culture and Society*, 4, 4 (Summer 1979), 695–718.

SPEIZER, JEANNE F. "Role Models, Mentors and Sponsors: The Elusive Concepts," *Signs: Journal of Women and Culture in Society*, 6, 4 (1976), 692–712.

SPENDER, DALE. *Women of Ideas.* London: Routledge and Kegan Paul, 1982.

———. *Man Made Language.* London: Routledge and Kegan Paul, 1980.

SPITZE, GLENNA, AND LINDA J. WAITE. "Labor Force and Work Attitudes: Young Women's Early Experiences," *Sociology of Work and Occupations*, 7 (1980), 3–32.

STEIN, PETER J. (ed.). *Single Life: Unmarried Adults in Social Context.* New York: St. Martin's Press, 1981.

STEWART, DEBRA W. *The Women's Movement in Community Politics in the U.S.: The Role of Local Commissions on the Status of Women.* New York: Pergamon Press, 1980.

STOCKARD, JEAN, AND MIRIAM M. JOHNSON. *Sex Roles: Sex Inequality and Sex Role Development.* Englewood Cliffs, N.J.: Prentice-Hall, 1980.

STRAUS, MURRAY, RICHARD GELLES, AND SUZANNE STEINMETZ. *Behind Closed Doors: Violence in the American Family.* Garden City, N.Y.: Anchor/Doubleday, 1980.

STROBER, MYRA. "Women and Men in the World of Work: Present and Future." In Libby Cater, Anne Scott, and Wendy Martynn, *Women and Men: Changing Roles, Relationships and Perceptions.* New York: Aspen Institute, 1976.

STROUSE, JEAN. *Alice James: A Biography.* New York: Bantam, 1980.

TARSHIS, BARRY. *The Average American Book.* New York: Atheneum, 1979.

TAYLOR, MARVIN J. (ed.). *Fact Book on Theological Education, 1981–82.* Vandalia, Ohio: The Association of Theological Schools in the United States and Canada, 1982.

TAYLOR, VERTA. "The Future of Feminism in the 1980's: A Social Movement

Analysis." In Laurel Richardson and Verta Taylor (eds.), *Feminist Frontiers: Rethinking Sex, Gender and Society*. Reading, Mass.: Addison-Wesley, 1983.

TERKEL, STUDS. *Working.* New York: Avon Books, 1974.

THOMAS, WILLIAM, I. *The Child in America.* New York: Knopf, 1928.

THORNE, BARRIE, AND NANCY HENLEY. *Language and Sex: Difference and Dominance.* Rowley, Mass.: Newbury House, 1975.

THORNTON, ARLAND, DUANE F. ALWIN, AND DONALD CAMBURN. "Causes and Consequences of Sex-Role Attitudes and Attitude Change," *American Sociological Review*, 48, 2 (April 1983), 211–227.

THORNTON, ARLAND, AND DONALD CAMBURN. "Fertility, Sex Role Attitudes, and Labor Force Participation," *Psychology of Women Quarterly*, 4 (1979), 61–80.

THORNTON, ARLAND, AND DEBORAH FREEDMAN. "Changes in the Sex-Role Attitudes of Women, 1962–1977: Evidence from a Panel Study," *American Sociological Review*, 44 (1979), 832–842.

TIGER, LIONEL. *Men in Groups.* New York: Vintage, 1970.

———, AND ROBIN FOX. *The Imperial Animal.* New York: Holt, Rinehart and Winston, 1971.

TINKER, IRENE (ed.). *Women in Washington: Advocates for Public Policy.* Beverly Hills, Calif.: Sage, 1983.

TOFFLER, ALVIN. *Future Shock.* New York: Random House, 1970.

TREIMAN, DONALD J., AND HEIDI I. HARTMANN (eds.). *Women, Work and Wages: Equal Pay for Jobs of Equal Value.* Washington, D.C.: National Academy Press, 1981.

TUCHMAN, GAYE. "Women's Depiction in the Mass Media," *Signs: Journal of Women in Culture and Society*, 4 (1979), 528–542.

———, ARLENE K. DANIELS, AND JAMES BENET. *Hearth and Home: Images of Women in the Mass Media.* New York: Oxford University Press, 1978.

TWAIN, MARK. *Tom Sawyer and Huckleberry Finn.* London: Dent, 1943.

U.S. Bureau of the Census. "Money Income of Families and Persons in the United States," *Current Population Reports*, Series 60-127. Washington D.C.: U.S. Government Printing Office, 1980.

U.S. Commission on Civil Rights. *A Growing Crisis: Disadvantaged Women and Their Children.* Clearinghouse Publication 78, Washington, D.C., 1983.

———. *Unemployment and Underemployment among Blacks, Hispanics, and Women.* Clearinghouse Publication 74, Washington, D.C. 1982.

U.S. Department of Education. *The Condition of Education.* Washington, D.C.: National Center for Education Statistics, 1983.

U.S. Department of Health, Education and Welfare. *Summary Data Vocational Education, Program Year 1978.* Washington, D.C.: Bureau of Occupational and Adult Education, 1978.

U.S. Department of Labor. *Employers and Childcare Establishing Services through the Workplace.* Washington, D.C., Women's Bureau, 1981.

U.S. Office of the Federal Register, National Archives. *Code of Federal Regulations.* Washington, D.C.: U.S. Government Printing Office, 1980.

U.S. President. *Employment and Training Report of the President.* Washington, D.C.: U.S. Government Printing Office, 1981.

VETTER, BETTY M., ELEANOR L. BABER, AND SUSAN JENSEN-FISHER. *Professional Women and Minorities: A Manpower Data Resource Service.* Washington, D.C.: Scientific Manpower Commission, 1982.

VIGUERIE, RICHARD A. *The New Right: We're Ready to Lead.* Ottawa, Ill.: Caroline House, 1981.

WAITE, LINDA J. *U.S. Women at Work.* Santa Monica, Calif.: Rand Corporation, 1981.

WALLACE, RUTH A. "Bringing Women In: Marginality in the Churches," *Sociological Analysis*, 36, 4 (1976), 291–303.

———. "A Model of Change of Religious Affiliation," *Journal for the Scientific Study of Religion*, 14, 4 (December 1975), 345–355.

———, AND ALISON WOLF. *Contemporary Sociological Theory*. Englewood Cliffs, N.J.: Prentice-Hall, 1980.

WALLERSTEIN, IMMANUEL. "Semi-Peripheral Countries and the Contemporary World Crisis," *Theory and Society*, 3, 4 (Winter 1976), 461–484.

WALSHOK, MARY. *Blue-Collar Women*. Garden City, N.Y.: Anchor, 1981.

WALUM-RICHARDSON, LAUREL, *The Dynamics of Sex and Gender*. Boston: Houghton Mifflin, 1981.

WARNER, MARINA. *Alone of All Her Sex: The Myth and Cult of the Virgin Mary*. New York: Vintage, 1976, 1983.

WEBER, MAX. *Economy and Society*, New York: Bedminster Press, 1968.

———. *The Methodology of the Social Sciences*, trans. Edward Shils. New York: Free Press, 1949.

———. *The Religion of China: Confucianism and Taoism*. New York: Macmillan, 1916/1969.

———. The Religion of India: The Sociology of Hinduism and Buddhism. Glencoe, Ill.: Free Press, 1916–1917/1958.

WEDEL, JANET. "Ladies, We've Been Framed: Observations on Goffman," *Theory and Society*, 5, 1 (1978), 113–126.

WEISS, ROBERT S. "Issues in the Adjudication of Custody when Parents Separate." In George Levinger and Oliver C. Moles (eds.), *Divorce and Separation: Context, Causes and Consequences*. New York: Basic Books, 1979, 324–336.

WEITZMAN, LENORE J. *The Marriage Contract: Spouses, Lovers and the Law*. New York: Free Press, 1981.

———, CAROL M. DIXON, JOYCE A. BIRD, NEIL McGINN, AND DENA M. ROBERTSON. "The Traditional Marriage Contract." In Laurel Richardson and Verta Taylor (eds.), *Feminist Frontiers*. Reading, Mass.: Addison-Wesley, 1983, 95–97.

WELCH, MARY SCOTT. *Networking: The Great New Way for Women to Get Ahead*. New York: Harcourt Brace Jovanovich, 1980.

WERTZ, RICHARD W. AND DOROTHY C. WERTZ. *Lying-In: A History of Childbirth in America*. New York: Free Press, 1977.

WHITEHOUSE, MARY. *Whatever Happened to Sex?* London: Wyman, 1977.

WOMEN'S INSTITUTE FOR FREEDOM OF THE PRESS. *1983 Index/Directory of Women's Media*. Washington, D.C.: Anaconda Press, 1983.

WOOLF, VIRGINIA. *A Room of One's Own*. Harcourt, Brace and World, 1929.

Working Women United Institute, "Speak-Out on Sexual Harrassment." Ithaca, New York, May 14, 1975 (typescript).

YENCKEL, JAMES, T. "Now's the Time for All Good Men to Aid Themselves," *Washington Post* (February 7, 1982) pp. c1–c5.

YOUNG, ANN M. "Going Back to School at 35 and Over," *Monthly Labor Review* (*July 1977*), *43–45*.

YOUNG, IRIS M. "Throwing Like a Girl: A Phenomenology of Feminine Body Comportment, Motility and Spatiality," *Human Studies*, 3 (1980), 137–156.

ZARETSKY, ELI. *Capitalism, the Family and Personal Life*. New York: Harper & Row, 1976.

ZEITLIN, JUNE H. "Domestic Violence: Perspectives from Washington." In Irene Tinker (ed.), *Women in Washington: Advocates for Public Policy*. Beverly Hills, Calif.: Sage, 1983, 263–275.

INDEX